T0291525

Why Democracy Failed

In this distinctive new history of the origins of the Spanish Civil War, James Simpson and Juan Carmona tackle the highly debated issue of why it was that Spain's democratic Second Republic failed. They explore the interconnections between economic growth, state capacity, rural social mobility, and the creation of mass competitive political parties, and how these limited the effectiveness of the new republican governments, and especially their attempts to tackle economic and social problems within the agricultural sector. They show how political change during the Republic had a major economic impact on the different groups in village society, leading to social conflicts that turned to polarization and finally, with the civil war, to violence and brutality. The democratic Republic failed not so much because of the opposition from the landed elites but rather because small farmers had been unable to exploit more effectively their newly found political voice.

James Simpson is Professor at the Universidad Carlos III in Madrid. Among his many publications are *Spanish Agriculture: The Long Siesta, 1765–1965* (1995) and *Creating Wine: The Emergence of a World Industry, 1840–1914* (2011).

Juan Carmona is Associate Professor at the Universidad Carlos III in Madrid. He has published widely on rural institutions, organizations, and conflicts, including, with James Simpson, the book *El laberinto de la agricultura Española* (2003).

Cambridge Studies in Economic History

Cambridge Studies in Economic History comprises stimulating and accessible economic history which actively builds bridges to other disciplines. Books in the series will illuminate why the issues they address are important and interesting, place their findings in a comparative context, and relate their research to wider debates and controversies. The series will combine innovative and exciting new research by younger researchers with new approaches to major issues by senior scholars. It will publish distinguished work regardless of chronological period or geographical location.

A complete list of titles in the series can be found at:
www.cambridge.org/economichistory

Why Democracy Failed

The Agrarian Origins of the Spanish Civil War

James Simpson
Universidad Carlos III de Madrid

Juan Carmona
Universidad Carlos III de Madrid

CAMBRIDGE
UNIVERSITY PRESS

CAMBRIDGE
UNIVERSITY PRESS

University Printing House, Cambridge CB2 8BS, United Kingdom

One Liberty Plaza, 20th Floor, New York, NY 10006, USA

477 Williamstown Road, Port Melbourne, VIC 3207, Australia

314–321, 3rd Floor, Plot 3, Splendor Forum, Jasola District Centre, New Delhi – 110025, India

79 Anson Road, #06–04/06, Singapore 079906

Cambridge University Press is part of the University of Cambridge.

It furthers the University's mission by disseminating knowledge in the pursuit of education, learning, and research at the highest international levels of excellence.

www.cambridge.org
Information on this title: www.cambridge.org/9781108487481
DOI: 10.1017/9781108766999

First published 2020

Printed in the United Kingdom by TJ International Ltd, Padstow Cornwall

A catalogue record for this publication is available from the British Library.

Library of Congress Cataloging-in-Publication Data
Names: Simpson, James, 1953– author. | Carmona, Juan (Carmona Pidal), author.
Title: Why democracy failed : the agrarian origins of the Spanish Civil War / James Simpson, Universidad Carlos III de Madrid, Juan Carmona, Universidad Carlos III de Madrid.
Description: Cambridge, UK ; New York : Cambridge University Press, [2020] | Series: Cambridge studies in economic history | Includes bibliographical references and index.
Identifiers: LCCN 2019059910 (print) | LCCN 2019059911 (ebook) | ISBN 9781108487481 (hardback) | ISBN 9781108766999 (ebook)
Subjects: LCSH: Spain – History – Civil War, 1936–1939 – Causes. | Spain – Politics and government –1931–1939. | Spain – Rural conditions – 20th century. | Agriculture – Economic aspects – Spain – History. | Land reform – Spain – History – 20th century. | Democratization – Spain – History.
Classification: LCC DP257 .S48 2020 (print) | LCC DP257 (ebook) | DDC 946.081/1–dc23
LC record available at https://lccn.loc.gov/2019059910
LC ebook record available at https://lccn.loc.gov/2019059911

ISBN 978-1-108-48748-1 Hardback
ISBN 978-1-108-72038-0 Paperback

A todos los que sufrieron durante la Guerra Civil Española

Contents

Figures

Maps

Tables

Acknowledgements

This book has been many years in the making, and we have accumulated numerous academic debts. We have been fortunate enough to benefit from several Spanish government grants (ECO2012-36213 and ECO2015-66196-P), which allowed us to prepare a number of papers, most of which have now been published. These were previously presented at meetings, including at the Agricliometrics in Zaragoza (2015); Asociación Española de Historia Económica in Madrid (2014); Asociación de Historia Contemporánea in Albacete (2016); Economic History Society in York (2013), Wolverhampton (2015), Cambridge (2016) and London (2017); European Rural History Organisation in Girona (2015) and Leuven (2017); European Social Science History Conference in Valencia (2016); GEHCEX, 'Congreso Extremadura durante la II República', Cáceres (2014); and SEHA in Lleida (2011), Badajoz (2013), Lisbon (2016), Santiago de Compostela (2018), and Madrid (2018). In addition, helpful comments were made on papers given at the departments of economic history in Pablo de Olavide, Santiago de Compostela (HISTAGRA), Sevilla, and Valencia, as well as during workshops on 'The state and agriculture in Spain (1920–1960): Continuity and change', at the Universidad Carlos III de Madrid (November 2014), and the 'Rabassa Morta and rabassaires (Siglos XVIII-XX)', at the Universitat de Barcelona (January 2017), organized by Josep Colomé and Francesc Valls-Junyent.

Special thanks need to be given to Francisco Albaladejo, Francisco Beltrán, Antonio Miguel Bernal, Elisa Botella Rodríguez, Paul Brassley, Salvador Calatayud, Thomas Christiansen, Francisco Cobo, Jean-Philippe Colin, Pep Colomé, Deborah Fitzgerald, Antonio Florencio Puntas, Domingo Gallego, Lina Gálvez, Juan García Pérez, Samuel Garrido, Luis Germán, Yadira González de Lara, Manuel González de Molina, Antonio Herrera, José Hinojosa Durán, Richard Hoyle, Iñaki Iriarte, José Ignacio Jiménez Blanco,

Mikeas Lana Berasain, David Lanero, Eric Léonard, Antonio López Estudillo, Antonio López Martínez, Socrates Petmezas, Vicente Pinilla, Jordi Planas, Pep Pujol, Ramón Ramón Muñoz, Tim Rees, Jaime Reis, Fernando del Rey, Francisco Sánchez Marroyo, Nigel Townson, Elizabeth Williams, and Alp Yucel Kaya for their comments. We have benefitted in particular from the long and enjoyable debates we have had with Ricardo Robledo over many questions discussed in this book.

Special thanks is also due to our joint authors, Eva Fernandez, Joan Rosés, and Enrique Montañés. Leandro Prados de la Escosura, as always, provided helpful comments and encouragement. Jordi Domenech was always highly supportive and made valuable criticisms.

James in particular wishes to thank his students who took the course *Casos de Historia Económica* between 2012/13 and 2018/19. They constantly made me rethink and rewrite the text. I hope they learnt as much as I did.

Juan presented four chapters at the CRH (EHESS) in the winter of 2017 and thanks Fabrice Bouadjaa, Nadine Vivier, Alain Chatriot, Pablo Luna, Laurent Herment, Niccolo Mignemi, and Bernard Vincent for their comments. Gérard Béaur was especially generous with his time and interest.

James is grateful to the Spanish Ministry of Education for financing a six-month sabbatical at the London School of Economics, where much of the final writing up has been done.

Finally, an earlier version of the manuscript was presented at a day-long workshop in November 2018 in the Universidad Carlos III de Madrid. Those who attended, Jordi Domenech, José Fernández Albertos, Lourenzo Fernández Prieto, Robert Fishman, Stefan Houpt, Markus Lampe, Pablo Martinelli, Juan Pan-Montojo, Sergio Riesco, Ignacio Sánchez Cuenca, and Antonio Tena, were not only kind enough to read the text in detail but provided many useful and suggestive comments.

Pilar Bravo Lledó and Pedro Jiménez Clemente greatly facilitated our work in the *Archivo de la Reforma Agraria* in San Fernando de Henares, and we also thank archivists at the *Archivo Histórico Provincial de Cáceres*. María Fernández kindly helped with the maps.

We would also like to thank Michael Watson, Emily Sharp, and Gayathri Tamilselvan for their encouragement and support at Cambridge University Press.

Finally, on a personal note, James thanks Pepe, Azucena, Carmen, Kate, Lindy, and Madeleine for their encouragement. He owes a special debt to Ángeles, who not only cheered me up when the going became rough but also made sure that the book was actually finished before the *obra* in Moralina!

Meanwhile, Juan thanks Carmen, Isabel, Merce, Mila, and especially Sergio for their support. In particular, he is indebted to his parents who, as many others, were exiled by the Spanish Civil War.

Notes on the Regional Division of Spain

Mainland Spain is made up of forty-eight provinces. Geographers and historians have divided Spain into regions and subregions in many different ways, depending on the nature of their research. In this work, we have incorporated two distinct approaches. First, the country is divided into two major sections: those provinces that have large areas of big estates (*latifundios*) and the rest of the country. Second, Spain is divided into four major regions, each of which is broken up into a number of subregions. Following Malefakis, thirteen provinces are identified as *latifundio* provinces in central and southern Spain: Albacete, Badajoz, Cáceres, Cádiz, Ciudad Real, Córdoba, Granada, Huelva, Jaén, Málaga, Salamanca, Sevilla, and Toledo.

The four regions are:

1. North: Álava, Coruña, Guipúzcoa, Lugo, Orense, Asturias, Pontevedra, Santander, and Vizcaya
   Subregions: Galicia (Coruña, Lugo, Orense, and Pontevedra), Asturias, Basque Country (Alava, Guipúzcoa, and Vizcaya), and Santander.
2. Interior: Albacete, Ávila, Badajoz, Burgos Cáceres, Ciudad Real, Cuenca, Guadalajara, Huesca, León, Madrid, Navarra, Palencia, Rioja, Salamanca, Segovia, Soria, Teruel, Toledo, Valladolid, Zamora, and Zaragoza
   Subregions: Castilla-León (Ávila, Burgos, León, Palencia, Salamanca, Segovia, Soria, Valladolid, and Zamora); Extremadura (Badajoz and Cáceres); Centre (Albacete, Ciudad Real, Cuenca, Guadalajara, Madrid, and Toledo); Upper Ebro (Huesca, Navarra, Rioja, Teruel, and Zaragoza).
3. Mediterranean: Alicante, Barcelona, Baleares, Castellón, Girona, Lleida, Murcia, Tarragona, and Valencia
   Subregions: Cataluña (Barcelona, Girona, Lleida, and Tarragona) and Levante (Alicante, Castellón, Murcia, and Valencia).

4. Andalucia: Almería, Cádiz, Córdoba, Granada, Huelva, Jaén, Málaga, and Sevilla

    Subregions: Eastern Andalucía (Almería, Granada, Huelva, and Jaén); Western Andalucía (Cádiz, Córdoba, Malaga, and Sevilla)

    For the purpose of this book the Canary Islands, Ceuta, and Melilla are not included.

Abbreviations

AAE	*Asociación de Agricultores de España/* Association of Spanish Farmers
APFR	*Agrupación de Propietarios de Fincas Rústicas/* Association of Landowners
CEDA	*Confederación Española de Derechas Autónomas/* Spanish Confederation of Autonomous Rightist
CEPA	*Confederación Española Patronal Agrícola/* Spanish Confederation of Farm Employers
CNCA	*Confederación Nacional Católica-Agraria/* National Catholic-Agrarian Confederation
CNT	*Confederación Nacional del Trabajo/* National Confederation of Labour
ERC	*Esquerra Republicana de Catalunya/* Catalan Republican Left Party
FNTT	*Federación Nacional de Trabajadores de la Tierra/* National Federation of Land Workers (Socialist)
IACSI	*Instituto Agrícola Catalán de San Isidro/* Catalan Agricultural Institute of San Isidro
IRA	*Instituto de Reforma Agraria/* Institute of Agrarian Reform
JAP	*Juventudes de Acción Popular/* Popular Action Youths
PSOE	*Partido Socialista Obrero Español/* Spanish Socialist Worker's Party
UGT	*Unión General de Trabajadores/* Socialist trade-union
USAC	*Unió de Sindicats Agraris de Catalunya/* Union of Agrarian Syndicates in Catalonia

Introduction

The popular enthusiasm that greeted the Second Republic in 1931 proved short-lived, and the military uprising of July 1936 led to a civil war that lasted three years, with the rebels finding themselves too weak to quickly finish the task they had initiated but too strong to be defeated by the government.[1] While the army was the 'ultimate cause of the breakdown' of this brief democratic experiment, it was the deep political crisis and the regime's loss of legitimacy that provided it with the opportunity to act.[2] The experience of a 'democratic breakthrough' quickly collapsing and the country turning to authoritarian rule has been all too frequent over the past century, with the 'Arab Spring' being the most recent example. In Europe, Spain was perhaps the extreme case rather than an exception. Ziblatt divides the Continent into two major blocks, with countries such as Britain, Belgium, the Netherlands, Norway, Sweden, or Denmark following a steady 'nearly linear' path to democracy over the course of the late nineteenth century and first half of the twentieth century and others, including Italy, Germany, Portugal, Spain, or France before 1879, taking major detours, experiencing frequent 'breakthroughs', followed by 'democratic breakdowns or coups d'état'.[3] Explaining why the Second Republic ended in civil war rather than a consolidated democracy remains as controversial today as ever. Many blame the traditional rural elite and highly conservative Church for refusing to relinquish power, while others point to the radicalization of a significant section of the Left and their revolutionary endeavours to protect what they considered as 'their' republic.[4] Few studies however have attempted to explain why moderate and often apolitical Spaniards became disillusioned in the first place and then attracted to these extremist policies. This book does just this by examining rural Spain, where over half the country's population still worked and lived in the 1930s.

---

[1] Juliá 2008, p.173.   [2] Linz 1978b.   [3] Ziblatt 2017, pp.9–15.
[4] See Moradiellos 2016, for a brief survey.

1

The contribution of economic historians in explaining revolutionary events or military uprisings is often marginalized in the literature, as knowledge about long-run growth, income distribution, or growing poverty is usually regarded as providing a background to events but cannot explain political change itself. Therefore, understanding the causes and economic consequences of the Great Depression is insufficient to predict why a liberal democracy became consolidated in countries such as the United Kingdom or France but gave way to social democracy in Scandinavia, or to fascism in Italy, Germany, and eventually Spain. Political scientists such as Juan Linz emphasize instead the importance of decisions taken by politicians at crucial points in time. For instance, there is no doubt that Spanish history would have been very different if, for example, Alcalá-Zamora, the President of the Spanish Republic, had asked right-wing political leader Gil-Robles to form a government in late 1935 instead of convoking elections. David Cameron's decision to call a referendum on Britain's membership in the European Union is another political decision that unleashed fundamental changes in a society.

Lawrence Stone used a three-stage model to understand radical political change in his study of the causes of the English Revolution between 1529 and 1642, dividing the period into 'preconditions, precipitations, and triggers'.[5] In this model, economic and social historians provide the 'structure' or background, leaving to political historians to discuss the partisan manoeuvres and pacts that determine the events that trigger the monumental changes. However, these attempts have been frequently criticized because the connections between the distinct phases are often not clear, and individual political decisions can only be understood by knowing the constraints under which they were made. Returning to Alcalá-Zamora, his authority to decide which politicians could form a government depended on the powers conferred upon him by the 1931 Constitution, a document that itself represented the interests and worries of those elected to the Cortes of that year. The 1931 elections were democratic, but the political interests of family farmers – a group that represented around a third of the country's electorate – went largely unrepresented. The Constitution would no doubt have been very different, and the President of the Republic would have faced very different constraints and opportunities to decide on a new Prime Minister in the winter of 1935, if small farmers had been better organized. Instead, the Constitution reflected the views of urban middle classes and organized labour, creating a 'Republic for the Republicans' as they claimed, rather than one representative of all Spanish society.

[5] Stone 1972.

This book begins by explaining how economic and political developments over the previous half century influenced the outcome of
the Second Republic (1931–6). In particular, it shows the interconnections between economic growth, state capacity, rural social mobility, and
the creation of mass competitive political parties, and how these limited
the effectiveness of the Republican governments, and especially their
attempts to tackle economic and social problems within the agricultural
sector. It then shows how political change during the Republic had
a major economic impact on the different groups in village society, leading to social conflicts that turned to polarization and finally, with the civil
war, to violence and brutality. The democratic Republic failed not so
much because of the opposition from the landed elites but rather because
small farmers had been unable to organize sufficiently to advance their
own political interests. Indeed, if Spanish politicians had followed Jules
Ferry's observations concerning France's Third Republic, and attempted
to build a democracy with the support of family farmers and created
a 'Peasants' Republic', the country's democracy might have enjoyed
wider support that would have given it a better chance of surviving.

On the eve of the Second Republic, many Spaniards believed that they
lived in a poor country, especially in comparison with their European
neighbours. Nevertheless, the half century prior to the Great Depression
was a period of long-run economic growth, resulting in living standards
being significantly above those found in poor countries today, and the
numbers living in absolute poverty declining, especially in the 1920s.
Other indicators, such as literacy and life expectancy, also suggest that
important improvements were taking place. Agriculture, far from being
backward, was also changing rapidly, and the growing rural exodus was
encouraging farmers to modernize farming practices. Yet by remaining
neutral during the First World War, there were few incentives for politicians to invest in state capacity, and this would severely handicap the
governments during the Second Republic to choose and implement
effective policies. This was particularly unfortunate given the high expectations that the new Republic would resolve social problems, which were
worsening because of the Great Depression.

In Spain, unlike much of North-Western Europe, economic growth
was accompanied by slow social mobility in rural areas, so that the
influence of the landed elites remained strong, and family farmers were
economically weak and politically unorganized on the eve of the Second
Republic. The two were connected, although not necessarily in the ways
that many contemporaries believed. Favourable movements in land
prices and wages from the 1870s allowed significant numbers of landless
workers to rent or buy plots of land, but these remained poor 'peasant

farmers', rather than prosperous 'free farmers'. Farm labourers were therefore able to get onto the farm ladder, but the distance between the lower rungs remained significant, keeping most in relative poverty. This, in part, was because of natural resources, as dry-farming methods had to be used on about four-fifths of the country's farm land, which severely limited farmers' ability to increase output and incomes by simply working the land more intensely. However, the slow appearance of autonomous organizations such as rural banks or cooperatives that could help farmers adapt to an increasingly competitive agriculture and create effective farm lobbies also limited social mobility. In most Western European countries the landed elites and the Church hierarchy organized rural voters and built farmer associations to create strong centralized political parties, because they had to participate in competitive elections, and defend themselves against the liberal's attacks in the national parliament. This did not happen in Spain because, even after male suffrage was introduced in 1890, elections were not free and politicians used corruption and bribery to determine outcomes. This allowed the landed elites and the Church to avoid the expensive task of having to build mass political parties and attract small farmers by offering them political and economic support. Instead, the political influence of the *caciques*, or village notables, was actually strengthened by the need to manipulate electoral results and the state's dependence on them to implement a growing range of policies. The result was that when the landed elites and monarchists finally became discredited in 1931, the interests of family farmers were limited in the new Constitution.

In Spain, the social consequences of the 1930s Great Depression had a greater rural dimension than in most of Western Europe. This was because agriculture was still the employer of last resort. In France for example, local farm workers benefitted because unemployed foreign migrants went home, but in Spain the number of farm workers actually increased as unemployed urban workers returned to their villages looking for work. For many contemporaries, especially in urban areas, the 'agrarian problem' became associated primarily with the high concentration of landless and near-landless labourers on the *latifundios* in Southern Spain. These were widely believed to be poorly cultivated, with their owners paying starvation wages. In fact, the causes of rural poverty were much more complex and originated from a combination of factors, including the difficulties of creating agricultural employment using dry-farming practices; the fact that most workers lived in large villages and towns, often at a considerable distance from the fields; and the limited rural exodus. With time, industrialization and high urban wages would reduce surplus farm labour, but this process was delayed in Southern Spain, not least because the area of cultivation continued to expand in some regions right up until the early 1930s. Unfortunately, the Second Republic coincided with economic depression and low farm prices, which encouraged commercial farmers to reduce labour inputs, just as the demand for work was increasing. The difficulties of improving yields and intensifying agriculture under dry-farming conditions made mechanization attractive for farmers to reduce labour costs.

The Second Republic significantly raised expectations that rural poverty could be alleviated in Southern Spain. Nevertheless, the decision of the new Left Republican-Socialist government to carry out a far-reaching land reform to create employment was both ineffectual and divisive. The weak state capacity that the government had inherited implied that it had virtually no information concerning how the latifundios actually operated, thereby severely limiting the debate on the feasibility of a reform. In particular, we show that, contrary to much of contemporary opinion, not only were the latifundios actually well cultivated by the standards of the day but there was very little new land that could be brought under the plough. Spain, in many respects, was already too rich for a traditional land reform, as converting pasture land to cereals would not only have created only limited amounts of employment but would reduce meat production, for which there was a growing demand, and increase wheat output, of which there was a surplus. But it was also too poor to fund a 'green revolution', which required large-scale investments in water storage and canals for new irrigation schemes, as well as the development of new plant-growing technologies, and the creation of the necessary food chains to process and transport high-value foods to consumers in distant markets. As a result, land reform settled fewer than 15,000 farmers on plots of land that were far too small to create a family farm, frustrating the hopes of many rural workers and poor tenant farmers, but also alienating small farmers who feared that future governments might extend the reform to incorporate their properties, especially following the Socialist-organized land invasions of March 1936.

While the threat of land reform directly challenged the traditional landed elites, the Left Republican-Socialist government's social and labour legislation of 1931 and 1932 risked increasing farmers' production costs at a time of weak farm prices. Among other things, it introduced collective bargaining, restricted the use of migrant labour, and required farmers to provide emergency assistance to workers through temporary land settlements. This legislation was highly contentious because its implementation at the village level was often arbitrary and highly politicized. When the Socialists controlled municipal governments, it was put into effect, and membership of its trade union soared. However, when the

Centre-Right won the elections in November 1933, landowners and farmers often ignored the legislation. The Socialists now faced the dilemma of having to either accept the legitimacy of the new municipal governments at a time when the living standards of its members were deteriorating or pursue illegal resistance and reject the authority of the state. Many chose the latter, resulting in the revolutionary uprising in the northern mining region of Asturias in October 1934.

Less visible, but affecting far more families, were the economic problems facing small farmers and tenants across the country, whose prosperity depended on both high farm prices *and* low wage costs, demands that were diametrically opposed to those of rural labourers and urban dwellers. Just as weak state capacity led to the Left Republican-Socialist government's failing to resolve the problems of landless labourers, conservative governments were now unable to intervene effectively in commodity markets to help family farmers. Instead, following the Right-Republican victory of November 1933, many farmers simply ignored collective bargaining agreements and blacklisted trade unionists. When the Popular Front won in February 1936, many small farmers, fearing that the Left-Republican government would again follow partisan policies, looked to more extreme alternatives.

There was clearly a class dimension to these rural conflicts, with the volume of unrest increasing or decreasing according to the political group in power, and whether policies favoured absentee landowners and farmers or landless workers and small tenants. Yet a second, less visible but more divisive cleavage was the fact that many small farmers and workers still depended economically on interlinked contracts and patron-client networks. This led many to continue to side with landowners, rather than joining the local labour syndicate. Others quite simply preferred to use their entrepreneurial skills and hard work to climb the farm ladder and become independent of both the village caciques and labour unions. The deep polarization of Spanish villages in 1936 was therefore caused by the clash between two very different ways of organizing rural society: the traditional patron-client hierarchical structures and the new class-based groups. Numerous conflicts took place over whether it should be the landowner or the Socialist FNTT that determined which groups of tenants should be given land, and which workers. There were also often disputes between neighbouring villages, while the conflicts between the socialist and anarchist syndicates at times, according to Manuel Azaña, the Republic's Prime Minister, descended into 'an authentic civil war'.

This book differs from most recent interpretations in three major areas. First, it argues that the low levels of state capacity that the Republican governments inherited were an important explanation for the failure of agrarian and social reforms during the Second Republic. This is illustrated by the inability of successive governments to widen the tax base, and in particular to fully implement an impartial land tax; by the limited information that was available to understand the extent that agriculture had progressed since the turn of the century; and by the lack of administrative capacity to implement legislation in a fair and objective manner. A second explanation is that agrarian policy was heavily biased towards the needs of landless workers and failed to respond to those of small farmers, who represented a third of the total electorate and who suffered from falling farm incomes at a time when government politics were pushing up their costs. Finally, historians have usually explained rural conflicts during the Second Republic in terms of either class or a clash between Marxist and Catholic ideologies. Although both arguments were used by the Left and Right to frame contentious policies and construct collective identities, they greatly simplify the nature of conflicts. In particular, they ignore the fundamental difficulties of trying to allocate impartially the inadequate amounts of land and employment during a major economic crisis. Conflicts broke out not just between workers' syndicates and farmers but also among different groups of workers, between those small farmers who joined a Socialist or anarchist syndicate and those who preferred to remain in a traditional patron-client relationship, and between neighbouring villages. Therefore, although none of these made civil war inevitable, most villages in Spain had become heavily polarized by the summer of 1936. A map following the military uprising of July 1936 suggests a country divided into two, with provinces where small family farmers predominated supporting the rebellion and those with latifundios remaining loyal to the Republic. In fact, this greatly simplifies the story, as the real divisions were *within* villages, in areas of both latifundios and small farms across the country.

The book is organized in five parts, each with two chapters. Part I provides the European context. From the mid-nineteenth century, Western Europe enjoyed an unparalleled period of economic growth and rising living standards, while increased state capacity saw governments widen their tax reach, experiment with central planning, and create a professional civil service. Changes in income distribution, rapid urbanization, rising literacy, windening of the suffrage, and the growth in trade unions led to significant demands for political change, especially following the First World War. By 1920, only Bolshevik Russia and Hungary of Europe's twenty-eight states were not democracies or had limited parliamentary systems. However, both the timing and sequencing of change varied significantly across countries. In particular, how governments responded to three major exogenous shocks – namely, the late nineteenth century 'grain invasion', the First World War, and the Great Depression – would have very different consequences across the Continent. By the 1930s, governments everywhere were in crisis, which helped strengthen liberal democracy in some countries (Britain, France) but led to authoritarian governments elsewhere (Soviet Union, Germany) or social democracy (Scandinavia).

Economic and social change were arguably as great in agriculture as in any other sector. In the late nineteenth century, agriculture was still by far the largest sector, and the influence of landed elites on national and local government remained essentially undiminished. However, the growing integration of international markets and domestic industrialization contributed to undermine the traditional elites' economic and political influence. At the same time, higher wages attracted large numbers of farm workers to the rapidly growing industrial cities, as well as the New World. Those who stayed behind benefitted from a combination of falling land prices and rising wages, allowing them to gain access to land and become farmers. Food shortages during the First World War led governments to prioritize increasing farm output, and government policies changed to favour farmers, rather than landowners. By the interwar period, family farmers in many countries accounted for a significant proportion of the farm vote and could potentially form a major political grouping to challenge the urban middle classes or organized labour. The political direction that small farmers took would have a major implication on whether liberalism prevailed, or the country turned to fascism, or social democracy.

Part II shows that Spain experienced rapid economic growth and enjoyed relative political stability in the half century before the Second Republic. Recent estimates suggest that GDP per capita increased by two-thirds between 1875 and 1931, by which time both Madrid and Barcelona had almost a million inhabitants, and Spain was becoming an increasingly modern European society. Agriculture played an important role in this change, with almost a million male and female workers, or a fifth of its workforce, leaving the sector during the two decades before 1931. Spain on the eve of the Second Republic had a much more dynamic economy than is usually suggested in the historical literature.

Although Spain had much in common with other Western European countries, a number of major differences emerged at this time. First, the Restoration settlement (1875–1923) provided the country with an unusual amount of political stability, undisputed national frontiers, and a marked absence of ethnic-racist nationalism. This was in contrast to the considerable disruption that the country had suffered following the highly destructive civil wars during the previous half century. But stability

came at a price. In particular, while universal male suffrage was introduced as early as 1890, no mass competitive political parties developed, as
parliamentary elections were fixed in advance by the political elite using
clientelism, corruption, and fraud. Trade unions were also frequently
banned. The association of parliamentary elections with patronage and
corruption would be difficult to erase, and politicians of all parties simply
adapted the system for their own ends during the Second Republic.

Another major factor was Spain's neutrality during the First World
War. This had obvious benefits, but it created no political demands for
governments to invest in state capacity. By contrast, the experience of the
Great War played an important role in state building in most Western
European countries and was valuable for when governments had to
respond to new problems, especially those associated with the 1930s
Depression.

Finally, agriculture differed to most North-Western European counties,
because of both the large numbers of landless labourers in Southern Spain
and the constraints imposed by dry-farming. This book challenges the
arguments that the nineteenth-century liberal land reforms failed to create
a society of small family farmers, but Spain remained essentially a 'peasant'
society, rather than one of small, economically viable family farmers. By the
interwar period, Spain was, therefore, predominantly a country of small
farmers, although large numbers of landless and near landless lived in
poverty in the regions of latifundios in the south. Dry-farming technologies
made it difficult for small farmers to introduce labour-intensive crops,
which was a major constraint that would restrict governments' responses
to the depressed international markets conditions of the 1930s.

Part III examines the links between the persistence of an economically
influential and politically strong rural elite and traditional Church, and
a peasant agriculture. For economists, small farms are seen as being competitive, because family labour is more productive than wage workers,
while political scientists believe that agrarian societies where family farms
predominate are more egalitarian and democratic than those with large
estates. Family farmers have to cooperate among themselves however, both
to take advantage of the growing economies of scale in some economic
activities and to create lobbies to channel their economic and political
demands. Many small farmers in Western Europe from the late nineteenth
century responded to the rapid industrialization and lengthening commodity chains by creating credit and producer cooperatives to reinforce their
competitive position. These were slower to appear in Spain, and provide an
institutional explanation for why family farmers were economically weaker,
and failed to create effective pressure groups to protect their interests. In
particular, it argues that there was a causal link running from weak farm

cooperatives to small farmers' limited political voice and representation in political parties before the Second Republic, and with the over-representation of the interests of urban republicans and organized labour in the 1931 Constitution, which resulted in the opposition of many small farmers to the Republic from the outset.

The limited presence of civic associations and farm cooperatives in Spain was not caused by a lack of social capital and trust as some historians have argued, as village grain banks were successfully operating since at least the eighteenth century, even in areas of latifundios. Instead we suggest that there was a lack of top-down support to create federations across wide geographical areas. In many northern European countries, the extension of the franchise encouraged urban-based liberal political parties from the 1870s to attack the privileges of both the Church and landed elites, leading them to create defensive alliances to build a mass conservative party to defend their interests in the national parliament. Their success at organizing small farmers led to new political entrepreneurs and Christian Democracy appearing, and a marked decline in influence of both the landed elites and Church hierarchy. However, the Restoration political settlement in Spain made it unnecessary for these groups to organize small farmers and build a mass political party before the Second Republic. Only in Catalonia did competitive regional party politics require politicians to intervene actively to help farmers, explaining the region's more dynamic associations and cooperative movement.

Part IV shows that many Spanish contemporaries believed that extremes of land inequality produced absentee landownership, poor farming practices, and widespread poverty among the landless. In fact this book shows that the land ownership structure in Southern Spain was not an obstacle to increasing farm output or improving living standards for most workers during the half century prior to the Republic. Instead, the agrarian problem is explained by the difficulties in creating employment for a growing number of workers during the Great Depression, at a time when weak farm prices encouraged farmers to reduce the area cultivated and cut labour inputs by mechanization.

The Second Republic created widespread expectations that it would end rural poverty and reduce inequality of opportunities. Central to this was the 1932 Land Reform Law which aimed to break up the large estates and create small holdings or collectives. However, only a few thousand families were settled, a tiny fraction of those in need, and these received far too little land to make them independent of the highly seasonal labour markets. The failure of land reform is usually explained by a combination of budgetary constraints, determined opposition from the landed elites, and a lack of commitment by urban-based politicians. Chapter 8 argues instead that most contemporaries did not appreciate the constraints to increasing employment under dry-farming conditions, or the difficulties in carrying out a land reform with the limited state capacity that the Republic inherited. In particular, although economic incentives were changed by giving land to landless workers, it was not possible to change crop rotations or increase the intensity of cultivation on small farms.

The difficulties for the 1932 Land Reform to settle more than a few thousand families contrasts with the massive land invasions involving over 100,000 individuals in the spring of 1936 in western Spain. The Left-Republican government responded by permitting most workers to stay and cultivate the land, in exchange for rent. However, the organizational advantages that this 'bottom-up' land reform offered the state, namely a land reform being carried out by those with detailed local knowledge of where under-cultivated land existed and which villagers were most in need, were offset by the problems of moral hazard (especially the over-cultivation by the occupiers of another person's land), and conflicts between those who already enjoyed user-rights to the land, namely live-stock farmers and other groups of tenants. Land invasions did not resolve the problem of insufficient land to cultivate.

Although land reform failed to resolve the chronic problems of unemploy-ment and poverty that Spain suffered during the Great Depression, it raised expectations among the landless and helped political groups of both extremes organize in the countryside. The Socialist FNTT in particular was able to make the problem of the landless the overriding social problem of the Second Republic, even though they represented only about 5 per cent of the nation's workforce. It also helped unite small farmers, who were often divided over commodity and regional issues, into a formidable group that became clearly identified with the conservative right.

Part V argues that most contemporaries and historians have associated Spain's agrarian problem with latifundios and explained the conflicts of the Second Republic in terms of class conflicts. Yet Andalucia was not Spain, and the deep polarization found in villages across the country in 1936 was caused as much by the major divisions among different groups of farm workers and small farmers, as a straightforward contest between the latifundistas and the workers. Conflicts arose from the clashes between two very different ways of organizing rural society, with the traditional patron-client hierarchical structures being confronted by new, class-based groups. There were two basic problems. First, the question of which groups of workers and tenants were to gain access to the insufficient land and work, and which ones would be excluded. A second, and related, problem was that legislation that improved work-ing conditions, either by raising wages or increasing the number of workdays, inevitably raised production costs not just for the larger farmers but also for those family farmers who depended on wage labour for part of their harvest work. Many of these small farmers earned little more than day-labourers.

Political power swung dramatically three times during the Republic, favouring the Socialist trade unions during the *Primer Bienio* (December 1931 to November 1933); the landowners and employers for the period of the *Bienio Conservador* (November 1933 to February 1936); and swinging back to the workers again after February 1936. As a result, employers and syndicates alternated in controlling local patronage and deciding whether to implement laws that benefitted their constituents. By 1936, the two Spain's were evenly balanced, with the Centre-Right coalitions doing almost as successfully in the elections as the Popular Front, even in areas of latifundios.

Over the five years the main parties on both the Left and Right moved away from the centre towards the political extremes. The anarchists had opposed the Republic from the outset, but the moderate Socialist Party (the PSOE) was instrumental in passing the wide-reaching social and labour reforms in 1931 and 1932. However, the Socialists were divided between orthodox Marxists and revisionists and, once out of power and in the face of belligerent landowners and farmers regaining their powers in the countryside at the expense of the FNTT, led to the party dividing and the extremists supporting the civilian uprising in Asturias in October 1934. The Right had a similar experience, with landowners and farmers gaining control of the countryside once more after the November 1933 elections and creating municipal governments that allowed them to ignore the labour reforms. The very narrow victory of the Popular Front heralded a return to the restrictions on hiring labour and higher wage costs.

The difficulties of implementing effective policies to improve conditions for the rural poor were therefore contradictory, as helping landless workers inevitably had a detrimental impact on the incomes of poor small farmers, who could not switch to higher-value crops. But there were major divisions even among these two groups, as some legislation benefitted some workers at the expense of others, while small farmers were often divided between those who identified with the left-wing syndicates and those that chose to remain in the traditional patron-client relations. The election results of February 1936 showed a highly polarized country, and even in areas of latifundios the Popular Front won by less than 1 per cent of the vote.

Part I

The European Experience: Economic and Political Development, 1870–1939

In June of 1922, King Alfonso XIII visited Las Hurdes, an isolated and very poor region stretching along the Portuguese border, where iodine deficiencies resulted in the population suffering from high levels of goiter and congenital hypothyroidism (cretinism). The visit was highly publicized and provided a stark contrast between a backward, rural region to the modern, vibrant cities of Madrid or Barcelona. While some farmers in Spain on the eve of the Second Republic still used the old 'Roman' scratch plough and lived in primitive housing, an increasing number of its citizens were driving cars, and intellectuals such as Ochoa, Ortega y Gasset, Marañón, Unamuno, Lorca, or Buñel, formed part of a wider, dynamic European society.

There were several overlapping sources of poverty found in Spain at the turn of the twentieth century. The first, and partly present in the extreme case of Las Hurdes, suggests a Malthusian scenario where population growth in villages with limited resources and few contacts with the outside world led to endemic poverty, the extent of which fluctuated with the size of the annual harvest and the precise moment of the farming year.[1] A second, and much more common cause by the 1920s, was the poverty and growing inequality produced by economic development and infrastructural improvements, leading to traditional industries and livelihoods disappearing because of competition from other regions, and making village workers unemployed. Indeed, in the case of Las Hurdes, it was the improvements in road communications that helped travellers, and their film crews, reach what had previously been an almost totally isolated part of the country. This 'uneven growth' would be resolved in time, either through the creation of new local employment or, more frequently, by outmigration to the growing cities. Finally, industrialization produced a new type of poverty linked to the business cycle, and the 1930s Great Depression sent unemployment and poverty soaring in both industrial

---

[1] In fact, Buñuel's film of 1932–5 suggests that Las Hurdes was connected to the outside world through temporary migration and the sale of honey.

and rural economies. Although traditional rural societies possessed some mechanisms to help alleviate extreme poverty, there was growing pressure on central governments to assume greater responsibilities with industrialization, and the switch from the agricultural to the business cycle.

Contrasts between the persistence of severe poverty and a dynamic urban society were not unique to Spain in the interwar period. George Orwell's description of the slums and malnutrition in England's industrial cities in the 1930s shocked his educated readers as much as Alfonso XIII's visit to Las Hurdes upset Spaniards. We cannot be sure whether living standards were actually significantly worse in either Wigan or Las Hurdes in the interwar period than they had been in earlier decades, but both received widespread national publicity and, in their different ways, led to political demands for greater state involvement in resolving the problems.

This section considers the economic and political changes in Western European countries over the seven decades or so before the 1930s, and provides a framework to understand better, in later chapters, how Spain differed. The first chapter begins by looking at the links between economic development, the creation of state capacity, the extension of the suffrage (and with it the erosion in influence of the autonomous power centres), and the growth of organized labour across Europe. Historians have argued that the timing and sequencing of these changes were often very different among Western European countries, greatly affecting their capacity to respond to events such as the First World War, and having a major influence on the nature of political regimes that would appear in the 1920s and 1930s.[2] In Spain, the combination of early male suffrage, the persistence of strong traditional elites and autonomous power centres, and weak state capacity, was perhaps unique in Western Europe in 1929.

Chapter 2 looks in more detail at European agriculture, and in particular rural social mobility and the consolidation of the family farm, and the changing nature of relations between the sector and the state. Traditional agriculture employed between a half and two-thirds of the active labour force, and the sector still accounted for between a quarter and a half in 1929 almost everywhere in Europe, with most males now enjoying the vote. Agriculture was rarely stagnant, as suggested in most two-sector models of the economy, but grew rapidly with industrialization.[3] Everywhere landowners, farmers, and agricultural workers had to adapt to rapid changes in factor prices and the demand for farm products brought about by a combination of domestic economic growth and the greater integration

---

[2] For the importance of timing and sequence of change on historical outcomes, see Pierson 2004 and Fukuyama 2014, p. 30.
[3] Ansell & Samuels 2014, p. 66, for example, assume that agriculture is stagnant and industry growing.

of global markets. Imports of cheap foods and beverages led to falling prices
and sparked conflicts between landlord and tenant over who should bear
the losses. In addition, farmers, especially the smaller ones, resented the
fact that consumer prices often fell less than farm gate prices, the difference
being absorbed by the middlemen in the lengthening food chains. At the
same time, farm workers found that their wages grew less than those in the
urban sector, and fell significantly at times of inflation, while employment
opportunities for some workers were threatened by mechanization.

Income distribution changed significantly *within* the agricultural sector,
leading to new social groups challenging the incumbent rural elites across
much of Western Europe. In particular, a major characteristic of the period
between the 1870s and the 1920s was the relative decline of landowners,
the growing scarcity of farm labourers, and the consolidation of the small
family farm. Industrialization played a major role in this, but so did
changes *within* agriculture itself, and the relative success of different farm
groups and organizations in influencing government policy. By the interwar period, the successful commercial farmers of industrial Europe had
little in common with the old traditional landed elites of the Old Regime.

1 The Modernization of European Societies

> As hard as it may be for us to credit, agrarian ideology is crucial if we are to understand, not the archaism of Hitler's regime, but its extraordinary militancy.[1]

> A socialist movement that mobilised a significant fraction of the rural proletariat (agrarian labourers and smallholders dependent on the labour market) contained the seeds of its own failure, for it would become enmeshed in rural class conflict and alienate the family peasantry.[2]

The period between 1870 and 1939 was one of long-run economic growth and unprecedented improvements in living standards across Europe, as well as of major social conflicts, rising nationalism, and experiments in new forms of political representation. Economic growth led to rising productivity and higher living standards, while rapid social mobility increased the size of the urban middle classes, consolidated the position of family farmers, and witnessed the appearance of organized labour.[3] These transformations led to demands for greater political voice and eventually full democracy, and by 1920, all but two (Bolshevik Russia and Hungary) of Europe's twenty-eight states were democracies or 'having restricted parliamentary systems'.[4] Yet as Charles Tilly notes, 'democratization is a dynamic process that always remains incomplete and perpetually runs the risk of reversal – of de-democratization'.[5] At no time was this truer than in the 1930s, as Europe split between authoritarian nation-statism and liberal democracies.[6] The experience of Spain of first achieving, and then losing, its democracy was therefore hardly

---

[1] Tooze 2006, p. 180.   [2] Luebbert 1991, pp. 285–6.
[3] Following Fukuyama 2014, p. 40, social mobility 'entails different parts of society becoming conscious of themselves as people with shared interests or identities, and their organization for collective action'.
[4] By 1939, half of them had 'succumbed to dictators with absolute powers', and by the end of 1940, the figure had diminished to just the United Kingdom, Ireland, Sweden, Finland and Switzerland. Casanova 2010b, p. 4. See also Mann 2004, p. 37, and Capoccia 2005, p. 7.
[5] Tilly 2007, p. ix.   [6] Mann 2004, p. 24.

unique in interwar Europe. For political scientists such as Luebbert or Fukuyama, it was the timing and sequence of key events, such as economic growth, social mobility, state building, or the extension of suffrage, that determined whether liberal democracy survived.

Democracy implies not just a parliamentary government, competitive party system, and universal male suffrage, but also fundamental changes in the nature and scope of the state and rule of law. In particular, states need reliable sources of revenue and good information in order to determine suitable legislation and to have the ability to enforce its laws and allocate impartially public goods such as education or social benefits to its citizens. The growth of state capacity is the result of political demands and especially the need to fight wars. From the mid-nineteenth century across Western Europe, the growth in party political competition, the Great War, and the 1930s Depression produced new demands that led to major changes in state capacity. In Western Europe, the size of the urban middle classes, organized labour, and the rural sector was such that, even if one of these groups had been sufficiently homogenous in their interests, it would still have been too small to control a majority on its own to win free elections. The strategic alliances of these distinctive groups, or their fractions, therefore determined the nature of government.

The chapter looks at the changing relations between political representation, economic development, and state capacity. It begins by discussing the difficulties of switching from a society run by the landed elites to that of universal suffrage and competitive party politics. This is followed by looking at state capacity and the massive demands produced by the First World War. This will be followed by two sections that consider the rapid economic growth that took place, and how a combination of industrial demand for unskilled labour, emigration, and international trade threatened to produce a major switch in income distribution away from the landed elites to urban workers. The chapter concludes by examining how the economic and social problems caused by the First World War and the collapse of the international economy in the 1930s led to the strengthening of liberal democracy in some countries, but the appearance of social democracy and fascism in others.

When Do Elites Give Up Power? The Rise of Democracy and the Modern State

Economic growth, beginning in the seventeenth century and accelerating from the mid-nineteenth century, threatened the financial and political interests of the traditional landed elites, and how these elites reacted to the new challenges had major implications for the nature of political development that subsequently took place. Everywhere the shift from hegemonic regimes to competitive oligarchies – and then to an expanded suffrage that first incorporated the middle classes and then the working classes – and democracy, took place in stages, sometimes violent ones. Historians and political scientists have made considerable efforts to understand under what conditions extending political participation took place, and in particular when traditional elites were willing to surrender political power and accept polyarchy.

One strand of this literature emphasizes the redistributive effects of democracy, and the belief that the fall in the average wealth of voters as suffrage is widened will lead, in the words of Frédéric Bastiat (1850), to the 'legalized plunder' of the rich's property through taxation.[7] Acemoglu and Robinson, for example, see an inverted U-shaped relationship between intergroup inequality and the transition to democracy, with the traditional elites in societies with high levels of income inequality opposing democracy, not just because they have a considerable amount to lose, but also because they have the resources and capacity to use the state to repress change. By contrast, in more 'equal societies', citizens would be 'not sufficiently attracted' to join a revolution and social unrest, because there was less to redistribute.[8] However, a significant literature questions whether democracies actually redistribute more than autocracies, or whether inequality is correlated with pressures for redistribution. In fact, the historical experience suggests that regime change has often taken place in societies with very different levels of income inequality.[9]

A second interpretation links political transitions to elite competition between groups at the top end of the income distribution, rather than between the rich and poor. In these models, economic growth creates new groups of rich individuals who demand to be included in government decision-making to protect their property from the whims of an autocratic state, rather than for reasons of redistribution. Ansell and Samuels distinguish between land inequality, which is inherited from pre-industrial societies, and income inequality produced by the growth in the industrial and financial sectors. Landed elites, they argue, 'prefer autocracy because they need the state's coercive authority to repress wage demands and keep labour in place, working the land', but the rising inequality associated with economic development is favourable for democracy, as the newly rich found in industry and finance will demand changes to the

---

[7] Cited in Ansell & Samuels 2014, p. 3. Most British contemporaries, however, believed the working class posed no redistributive threat. Ibid., p. 49. See Meltzer & Richard 1981, for the median voter theory.

[8] Acemoglu & Robinson 2006, pp. xii, 27 and 37. See also Boix 2003.

[9] Ansell & Samuels 2014, p. 5.

institutional framework to protect their gains from expropriation by an authoritarian state.[10]

The growth in the nonfarm sector, first through greater trade and then industrialization, offered Europe's monarchies new and potentially attractive sources of revenue. However, it was the state's need to increase its fiscal capacity to fight wars that gave the recently enriched citizens the opportunities to bargain taxes for a share in political power.[11] The classic example for constitutional commitment was the success of the new elites in disposing of two British monarchs and extending parliament's powers to protect their own commercial interests in the seventeenth century.[12] Yet the new elites showed no interest in establishing democracy or income redistribution, as both would have hurt them as much as it would have harmed the traditional landed elites.

The next stage in the drive from a political oligarchy to polyarchy and an increased opportunity for participation and contestation came from urban areas, where a growing share of the population lived (Table 1.1). In particular, the revolutions that swept Europe in the 1840s saw popular demands for new political rights and 'bottom-up mobilization converged to extract concessions from existing holders of power'.[13] In Sweden, organized labour by the end of the century demanded universal suffrage, although in countries where industrialization and urbanization had begun much earlier, such as Britain, the role of trade unions was much less important. The timing and sequence of events was essential because, as Chapter 9 notes, early male suffrage and competitive party elections helped encourage labour to participate in elections and allowed democratic revisionism to take root, while its delay often strengthened Marxist orthodoxy and, in the case of Spain, anarchism.

Another literature contrasts the concentration of landownership, rural poverty, and oligarchic forms of government found in Latin America with the family farm and inclusive societies that supposedly favoured the early appearance of democracy in North America.[14] The theories often suggest limited or no social mobility in agriculture, so that the economic and political powers of the traditional rural elites remain unchanged over

---

[10] Ibid., 2014, p. 12 and Fukuyama 2014, p. 405.   [11] See especially Tilly 2007, p. 173.
[12] North & Weingast 1989.
[13] Tilly 2007, p. 65. The revolutions of 1848 were not limited to just 'wars of progress'. The widespread unrest in the countryside was often directed against the sale and sometimes usurpation of common lands, while among urban workers it was often linked with artisans' opposition to new work practices and impersonal market forces, rather than the demands of the small numbers who comprised the new working classes. Bayly 2004, pp. 155–60.
[14] Most recently, Engerman & Sokokoff 2012 and Acemoglu & Robinson 2012. This is discussed in more detail in Chapter 7.

Table 1.1 *Socio-economic variables in Western Europe, c. 1920*

	A	B	C	D	E	F	G
	Active in ag. 1920	Workers in all sectors as % of active population	Urban population 20,000+	Importance of family farms 1920s	% of male population over 20 who could vote 1910	% of male population over 20 who could vote 1920	Central government spending as % of GDP
Austria	45.9	47.1	26	45	38	90	n.a.
Belgium	19.1	59.6	30	30	38	43	n.a
Denmark	35.2	50.0	29	49	30	70	8.8
Finland	70.4	39.9	11	47	75	74	n.a
France	34.9	45.9	28	35	43	43	29.8
Germany	30.5	50.4	41	54	39	95	n.a
Ireland	51.3		29	40		74	
Italy	55.7	51.0	31	22	15	49	36.1
Netherlands	23.6	64.2	45	40	26	39	14.9
Norway	36.8	52.8	18	82	59	80	12.8
Sweden	40.4	51.6	20	50	33	33	5.6
Switzerland	27.1	49.7	23	60	37	40	n.a
UK	7.6		61	25	29	75	27.4
Spain	55	Na	40	20	62	66	8.4

Column F: The figure for Switzerland increased to 88% in 1921 and in the Netherlands to 81% in 1922.
Bartolini 2000, pp. 133, 148, 165 for Columns A, B, and C; Vanhanen 1984, Column D; Flora 1983, Columns E and F. Spain: Carreras & Tafunell 2005, tables 2.23, 6.2, 12.2 and 14.6. Prados de la Escosura 2017, table S19.

centuries, and the possibility of the growth and consolidation of family farms, such as took place in Western Europe before 1939, were minimal. In fact, the nature of landownership changed dramatically in Western Europe before and during industrialization, so that the landed elites found under the Old Regime institutions were very different to those a century later, regardless of the levels of industrialization that a country had experienced. The autonomous powers of the Church and the military also declined sharply in most countries.[15]

However, the question of how and when the landed elites were willing to surrender political power peacefully is crucial. For Robert Dahl, a defining feature of successful polyarchies was that new rules, practices, and 'the culture of competitive' politics were established that allowed the landed elites to feel protected *before* the shift from non-party politics to party competition.[16] Ziblatt also suggests that traditional elites will only give up power and accept democratic elections peacefully when they believe a strong, well-organized mass political party exists to represent their interests, which is capable of winning elections. For this author, when a party could provide such safeguards *before* the extension of the suffrage, such as in Britain, then the elites were willing to embrace democracy. When it was absent, for example, in Germany or Spain in the interwar period, they opposed it and resorted instead to electoral fraud, clientelism, and corruption.[17]

By concentrating on the landed elites, the historical literature often ignores the growth and consolidation of family farms across Western Europe by the 1930s. The political potential of this group was significant because even though the *relative size* of the farm population started declining at an early stage of industrialization, agriculture still employed between a quarter and a half of the active population virtually everywhere on the eve of the Great Depression, and the numbers of family farmers were actually growing. Traditionally, small farmers had been often found in hierarchical patron-client networks, effectively giving them no independent voice. The rapid improvements in communications (transport, newspapers, voice), and the development of impersonal markets for both commodities and factor inputs (land, labour, capital) from the late nineteenth century, helped erode the usefulness of these networks for both the patrons and their clients. Family farmers also increasingly participated in autonomous civil associations, which political scientists often see as being

---

[15] For Tilly, for example, 'the fundamental processes promoting democratization in all times and places . . . consist of increasing integration of trust networks into public politics, increasing insulation of public politics from categorical inequality, and decreasing autonomy of major power centres from public politics'. Tilly 2007, p. 23.
[16] Dahl 1971, p. 36.   [17] Ziblatt 2017, pp. 26–7 and 34.

important to create mass political parties and democracy.[18] However, as Riley notes, the decline of landowners as a political group does not automatically imply the appearance of a strong network of autonomous associations of small farmers. Furthermore, networks of autonomous associations could be used to support fascism at times and not just democracy.[19]

The organization of large numbers of small farmers in civic associations offered the possibility for creating mass political parties that could match those of the growing urban middle class and organized labour. For Luebbert, the presence of well-organized groups of family farmers, and their decisions whether to align with the urban middle classes or with organized labour, would be a major factor in determining whether democracy survived, or whether the country turned to fascism.[20]

The Growth of State Capacity

The development of an effective state capacity is crucial for democracy to succeed. In particular, governments have to serve the interests of the electorate; possess sufficient capacity to manage and implement legislation; defend individuals from deprivation and unlawful infringement of their rights by others; and protect them from arbitrary and illegal abuse from the state itself. Besley and Persson suggest, for example, that 'historical accounts demonstrate vividly that state authority, tax systems, court systems, and democracy coevolve in a complex web of interdependent causality'.[21] The inability of governments to implement legislation because of weak capacity can therefore threaten democracy itself:

Many of the failures attributed to democracy are in fact failures of state administrations that are unable to deliver on the promises made by newly elected democratic politicians to others who want not just their political rights but good government as well.[22]

Historians have considerably widened our understanding of the nature of state building. Centeno and Ferraro, for example, identify several

---

[18] The literature is vast but, in particular, Tocqueville 1835–40/2000, Putnam 1993, North et al. 2007, and Tilly 2007.
[19] Riley 2019.   [20] Luebbert 1991.
[21] Besley & Persson 2011, p. 5. The authors quote Adam Smith, who wrote that the state needed to provide 'peace, easy taxes, and a tolerable administration of justice'. The importance of state capacity is underlined by the fact that '40 to 50 states' today 'suffer weakness or fragility'. Ibid., pp. 1–2.
[22] Fukuyama 2014, p. 38. He notes that Samuel Huntingdon talked of the 'gap that emerged between the expectations of newly mobilized populations and their government's ability or willingness to accommodate their participation in politics'. Ibid., p. 48.

dimensions of state capacity and strength.[23] First, *territoriality* is the state's ability to use coercive force to impose its 'preferred order', and requires both the security of frontiers and control over domestic 'rival claimants and subjugated groups'. *Economic* capacity involves the creation of institutions to promote economic growth and build an efficient fiscal system. *Infrastructural* or *cognitive* capacity represents the state's competence in amassing information and implementing policy.[24] Finally, *legitimacy* refers to the extent that citizens accept the state as an arbitrator in their daily lives.

Charles Tilly famously wrote that 'war made the state and the state made war', as external threats led not just to higher taxes, but also increases in the size of bureaucracies.[25] However, prior to 1914, the budgets of all Western European counties were very small relative to GDP, usually less than 10 per cent, and a significant part of expenditure was linked to military spending and interest payments on war debt. The First World War dramatically changed the scale and nature of state involvement in the economy, bringing industrial warfare and mass killings to nation states that were often still heavily rural. There were seven or eight million combat-related deaths, and almost as many among non-combatants. The war, which had been expected to be short, severely tested the ability of individual countries to sustain their armies in the field and to feed their citizens by the fourth year. The logistics were enormous, with, on average, 10,000 soldiers every mile along the 475 miles of the Western Front between the Swiss border and North Sea alone having to be supplied.[26] Government spending soared, reaching the equivalent of half of GDP in France and Germany, and a third in the United Kingdom.[27] The battlefield stalemate contrasted with the capacity of different countries to feed their urban populations. As Avner Offer has written, 'Germany did not run out of rifles or shells. It suffered badly from shortages of food. Likewise the Allies: their agrarian resources decided the war. So not only a war of steel and gold, but a war of bread and potatoes'.[28] The Great War forced governments not just to increase state capacity, but also to develop new relations with the agricultural sector (Chapter 2). The return to peace inevitably greatly reduced state spending, but the experience of war had taught governments of the need for planning and efficient implementation of laws, as well as the need for a better understanding of how their economies worked.

[23] Centeno & Ferraro 2013, pp. 10–13.
[24] See, in addition, Mann 1993 and Whitehead 1995.
[25] Tilly 1975, p. 42. For Italy, see Dincecco et al. 2011, and for Spain, Sabaté 2016.
[26] Mann 2012, p. 141.   [27] Broadberry & Harrison 1995, p. 15.   [28] Offer 1989, p. 1.

Yet while democracy is a 'dynamic process', always incomplete and in danger of reversing, state capacity has a tendency to move forward in the same direction. The importance of the First World War required governments not only to accumulate information concerning how their economies operated, which otherwise they might not have done, but also to learn to become more efficient, leaving them better prepared to adjust to new problems when they occurred, such as the Great Depression. Therefore, even if state needs and priorities changed over time, governments required the capacity to collect and process information, and the ability to implement their decrees efficiently and impartially. In addition, and crucial for the arguments here, because capacity is built up over time, new reforming governments are highly dependent on both the size of the investments made by previous governments and the nature of the capacity that these had created.[29] The problems facing Spain's reforming governments of the Second Republic were therefore twofold, as not only had the country's neutrality during the Great War led to low levels of investment in state capacity, but much of that which did exist left it ill-equipped to deal with the widespread poverty of the 1930s.

Finally, state capacity requires an explicit investment to create structures that could extend 'government communication and control continuously from central institutions to individual localities or even households, and back again'.[30] A crucial stage in the growth of the liberal nation state was the need to end its dependence on the use of patronage to collect taxes and implement polices locally. Unfortunately, as we shall see, in Spain, the increase in the scale of government and the growth in suffrage led to the development of clientelism and the appearance of complex hierarchical political machines based on the reciprocal exchange of favours, rather than the creation of impersonal mechanisms to collect taxes and allocate published goods (Chapter 3).[31]

Economic Growth and Structural Change

Western European economies grew at a historically unprecedented rate between 1870 and 1929, with GDP per capita income doubling in real terms (Table 1.2).[32] Population also grew rapidly and the rural exodus filled the rapidly expanding cities. As the industrial sector increased in importance, firm structure changed radically, with some factories

---

[29] Besley & Persson 2011, p. 12.   [30] Tilly 2007, p. 19.
[31] Fukuyama 2014, p. 86. See also North et al. 2007, p. 11.
[32] From $2,141 in 1990 international dollars in 1870 to $4,452 in 1929, and refer to the leading twelve nations (Austria, Belgium, Denmark, Finland, France, Germany, Italy, Netherlands, Norway, Sweden, Switzerland, and the UK). Maddison-Project, 2013.

Table 1.2 *Economic growth and structural change in selected European countries, 1870–1930*

	Per capita income (1990 $)		% labour force in agriculture		% of population living in cities of 20,000+		% of population literate	
	1870	1930	1880	1930	1880	1930	1870	1930
France	1,876	4,532	40	36	24	31	69	95
Germany	1,839	3,973	43	29	16	43	90	98
UK	3,190	5,441	22	6	56	70	75	98
Italy	1,542	2,631	57	47	23	37	31	77
Spain	1,207	2,620	66	46	na	31	28	71

Sources: Maddison-Project 2013; and Bartolini 2000, pp. 133, 165, and 195.

employing hundreds if not thousands of workers, and industrial concentration increasing considerably in some sectors.[33] In Eastern Europe, GDP per capita grew at similar rates, but the levels in 1929 were still below those enjoyed in the West in 1870, while at least half the labour force remained in agriculture.[34]

The causes and nature of economic growth were diverse.[35] In the first instance, a combination of institutional change and infrastructural investment greatly facilitated the integration of domestic markets. The abolition of local weights, measures, and currencies reduced transaction costs associated with internal trade, while the railways led to a major reduction in freight charges and facilitated planning by economic enterprises. By the interwar period, the internal combustion engine was producing another transport revolution and becoming important even in the poorer economies. Information flows improved greatly with the telegraph, postal services, and telephone, while newspaper readership soared. The reduction in freight and information costs helped integrate global markets, which, by the late nineteenth century, threatened to flood European countries with cheap food and manufactured goods leading to demands for government intervention to protect 'infant' industries and traditional agriculture.

---

[33] In Spain in 1920, for example, four firms accounted for 96 per cent of paid up capital in the steel industry, 68 per cent in mining, 45 per cent in electricity and 44 per cent in banking. Ceballos Teresi 1931, cited in Fraile Balbín 1991, p. 51.

[34] The increase was from $952 to $1,982 (1990 international dollars). Countries include Albania, Bulgaria, Czechoslovakia, Hungary, Poland, Romania, and Yugoslavia. Maddison-Project, 2013.

[35] See, for example, Allen 2011, pp. 41–2.

In a number of countries, 'universal' investment banks played a major role in attracting small savers deposits, and then investing funds in companies specializing in transport or heavy industries, such as steel, chemicals, or engineering. In others, such as Russia, the state played a major role, leading Gerschenkron to argue that planning and hierarchical structures substituted for markets in more backward countries.[36] By the interwar period, state-driven economic development was not limited to just the Soviet Union, but was becoming increasingly important in countries such as Nazi Germany, Italy, or even France.

Levels of schooling increased everywhere, so that by 1930 most adults were literate in North-Western Europe, and significant gains were also being found further south (Table 1.2). Higher levels of literacy helped increase workers' skills that, when accompanied by technological change, produced important productivity increases. Compulsory, free schooling was also used to build national identities, so that if French was still a foreign tongue to half the country's citizens in 1870, it had become their first language half a century later.[37]

With economic growth came improvements in real wages and a shorter working week, allowing families to dedicate an increasing amount of their income to buying new consumer goods and leisure activities. Figures for mortality fell significantly, partly because of a reduction in the exposure to diseases achieved by investment in clean water supplies, improved sanitation, and better housing. According to Millward and Baten, after 1900, infant heath movements 'swept the continent' and led to the greater use of midwives and improved hygiene.[38] Diets improved and famines were relegated to history, with the exception of war zones and the USSR's collective experiments in the 1930s. Birth rates declined, with the 'decisive' falls of the 1920s and 1930s affecting even periphery countries such as Russia, Spain, and Portugal.[39] As mortality levels fell earlier and faster than birth rates, population growth was rapid. Europe was a young Continent in the 1930s, and in Spain half the population was 24 years old or younger.[40]

Economic growth was reversed in most countries during the First World War, but then accelerated rapidly during the 1920s, as technical change helped increase labour productivity, both by lowering energy and transport prices and by encouraging surplus farm labour to move to the more productive industry and service sectors.[41] The Wall Street Crash in

---

[36] Gerschenkron 1966. See also Harley 1991.   [37] Weber 1977, pp. 70 and 79.
[38] Milward & Baten 2010, p. 239.   [39] Ibid., p. 243.
[40] Almost three-fifths were 30 years old or younger. Calculated from Nicolau 2005, p. 145.
[41] Roses & Wolf 2010, pp. 203–4.

Table 1.3 *World production and prices between 1929 and 1932*

	Production		Prices	
	1929	1932	1929	1932
Industry	100	64	100	64
Food	100	100	100	52
Raw materials	100	75	100	44

Source: Feinstein et al. 1997, table 6.2.

October 1929 was caused by investors responding to the Federal Reserve Board's attempts to cool the overheating domestic economy by raising the discount rate to reduce the money supply. Although perhaps a logical response to domestic problems, it was the exact opposite of what was needed for the international economy, given that the United States owned a significant share of the world's gold reserves. The Great Depression was therefore made considerably worse by a falling money supply, deflation, and a growing tariff war. The value of world trade collapsed by 61 per cent between 1929 and 1932 and food prices halved (Table 1.3). Official unemployment rates rose sharply, especially in the industrial economies of Germany and the United States. In general, the depth and length of a country's depression was less if governments left the Gold Standard early and intervened to increase economic activity.[42]

The demands on state capacity in the 1930s were very different from those associated with the Great War, and the deep crisis challenged the nature of traditional liberal thinking on the role of the state. The high levels of involuntary unemployment and its associated poverty led to popular demands for new policies and social transfers, although the results were often limited (Table 1.4).

Finally, the first third of the twentieth century saw a decline in income inequality in many European economies.[43] Following Kuznets, highly rural societies had low income inequalities, but growing commercial and industrial activities increased the possibilities for personal gain, leading to the growth of professional classes and a labour 'aristocracy'. This curve then began to move downwards in response to rising real wages and the growth of the state and redistributary policies, leading to higher levels of education, social transfers, and progressive taxation.

---

[42] Feinstein *et al.* 1997, p. 170, and table 9.3.   [43] See especially Milanovic 2016, ch. 2.

Table 1.4 *Changes in social expenditures as percentage of GDP, 1930 and 1933*

	Social spending as % of total spending	
	1930	1933
Belgium	1.83	5.85
France	2.49	3.97
Germany	11.15	11.41
Italy	1.40	1.40
Netherlands	1.61	6.56
Norway		4.72
Sweden	3.84	6.02
UK	6.52	7.70
Spain	0.48	1.05

Source: Espuelas 2015, appendix 1.

The International Economy, Income Distribution, and Government Intervention

The growth of the international economy also had a major impact on both living standards and income distribution. Over the centuries, between about 1500 and 1815, European farm rents and food prices tended to move in line with population growth, with real wages in the poorer countries often stagnant or falling.[44] Landowners benefitted both from higher farm prices and rents because of the combination of rapid population growth, limited food imports, and a relative fixed area of arable land, but also from the possibilities to consume cheap labour-intensive luxury goods, and pay for large numbers of inexpensive servants.[45] Farm profitability recovered quickly after the post-Napoleonic slump, and European farm rents remained high until the 1870s, leading Koning to write that, 'not without reason, Ricardo, Marx and other nineteenth-century economists highlighted rising land rents while assuming parity between agricultural and industrial profits'.[46]

The arrival of cheap foods and raw materials from the land-abundant and labour-scarce New World from the 1870s threatened to reverse this long-run trend, by changing not only relative factor prices (land and labour) in Europe, but also income distribution, land ownership, political power, and even the role of the state. New World farmers quickly expanded output in response to lower transport costs caused by the

[44] Allen 2011, figure 3.   [45] Hoffman et al. 2002.   [46] Koning 1994, p. 14.

railroad expansion and the drop in international freight costs, so that transatlantic commodity prices converged, with the difference in wheat prices between Liverpool and Chicago falling from 58 per cent in 1870, to just 18 per cent by 1895. Wheat production in New World wheat-exporting counties increased by two and half times between 1885–9 and 1929–34, compared to just under a third in Europe.[47] Other foods were also affected, and the new refrigeration technologies, for example, caused the price gap for meat and animal fats to fall from 92 per cent to 18 per cent between London and Cincinnati between 1895 and 1913.[48]

According to Ricardo's theory of rent, the cost of adapting to lower European food prices would be made up by landowners through rent reductions, allowing farmers to remain competitive.[49] However, facing this potentially significant drop in their rents and profits, the landed elites demanded government intervention, and many countries in the 1870s and 1880s created parliamentary commissions to look into the nature of the agrarian crisis, and propose solutions.[50] Although previous market intervention had usually been directed at protecting consumers from high prices and guaranteeing supplies of unadulterated food, farmers now demanded higher prices.[51] The question of using tariffs to protect farmers' profits (and landowners' rents) was especially controversial in a period when mass politics and growing urban populations were becoming important. Government market intervention had profound implications for income distribution, and European governments split over the issue.

Britain opted for free trade, and rising wheat imports led to domestic production covering just 19 per cent of the nation's needs in 1910–14, compared to 74 per cent in 1850–4.[52] However, the British case was exceptional because the small size of its farm sector had already greatly reduced the political influence of its landed elite. Elsewhere, most governments increased tariffs in varying degrees, in theory to give farmers time to adapt. European wheat prices therefore showed significant variations, falling by 38 per cent in Britain between 1869/73 and 1909/13, but increasing by 5 per cent in heavily protected Spain.[53] Government decisions on whether to intervene to restrict international competition had a much greater impact on both living standards and income distribution, than their attempts to introduce progressive taxes or social spending

[47] Malenbaum 1953.   [48] O'Rourke & Williamson 1994, table 2.
[49] Pasour & Rucker 2005.   [50] Vivier 2014.
[51] Britain, and it's 'Corn Laws', was the notable exception. See especially Lindert 1991, pp. 29–83.
[52] Perren 2000, table 17.1.   [53] Calculated from GEHR 1980, table 14.

(pensions, health, welfare, and unemployment) before the Great Depression.[54]

High wages in the New World also attracted around 50 million Europeans over the nineteenth century, with most leaving after the 1870s.[55] Initially, most emigrants originated from the North, but cheaper tickets and growing living standards helped make Southern Europe a major contributor by the turn of the twentieth century. Many were 'target earners', who returned home after a few years with their savings to invest on the family farm. This combination of growing industrialization, falling food prices, and emigration, reduced domestic competition for farm work, and helped push up wages for those labourers who remained. In addition, the growing concentration of labour carrying out similar tasks in factories and mines greatly facilitated the possibilities of trade union activities and, when legal, these helped improve working conditions. Between 1870 and 1913, Europe's unskilled urban workers saw an unprecedented 1.4 per cent annual increase in real wages.[56]

The Threats to Liberal Democracy in the Interwar Period

While the Great War undermined liberals' faith in reason, progress, and science, the Depression highlighted the limits of the market economy.[57] Now, instead of the perpetual expansion of supposedly self-regulating market relations, societies attempted to protect themselves from their undesirable consequences. Economic recovery on its own was often not enough to resolve the popular discontent. For Silver, the New Deal, Swedish Social Democracy, Soviet Five-Year Plan, Fascism, Nazism, and Japanese militarism were 'different ways of jumping off the disintegrating world market into the life raft of the national economy'.[58]

The social mobility produced by structural change and industrialization, and the extension of the franchise that now allowed these groups to vote, had important electoral consequences. Yet far from handing power to the Left as many had originally expected, the widening of democracy required different groups to negotiate and make pacts with each other. Although Table 1.1 suggests that a broad definition of the working classes including both farm and industrial workers might account for half the electorate, the political interests of these and other groups were highly heterogeneous, making it difficult to create effective alliances. Depending

[54] See especially Lindert 2004 and Espuelas 2015.   [55] Baines 1994.
[56] O'Rourke & Williamson 1997, table 2.   [57] Luebbert 1991, p. 194.
[58] Silver 2003, p. 143, cited in Mann 2012, p. 238.

on the level of development, societies became divided into three broad groups: around the farm sector, manufacturing and urban workers, and professional middle classes.

National histories inevitably stress a country's distinct experience. Therefore if fascist and authoritarian governments were common in the 1930s, the brutality and inhumaneness of the Nazis makes the Germany experience unique.[59] Spain's neutrality during the two World Wars, along with the bitter civil war between 1936 and 1939, also suggest that the country had a very different historical experience to other European countries. However, the need to respond to challenges brought about by economic modernization, globalization, nationalism, or the growth in mass politics were common across the Continent, fuelled by new ideologies that quickly crossed political frontiers. A growing historical literature attempts to explain the paths taken by different countries by examining the timing and sequencing of their responses to these types of problems, to understand why a particular country stayed with liberal democracy or embraced instead National Socialism or social democracy.

For Luebbert, liberal democracies survived because the political and trade union aspirations of the working classes had been respected *before* the First World War, as liberal parties first entered into interclass coalitions with workers, and later participated in formal alliances with workers' parties. In Britain, France, and Switzerland, these pacts led to labour politics being defined in terms of sectorial and union interests, rather than those of class, and workers' aspirations were recognized as being legitimate, even though gains were often modest.[60] Consequently, there was no appreciable shift in the balance of class power, as working-class movements remained politically marginalized, trade unions failed to end market-driven wage settlements, and government policy was essentially market orientated.[61] When labour parties did come to power (Britain in 1924 and 1931; France in 1936), the policies they followed were extremely moderate.

By contrast, where liberalism had failed to capture sufficient middle-class support, or been unwilling or unable to form alliances with workers' groups before 1914, countries turned to social democracy or fascist dictatorship. In Norway, Sweden, and Denmark, social democracy involved political bargains substituting for market-determined wage and

---

[59] The so-called Sonderweg School. See Berman 2006, p. 136.

[60] Legal rights for trade unions, collective bargaining, and the right to strike were granted between 1867–75 in Britain and in 1884 in France. The important element in these countries was not the electoral system, but voters' behaviour, and whether they were willing to form interclass coalitions. Luebbert 1991, pp. 15 and 28–29.

[61] Ibid., p. 191.

price settlements, and labour market peace and discipline was secured through a social compact rather than trade union weakness. This Scandinavian solution was achieved by political alliances in the 1930s, with urban workers accepting farmers' demands for price-support for their products, interest rate reductions, tariffs, and tax relief, in exchange for programs that increased public works and expanded employment and other social costs, which raised farmers' labour costs. For Luebbert, the agreement was possible because, although smallholders and farm workers benefitted only marginally compared to the middle peasantry, the 'distribution of wealth within the countryside was not an issue'.[62]

Finally, in fascist societies, the socialist working class was crushed, and an alliance established between the urban middle classes and the family farmers. In Germany, the liberal movement had been important before 1914, but was 'crippled by divisions' over 'national territory, religion, the centre versus the periphery, the city versus the country', and the creation of a national movement became highly divisive. In Southern Europe, class-based organizations developed, but these lacked the interclass alliances found in liberal societies. Fascism therefore became important when both liberalism and social democracy had failed to accommodate the family peasantry.[63]

A common theme everywhere was therefore the importance of the farm sector in determining whether liberal democracy survived or whether social democracy or fascism appeared instead. This was not surprising, given that agriculture still employed between a quarter and half of the active workforce in 1930. However, while for some authors, such as Barrington Moore, the crucial support for fascism came from the landed elite, for others, such as Tooze, the decisive support came instead from family farmers.[64] By contrast, in both Italy and Spain, and to a lesser extent Germany, farm labour also offered socialist parties and trade unions 'a vast reservoir of potential support'.[65]

Conclusion

The 1930s were a desperate time for all European countries. Following the Continent's first major war for a century, economic recovery was short-lived, as the Great Depression sent unemployment soaring to unprecedented levels, and poverty returned to levels that many contemporaries believed had been consigned to history. The failure of the new

[62] Ibid., p. 268.   [63] Ibid., pp. 63 and 283.   [64] Moore 1967 and Tooze 2006.
[65] Luebbert 1991, p. 295. However, organized labour faced a dilemma as many farm workers, unlike industrial workers, could realistically aim to become independent entrepreneurs rather than remain part of the proletariat. See Chapter 9.

liberal democracies to deal with these extraordinary problems led many to turn to different forms of political organizations, where the state played an active rather than passive role in economic activities. From 1939, Europe and the World were plunged once more into a bitter, and bloody, war.

The fact that Spain remained neutral in both wars suggests a very different history to that of most other European countries. Yet as we shall see, there was also plenty that all it did have in common with other Western European countries, including the experience of economic development, better living standards, the initial shift from competitive oligarchies to democracy, or the growth in state capacity. In fact Spain, in its own way, also experienced the cycle of government failure at resolving the economic and social problems of the 1930s, leading to a growing rejection of liberal democracy, and finally to war.

2 European Agriculture in an Age of Economic Instability

From the mid-nineteenth century, if not before, all Western European societies embarked on a process of economic development, which saw growing numbers of farm workers and small farmers moving to the cities or emigrating in search of higher wages. At the same time, governments switched from competitive oligarchies, where the landed elites enjoyed considerable influence, to one of mass political parties and free elections. By 1920, the process was well advanced in North-Western Europe although, with the exception of the UK, agriculture still employed between a third and a half the population in most countries (Table 1.1). As labour left the land and food imports pushed farm prices lower, at least in real terms, farmers looked to cut costs by mechanizing simple farm operations, or switching to labour-intensive, higher-value crops, to protect their incomes.

The half-century prior to the First World War also saw unprecedented social changes in the countryside. As Chapter 1 showed, the economic position of these elites were now threatened, by free trade and the import of cheap foods; politically, by urban demands for cheaper food and an extension of the suffrage; and socially, as more efficient factor and commodity markets eroded the benefits of the traditional patron-client networks. By contrast, the family farm became increasingly important. The family farm is the predominate form of organization found in agriculture throughout history, and indeed across much of the world today.[1] Not only are family farms highly efficient in labour-intensive agriculture, but a high degree of equality in land distribution is often seen as helpful in creating democracies. Yet there were important differences between the self-sufficient 'independent' family farms found in areas such as the United States or Scandinavia in the interwar years, and the 'peasant' farms found in Eastern and Southern Europe. Furthermore, although the growth of an 'independent' family farm sector is partly a consequence

---

[1] Allen & Lueck 2002, p. 167–8.

of the decline in the landed elites, there were other factors involved, as later chapters will show.

The relation between the agricultural sector and government also changed fundamentally with the integration of the Atlantic economy, and the flood of cheap food imports, especially from the 1870s and 1880s. Tariffs were the ideal solution for the landed elites, as they not only raised farm prices, but also avoided governments intervening in agriculture itself. The First World War changed these relations, as governments suddenly had to find more food, and ensure that it could be distributed efficiently to where it was most in need. As a result, governments to a greater or lesser extent everywhere began to look to farmers, as oppose to landowners, to help the war effort by producing more. The problem of wartime food shortages contrasted with the surpluses of the 1930s, with farmers now demanding state intervention instead to control prices. Hitler, among others, realized that the family farmer could provide vital political support, as well as the supplies and the soldiers that his new armies needed.

This chapter looks at the agrarian question in an international perspective. The first section examines the problems and opportunities for the farm sector produced by industrialization and the greater integration of the Atlantic economy after 1870 and, in particular, the downward pressure on European land prices (and rents) and rising real wages. This is followed by a discussion on how the impact of the First World War changed government attitudes towards the sector. The third and fourth sections examine social mobility and the importance of the family farm, and the impact of the First World War and the Great Depression on the farm sector, and especially the demands for greater government intervention.

European Agriculture and Economic Growth

Economists and politicians have sometimes drawn very different conclusions over the role to be played by the agricultural sector during economic development. Some see agriculture as being subservient to industry, and its function limited to supplying cheap food for the rapidly growing cities; obtaining foreign exchange through its exports; paying taxes to be invested in infrastructure and industry; creating a source of demand for consumer and capital goods; and finally, supplying cheap labour to allow industry to compete internationally.[2] However, economists from the days of Adam Smith have also emphasized the complementary nature of agriculture and

---

[2] The classic contribution is Johnson & Mellor 1961, pp. 571–81. For Spain, Tortella 1985.

the industrial and service sectors during the development process.[3] In these models, urban growth and higher incomes encourage greater farm specialization, leading to higher agricultural productivity, rising rural prosperity and, in turn, an increased demand for industrial goods. This dual growth is dramatically illustrated in China's recent history, where as late as the 1970s the agricultural sector still employed about 70 per cent of the labour force, but provided consumers with less than 2,300 calories per capita per day. Over the next three decades, as the country's annual GDP grew at over 8 per cent, farm employment fell to a quarter, and the Total Factor Productivity (TFP) in the farm sector soared to a massive 4 per cent a year.[4] The experience of Western European countries after the Second World War also illustrates the inter-relationship between a rapid rural exodus, rising GDP, and growing TFP in agriculture.[5]

Something on a more modest scale happened in parts of Europe during the half-century prior to the Second World War. In general, those countries with relatively few workers in the farm sector enjoyed the highest living standards, with Western Europe at the top, and Eastern Europe at the bottom, and the Mediterranean countries occupying the middle ground (Figure 2.1). As Van Zanden notes, European agricultural development even by the 1870s was 'highly dependent on the extent of the structural transformation of the economy and of the level of demand from the urban sector. To put it more bluntly, a highly productive agriculture was always part of a well-developed economy.'[6]

In general, the more advanced European countries had a prosperous agriculture because either output per hectare was greater, or workers had access to more farmland than in poorer countries. Average farm size and the number of hectares per farm worker are greater among the countries towards the top of Table 2.1, and these nations also often enjoyed higher wheat yields and had a greater density of cattle and pigs. The lower productivity found in countries such as Poland or Bulgaria compared, for example, to those of Belgium or Germany, was partly caused by such factors as lower levels of capital inputs per worker or poorer schooling and literacy. However, the major causal explanation was that production

---

[3] Adam Smith wrote in *The Wealth of Nations* that 'through the greater part of Europe the commerce and manufacture of cities, instead of being the effect, have been the cause and occasion of the improvement and cultivation of the country'. Smith 1776: 1970, p. 515.

[4] Zhu 2012, p. 109 and tables 1 and 2. Agriculture's contribution to GDP tumbled from 30 to 10 per cent, as predicted by Mellor's law, which states that the faster a country's agriculture grows, the faster its relative size declines. Mellor 1995, p. 1, cited in Olmstead & Rhode 2009, p. 2.

[5] Economic growth had historically been faster in those countries where a large agriculture sector existed, such as China in 1978, or Spain in 1950. For Europe, see Temin 2002.

[6] Van Zanden 1991, p. 226.

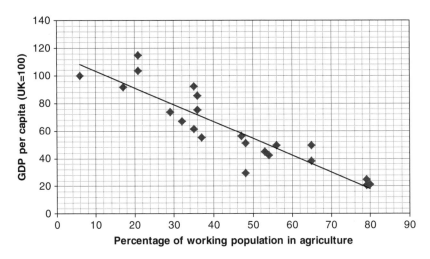

Figure 2.1 Levels of GDP per capita and share of labour force in agriculture in Western Europe, 1929
Source: Based on Feinstein et al. 1997, p.57.

opportunities for farmers differed greatly between both Western and Eastern Europe, and between Northern and Southern Europe.[7]

Economic development and rising incomes after 1870 offered significant economic possibilities for some farmers but challenged the very survival of others. While demand was influenced by Engel's law, which suggests that consumers spend relatively less on food and beverages as incomes increase, technological change and greater market integration were helping farmers increase output. Persistent overproduction in the traditional economies had been limited because of storage and transporting difficulties and implied that shortages and gluts caused by weather or disease followed each other in quick succession. By the late nineteenth century, however, the railways had significantly reduced the influence of local conditions on farm prices, and better storage allowed surpluses to be kept over from one year to the next. By the early 1900s, even tariffs could not resolve serious structural imbalances between supply and demand that left some European farmers facing ruinous prices for a wide range of products including wine, olive oil and sugar. This long-run tendency towards overproduction was eliminated by the First World War, but returned dramatically again in the late 1920s and 1930s.

---

[7] As Theodore Schultz noted, 'once there are investment opportunities and efficient incentives, farmers will turn sand to gold'. Schultz 1964, p. 5.

Table 2.1 *Characteristics of European farming, c.1930*

	% in agriculture	GDP per capita($), 1990	Average size of farm in hectares	Average number of workers/farm	Hectares per farm workers	Wheat yields 1930–4	N° of cattle per 100 hectares	N° pigs per 100 hectares
UK	6	5.195	32.7	2.7	12.3	16.6	44	23
Belgium	17	4.873	1.5	0.5	2.8	24.3	109	75
Switzerland	21	6.160	11.0	2.0	5.5	20.2	72	50
Netherlands	21	5.467	11.5	3.5	3.3	22.3	113	65
Germany	29	4.049	9.6	3.1	3.1	17.3	65	79
Austria	32	3.610	10.7	2.5	4.3	15.1	54	65
Denmark	35	5.138	15.5	3.0	5.2	17.4	99	99
Norway	35	3.377	3.0	1.0	2.5	17.8	127	54
France	36	4.489	8.7	1.9	4.5	11.5	45	20
Sweden	36	3.937	8.2	1.7	4.9	19.0	60	30
Czechoslovakia	37	2.926	5.3	1.7	3.1	17.5	51	47
Italy	47	2.814	5.1	1.9	2.7	13.5	33	15
Portugal	48	1.600	na	na	na	7.4	37	49
Ireland	48	2.950	11.7	1.7	6.7	19.5	86	20
Hungary	53	2.404	5.8	1.5	3.8	11.3	22	33
Greece	54	2.300	na	na	1.5	8.0	44	27
Spain	56	2.802	12.2	1.4	8.7	9.3	10	14
Poland	65	1.994	7.8	3.1	2.5	11.2	36	28
Yugoslavia	79	1.325	na	na	2.9	8.4	28	20
Romania	79	1.219	5.7	2.0	2.8	9.2	24	17
Bulgaria	80	1.284	5.9	3.6	1.6	10.8	44	24

Sources: Feinstein et al. 1997, table 4.1, Maddison 1995, International Institute of Agriculture, Warriner 1939, p. 3, and Germany. *Statistisches Jahrbuch für das Deutsche Reich,* 1937.

An additional problem was that although the relative share of those employed in Western European agriculture fell during industrialization, absolute numbers often continued to increase before 1914, before stagnating until the Second World War.[8] As most areas had limited supplies of new land that could be easily brought under the plough, farmers had to increase the intensity of their operations if labour was to be kept fully employed. When farmers did not have access to sufficient land, and could not pursue labour-intensive farming, they were forced to search for temporary off-farm employment. Problems of surplus farm labour were made worse during major economic downturns as unemployed workers drifted back to their villages in search of work and food. The local supply of farm labour therefore could experience a substantial increase during economic depressions, just when farmers were trying to cut costs because of low farm gate prices in an attempt to remain profitable.

Yet many farmers benefitted from economic growth, especially as demand elasticity varied significantly within the food and drink sectors, so that falling consumer demand for basic foodstuffs, such as bread or potatoes, were offset by the rapid increase for those rich in proteins, fresh fruits or vegetables. Northern Europe's richer consumers also offered some farmers, especially in the Mediterranean, the possibility to specialize in high-income, labour-intensive market-gardening. Governments helped by sponsoring research and extension services; investing in infrastructure, including roads and irrigation systems; as well as resolving market information problems for consumers by setting new standards in food quality and implementing veterinary controls. After 1870, the challenge facing Europe's marginal cereal producers, for example, was how to switch to these higher-value products.

The speed of farm mechanization was often closely correlated with wages, and mechanical reapers were already being used to collect virtually the whole cereal harvest as early as 1880 in labour-scarce United States. If change was slower in Europe, this was often simply because farmers faced very different cost structures, and explains why the area collected by mechanical reapers was only 56 per cent in Britain in 1874, 12 per cent in France (1892), 6 per cent in Germany (1895) and even less in Spain.[9] By the 1920s, the tractor was also becoming increasingly common in US

---

[8] Federico 2006, table 4.16.

[9] Figures in Collins 1969, table 3, and for Spain, Simpson 1995. Other factors were also important, including energy costs, and the mechanical support provided by the developing manufacturing industry. See Chapter 4.

agriculture, resulting in a massive saving of labour, but also releasing large areas of land that had been used to feed work animals.[10] Again, the speed of diffusion was slower in Europe but the tractor, together with other labour-saving farm equipment, was threatening to change the nature of farm work, even in Southern Europe, on the eve of the Great Depression (Chapter 7).

Growing urbanization and cheap transportation led to a major increase in market size, so that many farmers found themselves increasingly separated from the consumer as the commodity chains lengthened, and the number of intermediaries grew. Not only did farmers receive a declining percentage of retail prices, but they also faced significantly greater income volatility, and, at times of severe overproduction, merchants were sometimes unwilling to buy at any price.[11] Nevertheless, the weakness of small farmers in the market place was compensated in part by their greater political voice caused by the extension of the suffrage and the appearance of mass political parties. Farmers began to create new forms of organizations, such as cooperatives, which allowed them to enjoy the efficiency of the small family farm, with the ability to integrate some production processes into much larger businesses to benefit from their economies of scale (Chapter 5).

How farmers responded to these problems varied significantly both across and within countries. However, two very general points can be made now. In the first instance, agriculture was more prosperous in industrial Europe because tariffs in the 1930s kept food prices roughly double those of world markets, and surplus farm labour found employment in the growing cities. Labour was only retained in agriculture when it could be profitably employed. A second factor was the constraints imposed by the seasonal distribution of rainfall. In general, the abundant and summer peaks of rain in North-West Europe permitted a wider variety of crops and intensive livestock farming than elsewhere. It also offered more employment for both labour and work animals throughout the year, and lower volatility in crop yields.[12] Consequently, workers were

---

[10] Farm draft animals consumed roughly 22 per cent of all cropland harvested over the 1880 to 1920 period, peaking in 1915 at about 93 million acres (with another 14 million for off-farm animals in cities and mines). By 1944, the tractor saved about 8 per cent of total labour requirements; Olmstead & Rhode 2001, pp. 664–5. Steckel & White 2012 suggest savings from the tractor and related machinery as being equivalent to 8 per cent of total US GNP by 1954.

[11] This was a common complaint among winegrowers in the Midi during the 1900s. Simpson 2011.

[12] As Doreen Warriner (1939, p. 151) writes, 'wherever intensification by increasing livestock production was possible ... the extension of peasant farming meant an improvement in the welfare of the peasant community, since it implies more employment'.

often employed on annual contracts, and labour considered a fixed, rather than variable cost, encouraging farmers to find year-round employment to keep their workers fully occupied.[13] By contrast, in the Mediterranean regions, there were few annual labour contracts. The vine and the olive were ideal crops for small farmers, providing large amounts of work, but demand was stagnant and prices falling by the late 1920s. Despite their low yields, dry cereal farming *could* also be highly competitive when farmers had a sufficiently large area to mechanize production. However farming conditions in Southern Europe, especially Spain, were often unsuitable for labour-intensive agriculture and insufficient land existed for family farmers to benefit from the growing economies of scale found in modern cereal production.

Agriculture and the Demands and Legacies of the First World War

The social tensions in European society set off by industrialization and globalization were greatly accentuated by the Great War and the 1930s Depression. War highlighted the strengths and weaknesses of Europe's different farming systems, and countries with large peasant populations such as Russia, Italy, Austria-Hungary, the Ottoman Empire and Germany, had greater difficulties to increase food supplies for urban centres and the army.[14]

Britain initially seemed by far the most vulnerable, as not only had it made few preparations for war, but less than 10 per cent of its active population were still in agriculture, and it imported 65 per cent of its calorific needs, compared to just a fifth by Germany in 1914.[15] Nevertheless, British farmers were accustomed to adapting quickly to rapidly shifting markets because of their lack of tariff protection, and the county's high dependence on food imports implied that an ample storage and a centralized system of food distribution already existed in 1914, unlike the distinctly small-scale systems found in Germany. The switch into livestock production and 28 per cent reduction in the area of cereal cultivation between 1873 and 1913 had also created a natural 'soil bank' of fertile land that could now be used to increase arable

---

[13] The tradition of farm servants was much more pronounced in Northern than Southern Europe. Reher 1998.

[14] Broadberry & Harrison 1995, pp. 18–22.

[15] The United Kingdom imported four-fifths of its wheat and flour, and more than 50 per cent of food (by value) on the eve of war, while Germany imported 27 per cent protein and 42 per cent fats. Offer 1989, pp. 25, Olson 1963, p. 74, and Turner 2000, pp. 224–5.

production.[16] By contrast, the area of arable land increased in Germany in the run-up to the war, leaving farmers dangerously dependent on mineral fertilizers, which now became scarce. The British government only started intervening following the poor harvest in 1916 and the unrestricted submarine warfare from February 1917 but, by the end of the war, it bought and sold 85 per cent of the food consumed in the country, and 'producers, middlemen, and consumers alike were forced to fit into a program geared to defend the nation against the German food blockade'.[17] Unlike Spain in the early 30s, British farmers responded to new laws requiring them to increase production by cultivating pasture and meadow land, and there were only 254 prosecutions and 317 tenancies terminated following the 100,000 orders made to farmers.[18] The result was that while British males enjoyed a daily diet that averaged around 3,400 calories throughout the war, the figure in Germany had fallen by half by 1918.[19] Germany's inability to allocate supplies to those most in need led to a rampant black market accounting for between a fifth and a third of total production, causing widespread hunger.[20]

The wartime experience saw most governments attempt to organize employers and workers in a single state-coordinated administration, and suggested how state intervention and planning might be used in the future.[21] Strikes were made illegal in key industries, and trade unions sometimes co-opted into decision-making committees. Government intervention required vast amounts of information, and planning suffered because of limited state capacity. In Germany, for example, the statistical returns by farmers during the war were 'chronically unreliable', and reports issued by the Food Office known as 'tables of lies'.[22] The war experience greatly influenced thinking about agriculture and food policy, and both Stalin and Hitler introduced major changes to the food chain by the late 1930s to avoid the threat of starvation in a future war. The Nazis established a highly impressive statistical service to measure economic activity and allowed radical planning experiments. In September 1933, the *Reichsnaehrstand* (RNS) or State Food Corporation was created, which set prices and exercised more or less direct control over 25 per cent of Germany's GDP, regulating the whole food chain from the farm to the table, and effectively ending the free markets for

[16] Afton & Turner 2000, pp. 1770–2.   [17] Olson 1963, pp. 87 and 95.
[18] Ibid., p.98. For Spain, see Chapter 8.   [19] Mann 2012, p. 160.
[20] For rationing and hunger, see Offer 1989, ch. 4. During the War there were 769,000 more civilian deaths in Germany than expected. Olson 1963, p. 79.
[21] Mann writes that, 'in all countries except Russia, the crucial production committees were staffed jointly by industrialists and financiers working alongside ministers, civil servants and generals'. Mann 2012, p. 154.
[22] Tooze 2001, pp. 70–1.

agricultural produce.[23] All individuals and existing organizations involved in food production and its distribution were obliged to join. Higher prices encouraged farmers to increase production, making Germany 83 per cent self-sufficient in food by 1937, despite rising per capita consumption, and Hitler now enjoyed 'all the necessary machinery' for controlling food supplies and prices.[24]

Russia had been a major food producer before the First World War, but the state's inability to provide the basic needs for urban consumers led to food protests and contributed to the 1917 Revolution.[25] The massive land invasions by small farmers were initially welcomed by the Bolsheviks, but the government saw the failure of peasant agriculture to supply sufficient cheap food to the cities as a threat to the Revolution.[26] Collectivist agriculture, by contrast, allowed the state to plan the production and distribution of food on a massive scale.[27] The collectives were huge and highly mechanized, averaging around 80,000 hectares, and some US experts initially saw them as a model for their own country's future.[28] Urban consumption of basic foods such as bread, potatoes and cabbage rose, but that of higher-value foods fell. However, increased urban consumption was not achieved by rising farm output, but rather by the decline in rural consumption, and the significant fall in livestock numbers and the land required to feed them.[29] The 1932 famine left perhaps 10 million dead, but by 1934 the state was in a position to determine cropping patterns, collect surpluses, and control the countryside, leaving the country better prepared for any future military threats. In the Soviet Union, the collectivization of agriculture replaced market relations with state coercion and violence.[30]

By contrast, in liberal democracies such as Britain or France, the interwar experience of agriculture was very different, but there were also important breaks with the past. Both governments attempted to increase efficiency by creating new farm organizations which allowed informal contacts between the sector and government to determine and implement policy, without abandoning the market. In England and Wales, the National Farmers' Union (NFU), became the official client group

---

[23] The state controlled imports through the *Reichsstellen* and, although not formally part of the RNS, 'formed an indispensable component to its action'. Tracy 1989, p. 193.
[24] Ibid., p. 199.   [25] Gatrell & Harrison 1993, p. 445.
[26] Ellman 2014, p. 182, Allen 2003, p. 46.
[27] In addition, collectivist agriculture was to supply a major share of the resources needed for investment during industrialization. Ellman 2014, p. 185.
[28] Fitzgerald 1996, pp. 459–86.
[29] Ellman 2014, p. 195. Allen 2003, pp. 135–6, suggests that the slaughter of 15 million horses between 1929 and 1933 freed enough land to feed about 30 million people.
[30] Ellman 2014, ch. 6.

representing the sector.[31] The NFU had been founded in 1908 to protect the interests of tenant farmers, but quickly included owner-occupiers as well.[32] The organization played a major role in formulating and implementing policy during the Great War, helping survey farms, assess labour needs, and promote food production. However, it rejected attempts to become an official government body when it resigned from the Council of Agriculture for England, and instead remained independent, widening its support base by including landowners and workers. By the 1920s it had acquired a level of organizational capacity and monopoly of representation that allowed it to represent the sector in its negotiations with the state.[33]

Although the influence of the NFU should not be exaggerated before the Second World War,[34] its success in becoming the official client group allows us to identify some of the difficulties to create a centralized farm lobby in other countries during the interwar period. Four factors in particular appear to be crucial. First, independent farm groups were already organizing freely in England by the mid-nineteenth century, reflecting the competitive nature of party politics. Second, agrarian class conflicts were relatively low, as landowners had already lost considerable economic and political influence by 1914, and surplus rural labour left the sector for high urban wages. Third, farming regions and land-tenure regimes were relatively homogenous, helping produce a unified lobby, especially after Ireland's independence. Finally, the fact that Britain was essentially an industrial economy implied there was no danger that a farm lobby could control the legislature, while free trade implied that urban workers benefitted from low food prices and were not threatened by a flood of cheap farm labour reducing urban wages.

Only the first of these factors was present in France, where endeavours to create a national farm organization came to nothing prior to the Second World War. French political parties were weak, but competition between the conservative Right and republican Centre-Left groups to organize in the countryside led to the creation of 2,069 farm syndicates with 512,000 members by 1900. The *Fédération nationale de la mutualité et de la coopération agricoles* was founded in 1910 to consolidate credit, insurance, and cooperative societies and, by 1929, there were 15,000 syndicates and

---

[31] Unions were also created in Scotland and Ulster, but the one in England and Wales was the largest, and took the lead in representing farmers throughout the United Kingdom. Self & Storing 1963, p. 37.
[32] The landowners' Central Chamber of Agriculture, founded in 1865, had traditionally represented the interests of the sector in parliament.
[33] Cox et al. 1991, p. 41–7.   [34] Tracy 1989, pp. 130 and 157.

1.5 million members.[35] However attempts by both the Left and Right to establish a strong centralized system failed. Instead, power lay in the strong regional associations and, from the 1920s, with specialist organizations for major commodities such as wheat and wine.[36]

In Northern Europe especially, the state became involved in helping farmers raise output, and invested in scientific research and extension services, as well as encouraging the creation of new organizations such as producer cooperatives or rural banks.[37] The Great War everywhere brought demands for a fairer society, although hungry urban dwellers resented the supposed abundance of food in rural areas, while farmers believed many industrial workers had been able to escape the draft.[38] These tensions contributed to the lack of post-war class unity between peasants and workers in some countries.[39] Government policies increasingly had a bias towards helping small farmers, as political parties competed for their votes, and switched away from supporting the interests of landowners to those of farmers. This was caused both by a decline in the state's dependence on the rural elites for enforcing policy locally, and by its growing interest in increasing farm output. As we shall now see, it helped contribute to major social changes in some countries.

The Family Farm and Rural Social Mobility

A number of influential eighteenth and nineteenth century writers, including the Physiocrats, Arthur Young, Albrecht Thaer, and James Caird, argued that England's large-scale capitalist farms were more efficient that the small family farms found over much of France. Large farmers, unlike smallholders, were financially able to fully stock their farms and had the skills to modernize their farm operations by following the technical advances of the day that were reported in the farming press.[40] The twentieth century, with the

---

[35] Politicians therefore found it difficult to mobilize the rural vote nationally, but used it instead to create networks of local support among elected administrative officers such as mayors. Sheingate 2001, p. 44, 66 and 92.

[36] Cleary 1989, pp. 49–51.

[37] However, Augé-Laribé 1950, pp. 124–31, described French agricultural research and extension as 'the regrettable failure of agricultural policy'. Sheingate 2001, p. 73. There were however some important exceptions. For a more positive interpretation of the wine sector, see Paul 1996.

[38] Olson 1963, p. 81 and Augé-Laribé & Pinot 1927, p. 2.   [39] Mann 2012, p. 148.

[40] One notable exception was wine, and Arthur Young calculated that in France a vineyard produced on average £9 per acre compared to £6 or £7 for the best land in England. Simpson 2011, pp. 7 and 8.

appearance of the 'factory farm', appeared to reinforce the advantages of scale.[41]

However, family-operated farms also had their defenders, and not just because there were actually few economies of scale in most forms of agriculture before 1914. In particular, the success of the family farm was due to its low monitoring costs of labour, and because they were better placed to allocate their time efficiently between work and leisure.[42] Much of agricultural work is unspecialized and its timing depends on weather conditions, creating difficulties for employers to check whether the work has been adequately carried out.[43] For the family farm, these problems are significantly reduced because members benefit directly from the effort and care that they invest on their land. Only for a small number of highly specific tasks, such as harvesting, are monitoring costs sufficiently low to encourage farmers to use wage labour. Small farmers can also enjoy a detailed knowledge of their land, allowing them to adjust cultivation techniques over relatively small areas to maximize quality or quantity of specific crops.[44] Farmers with access to their own land can also use their own entrepreneurial skills to build up a small business, an important factor when discussing future reforms.[45] Finally, cooperatives from the turn of the century offered small farmers the possibility to integrate upstream and downstream activities as economies of scale became important in activities such as the bulk buying of fertilizers, or the making and marketing of wine.

Liberal land reforms from the mid-eighteenth to mid-nineteenth centuries changed the nature of land ownership in many countries by ending feudal dues, the use of strict settlement, and sales of large areas of church and municipal lands. These changes did not significantly reduce land inequality, and often a relatively small number of families continued to own a high percentage of the land, leaving the majority of those employed in agriculture as landless or farming plots that were too small to maintain their families. However, the reforms did allow a new generation of landowners (the 'bourgeoisie') to replace the old aristocratic houses and institutional landowners and, by widening the land market, offered possibilities of a 'farm ladder' to develop. The farm ladder, in theory, allowed young people to work as wage labourers and save money and gain

---

[41] Augé-Laribé 1907, for France, and Scott 1998, pp. 164–8, for a discussion on Lenin's 'high-modernist state'.

[42] De Vries 2002, and Scott 1998, pp. 299–300.

[43] Allen & Lueck, 2002, p. 143, note that 'for many farm labor tasks, the gains from specialization are limited because stages of production tend to be short and require different skills from stage to stage. As a result, farmers tend to be unspecialized "jacks of all trades".'

[44] Carmona & Simpson 2012, p. 889.   [45] See Chapter 8.

experience to be able to either rent or sharecrop some land. With hard work, favourable shifts in factor prices, and perhaps luck, they became owners of small plots of land, enjoying sufficient property to become rentiers in their old age.[46] The possibilities for earning some cash was crucial to help young workers establish themselves on the farm ladder, or supplement the income of small farmers, and today between 30 and 40 per cent of income in rural areas of developing countries is estimated to come from non-agricultural sources.[47]

Between 1870 and 1930, across Europe there was a major growth in the number of family-owned farms, and an accompanying decline in the numbers and size of landed estates. As noted in Chapter 1, industrialization and the greater integration of global markets led to rising real wages and falling food prices, especially when tariffs were low or non-existent. At the extreme, in England and Wales, rents fell by 27 per cent and ordinary farm wages rose by 31 per cent between 1870 and 1913.[48] The result was that the real cost for labourers to buy or rent land declined over time. Yet despite these shifts in market forces, land rents and wages were often 'sticky', because landowners were able to resist changes.[49] In addition, and as Koning notes, because of rising real wages, Northern European landlords often benefitted from an *increasing* demand for land despite falling grain prices, as classical economic theory failed to reckon with the self-exploitation of family farmers who, on occasion, worked for less than casual labourers.[50] Just as landowners were reluctant to accept rent reductions, farmers also tried to slow the exodus of their labourers. In particular, 'paternalistic' contracts remained common in many regions, and these provided security (but low wages) to discourage workers from leaving, while elsewhere landless workers were given tenancies or became sharecroppers.[51] When this failed, farmers turned to foreign workers, and by the turn of twentieth century Italian and Spanish workers were widely found in southern France,[52] while in Eastern Germany the departing German labourers were replaced by Russian-Polish workers.[53] While farm labourers were often quick to leave for higher urban wages, they

---

[46] Augé-Laribé & Pinot 1927, p. 116, talk of a proletariat constantly disintegrating, 'as members break away, either to become landowners or join the industrial proletariat in the manufactories' in France.
[47] Haggblade et al. 2007, in Lipton 2009, p. 141. See also Banerjee & Duflo 2007.
[48] Rents refer to England only. Afton & Turner 2000, tables 39.6, 42.9 and 42.10.
[49] Offer 1989, p. 102.
[50] Koning 1994, p. 27. For 'an industrious revolution' which failed to change consumption habits, see Marfany 2012, pp. 13–19, for Catalonia, and Allen & Weisdorf 2011 for England.
[51] For the Midi, Carmona & Simpson 2012, pp. 902–4.
[52] Smith 1975, p. 373, and Frader 1991, table 9.   [53] Koning 1994, p. 104.

were usually reluctant to permanently move to other agrarian regions, so that the weakly integrated labour markets resulted in farmers in some parts of a country suffering from labour shortages, while there was a scarcity of wage-earning opportunities elsewhere.[54]

Although landlords attempted to avoid having to cut rents or pay higher wages, the widening suffrage led to governments legislating to protect tenants and the small, family-operated farm. The process of social change was sometimes spectacular. Ireland, for example, switched from having just 3 per cent of farms belonging to owner-occupiers, and 97 per cent rented in the 1870s to a complete reversal by 1929, with 97 per cent owner-occupied and 3 per cent rented.[55] The Irish Land Question and the country's fight for independence were major forces behind these changes, but in England falling rents and the introduction of death duties also spelt the end of the traditional landed estate, and between 1918 and 1921 there was 'a revolution in land ownership', with a quarter of all the country's land being sold, mostly to the owners' tenant farmers.[56]

The structure of farm ownership has often been seen as a crucial factor in determining income distribution and the nature of political organizations. For Robert Dahl, traditional peasant societies had 'a very high propensity for inequality, hierarchy, and political hegemony' compared with the 'free farmer' societies, found in countries such as Switzerland, Norway, or the United States, which were 'egalitarian and democratic'.[57] Growing nationalism from the late nineteenth century also found strong rural roots, idealizing the family peasant farmer, rather than the landlord. Following the First World War and the break-up of central European empires, land reforms and the division of the great estates were an integral part of the creation of new states in countries such as Rumania, Poland, Czechoslovakia, and Yugoslavia (Chapter 8).[58]

Vanhanen provides the only truly comparative picture for the growth of the independent family farm in this period and, although the figures have to be used with extreme caution, they are widely cited in the literature (Table 2.2).[59] In fact the limited statistical information available in most countries makes it is almost impossible to measure the growth of the family farm with any accuracy, especially as rapid shifts in farm prices

---

[54] For Denmark, see Henriksen 2014, p. 233.

[55] The figures in 1916 were 64 per cent (owners) and 36 per cent (tenants). Hooker 1938, p. 120. The 1929 figures are based on land area, and the others on the number of landholders.

[56] Thompson 2009. See also Beckett & Turner 2007.   [57] Dahl 1971, p. 53.

[58] Brassley 2010, p. 156.

[59] Vanhanen (1984, p. 35), defines family farms as providing employment for up to four people, including family workers. Tenancies are included, when 'they do not make the tenant cultivator socially and economically dependent on the landowner'.

Table 2.2 *Relative importance of family farms in European agriculture between the 1880s and 1950s*

	% employed in agriculture (1930)	GDP 1929 per capita (in 1990 $)	Family farmers as % of farm population 1880s	1910s	1930s	1950s
UK	6	5,503	8	20	30	48
Belgium	17	5,054	22	22	40	90
Switzerland	21	8,636	45	55	69	85
Netherlands	21	5,689	25	26	50	92
Germany	29	4,051	48	51	54	90
Austria	32	3,669	40	41	45	60
Denmark	35	5,075	35	44	60	87
Norway	35	3,387	71	80	84	88
France	36	4,710	29	29	45	70
Sweden	36	4,063	35	41	60	79
Czechoslovakia	37	3,042	na	na	65	60
Italy	47	2,778	18	18	27	33
Portugal	48	1,610	20	20	20	26
Ireland	48	2,824	na	na	58	74
Hungary	53	2,476	39	40	41	68
Greece	54	2,342	35	30	45	75
Spain	56	2,739	15	18	22	22
Poland	65	2,117	na	na	65	81
Yugoslavia	79	1,256	na	na	62	77
Romania	79	1,152	26	35	54	60
Bulgaria	80	1,227	na	53	75	60
Russia/USSR		1,386	33	43	18	1
USA	22	6,899	60	60	61	72

Sources: Feinstein et al. 1997, table 4.1; Maddison project 2013 version, and Vanhanen 1984, appendix.

led to significant income volatility and make any meaningful description difficult. Farmers' living standards, as already noted, were also influenced by a country's level of economic development, and growing industrialization magnified regional differences. The figures in Table 2.2 therefore provide only a very rough order of the magnitude, and direction of change, of the farm structure over time. However, two conclusions are clear: family farms were either already dominant by the 1880s, or they rapidly increased in importance everywhere over the next half-century, with the notable exceptions of Spain, and other Southern European countries, a subject discussed later in the book. Furthermore, the landownership structure and a country's level of economic development would have important implications for government policy during the Great Depression of the 1930s.

Agriculture and the Economic Response to Instability in the 1930s

The problems facing the agricultural sector during the Great Depression were totally unlike those of any previous crisis. During the late nineteenth century, growing food imports threatened to significantly lower prices, but governments could respond by raising tariffs and restricting foreign competition. An important safety valve also existed for surplus farm labour, as they could migrate to the growing manufacturing cities, or emigrate to the New World. The problems during the First World War were very different, and concerned how to increase farm output and control rising food prices for urban consumers. By contrast, the 1930s witnessed massive overproduction, rapidly falling farm prices and incomes, and widespread unemployment, none of which could be resolved by just higher tariffs.

The food shortages and the high prices immediately following the Great War encouraged farmers to increase output whenever possible, especially as chemical fertilizers were readily available once more. In Italy, for example, Mussolini launched his 'Battle for Wheat' in 1925, and quickly succeeded in making the country virtually self-sufficient. However, just as European and New World farmers were increasing wheat output, demand was beginning to fall in many countries. Between 1909/13 and 1924/9, per capita consumption fell by 16 per cent in the United States, 13 per cent in France, and 8 per cent in Spain and the UK,[60] and on the eve of the Great Depression the world's unsold stocks had swollen to the equivalent of a year's exports from all exporting countries.[61] Farm prices fell dramatically as lower incomes led to falling demand, not only of basic commodities, but also for superior foods such as butter and meat (Figure 2.2).

A second, related problem was that agriculture was still the employer of last resort in most European countries. Therefore, not only did the falling urban demand for labour slow the rural exodus, but rising urban unemployment led to some workers returning to their villages. Even in an industrial economy, such as the United States, 'the failure of industrial output to expand during the thirties was the basic factor in the worsening of

[60] Malenbaum 1953, p. 245. In Italy by contrast, per capita consumption rose 11 per cent.
[61] Tracy 1989, p. 119.

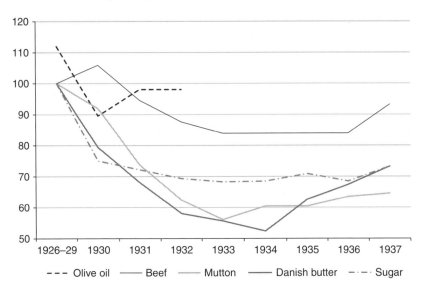

Figure 2.2 Prices of major foodstuffs on world markets (1927/29 = 100)
Source: Based on Tracy 1989, figure 6.1.

the agricultural situation. The main cause of the unproductive employment and low earnings in agriculture was the unemployment in industry'.[62]

The consequences of this growth in surplus farm labour varied, according to both the nature of agriculture and social structure in each region. Family farms were best suited to absorb surplus labour, as it was the family unit that redistributed both work and consumption opportunities among its members. However, because land was fixed and off-farm work opportunities limited, small farmers responded to low prices by working harder to produce more and maintain their incomes. This risked mounting agricultural surpluses and prices falling by even more. Large farmers by contrast looked to reduce costs by cutting labour inputs. In areas where large estates and wage labour predominated, there was sometimes a tension between the private rights and the social obligation of landowners. In particular, it highlighted the moral question of whether landowners could deny access their land to the local, landless villagers at times of social hardship. The debate was not new, as the Highland clearances in the eighteenth and nineteenth centuries had shown, but in the 1930s, the landless peasants of Andalucia and Extremadura in Spain questioned the legitimacy of the latifundia.[63]

[62] Schultz 1945, p. 113.   [63] Lipton 2009, p. 3, and Bayly 2004, pp. 295–300.

Given the political importance of agriculture and the extent of the economic shock, governments were forced to intervene. There was, however, little attempt to co-ordinate policies internationally, and domestic polices often benefitted one farm group at the expense of another. In general, two distinct policy areas can be identified: market intervention to alleviate the problems produced by low and highly volatile farm-gate prices, and the provision of unemployment relief for farm workers.

The importance that many European governments attached to achieving a secure food supply, and the growing political influence of family-operated farms led to experiments in market intervention. Many governments resorted to tariffs, milling ratios, and import quotas to raise domestic prices of bread grains above international levels. As these were usually insufficient, they also turned to other mechanisms to remove market surpluses, and legislated to guarantee minimum prices. These are discussed in detail in Chapter 6, but it is worth noting here two problems that quickly emerged. First, even when merchants agreed to pay a minimum price, they could not be obliged to buy farm produce that they did not want. Therefore, if Spanish wheat farmers appear to have had few problems during the Great Depression, with official retail prices in 1931 being only 6 per cent below their 1927–9 levels, small farmers frequently complained that they could find no buyers.[64] A second problem was that when policies succeeded in raising prices, this inevitably led to farmers attempting to increase production, unless governments could also introduce, and *enforce*, policies to limit farm output.

There were also demands, especially in those countries with large numbers of landless, or near landless workers, to alleviate unemployment and low wages. Poor relief everywhere was traditionally considered the responsibility of local, rather than national government, but the scale of the problem in the 1930s was simply too great for these traditional systems. This led to social transfers increasing in most European countries, although from very low levels (Table 1.4). Unemployment benefits were limited and governments often used work programs instead, although these were usually restrained by the self-imposed budgetary constraints of orthodox monetary policy.

The relative importance given to these different policies varied between North-Western Europe, where they were designed to help the farmers, and Southern Europe where they appear more biased towards the landless and near-landless labourers. To a certain extent, the two polices

---

[64] Farm-gate prices are not available. The barley price was 7 per cent and olive oil price 15 per cent lower, but wine had recovered by 4 per cent, beef by 7 per cent and potatoes 13 per cent, in Carreras & Tafunell 2005, Vol. 1, p. 337.

produced contradictory results. Government intervention that helped small farmers rarely led an increase in wage employment, as farmers attempted to reduce costs by working family members harder and not employing wage workers. By contrast, if attempts to increase wage employment, such as Italy's *bonifica integrale* or Spain's *intensificación de cultivo*, were to be successful, they would result in increased farm output and consequently risked reducing farm prices, affecting both large and small producers. We shall return to these problems in later chapters.

The response to economic depression and the search for food security reached extreme levels in authoritarian states, where a mixture of 'high modernism' and military preparations led to state control over the whole food chain. For Germany, Adam Tooze links the Nazi's agrarian ideology with the 'extraordinary militancy' of the Hitler's regime, as for the National Socialists, the farmer was considered not just an entrepreneur in the usual sense, but rather as the backbone of German society.[65] This was recognized in the Erbhof Law of September 1933, which attempted to create a network of family farms that protected their Germanic owners from the vagaries of the market through a new system of entail, so that farmers could not go bankrupt, and the whole farm passed from one generation to the next through a single male heir. The farm was supposed to be of sufficient size to sustain a German family. Unfortunately, given the level of farm prices, there was insufficient land, encouraging Hitler to seek *Lebenstraum* to the east. The 9.3 million employed in German agriculture, equivalent to 29 per cent of the total labour force, formed an important part of National Socialist's support but, as Tracy has argued, farm policy was not 'merely based on a desire to pander to the agricultural interest and gain its support' but rather contained a strong internal logic to increase, by force, 'the strength of the German nation'.[66]

Small farmers not only provided significant support to Italian fascism and Germany Nazism, but almost everywhere in Western Europe they supported conservative political parties.[67] There are various explanations but, as the Spanish case illustrates, a major factor was their weak political representation, and the contradictory demands that democratic governments faced during the Great Depression. In particular, farmers wanted high prices and low wage costs, demands that were diametrically opposed to those of industrial workers and urban middle classes. Furthermore, all governments found it difficult to intervene in commodity markets and support farm prices, while lower farm wages could only be achieved by

[65] Tooze 2006, p. 180.   [66] Tracy 1989, p. 200.
[67] For fascism, see, for example, Snowden 1989 (Tuscany) and Paxton 1997, especially ch. 5.

restricting trade union activities. Farmers often believed, therefore, that governments supported urban, rather than rural interests. In fact, the benefits of supporting fascism were short-lived because, as Paxton has noted, 'triumphant fascism subordinated peasant society to industrial growth, just as liberalism had done and as Soviet communism was doing, in a far more bloody manner, at the same time'.[68]

Conclusions

Economic development and globalization from the 1870s had major implications for the agrarian social order in Europe, ending the land scarcity that had benefitted landowners for several centuries, and causing lower farm prices and rents, and rising wages. On the eve of the First World War, Europe's rural elites faced not just falling incomes, but also a major challenge to their political influence as the extension of the suffrage gave other farm groups unprecedented opportunities to influence the political agenda in their countries. The Great War itself showed the possibilities of state planning and direct market intervention, as well as the necessity of governments to secure adequate food supplies. These facts, combined with the growing weakness of the farmers' bargaining position in the increasingly competitive market place, and the political importance of a sector which accounted between a third and a half of the electorate in most Western European economies, implied that new links began to be established between the farm sector and the state. In some countries, these had produced an openly corporatist arrangement by the Second World War. As Sheingate writes, 'intervention in the operation of agricultural markets after World War I redefined the relationship between farmers and the government; regulation changed the boundary between state and society'.[69]

Yet the demand for change in farm policies produced diverse results across Europe, depending in part on the political influence of different groups in each society (landowners, small farmers and tenants, farm workers, or the non-farm sector), as well as the capacity of the state to provide tangible goods that political parties could trade for electoral support. Traditional agrarian elites had preferred low levels of state capacity, making governments dependent on them to implement

[68] Paxton 1997, p. 158.
[69] Sheingate 2001, p. 79. Theodore Lewis argued for a later period that 'Agriculture is that field of American government where the distinction between public and private has come closest to being completely eliminated. This has been accomplished not by public expropriation of private domain ... but by private expropriation of public authority'. Lowi 1979, p. 67, quoted in Sheingate 2001, p. 7.

legislation and maintain law and order locally. This was changed by the First World War, as governments needed to increase output, and consequently turned to farmers rather than landowners as their representatives in the countryside. By the 1930s, the state in a growing number of countries in North-Western Europe was learning to work with small farmers to intervene at the farm level to control output. The combination of responding to economic depression and the search for food security reached extreme levels in authoritarian states, where a mixture of 'high modernism' and military preparation led to state control over the whole food chain. Almost everywhere, the slowly declining agricultural sector played an important part in determining political outcomes during the interwar period. The next chapter looks in detail at Spain.

Part II

Spanish Agriculture, Economic Development, and Democracy

> For the man in the street the Republic did not merely consist in seeing hundreds of middle-class Republicans take over civil governorships and others posts formerly held by hundreds of middle-class Monarchists. By Republic the man in the street meant the disappearance of feudalism; the disappearance of the hegemony of the Church, the landed proprietors, the Army, the Civil Guard, the Crown.[1]

Spain was at war when the Cadiz parliament approved one of Europe's most liberal constitutions in 1812, with half the country occupied by French troops. It was not an auspicious beginning, and over the next half-century the country suffered three bitter civil wars and frequent political intervention by military leaders (*pronunciamientos*). The Restoration and 1876 Constitution ended this instability, and for almost half a century the two dynastic parties manipulated the electoral system so that, despite universal male suffrage, voters did not choose governments, sparing politicians the expense of having to build mass parties. The absence of competitive politics also limited incentives to invest in state capacity, especially as Spain remained neutral during the First World War. This inheritance of a weak party system, limited state capacity, and the persistence of the traditional elites, had immensely negative consequences for the democratic experiment during the Second Republic.

The Restoration also ushered in a period of comparatively strong economic growth, with recent estimates suggesting that GDP increased by around two and half times, and GDP per capita by two-thirds, between 1875 and 1931, slightly closing the gap between Spain and the leading European economies. Incomes also rose, and equality probably fell. The nature of economic development however was influenced by the prevailing political system, and the restricted access to power helped economic agents capture the state to increase their rents and restrict competition.[2] As Henry Buckley's comment suggests, many contemporaries believed that the problems of unemployment and poverty in the 1930s were caused by

---

[1] Buckley 1940: 2014, p. 64.   [2] See especially Fraile Balbín 1991.

socioeconomic factors that the Second Republic inherited, rather than the economic depression.[3]

The contrast between a relatively dynamic economy existing alongside the presence of traditional power relations was especially strong in the countryside. Spanish agriculture was one of Europe's most protected, but it made an important contribution to economic growth, not only by feeding a growing population, but improving their diets and living standards. Furthermore, this was achieved with fewer workers, as between 1910 and 1930 almost a million workers left the sector, equivalent to virtually a fifth of its workforce. As in other Western European countries, the combination of a growing integration of the global economy, rapid industrialization, and rising wages benefited farm workers. In particular, between 1860 and 1930, the number of owner-occupiers and tenant farmers increased by about a quarter, and the numbers of landless workers fell by half. Yet there were still many landless workers in the regions of latifundios, and a high proportion of family farmers remained poor 'peasant' farmers, as opposed to the self-sufficient, independent family farmers increasingly found in Northern Europe. For many farmers the threat of acute poverty was just one poor harvest away. By contrast, the rents of landowners and profits of commercial wheat farmers were protected by high tariffs.

A major difference between Spanish agriculture with that of Northern Europe was the restrictions imposed by the need for dry-farming over about four-fifths of the country. In particular, farmers who lacked sufficient land found it difficult to increase yields through more intensive cultivation, or switching into new labour-intensive crops. Small cereal farmers in particular struggled, as large producers were increasingly able to reduce labour inputs and costs by mechanizing. Therefore, the 1930s depression exposed the limits to Spain's agricultural growth model, not just for the landless workers of the south, but also for small peasant cereal farmers everywhere.

This section begins by looking at long-run political and economic change in Spain over the century prior to the Second Republic, followed by a detailed study of agricultural change, and especially the restrictions imposed by the need to follow dry-farming practices over large areas of the country. Finally, it considers some of the regional diversity in agriculture, and localized land-tenure regimes. The third section will look at the political explanations for why small farmers remained poor, and why the landed elites and the Church continued to control village society.

---

[3] Henry Buckley was a British journalist in Madrid.

3 The Limits to Spanish Modernization, 1850–1936

Between 1808 and 1843 the entire socio-economic order of the Spanish Ancien Regime was dismantled. The nobility and the clergy lost their legal privileges and the equality of all male citizens before the law was proclaimed. Entails, seigneurial rights and the tithe were abolished. The lands of the Church were disentailed and sold at public auction, the guilds were suppressed and economic freedom established. The Inquisition was dissolved and the Church's legal jurisdiction in civil affairs eliminated. The absolute power of the monarch was replaced by a parliamentary system based on popular sovereignty.[1]

Spain was a relatively prosperous and fast-growing European economy on the eve of the Second Republic. Per capita income doubled between the 1870s and 1930s, by when the urban populations of Madrid and Barcelona were each approaching a million inhabitants. Industrialization was especially strong in Catalonia and the Basque Country, leading to fundamental changes in the production, distribution, and marketing of goods. Yet economic growth in Spain, as in most countries, remained highly uneven, resulting in some regions and social groups being left behind.[2] Poverty was still widespread, especially among the landless and near-landless workers of the south. Government expenditure on social transfers was equivalent to just 1 per cent of GDP in 1929. Although the Church sometimes acted as a substitute, it imposed conditions which were considered unacceptable to an increasingly large part of the population that was anticlerical.[3] Universal male suffrage was introduced in 1890, but voters could not change governments, political voice was limited, and labour organizations were either often banned or severely repressed. State capacity increased to some extent, but remained weak in a number of important areas, so that when unemployment surged during the Second Republic, governments had considerable difficulty in responding to the new challenges. Indeed, this combination of limited party development and weak state capacity in 1931 goes a long way to

---

[1] Burdiel 2000, p. 17.   [2] Rosés & Wolf, 2019.   [3] Arenas Posadas 2009.

explaining why the democratic experiment of the Second Republic would fail. Unfulfilled expectations of government land and labour market reforms not only disillusioned many but led to a growing rejection of liberal democracy, which the strong autonomous power centres such as the landed elites, Church, and military were able to exploit.

This chapter begins by examining the political transition from the Old Regime to the liberal state, and the considerable divisions and violence that this produced. This is followed by a review of the nature and speed of industrialization and structural change, the growth in living standards, and a decline in income inequality between the two Republics. Then we look at the political developments during the Restoration Period (1875–1923) and show how the state's continued dependence on local elites to manipulate elections and implement policy helped them perpetuate their power, while the absence of genuine mass political parties removed the incentives to create state capacity. The chapter concludes with a look at the economic and political problems that confronted the new Republican government in 1931.

From the Loss of Empire to the Creation of the Liberal Nation State (1808–76)

The liberal 1812 Constitution would deeply divide Spanish society for well over a century. Civil wars of one description or another plagued the country in one of every four years over the nineteenth century, and military uprising or *pronunciamientos* occurred at even great frequency, once every twenty-three months on average (Tables 3.1 and 3.2). The First Republic (1868–74) was established by a military coup, and ended by another. Only with the Restoration (1875–1923) was a period of relative political stability and economic growth achieved.

However, it is too simple to view the first half of the nineteenth century as only a battle between the forces of liberalism and reaction. The liberal state succeeded, at least in part, in developing the physical and legal infrastructure necessary to transform land and labour markets, integrating the national economy, and allowing the country to participate in the increasingly global system of exchange. Nevertheless, success was only achieved at the cost of an increase in political clientelism.[4] Indeed, as we will argue, the massive sales of Church land was both a government response to the acute financial difficulties caused by a civil war, and a means to widen its political support among a new elite. Rather than simply a struggle between liberals and conservatives, the political history over much of the period was one of

---

[4] For an excellent comparison between the experience of state building in Spain and Latin America during the nineteenth century, see Centeno & Ferraro 2013, ch. 1.

Table 3.1 *Spain at war, 1808–1939*

	1808–1899		1900–1939	
	Number of wars	Years at war	Number of wars	Years at war
Colonial – independence	6	19.5	–	–
Colonial – expansion	6	8.5	1	19
Civil Wars	6	19.0	1	3
Peninsula War	1	6.0		

Source: Vallejo Pousada 2014, table 9.3.

Table 3.2 Pronunciamientos *and military uprisings*

	Number	Frequency every x months
Fernando VII (1808–33)	14	21.4
Isabel II (1833–68)	25	16.8
Sexenio Democrático (1868–74)	4	18.0
Restoration (1874–1923)	4	147.0
Primo de Rivera (1923–30)	6	14.0
Second Republic (1931–9)	2	48.0

Source: Linz et al. 2005, cuadro 14.6.

a realignment of traditional elite groups to new market opportunities. As Carolyn Boyd has written,

The so-called 'liberal revolution' was … not a response to the demands of a growing and self-confident bourgeoisie, nor to a profound transformation of Spain's economic and social structure. Rather, it was the result of the military victory of a small, but politically significant, elite over its traditionalist opponents.[5]

The most dramatic opposition to the new liberal state were the three Carlist Wars, in 1833–40, 1847–9, and 1868–76. Historians have struggled to explain adequately how the 'reactionary' Carlist forces were not only able to pursue these wars, but were actually intriguing for another one long before July 1936. Carlism represented not just the defence of absolute monarchy and the traditional Church, but also the rejection of liberal and urban ideas that were considered as alien to village society. In the upland areas across northern Spain, and especially in

[5] Boyd 2000, p. 73.

Navarra, rural inequality was limited and the local clergy played a leading role in village society. The demands of the new liberal state challenged the region's system of self-government, undermined the role of the Church, endangered the common lands, and imposed new taxes, while greater market-integration exposed marginal farming and threatened mass migration. Liberal reforms affected not just the local landed elites and Church, but also the very fabric of village society and economic organization.

Radical new ideas associated with the Enlightenment questioned the legal nature of landownership against a background of growing population and rising demand for food. Jovellanos was Spain's most influential writer, and in his *Ley Agraria* (1793) argued that landownership should be a reward for economic efficiency rather than privilege, thereby directly challenging the institutional order of the Old Regime.[6] Landowners faced a more immediate threat with the Peninsular War, which saw a breakdown in law and order, the widespread invasion of common lands, tithe strikes, and the slaughtering of animals belonging to members of the Mesta sheep guild. The governments' reforms of 1811 and 1820 were quickly reversed, but those introduced in the 1830s and 1850s legitimized the de facto changes that were taking place, and significantly advanced the reform process. Access to land was now to be market, rather than authority based, and the *dominium utile* and *directum* joined in a single individual, rather than being divided.

Sales of Church lands began in 1798, but the great bulk took place following the Mendizábal Laws of 1836 and 1837, while the tithe was abolished in 1841. The traditional nobility were given the possibility to sell their lands with the ending of entail (*mayorazgos*), while the abolition of the Mesta (1836) allowed landowners over large areas of central Spain to raise rents, or turn pasture land into arable.[7] The size of the land market was greatly increased, and some 18.4 million hectares or 36 per cent of Spain's land area, changed hands between 1766 and 1924.[8] Contemporaries such as Jaime Balmes and Claudio Moyano noted that the state had created new property rights by arbitrarily destroying old ones.[9] The debate over state authority and the limits to property rights would return with the land reform debate during the Second Republic.

---

[6] Unlike earlier proposals for reform during the reign of Carlos III (1759–88), Jovellanos was the first to attack entail and church property. Ruiz Torres 1996, pp. 208–14.

[7] García Sanz 1985 and Villares Paz 1997.

[8] Some 10.2 million hectares resulted from disentail laws. Ruiz Torres 2004 and Pan-Montojo 2009, p. 139.

[9] Costa 1904.

The elimination of seigneurial property (*señorios*) and the nationalization and sale of municipal lands represented key elements in the growth of the modern, centralized Spanish state, as only a third of the country, and half the population, had previously been under direct royal jurisdiction.[10] The liquidation of the Old Regime not only greatly increased the size of the land market, but gave governments greater powers to determine the nature of the rules and regulations of property use.[11] However, feudal society had been highly heterogeneous and its abolition modified, rather than eliminated, the diverse system of land-tenure relations across the country. As a result, the reforms were still highly contentious in the 1930s, especially as although they had changed the nature of the Church's and nobility's assets and income, their economic and political powers appeared, at least superficially, largely undiminished. The Church was financially compensated for its losses, and its considerable influence over village life in large areas, especially in the North, continued until well into the second half of the twentieth century.[12] The traditional noble households had sold large parts of their patrimony, but it was widely believed that they had illegally used their seigneurial powers to usurp significant areas of common lands to create their latifundios, while the presence of a new class of *latifundistas* appeared to manipulate local politics.[13] Reformers such Rafael Altamira or Pascual Carrión therefore blamed the liberal land reforms for perpetuating a system of large estates in the south of the country, which they thought led to inefficient farming and that kept large numbers of landless workers underemployed, delaying economic and political development.

Another problem was that property rights in both Galicia and Catalonia were divided between landowners who received rent, and farmers who enjoyed perpetual rights to cultivate the land (Chapter 9). Finally, Joaquín Costa linked the difficulties that many small family farmers were experiencing in the late nineteenth century with changes brought about by the growth of the market and their loss of common rights. In areas of small property, the liberal revolution was often seen as producing high taxes, price volatility, and widespread usury, in contrast to a supposed idyllic peasant society that had previously existed. Costa's views were still widely influential during the Second Republic.

---

[10] Shubert 1990, pp. 57–9.   [11] Boone 2014, p. 67.
[12] Alonso 2011, Lannon 1987, and Callahan 2000.   [13] Bernal 1979.

The Restoration Political System: *Caciques* and the *Turno Pacífico*

Following the frequent civil wars and military *pronunciamientos* of the early nineteenth century, the 'Restoration' period (1875–1923) provided remarkable political stability under a constitutional monarchy. The 1876 Constitution created one of the most advanced liberal regimes in Europe, and integrated into the political system the various groups 'who had previously wrought havoc on the country'.[14] Adult male suffrage was achieved as early as 1890, and important civil liberties such as freedom of association (1887) of speech, of the press, or the right to strike (1909) granted. Yet these changes failed to produce a real party system, restrict the powers of the Monarchy, democratize the senate, or restrain the army.[15]

The central state in the early nineteenth century had faced considerable problems in exerting its authority in the regions, and the Restoration system depended on the powers of local political bosses (*caciques*) to both implement its policies and produce the electoral results demanded from Madrid. The *caciques* were usually associated with commercial agriculture, or the processing and marketing of farm produce, and not the old landed elites.[16] They formed the link between the village and the wider world, using a mixture of private and public patronage to exert power, as their control of the political machinery – the town hall, the representation to national government, and the taxes paid and distribution of funds – allowed them to reinforce their networks. Just as in Italy, the Restoration governments made extensive use of the patron-client networks, 'to accomplish political work which, in constitutional principle, should have been carried on by independent citizens, representative assemblies, bureaucrats, and public-minded public officials'.[17]

The Restoration achieved political stability only because the two main dynastic parties (the conservatives and liberals) took it in turns to form governments in what became known as the *turno pacífico*. This worked because the incumbent party resigned when it could no longer govern, allowing the opposition to organize new elections and assign sufficient seats to obtain a parliamentary majority *before* the elections took place. The chosen candidates then resorted to extensive vote buying, coercion, and mass fraud to achieve the required electoral results in their constituencies.[18] Both the conservative and liberal parties were willing to surrender power in this way because the system guaranteed that their time in opposition would

---

[14] Jacobson & Moreno Luzón 2000, p. 98.   [15] Linz 1967, p. 202.
[16] Moreno Luzón 2007, pp. 427–8.   [17] Tilly et al. 1975, pp. 90–1.
[18] Curto-Grau et al. 2012, p. 771.

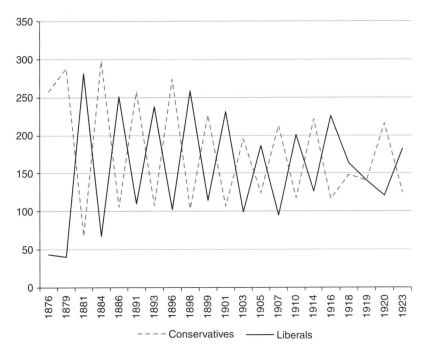

Figure 3.1 The *turno pacífico* of the dynastic parties in the Congress of Deputies (number of parliamentary seats)
Source: Based on Jacobson & Moreno Luzón 2000, p. 99.

be only temporary, as their opponents were trusted to 'respect the rules'. Despite universal male suffrage, therefore, democracy became associated among both urban and rural populations with political corruption and an absence of competitive party politics. The electoral results, with each party taking it in turn to rule, reflect the successful operation of the system, especially before the turn of the century (Figure 3.1). As a result, neither the liberals, nor the conservatives, needed to build a genuine party with a centralized bureaucracy for winning votes in democratic elections.

The difficulties of incorporating new social groups within the system were the Achilles heel of the *turno pacífico*. At first these were few, as some were bought off and incorporated within the *turno*, while republican, socialist parties were sufficiently marginalized, and trade union activities restricted, when not openly repressed. However economic development and structural change led to new political demands, and vote rigging proved much more complicated in urban than rural areas. In particular, the Cuban 'disaster' of 1898 led to a general dissatisfaction among many intellectuals, especially with the 'Montjuic affair', and the widespread use of torture on political activists. Alejandro Lerroux now turned his small republican party, organized around urban intellectuals, into a mass movement embracing the need for social reform. It contained a strong anticlerical element, which blamed the Church for the failure of the country to modernize. Yet while the Dreyfus Affair helped consolidate French democracy in an increasingly industrial society, in Spain there was to be no review of the Montjuic case until the Second Republic. Furthermore, Lerroux's radical republicanism did not pretend to establish a representative and impartial political system, but aimed rather at creating a new form of *caciquismo*, which was urban rather than rural.[19]

The difficulties of incorporating new social groups within the *turno pacifico* were highlighted by the so-called 1917 Crisis, when the government seemed unable to respond to the threats from different military factions, various political lobbies, and the revolutionary strikes, that would persist during the Bolshevik Triennium (1918–20). Catholic and employer groups increasingly rejected the system, and the government's attempt to widen support with social and political reforms ended with the bloodless coup by Primo de Rivera in 1923. This was initially supposed to last three months to restore order, but the Dictatorship became consolidated, and institutionalized as a corporatist regime, somewhat influenced by Italian fascism. The Dictatorship (1923–30) ended any attempt to transform an oligarchic to a democratic parliamentary system under the 1876 Constitution, while the fate of the Monarchy was sealed by King Alfonso XIII's support for Primo de Rivera.

Long-Term Economic Development and Changes in Living Standards

Although Spain's leading intellectuals reflected bitterly on the country's perceived failures compared with Northern Europe following the loss of Cuba in 1898, the next three decades saw remarkable economic and social change, as the economy grew by an annual 2.6 per cent in real terms, a per capita growth of 1.6 per cent (Figure 3.2).[20] Structural change, which involved farm workers moving off the land to work in the industrial and service sectors where productivity was higher, occurred relatively late. Even so, the farm population fell from around two-thirds of the active population as late as 1910, to just under a half by 1930.[21] Living

---

[19] Álvarez Junco 2002, pp. 173–5.
[20] Calculated from Prados de la Escosura 2017, table S27, for the years 1898–1929.
[21] Ibid., p. 159, calculates that approximately half the annual 0.7 per cent increase in labour productivity between 1883 and 1929 can be accounted for by this reallocation of workers.

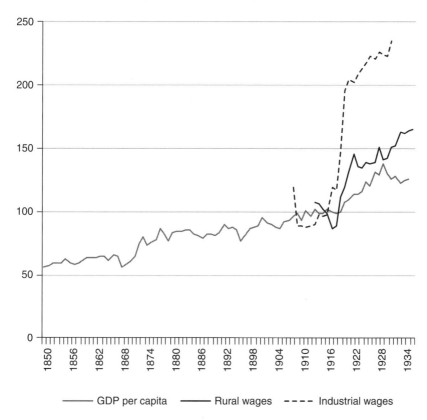

Figure 3.2 Changes in Spanish GDP per capita and real wages, 1850–1935 (1913/17 =100)
Sources: GDP per capita, Prados de la Escosura 2017, S27 and Maluquer de Motes & Llonch 2001, table 15.21.

standards by the 1930s were significantly above those found in many of the world's poorer countries at the end of the twentieth century. In 1900, average incomes in Spain were double that of a poverty line defined as $2 per person per day (expressed in 1985 purchasing power–adjusted international dollars), and triple this figure in 1930. The numbers who lived below this poverty line halved from 24 to 12 per cent of the population between 1900 and 1935, before climbing to 24 per cent again in 1950.[22]

Population growth was also impressive, growing from 15 million in 1850 to 24 million by 1933, although again the rate was also slower than

[22] Prados de la Escosura 2008, p. 306 and figure 9.

most Western European countries, primarily because of higher levels of mortality. However, if mortality figures were still 29 per thousand as late as 1900, they had fallen to 17 per thousand by 1930, with infant mortality dropping from around 200 to 120 per thousand.[23] Urban growth was significant, with the percentage of the nation's population living in towns of more than 5,000 inhabitants increasing from 29 to 37 per cent during the first third of the century.[24] Yet care is needed in interpreting the economic significance of urbanization, as farms in Northern Spain were widely scattered across the countryside and the region's relatively small settlements had important service sectors, exactly the opposite to what was found in the South, where population was concentrated in large villages or towns, and significant sections of the population worked in a variety of low-skilled activities in different sectors.[25]

Literacy levels, as elsewhere in Southern Europe, remained half those of the industrial 'core' and Northern Europe on the eve of the First World War, but again change was happening rapidly, with figures doubling between 1880 (35 per cent) and 1930 (69 per cent).[26] Levels were higher in urban rather than rural areas, and the literate were more likely to emigrate, or move to the city than those with no education.[27] The growth in literacy and urbanization encouraged a rapid increase in the newspaper industry, itself the result of the mechanization of printing, the telegraph, the mass production of cheap paper, and news agencies. By the 1890s, Madrid could boast of between thirty and forty daily newspapers, although only a handful had a circulation of more than a few hundred.[28] Provincial cities and towns were also increasingly well served by the turn of the twentieth century.

Evidence for real wages is poor, but they appear to have grown slowly over the last third of the nineteenth century, and then accelerated during the first third of the twentieth (Figure 3.2). Information concerning family incomes is virtually non-existent, although crucial to understand

[23] Nicolau 2005, pp. 125 and 130–1.
[24] Carreras & Tafunell 2005, pp. 125, 130–1, and 488.
[25] Brenan 1962, 4th edition, pp. 118, writing in 1943, notes for towns such as Osuna (population 16,000) or Carmona (22,000), that 'the first impression is one of decay and stagnation. A few wretched shops selling only the bare necessities of life: one or two petty industries – soap making, weaving of esparto mats, potteries, oil distilleries that between them employ some couple of hundred men'.
[26] O'Rourke & Williamson 1997, table 4, and Tortella 1994.
[27] Spain. Censo de Población, 1891. Quiroga Valle 2003b, p. 600, finds that literacy was 25 per cent higher for those living in provinces other than their birth province for the years 1893 and 1899. Around 74 per cent of Spaniards of over seven years of age living in Argentina in 1914, and 80 per cent of those arriving in Cuba between 1903 and 1927, were literate, compared to 50 per cent in Spain in 1910. Sánchez Alonso 2000, p. 734.
[28] Álvarez Junco 2002, p.15–7.

long-term shifts in consumption and poverty. Prados de la Escosura has maintained that slow growth and rising inequality led to an increase in absolute poverty in the period 1880–1920, but that this was then reversed during the years between 1920 and 1935.[29] As this book will argue, this seems unlikely for a number of key groups in agriculture during the 1930s, because if labour legislation increased hourly take-home wages for some workers, this was offset by falling employment opportunities, while weak farm-gate prices affected negatively the incomes of the hundreds of thousands of family farmers.

Given the limited information on wages and employment, historians have also looked to other indicators to better understand long-term changes in living standards. These often reinforce the idea of a limited, but positive growth in the decades prior to the Civil War. For example, there was a modest increase in the average height of the military recruits born between 1893 and 1930 (from 163.8 to 165.4 cm), although figures hide some significant variations across social groups and regions.[30] Furthermore, not only were Spanish recruits some of the shortest in

Table 3.3 *Indicators of European living standards, c.1930*

	Spain	France	Italy	Great Britain	Germany	Portugal
GDP per capita	2,620	4,532	2,918	5,441	3,973	1,571
% working in agriculture	46	36	47	6	29	55
Ag. output per worker	39	88	43	100	104	na
Real wages	57	71	55	103	99	24
Mortality per 1000	17	16	14	13	11	17
Infant mortality per 1000	117	84	106	65	85	144
Literacy	68	95	78	100	100	40
Mailed items per capita	33	153	59	146	94	23
Stature (mm)	165.1	169.1	167.2	173.6	173.0	165.4

Sources: GDP per capita (1990 international Geary-Khamis dollars) in Maddison 2003; agricultural output per male worker compared to pre-1922 United Kingdom, O'Brien & Prados de la Escosura 1992, table 6; employment in agriculture and mailed items per capita, Mann 2004, table 2.1; real wages shown as a percentage of Great Britain in 1927, Williamson 1995, p. 181; total and child mortality (under one year), Mitchell 1992, p. 75; literacy, UNESCO 1953; and stature, Hatton & Bray 2010, p. 411.

[29] Prados de la Escosura 2008, especially pp. 309–10.
[30] Nicolau 2005, cuadro 2.16, and especially Quiroga Valle 2001.

Europe in the mid-nineteenth century, but the gap actually widens over the following century.[31]

Finally, the combination of large numbers employed in agriculture and low labour productivity implied limited food consumption, a feature that is common in many poor countries, even those on the verge of rapid economic growth.[32] Spanish diets improved slowly, with the average per capita calorie consumption increasing from roughly 2,100 per day in 1897/1901 to 2,400 in 1929/33, but there were important increases in the consumption of meat (+63 per cent), dairy products (+122 per cent) and sugar (+153 per cent), albeit from low levels in all cases, and perhaps benefiting primarily urban consumers. By contrast, there was a modest decline in bread consumption.[33]

The Growth and Limits to State Capacity

Spanish contemporaries after 1898 frequently commented on the weakness of state institutions, most notably Ortega y Gasset in his highly influential *España invertebrada* (1914). Governments had liberalized internal markets, changed the nature of property rights and enforcement of contracts, and improved communications (the railways and telegraph), but its influence remained weak. As James Scott has noted for pre-modern states in general, government in 'many crucial respects', was 'partially blind; it knew precious little about its subjects, their wealth, their landholdings and yields, their location, their very identity'.[34] Aside from basic information on demography and foreign trade, the Spanish government in the mid-nineteenth century was ignorant of much concerning the economy and its citizens.[35] There are virtually no contemporary statistics on agricultural output until almost the last decade of the century, and those that existed, such as the *Junta General de Estadística*'s estimates of wheat production in 1857, were not considered 'fit for publication', although this did not stop Fermín Caballero a decade later 'correcting' the figure by multiplying it by 3.6![36]

As noted in Chapter 1, the state's capacity to tax was initially closely linked to the need to finance war. Spain had participated in every major Continental war between the sixteenth and eighteenth centuries, but it

---

[31] Martínez-Carrión 2011, figure 5 and table 1.   [32] See Chapter 2.
[33] Simpson 1989, cuadro 5.   [34] Scott 1998, p. 2.
[35] The population census of 1857 was the first since 1797, and considered by demographers as being reasonably reliable. Pérez Moreda 1985, p. 27. For trade statistics, see Tena 2005.
[36] Tortella 1985, p. 77.

was then absent in all of them during the next two centuries.[37] The nineteenth century civil wars split the country, and did little to increase state capacity, while at the same time Spain lost much of its empire, just as the leading European countries were rapidly increasing their colonial possessions.[38] However, government spending everywhere in Europe remained low before the First World War, and Spain's disastrous Cuban war saw the start of important tax reforms.[39] It is not inconceivable therefore that if the country had participated in the First World War, state capacity would have grown much faster.

During the first third of the twentieth century, Spain suffered from both a low total tax take and a relatively high dependence on indirect taxes, tariffs, and monopolies (Table 3.4), explained by the high economic and political costs of increasing fiscal capacity. By contrast, on the expenditure side, a significant proportion of income was spent on interest payments and the military, with relatively little for capital formation. Spanish social transfers, taken to include education, health, pensions, and social security expenditure, accounted for just 11.3 per cent of government expenditure.[40]

The state's failure to increase its tax capability is most apparent with the land tax (*contribución territorial*) which was introduced in 1845 and accounted for between 20 and 25 per cent of revenues before 1900.[41] Individuals were assessed by village commissions (*juntas periciales*) composed equally of elected councilors and the largest local taxpayers, who drew up lists of all agricultural property, and estimated each villager's income by taking into account the type of crops and land quality (*cartillas evaluatorias*).[42] Once the government decided its financial needs, it allocated sums to each province, and the demands were then divided between the different villages. The arbitrary nature of this method is highlighted by the fact that Laureano Figuerola, when he became Minister of Finance in

[37] Álvarez Junco 2013, pp. 315–16. See Grafe 2012 for the failure to create a unified tax system in Spain in the eighteenth century, and Johnson & Koyama 2017 for problems of building a centralized state in the European context
[38] Blattman & Miguel 2010, p. 42, note that, 'The historical evidence ... that war enables the development of capable government institutions in Europe may not generalize to civil war cases', as 'government may lose legitimacy, while victors and vanquished (and victims) are condemned to coexist in the same society, potentially exacerbating political and social divisions'.
[39] In 1913, central-government spending in France, Germany, and the United Kingdom averaged between 8 and 10 per cent of GDP. Broadberry & Harrison 1995, table 1.5. For Spanish tax reforms, see especially Cabrera Calvo-Sotelo & Comín 1989.
[40] Comín & Díaz 2005, table 12.18. Even so, pensions, accounting for approximately half the total, were for civil servants and not therefore strictly social transfers. See also Espuelas 2015.
[41] Ibid., p. 883.
[42] This paragraph is based on Pro Ruiz 1995. The *amillaramientos* were supposed to be recalculated every ten years, although this rarely occurred (pp. 105–6).

Table 3.4 *Tax revenue and expenditure in Spain, 1860–1930*

	Government expenditure as % GDP	Nature of taxes as % of total			
		Indirect	Direct	Monopolies	Other income, excluding loans
1860	10.9	26.3	24.3	29.3	13.0
1901	9.7	40.8	37.3	14.5	9.5
1923	12.7	38.9	33.5	11.7	9.9
1935	13.5	31.9	34.4	16.3	12.8

Specific expenditures as a % of the total

	Goods & services	Salaries & wages	Interest payments	Capital formation	Military expenditure + interest payments*
1860	37.6	36.0	13.1	4.8	47.2
1901	15.5	36.4	38.5	2.5	57.6
1923	26.0	31.6	18.6	4.7	43.6
1935	16.8	37.4	21.1	7.4	37.1

* includes payments in previous four columns.
Source: Comín & Díaz 2005, tables 12.1, 12.16, 12.17, and 12.18.

1868, found that tax records existed in Madrid for less than half (23) the country's provinces. The extent of fraud was exposed by the *Instituto Geográfico y Estadísticos*'s study of eight southern provinces between 1872 and 1893, which calculated 2.77 million hectares, or 26 per cent of the total land area, went undeclared. The actual level of fraud was considerably greater, as the economic use of the land was frequently misreported. In the province of Cádiz, for example, 48 per cent of irrigated land, 52 per cent of olives, 25 per cent of vines, 22 per cent of cereals, and 9 per cent of low-value grazing land (*montes y pastos*) went undeclared. To compensate, the area with no agricultural value was *over* declared by 67 per cent![43]

The character and the extent of fraud made it difficult for the government to adequately determine the country's wealth and increase its fiscal capacity. Yet the consequence of the poorly collected land tax extended well beyond that of diminished revenue, as the system increased the power of the local elite at the expense of the central state. Tax lubricated a patronage system that ran from Madrid to the country's most isolated settlement, with the provincial *caciques* determining which villages paid

[43] Ibid., cuadro 3.

most taxes, and the village *cacique* which taxpayers were to be 'rewarded' for their loyalties, and which 'punished'.[44]

Work began on the cadastre in 1895, and it was estimated by 1923 that the *amillaramientos* had under-calculated land taxes by half. However, a well-organized campaign by landowners through the *cámaras agrícolas* demanded greater vigour in calculating land values, effectively forcing the government to allocate more resources to compiling the cadastre, and successfully slowing its advance to a crawl. By 1930, only 22 million hectares, or less than half the country, had been surveyed, and even so the cadastre failed to reflect changes in annual output or farm prices. In Spain, central government taxation was equivalent to only 8 per cent of GDP in the 1920s, compared to 32 per cent of GDP in France, or 26 per cent in the United Kingdom.[45] As Comín notes, 'in the thirties there were no tax statistics on income and wealth, or a Treasury capable of creating them and managing the new (income) tax; in fact, it could not even collect effectively the traditional taxes on production'.[46]

The low level and nature of government taxation and expenditure was matched by a notoriously inefficient civil service and military, the absence of meritocracy in the selection of personnel, and an unwillingness to vote the necessary funds to improve government information and capacity.[47] This failure to create a structure that allowed central institutions to operate independently helped local elites continue to play a major role in transmitting and enforcing government policy in villages. So while major shifts in factor prices and the production needs of the First World War helped erode the social and economic power of the landowner in favour of the entrepreneurial farmer over large areas of Western Europe, the process was much slower in Spain.

The Spanish state also suffered from a lack of legitimacy, in part the failure to create a strong national identity. Eugene Weber has shown for France that from the 1870s the building of a railway network, the provision of free, lay, and compulsory education, and military service, all helped turn regional peasants into Frenchmen, reinforcing the central state, and diminishing the power of autonomous power centres. In Spain nationalism took a very different path, initially being associated with the struggle against Napoleon and the liberal revolution, and demands for modernization and polyarchy.[48] However, much of society did not share

---

[44] Therefore, in Cadiz province, the village of Alcalá del Valle was taxed for an area that was 62 per cent *greater* than physically existed. Ibid., cuadro 2.

[45] Comín & Díaz 2005, table 12.2.

[46] Comín 1996, p. 84. See also Cabrera Calvo-Sotelo & Comín 1989 for attempts at reform.

[47] It was only in 1918 that civil servants could not be dismissed for political reasons.

[48] Álvarez Junco 2013.

these ideas, and the Church in particular resented any restrictions over its influence in questions of education and the family, both of which were protected in the 1876 Constitution. The loss of credibility of the political elites, military, and Church following the debacle of 1898 also contributed to the growth of Catalan and Basque nationalism, as well as growing class conflict. By the 1930s, Spanish nationalism, as elsewhere in Europe, had ceased to be liberal, and instead was a reactionary movement that looked to unite a divided country under the Catholic banner.

From Boom to Slump: Poverty and Democracy in the 1930s

Economic historians have often argued that Spain suffered less than most Western European countries during the Great Depression, not because of some enlightened economic policy, but rather because of its weak export sector, its limited dependence on international financial markets, and the country's failure to join the Gold Standard.[49] However new estimates suggest that per capita income fell by 11.5 per cent between 1929 and 1933, compared to 12.2 per cent in Germany and 10.0 per cent in France.[50] As Francisco Comín has written, 'the Second Republic economy followed the international trend, but with the peculiarities of a backward country, and the special problems associated with a newly established democracy'.[51] The fact that many contemporaries preferred to ignore the international context behind Spain's economic problems and blamed the Republican governments instead, should not disguise the importance of the slowdown.

Spain's tariffs limited the impact of world food prices halving between 1929 and 1932 (Table 1.3). Farmers, while experiencing a particularly sharp fall in 1930, benefited from the exceptional cereal harvests of 1932 and 1934, with contemporaries noting that large harvests produced a strong domestic demand for consumer goods (Table 3.5).[52] However, the price data corresponds to 'official' prices and small farmers often had difficulties selling at these levels, while export crops such as olive oil saw prices fall by 20 per cent. Agricultural output in 1933 was 20 per cent lower than in 1929. This drop in farm incomes however was accompanied by rising production costs, as the official statistics suggest that wages edged upwards. As Malefakis has noted, Spain was perhaps the only Western European country where nominal farm wages actually

---

[49] Palafox 1991, pp. 156–7.   [50] Prados de la Escosura 2017, table S27, p. 359.
[51] Comín 2012.   [52] Flores de Lemus 1926: 1951 and Zumalacárregui Prat 1934.

Table 3.5 *Index of GDP and its major components, at 1929 prices*

	Agriculture	Industry	Construction	Services	GDP	GDP per capita	Mining
1929	100	100	100	100	100	100	100
1930	86	100	104	102	96	94	94
1931	92	90	76	102	94	91	82
1932	103	88	65	103	97	92	71
1933	92	88	76	105	95	88	66
1934	103	88	71	106	99	91	63
1935	102	92	74	111	100	91	71

Sources: Prados de la Escosura 2017, tables 16 and 27; mining, Prados de la Escosura 2003, A5.9.

Table 3.6 *Prices of farm commodities and factor inputs*

	1880/85	1913/14	1925/29	1931/35
Wheat	92	100	160	156
Olive oil	88	100	181	143
Wine		100	96	113
Meat (beef)		100	191	175
Wage labour (1)	92	100	233	259
Wage labour (2)	88	100	261	280
Rent	56	100	144	152

(1) Coastal Catalonia and (2) Spain
Sources: Barciela López et al. 2005, pp. 336–7, Garrabou & Tello 2002, and Bringas Gutiérrez 2000, pp. 57 and 96.

increased during the Great Depression.[53] Yet while higher wages were no doubt welcome, the real problem for most farm workers in the 1930s was actually finding work. For small farmers in particular, the combination of lower prices and rising harvest wages squeezed household budgets. The political consequences of this are dealt with later.

Just as in other countries, many of the problems facing Spanish agriculture in the 1930s originated in industry. Over the two decades between 1910 and 1929, while GDP grew by 69 per cent, industrial output increased by 91 per cent, and agriculture by 48 per cent. The numbers

---

[53] Malefakis 1970, p. 329. However, both the official farm prices and wages were probably often above those actually contracted at the farm level. See Chapter 10.

employed in agriculture declined by 20 per cent from 5.1 to 4.1 million, but the sector's contribution to GDP fell only from 28 to 26 per cent, as farm labour productivity grew by 57 per cent.[54] A dynamic industrial sector therefore attracted underemployed farm labour, encouraging farmers in turn to introduce new technologies to increase output and reduce labour inputs. The opposite scenario happened during the 1930s. Between 1929 and 1935 industrial output declined by 11 per cent, and construction and mining fell by a massive 27 per cent (Table 3.5). Accurate unemployment figures for these sectors are unavailable, but even a relatively small increase had a negative impact on agriculture because, as unemployed workers returned to their villages to look for work on the family farm, or compete with local workers for seasonal

Table 3.7 *Changes in labour demand and supply for major crops during the 1930s*

	Cereal-area sown	Demand for harvest labour				Total change in labour demand	Number of farm workers	Changes in per capital work
		Cereals	Olives	Vines	Total			
1926/30	100	100	100	100	100	100		
1930	102	107	31	83	93	98	100	100
1931	103	98	94	88	96	101	103	98
1932	104	131	94	98	122	114	106	107
1933	102	103	78	91	98	101	109	92
1934	103	134	84	100	123	114	113	101
1935	101	111	118	79	109	106	116	92
1931/5	103	116	97	91	109	107		

Notes and sources: sown area includes wheat, barley, oats, and rye on irrigated and non-irrigated land. Cereal and wine harvest labour: the average harvest yield has been calculated for the period 1926/30 (olive 1926/35). Harvest demand is then calculated by multiplying the area cultivated each year by a fixed quantity of labour (wheat, 13.5 days per hectare; barley, 15.5 days, and oats and vines, 10 days) together with the amount that the annual harvest deviated from the 1926/30 average. For the olive, estimates have been made for the provinces of Cordoba, Jaen, and Seville using traditional technologies, and extended to the rest of the country. See Simpson, 1995, table 5.10. Total changes in labour demand use the same fixed coefficients as harvest demand (i.e., wheat 13.5 day per hectare), and the figure added to harvest demand.
Farm workers: figures assume that the number of farm workers grew by an annual 2.9 per cent, of which 1.9 per cent was caused by population growth, and 1.0 per cent by non-farm workers looking for employment in the sector.

[54] Prados de la Escosura 2003, pp. 291–2, 388–9, and 609.

employment on the large estates.[55] At the same time, rising urban unemployment discouraged farm workers moving to the cities. An indicator of this potential for disrupting labour markets can be illustrated by the fact that a projected net figure of 1.7 million workers joined the Spanish labour market between 1930 and 1936, equivalent to over 40 per cent of the 4.1 million of all ages employed in agriculture.[56] Table 3.7 suggests that it was the growing farm population, which is estimated to have increased by 20 per cent between 1930 and 1936, rather than any decline in the area cultivated or poor harvests which caused most rural hardship. At the village level, of course, harvest volatility could be significant, and new labour legislation had a major impact on which groups of workers were employed, and which were not (Chapter 10).

Conclusion

The political stability that the *turno pacífico* provided until the First World War came at a high cost, as it strengthened the influence of local elites who were able to use central government funds to build and consolidate their clientelistic networks. As a result, the Spanish state remained a weak administrative unit, 'centralized on paper but limited in its capacity to impose executive decisions from above, depended on local elites to implement policies'.[57] The political system could only work if sufficient citizens identified with the two parties, but opposition increased after 1900 among organized labour in the growing cities, republican groups, and nationalists in Catalonia and the Basque Country. By contrast, opposition from small farmers was strictly limited, as explained in Chapter 6.

Spain's neutrality during the First World War had important consequences in terms of creating state capacity. Governments found it harder to intervene effectively in the economy, so even if the 1930s economic depression was less severe than in some other European countries, the response by central government was often ineffective. The fact that the Second Republic significantly raised expectations that the new government would resolve the social problems, therefore, inevitably led to deep frustration among many groups, not just the landless workers, when it failed.

---

[55] For industrial unemployment, see Palafox 1991, pp. 264–5.
[56] Nicolau 2005, pp. 145–7, our calculations. The labour force is taken as all individuals aged between fifteen and sixty-four. It assumes that 2.73 million aged between ten and fifteen entered the workforce between 1930 and 1936, and the 1.01 million aged between fifty-nine and sixty-four ceased to work.
[57] Jacobson & Moreno Luzón 2000, p. 99.

4 Agricultural Growth, Regional Diversity, and Land-Tenure Regimes

> The latifundios ... have no relation whatsoever with the natural condi-
> tions of these regions, and their origin is in the Reconquest and the liberal
> land reforms. They explain the depopulation of the countryside; deficient
> cultivation; low wages; high rents; scarce and rickety livestock and, in
> general, the precarious situation in which a third of the country is found.[1]

> The agricultural progress since the beginning of the century has been
> enormous. The use of chemical fertilizers and modern machinery is to be
> found in all the villages. Some farms, with respect to machinery at least,
> are at the same level as the most progressive countries. The production
> of cereals and legumes has doubled in the last twenty years.[2]

Many historians argue today that Spanish agriculture in the half-century
prior to the Civil War was a success story.[3] In particular, between 1910 and
1930, land output increased by 31 per cent and labour productivity by
65 per cent, and the sector made an important contribution to economic
growth. In 1929, Spanish consumers were largely fed by their farmers, and
although food and beverages accounted for around a fifth of all imports,
farm products represented over half of exports.[4] Mechanization and the use
of artificial fertilizers were becoming increasingly important, and large-
scale irrigation projects were being planned and constructed. Yet many
Spaniards on the eve of the Second Republic believed otherwise, and
associated rural poverty, especially in southern Spain, with poor farming
techniques, which they blamed on land inequality, and the supposed
obstacles that latifundios placed on the country's economic development.[5]
    This chapter looks at agricultural performance, landownership, and farm-
ing systems at the national and regional levels. As in many European
countries, the 'long nineteenth century' saw massive sales of Church and
municipal lands, as well as changes in the nature of land-tenure regimes as
liberal governments dismantled the Old Regime, and set about building

---

[1] Carrión 1932: 1975, p. 347.   [2] Díaz del Moral 1928, 1973, p. 37.
[3] The debate instead has centred on the degree of change. See especially Garrabou et al.
1986, Simpson 1995, and Pujol et al. 2001.
[4] Figures refer to 1926. Tena 2005, p. 611.
[5] de los Rios 1925 and Senador Gómez 1915: 1993.

a modern, centralized state. Transport improvements, especially the railways, opened up new markets benefiting some farmers, but producing unwelcome competition for others, a process that was accelerated by globalization and economic development. However, the distribution of farm income depended not only on economic factors such changes in international commodity and factor prices, but also on political decisions on tariffs that protected landowners (and farmers) at the expense of consumers. In Spain, this not only helped the landed elites, who were more successful at maintaining their political and economic privileges than those in Northern Europe, but it also kept resources in traditional Mediterranean crops such as cereals and vines.

The need to use dry-farming methods also had political consequence because although Spain was becoming increasingly a country of small farmers, many had problems intensifying cultivation and climbing the farm ladder. Furthermore, the distinctive land-tenure regimes and cropping systems, as well as the difficulties in creating new farm organizations to help participate in an increasingly competitive market place, produced deep cleavages within the sector. Therefore, although specialist producers might face similar crop-specific problems, it could lead to very different forms of collective action. For example, wine producers everywhere complained about fraud, high taxes, and low prices in the 1920s, but the nature of contention and organization followed very distinctive paths in the two major producer regions of Catalonia and La Mancha. Likewise, the nature of social discontent in areas of small-family cereal producers in Castile-Leon was very different to that found in areas of latifundios in southern Spain. This chapter provides an introduction to the background to some of these problems, and leaves to following chapters to trace the nature and development of these conflicts.

The chapter is divided into four major sections. It begins by looking at the long-run growth in farm output and productivity, followed by a discussion on the access to land and the nature of rural settlements. It shows that long-run shifts in land prices and farm wages allowed a considerable increase in the numbers of farm tenants and owner-occupiers. This is followed by examining the difficulties of increasing labour-inputs using dry-farming techniques. Finally, section four shows the major characteristics of the 'agrarian question' in the early 1930s.

Explaining Long-Run Change: From Traditional to Modern Farming

Spanish agriculture, after making relatively slow progress over much of the nineteenth century, accelerated during the three decades before the

Civil War. As in many developing economies, rising urban incomes and the growing rural exodus created a stimulus for farmers to change production systems and raise productivity. Nevertheless, on the eve of the Second Republic both labour productivity and land yields remained at a considerable distance to those found in Northern Europe, and the diets for many Spaniards were still meagre in nutrients and poor in meat and dairy produce.

Spain's population increased from 9 to 17.5 million between 1750 and 1890, implying that domestic output had to double just to maintain consumption levels, as both imports and exports were small. The fact that real wages and per capita incomes showed a small increase between the two dates, suggests that diets might actually have improved, but any change must have been limited as the average calorie intake in 1900 was still only 2,096 per capita per day (equivalent to 2,733 calories per equivalent adult male units).[6] This doubling of farm production was achieved by extending the area cultivated and product specialization, rather than technological change.[7] Two factors appear crucial: the increase in farm prices between the 1820s and the 1880s for the country's major crops (wheat, wine, and olive oil), and the availability of large areas of new land that could be brought into cultivation following the massive sales of municipal and church lands, as well as the abolition of institutions such as the Mesta (1836), tithes (1841), or entail (1836–41). One estimate shows the area of cereals alone increasing by 40 per cent between 1800 and 1900.[8]

Population growth helped push up food prices, while better roads and railways reduced transport costs, encouraging farmers to extend the area cultivated, especially in areas previously considered as too marginal, such as Extremadura or the Cinco Villas (Zaragoza). The combination of abundant supplies of uncultivated land and cheap labour led some contemporaries in the mid-nineteenth century to believe that Spain could become Europe's granary following the blockade of Ukraine's exports during the Crimean War. It proved short-lived, not least because of the high transport costs, despite new railways linking the country's main grain-producing regions to the coast, but also because wheat yields were only a third of those

---

[6] Simpson 1995, p. 284. See also Prados de la Escosura 1989.

[7] A word of caution is needed because although there were no obvious technological changes in cereal production, virtually no information is available on the possible biological changes in wheat varieties. See especially Pujol-Andreu 2011 and Olmstead & Rhode 2002.

[8] Gallego 2001, p. 186. Garrabou & Sanz 1985b, p. 103, suggests the farm area increased by 18 per cent between 1860 and 1910.

found in Northern Europe.[9] Instead, contemporary optimism switched to other crops, especially vines and olives, which saw their area grow fourfold between 1795 and 1888.[10] The olive became increasingly planted for its fruit and oil rather than as just a source of cheap wood and energy, and new technologies from 1900 allowed the country to become a leading exporter of edible oils.[11] Even more spectacular was viticulture, as wine represented over 40 per cent of all exports in the 1880s, leading Joaquin Costa to suggest that Spain could become the world's *bodega* after French production collapsed because of phylloxera.[12]

Although cereal tariffs protected Spanish farmers, the late nineteenth century 'grain invasion' illustrated that, due to its limits, a farming model that relied on employing more land and labour rather than capital to increase output, and which failed to increase factor productivity through technological advances, was no longer feasible. The increase in cereal cultivation led to widespread deforestation and the ploughing up of pastures, leading to a collapse in livestock numbers, which reduced the supply of manure needed to fertilize the land by 40 per cent. Because of population growth, the area of cultivable land per worker fell from 4.5 to 4.1 hectares between 1860 and 1890.[13] Even before the cereal invasion, there were indications of falling yields and diminishing returns to labour in some areas of Castile and Aragon.[14] However, there were difficulties in switching immediately from a traditional, 'organic' agriculture to one than involved the use of artificial fertilizers, new farm machinery, and improved 'scientific' farming methods. The growing integration of global markets for farm products made most of Spain's cereals, livestock production, and olive oil uncompetitive, while wine exports collapsed once French domestic production recovered, and phylloxera destroyed Spain's vines. As high farm prices had benefitted landowners and, to a lesser extent, farmers, it was these groups, rather than small tenants and landless workers, that were now most threatened.

---

[9] For wheat yields, Simpson 1995, p. 17, and Robledo 1993, pp. 71–5, for the contemporary debate.

[10] By a factor of 3.7 and 4.0 respectively. Garrabou & Sanz 1985a, p. 130.

[11] Infante Amate 2013 and Ramón Muñoz 2000.

[12] Joaquin Costa noted in 1880 that 'Spain is not, and cannot be, Europe's breadbasket, but can aspire to be its winery', cited in Robledo 1993, p. 77. For the influence of French demand in the 1880s on Spanish production, see Pan-Montojo 1994 and Simpson 2011.

[13] Carmona et al. 2019, table 1 and Simpson 1995, table 5.1. For changes in livestock numbers, see especially García Sanz 1991 and GEHR 1978–9. For recent comments on the effects of land sales on efficiency, see Beltrán Tapia 2015 and González de Molina Navarro et al. 2014.

[14] Nadal 1975, p.78,

The optimism of the 1860s and 1870s was shattered, and contemporaries talked now of the country's supposedly poor resource endowments. Lucas Mallada (1890), for example, wrote that only 10 per cent of land 'leads us to suppose we have been born in a privileged country', a further 45 per cent was moderately productive, and the rest had either very low productivity because of altitude, lack of water or poor soil, or was totally unproductive. Mallada was a forerunner of the 'Regeneration' movement which, following the loss of Cuba in 1898, identified agriculture as a major cause of Spanish backwardness compared to the rest of Western Europe. Joaquin Costa would go even further, linking skewed landownership, and an undemocratic political system to the country's poor economic performance.

Farmers in all countries had to adapt to the growing global economy for food, but while cereal producers in the United States could continue to expand the farm area profitably, those in Northern Europe were forced to increase output per hectare, or reduce labour inputs through mechanization. Traditional Spanish agriculture on the eve of the First World War consisted of cereals, legumes, potatoes, wine, and olive oil, which still accounted for 55 per cent of crop output, a figure that increased to 84 per cent of total output when livestock was included. Unlike Northern Europe, the need to use dry-farming technologies made it much more difficult for Spanish farmers to intensify farm production, while the growing farm population delayed mechanization. Instead, higher tariffs from 1890, and the depreciation of the peseta, helped keep resources in traditional agriculture and benefit landowners at the expense of wage earners and urban consumers until the turn of the century. Labour productivity remained stagnant because of the restrictions imposed by dry-farming, the weak demand for higher value agricultural products because of low per capita incomes, and the high feed costs for livestock farmers.

The growing use of artificial fertilizers over the first third of the twentieth century contributed to another significant increase in the area of wheat cultivation, while labour started leaving the land in large numbers, and farmers switched very slowly to new crops. From the 1890s, annual production statistics allow a better understanding of these transformations, and the period between 1900 and 1930 suggests an unprecedented rapid growth historically (Table 4.1).[15] In particular, total output grew by 43 per cent and, because the area of farmland increased only slowly (10 per cent), output per hectare rose by almost a third (31 per cent).

---

[15] The fact that contemporaries had only a poor knowledge of the area cultivated suggests that these estimates should be treated with caution. Pro Ruiz 1995, p.,107. See Appendix 1 for a discussion on Spanish agriculture statistics.

Table 4.1 *Agricultural change in Spain, 1891/5 to 1929/33*

	Agricultural output millions pesetas	'000s males employed in agriculture	Output per male worker/ pesetas	'000 hectares agricultural land	Output per hectare/ pesetas
1891/5	3,299	4,033	818	23,934	138
1897/1901	3,308	4,392	753	25,898	127
1909/13	3,710	4,680	793	26,832	138
1929/33	4,741	3,827	1,239	28,567	166
Growth 1900 1930			+65%		+31%

Source: Simpson 1995b, p. 181–6.

As the male workforce fell by almost a million (–13 per cent), labour productivity increased by two-thirds (65 per cent). In the half-century leading up to the Second Republic, the share of labour in agriculture fell from 63 to 45 per cent, and the sector's contribution to GDP fell from 39 to 24 per cent.[16] Agriculture therefore appears to have made an important contribution to economic growth by producing a consistent supply of food at affordable prices to the growing population; releasing labour to the more productive industrial and service sectors; accumulating capital for domestic industry; and providing markets for both its capital goods (machinery, fertilizers, etc.) and consumer products (textiles, etc.), as well as earning foreign exchange through exports.[17] Yet the agricultural performance needs to be also seen in a wider context. Labour productivity remained significantly below that of other Western European countries, reaching only 24 per cent of Denmark's, 38 per cent of Germany's, 44 per cent of France's, or 91 per cent of Italy's in the 1930s.[18] Furthermore, although living standards improved and acute hunger was a historical memory for most Spaniards by 1931, food consumption remained low, and deprivation and malnutrition quickly returned following the Civil War. As Leandro Prados de la Escosura has aptly noted, the half-century before the Civil War combined both economic growth and growing backwardness with the leading European economies.[19]

[16] Figures for 1882 and 1931, Prados de la Escosura 2003, table A.11.4 and A.2.8.
[17] Johnson & Mellor 1961. For Spain, see especially Tortella 1985, p. 64–7, and Clar & Pinilla 2009, pp.,325–8. For relative farm and industrial prices, Prados de la Escosura 2003, pp.,215.
[18] O'Brien & Prados de la Escosura 1992, table 6.   [19] Prados de la Escosura 1988.

Most Spaniards certainly believed both that the rate of change was too slow, and the benefits were enjoyed by only a small section of society. In particular, the latifundios were considered to be poorly cultivated which produced widespread structural unemployment over large areas in central and southern Spain, and severely limited work opportunities and social mobility among the rural population. Although there were in fact other 'agrarian questions' as we shall see, it was to the latifundio question that would preoccupy most contemporaries during the Second Republic.

Access to Land and the Nature of Rural Settlement

The Spanish Reconquest, which began in the ninth and tenth centuries but was only completed in 1492, strongly influenced the nature of settlement and landownership and, although modified with the nineteenth century liberal reforms, still persisted in many respects in 1931. Spanish land ownership is usually divided into two distinct geographical areas, with large estates in the centre and south of the country, and small holdings especially in the north and along the Mediterranean coast (Map 4.1). The thirteen latifundio provinces accounted for 42.7 per cent of the country's farm land, employed 37.8 per cent of the farm population, and produced just 29.5 per cent of farm output. In these provinces, holdings of over 100 hectares accounted for 46 per cent of the total land area, while just 0.6 per cent of holdings accounted for 52.4 per cent of the land and were responsible for 38.3 per cent of the land tax (Table 4.2).[20]

Landownership is not the same as farm size, and a significant numbers of landowners did not work the land themselves. Instead small family-operated farms were common, especially over much of northern and eastern Spain, being less important in the centre and south, where wage labourers worked the large estates. Traditionally the Spanish agrarian question has been associated with the latifundios, and the inefficiencies that these farms supposedly created in terms of deficient cultivation and structural unemployment. By contrast, the problem on small farms was often excessive fragmentation, and a typical family farm of 30 hectares in Castile-Leon could be divided into 40 different plots.[21] Further north, especially in Galicia, *minifundios* were the norm, and in 1959, when relatively accurate figures are finally available, there were reportedly

---

[20] Carrión 1932: 1975, table 2.
[21] EPAPM 7 /1/1909, no 610, p. 3. Cascón recommended that holdings be consolidated and tenancy laws reformed.

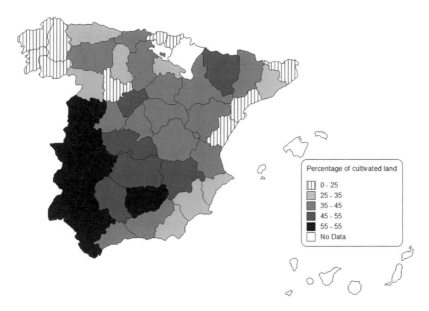

Map 4.1 Area held by large owners in possession of a minimum of 250
hectares
Source: Malefakis 1970, map 3.

Table 4.2 *Landownership in 1930s*

	≤ 10 hectares		10–99 hectares		100+ hectares	
	Spain	South	Spain	South	Spain	South
Number of holdings (%)	99.1	96.6	0.8	2.8	0.1	0.6
% of total area of land	46.5	27.9	24.9	19.8	28.6	52.4
% of taxable income	60.2	41.1	21.5	20.6	18.7	38.3

Notes: Includes information for the North that was only available in 1959.
Source: Malefakis 1970, tables 1, 2, and 3.

15 million tiny plots, a figure which outnumbered the total active population by 26 to 1, and the peasant proprietor class by 40 to 1.[22]

A significant, but unknown amount of the land was rented. According
to the cadastral in 1928, which covered about a fifth of the country's area,

---

[22] Malefakis 1970, pp. 17–18.

a third of all land was rented or sharecropped, although in areas of small property the figures were higher, reaching 41 per cent of land in Castile-Leon.[23] In Catalonia, the combination of large estates and high farm wages, the result of early industrialization, encouraged owners to rent their lands rather than work it themselves, while in Andalucia, the presence of an abundant labour supply often led to direct cultivation.[24]

This description provides a static picture in what was essentially a dynamic process, as the size and nature of land ownership changed over time, even in the south (Chapter 7). In particular, it takes no consideration of the changes in the numbers of rural families who had access to land, either as owners or tenants, and those who remained landless. In the decade or so before the First World War, almost two million Spaniards emigrated, providing many labourers with the possibilities to accumulate savings to rent or buy a farm, with numbers being much greater in the areas of small property in the north of the country (Map 4.2). Although opportunities to emigrate declined after 1914, the urban pull more than compensated, and the total number of men and women employed in the farm sector fell from 5.1 million in 1910 to 4.1 million in 1930, thereby reducing the competition for land among the landless, with all regions participating, except some southern provinces (Map 4.3).

The combination of fewer farm workers and rising wages led to an important growth in the relative number of landowners and tenants, and a sharp fall in landless workers. Information is lacking for the north, where landownership and rental contracts were common, and wage labourers had always been few, but in the rest of the country there is no doubting the direction of change, especially in the years leading up to the Second Republic.[25] Landless male workers, as a share of the total farm population in central-eastern Spain, fell from just over half in 1860 (52 per cent) to under a quarter by 1930 (23 per cent) (Table 4.3). The decline in the regions with large estates is less spectacular, but still significant, falling from 63 to 39 per cent. As in other European countries, land markets were adapting to

---

[23] Across Spain, 65 per cent of land was directly cultivated, 29 per cent rented, and 6 per cent sharecropped. In the provinces of Granada and Malaga, 50 per cent of the land was either rented or sharecropped (with 99 per cent of the farm area surveyed); 46 per cent in Badajoz and Caceres (59 per cent of the area); 44 per cent in Almeria and Murcia (55 per cent); 42 per cent in Castile-Leon (36 per cent); 32 per cent in Bética (88 per cent); 28 per cent in Albacete, Toledo and Ciudad Real (100 per cent); 25 per cent in Cuenca, Madrid and Guadalajara (39 per cent), and 22 per cent in Alicante, Castellón and Valencia (67 per cent). Carmona & Simpson 2003, p. 63, based on Ministerio de Hacienda, 1931, pp. 42 and 92–103.

[24] Sharecropping contracts were used in response to rising wage costs in parts of Andalucia during the 1920s. Naredo et al. 1977.

[25] In the North, tenants (*subforos*) were wrongly classified as workers in 1860, thereby distorting the true picture of farm organization.

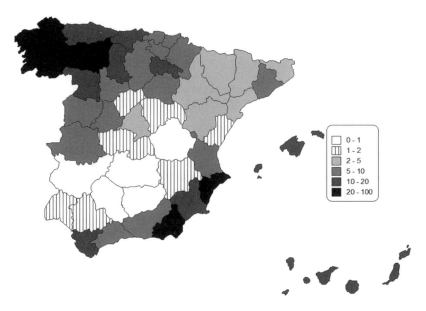

Map 4.2 Gross provincial emigration rates per thousand inhabitants, 1911–13
Source: Sánchez Alonso 2000, figure 4.

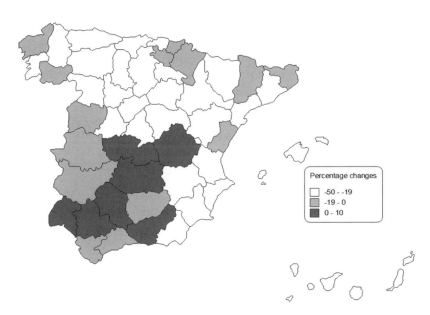

Map 4.3 Percentage changes in numbers employed in agriculture, 1910–30
Source: Simpson 1995b.

Table 4.3 *Numbers of male landowners, tenants, and workers in Spain (in thousands)*

	1860	1890	1910	1930
Owners and tenants				
Central & Eastern Spain	1,083	1,322	1,452	1,315
Latifundio Spain	500	616	739	902
North	550	795	529	481
Total	2,133	2,733	2,720	2,698
Landless workers				
Central & Eastern Spain	1,238	1,030	780	399
Latifundio Spain	849	815	809	569
North	250	337	146	46
Total	2,337	2,182	1,735	1,014
Number of hectares of farm land per male worker in Spain				
	4.5	4.1	4.6	5.7

Source: Carmona et al. 2019, tables 1, 2, and 3. Figures for the North assume 70 per cent of the farm population were owners or tenants.

the changing relative prices of land and labour that benefitted wage labourers (Table 2.2).

Yet although long-run changes were favourable, the plight of the landless was a very real one in the 1930s. In particular, and as Chapter 7 will show, many small farmers had insufficient land to feed their families, especially when the urban unemployed returned to their villages.[26] In particular, many of those at the foot of the farm ladder could not rent or buy land because they were young, lacking both capital and experience. Figures are not available for the Second Republic, but in 1950, when the size of the active population in agriculture was similar to that in 1930, 43 per cent of all farm labourers were under 24 years of age, compared to only 7 per cent of owners and tenant farmers.[27] In developing countries today, a third of rural poverty is age-related, a figure that perhaps was not so different for Spain in the 1930s.[28]

[26] According to Pascual Carrión, in the south, 95 per cent of landowners earned less than a peseta a day after costs and taxes from their land, 4 per cent (73,000) about 5,000 pesetas; less than 1 per cent account for almost half the taxable income. Carrión 1932: 1975, p. 104.
[27] Carmona & Simpson 2003, p. 91.
[28] World Bank 1990, p. 35, cited in Lipton 2009, p. 18.

Furthermore, although the numbers with access to land increased in Spain over the half-century or so before the Second Republic, many failed to become prosperous, independent family farmers, which political scientists have sometimes identified as being necessary for a well-functioning democracy in rural societies.[29] This failure to create a society of prosperous family farmers marked an important difference between Spain and most other Western European countries. In particular, Spanish governments showed much less interest in strengthening the negotiating position of tenants, or consolidating the family-operated farm. The issue of tenant rights was a persistent source of conflict in regions such as Galicia, Catalonia, or the Levante, while farmers faced a number of important obstacles to climb further up the farm ladder, especially the lack of cooperatives to provide cheap working capital or process their harvests (Chapter 5), and the failure of political parties to pass legislation to improve tenant rights (Chapter 9).

Why Was Rural Poverty So Widespread? The Limits to Intensive Farming Systems in the 1930s

Despite the economic growth that took place over the first third of the twentieth century, half of all workers remained in the farm sector, and low productivity implied that a significant, but unknown number still lived at around or even below subsistence levels on the eve of the Second Republic. One explanation, as Doreen Warriner noted during the 1930s, was that higher farm prices and productivity had made Western European farmers more prosperous than those in Eastern Europe.[30] This in turn can be partly explained by the possibilities to specialize in higher value products, encouraging greater capital inputs per hectare. In some respects, farmers in large areas of Spain suffered similar problems to those in Eastern Europe at this time.

Yet weak demand was only one factor. A large number of historians have argued that Spanish farmers were efficient and operating close to the production frontier, but growth was restricted by unfavourable natural resources.[31] Nevertheless, 'good' or 'poor' natural resources can only be fully understood when other factors such as the nature of technology, marketing systems, consumer demand, and property rights are also considered.[32] These factors were not imposed by nature, but were often

---

[29] For example, Dahl 1971.   [30] Warriner 1939, pp. 26–7.
[31] For example, Pujol et al. 2001, especially the chapters by Garrabou and Gallego.
[32] Wright 1986, pp.6-7.

the result of political decisions taken in areas such as tariffs, taxes, land tenure reform, incentives to create cooperatives and rural banks, or government investment in research and development. This section looks at the nature of some of the restrictions to increasing farm output and productivity, leaving to later sections in the book to understand why governments had been reluctant or unable to help remove these obstacles before the Second Republic.

A major constraint on Spanish agriculture was the lack of rainfall and, in particular, the long summer droughts which affected about four-fifths of the country's land. In these regions of *secano*, farmers were obliged to use dry-farming techniques and limit cultivation to extensive cereal and livestock farming, or drought-resistant crops such as the olive or vine. Dry-farming required winter rather than spring planting, and a period of fallow that allowed a cereal harvest only once every two or three years. The growing of artificial grasses such as clover or lucerne (alfalfa) was impossible at this time, resulting in low livestock densities. When irrigation was available, farmers could cultivate the land much more intensely and in areas with mild winters, grow high-value products such as oranges or rice. By contrast, in the North, sufficient rainfall and cooler summers allowed for more intensive cultivation and greater livestock densities (Map 4.4).

Most of our information on agricultural output is only available at the provincial level, and using this allows us to divide Spain into four major political regions: the North (Galicia, Asturias, Santander, and the Basque Country); the Mediterranean (Catalonia, the Baleares, the Pais Valenciano, and Murcia); Andalucia (the eight provinces), and the rest, which is called the Interior.[33] Table 4.4 shows that output per hectare of farm land was higher in the North and Mediterranean than the Interior and Andalucia. Differences in labour productivity across regions were less, but an important consequence of the *secano* was that labour demand was highly seasonal, resulting in relatively few workers being hired on annual contracts.[34] This was particularly noticeable in areas of latifundios, and perhaps only one in four wage labourers in western Andalucia was employed full time (Chapter 7). The high seasonality of labour demand encouraged workers to congregate in large villages or cities and in Cordoba, for example, 85 per cent of the province's population lived in urban areas, significantly increasing the cultivation costs on fields

[33] The Canary Islands are excluded.
[34] Reher 1998 links the presence of hired farm servants to 'weak' and 'strong' family regimes, rather than rainfall distribution in agriculture.

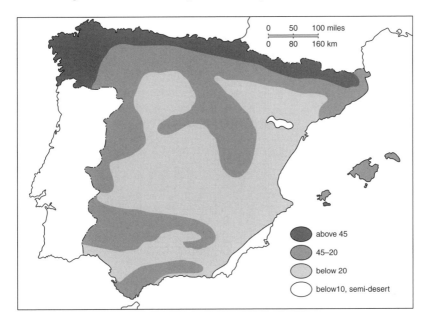

0   50   100 miles
0   80   160 km

above 45

45–20

below 20

below10, semi-desert

Map 4.4 Index of aridity
Source: Brenan 1969, p. 333.

in those areas found furthest away from settlements.[35] Without
irrigation or a massive rural exodus, severe restrictions existed to
increasing labour productivity by intensifying cultivation in regions
of *secano*. Rural poverty in much of Spain was caused essentially by
long periods of underemployment.

Cereal-legume rotations under dry-farming conditions covered well
over half the nation's crop area, making the country virtually self-
sufficient in bread grains by the Second Republic. Rather than enjoying
a comparative advantage, farmers depended on high tariffs, which left
bread prices significantly above world levels. The greater use of artificial
fertilizers from the turn of the twentieth century led to wheat output
growing by 34 per cent, although two-thirds of this increase was achieved
by extending the area cultivated, rather than higher yields or shorter
fallow.[36] Yields in dry-farming remained low everywhere because of the
weak response of traditional seeds to nitrogen and phosphate fertilizers,

---

[35] Carmona & Simpson 2003, p. 113.
[36] Simpson 1995, table 5.6. There were important regional differences, as discussed in
Chapter 7.

Table 4.4 *The nature of Spanish regional farming in 1929/33*

| | % of nation's agricultural area | % of nation's farm output by value | Output per hectare (pesetas) | % of total regional output | | | | Hectares/ male worker | Output per male worker (pesetas) |
				Cereals	Vines and olives	Other crops	Livestock		
North	7.6	18.5	797	17.4	2.7	26.7	53.3	3.4	2,739
Interior	60.1	38.9	211	41.1	13.1	23.3	22.5	10.9	2,315
Andalucia	19.0	16.7	288	28.4	27.5	23.6	20.5	5.7	1,630
Mediterranean	12.6	23.5	607	17.2	17.2	47.2	18.4	4.3	2,610
Spain	100.0	100.0	327	28.1	14.3	31.0	26.7	7.0	2,303

Source: Simpson 1995, tables 2.3 and 2.4.

technical problems that were not resolved until the second half of the twentieth century.[37]

Low yields however were not necessarily synonymous with low competitiveness, as the major New World exporting nations also used dry-farming techniques, and had similar yields to those found in Spain. By contrast, wheat-importing nations of northern Europe actually enjoyed higher yields because they were not constrained by summer droughts.[38] New World cereal producers were competitive because they used labour-saving technologies, such as reapers, threshing machines, tractors, and even combine harvesters, which offered the possibility to smooth peaks in seasonal labour demand, significantly increase farm size, and reduce unit costs. On the large estates in southern Spain, the presence of unemployed landless workers made this option highly controversial, especially during the 1930s (Chapter 7). The potential impact of mechanization was more complicated in areas of family farmers, as it promised to help them cultivate more land rather than cut costs. Although the size of family farms in Castile-Leon grew because of the rural exodus, their excessive fragmentation and the lack of cheap credit restricted mechanization.

Dry-farming conditions also led to extensive livestock farming because of the limited summer grazing. Given the economies of scale in moving animals over large distances, employment opportunities were limited.[39] In Northern Europe, cattle played an important role not just in commercial milk farming, but also in household economies. In England, for example, output per worker in the mid-nineteenth century in animal husbandry was 80 per cent higher than in arable cultivation.[40] By contrast, the poor-quality summer pastures over much of Spain made labour-intensive milk production unprofitable, and 70 per cent of production was found in Northern Spain, where summer rainfall was abundant.[41]

---

[37] As late as 1960, unsown fallow still occupied 40 per cent of all of Spain's cereal rotations, and wheat yields remained little more than those of the 1930s. Spain. Dirección General de Agricultura 1980, p. 27.

[38] Spanish wheat yields in 1925/9 were 0.92 tons per hectare, and the country imported 3 per cent of its needs. In Argentina, Australia, Canada, and the United States average yields were 0.97 tons, and these countries exported 44 per cent of production. Yields in France, Germany, and Italy were 1.47 tons, and imports accounted for 32 per cent of their needs. International Institute of Agriculture, 1933–4.

[39] Rosique Navarro 1988, p. 268, gives a figure of three men and a youth to manage a flock of 500 sheep and Torrejón y Bonete 1934, pp. 578–9, two adults and three children for 600 sheep. See Chapter 8 for the complaints over the employment priorities of keeping extensive livestock farms in areas of increasingly marginal cereal production.

[40] Clark 1991, p. 231, but for Britain see Turner 1991, p. 417, fn.19.

[41] Spain. Ministerio de Agricultura. Dirección General de Agricultura 1934, pp. 98–9. Figures refer to cows' milk.

The olive and vine thrived in areas of dry-farming, especially in central and southern Spain and, although labour requirements were also highly seasonal, they offered considerably more employment than with cereals, and output per hectare was about double.[42] Both crops were often found on marginal land, and planting required large amounts of labour and minimal quantities of capital, giving poor farmers the opportunity to create an asset that was not possible with cereals.[43] The skilled work required with these crops also encouraged the use of family, rather than wage labour.[44] However, production was geographically concentrated, with just five provinces accounting for 61 per cent of olive oil production, and 39 per cent of wine in 1930.[45] In addition, and as Lewis argued for tropical products in the period before the First World War, the supply of cheap, marginal land and large amounts of underemployed labour was common across the Mediterranean region. Any upswing in farm prices simply encouraged new plantings across the region.[46] By contrast, the high labour investment required to establish vineyards and olive groves made farmers reluctant to reduce capacity by uprooting plants at times of economic downturn, thereby prolonging production slumps. The low prices for both olive oil and wine during the 1930s discouraged farmers from extending the area of production to combat the high levels of cyclical unemployment.

Irrigation promised to significantly raise land output and create more employment. In fact in some areas, Spain was a world leader and, by 1932, irrigation covered only 5 per cent of farm land, but contributed 29 per cent of crop output.[47] Two basic types of irrigation were found. The first, and most important in terms of the area irrigated, involved diverting rivers, streams, and spring water using canals and gravity, helped by simple pumps. On the Valencia and Murcia plains, for example, there were long traditions of irrigation and highly complex institutions had developed over time to allocate the water among users. In many areas, however, flow irrigation systems lacked sufficient water during the summer months, leaving farmers with little option but to follow

---

[42] Tax returns (*cadastral*) suggest a gross income of 350 pesetas / hectare with cereals (two field rotation – *año y vez*), 700 pesetas for intensive olives, and 495 for extensive vines. See Carrión 1932: 1975, pp. 341–2.

[43] For viticulture, the classic example is the *rabassa morta* sharecropping contract in Catalonia. Sharecropping was also used to plant olives in Jaen. Carmona & Simpson 1999a and Simpson 1985, p. 227.

[44] Carmona & Simpson 2012.

[45] The figure rises to 60 per cent for the ten largest provincial producers of wine.

[46] Lewis 1978, p. 189, writes that, 'price in the short run is determined by current demand and supply. Price in the long run moves to the level determined by alternative opportunities'.

[47] Simpson 1995, pp. 147 and 261.

traditional cereal-legume rotations, rather than introducing higher-value crops. The obvious solution was to build storage capacity to capture the winter and spring rains, and release the water to farmers when it was needed. Progress was slow before the 1930s because of the enormous costs associated with major construction projects in remote parts of the country at a time when earthmoving equipment and cement technologies were still in their infancy.[48] The problems were exacerbated by the nineteenth century deforestation and risk of flash floods, which threaten to wash large quantities of topsoil into the reservoir. In fact, the high capital costs involved often made reservoir construction unprofitable for agricultural use, and it was the demand for hydroelectricity that led to reservoir capacity increasing from 78 million cubic metres in 1900 to 3,620 million by 1940, before major construction programs took the figure to 42,201 million in 1980.[49]

The second form of irrigation was associated with tube-well technologies, which allowed farmers to exploit aquifers at increasingly greater depths from the late nineteenth century. These grew out of the simple *norias* or waterwheels, but by the interwar period, private companies and cooperatives were using industrial technologies to extract large quantities of water. Production costs were expensive, making irrigation profitable only for high-value crops.[50] In particular, they played an important role in the expansion of orange cultivation, which quadrupled between 1902 and 1932.[51] Oranges produced a gross output of almost 4,000 pesetas per hectare, or ten times the figure for intensive cereals, and also considerably more than either the vine or olive.[52]

Irrigation allowed family farmers much greater flexibility to organize crop production to best utilize their labour and reduce the seasonal peaks in its demand. However, successful irrigation farming needed not only a good seasonal distribution of water, but also a favourable climate for high-value crops; investment in research and development to improve crop varieties; extension services to educate farmers; and efficient processing and marketing systems that could guarantee product quality for consumers. A number of local research stations enjoyed significant success, including the *Estación Arrocera de Sueca* that developed hybrid rice in 1924, helping farmers achieve the world's highest yields, or the *Granja-Instituto de Zaragoza*, which facilitated the introduction of red clover,

---

[48] Gómez Navarro 1932, Vol. 2.

[49] Spain. Dirección General de Agricultura 1980, p. 10. Minimum reservoir size is taken as 500m³.

[50] Font de Mora 1954, pp. 305–7. For tube-well technology, see especially Calatayud 1990 and Calatayud & Carrión 1999.

[51] Simpson 1995, table 6.7.   [52] Carrión 1932: 1975, p. 324.

alfalfa, and especially sugar beet in the Ebro valley.[53] Private commercial companies also played an important role in developing sugar beet and rice production, education, and supplying inputs to farmers.

Yet irrigation was far too localized to create sufficient employment to resolve the economic and social problems faced by governments during the Second Republic. In theory, major state intervention along the lines of the Tennessee Valley Authority might have absorbed some of the unemployed, while the large-scale construction of dams and other infrastructure projects promised multiple benefits, including not just irrigation, but also flood control and electricity.[54] The 1933 Plan of the Ministry of Public Works envisaged increasing the irrigation area by a massive 1.2 million hectares over just twenty-five years, but almost two-thirds of the land was to be used for cereals, presumably because sufficient water could not be guaranteed during the summer droughts.[55] In conclusion, only with a guaranteed water supply, significant advances in R&D, the creation of modern marketing systems for perishable fruit and vegetables, and higher consumer incomes, would farmers be able to use the new irrigation systems to radically change farming methods and increase labour productivity.

Finally, labour productivity in the North doubled between 1910 and 1930, despite the fact that miniscule, fragmented holdings and poor communications with the rest of the country limited market opportunities for many farmers (Table 4.5). The extent and nature of change can be appreciated in Galicia, where the problem of *minifundios* was greatest. The abundant summer pastures allowed a form of mixed husbandry to be practiced, and livestock produce accounted for about 44 per cent of farm output. Livestock improvements at this time included selective breeding; the adaptation and diffusion of hybrid maize; improvements in pasturelands; and veterinary services, all of which were provided by a mixture of public (municipal) and private bodies. The shortage of land led to highly labour-intensive cultivation, with farmers collecting vegetable matter from common lands to produce compost, improving both yields and the density of cultivation. Yet the most surprising advances were in the area of labour-saving mechanical technologies. By the 1930s, although Galicia had only 5 per cent of Spain's area of cereals, it accounted for about a fifth of the nation's threshing machines, with one found on average in every two parishes.[56]

---

[53] Simpson 1995, table 6.5 and pp. 137–8 and 145.
[54] Kitchens & Fishback 2015 for the impact of electricity on US agriculture during this period.
[55] Simpson 1995, p. 146.
[56] Fernández Prieto 1997, pp. 139–42. By contrast, the small size and uneven nature of fields made the use of mechanical reapers very difficult.

Table 4.5 *Changes in regional agriculture between 1910 and 1930*

	% change in area cultivated	% change in labour supply	% change in hectares per worker	% labour productivity growth 1909/ 13 to 1929/33	% change in output per hectare
North	-7.4	-26.0	+25.2	89.5	51.4
Interior	+20.5	-19.8	+50.3	60.0	6.5
Andalucia	+7.8	-2.6	+10.6	24.1	12.1
Mediterranean	+12.6	-25.9	+51.8	94.4	28.0
Spain	+13.8	-19.2	+40.8	64.5	16.9

Source: Simpson 1995b table 7, and Simpson 1995, table 2.4.

These played a crucial role in reducing the exceptional summer peaks in labour demand on the tiny family farms caused by tasks such as milking, harvesting, and haymaking coinciding.[57] Intensive farming and technological change cannot be separated from the wider changes in Galician society, which included large-scale emigration and remittances, the growth of independent civil associations, or the legal changes that allowed farmers to buy their land.[58] Yet the rapid diffusion of a labour-saving, complex technology such as a threshing machine in Galicia, illustrates the capacity of farmers to introduce modern production methods when adequate incentives were present. In dry-farming areas, family farmers did not face similar seasonal demands for their labour, limiting the incentives to acquire the machines.

The Agrarian Question: From Joaquin Costa to the Second Republic

The best-known writer on the nature and challenges facing Spanish agriculture in the half-century before the Second Republic was Joaquin Costa (1846–1911). Costa, as early as the 1880s, argued that dry-farming cereal cultivation was unprofitable under Spanish conditions, and soon urged the massive construction of reservoirs and canals for irrigation. These, he believed, could be undertaken using private capital but, if this failed, it should be provided by the state. To be successful however the state had also to invest in research facilities and teach farmers how to grow new crops. Costa was also critical of the latifundios, especially those

---

[57] Threshing was traditionally done in northern Spain by beating the grain, rather than the use of threshing boards as in the rest of Spain.
[58] See especially Villares 1982. Chapter 6 discusses civic associations.

belonging to absentee owners, which he believed were poorly cultivated. Instead he favoured the small family farm, and believed that its economic feasibility had been seriously damaged by the liberal reforms of the nineteenth century, especially following the sale of common lands. Finally, following a short period as a parliamentary deputy, Costa, in his book *Oligarquia y Caciquismo* (1901), argued that the country's economic backwardness, the landownership structure, and the unrepresentative and corrupt nature of the political system, were all interlinked. The volume of Costa's writings was immensely influential, but unfortunately much was originally published in obscure articles, which were not easily available before they appeared in collective volumes after his death.[59] The result was that Spaniards during the Second Republic debated Costa's ideas for agricultural reforms that had been written as much as half a century earlier.

There were few contemporaries who could match the range of Costa's thinking, but the nature of the political system and weak party system discussed in the previous chapter allowed parliamentarians for the most part to ignore his ideas until the Second Republic. The 1880s 'agrarian depression' and lower prices affected all farm groups, but higher tariffs limited imports, protected landowners' rents, and eventually led to farmers increasing output. Yet, at a local level, disruption was often significant. In the first instance, small farmers found an increasingly competitive market place, especially as growing market integration separated farmers from their consumers, and produced complaints that middlemen charged high prices for inputs (seeds, fertilizers, etc.), but paid them low prices for their farm produce. In addition, although greater market integration benefitted farmers in those areas with a comparative advantage (western Andalusia, for wheat; La Mancha, for wine, etc.), those in more marginal areas now found it increasingly difficult to compete. Family farmers attempted to form associations and create producer and credit cooperatives but, and for reasons explained in the following part, these were often slow to appear.

The presence of highly diverse local land-tenure regimes and the persistence of high rents led to calls for legislation to protect tenants. In some cases, this involved demands to join the *dominium utile* and *directum* in a single person (Catalonia, Galicia), but in most cases they reflected those found throughout Western Europe. In particular, they revolved around the so-called three Fs: fair rent (set by an independent tribunal); fixity of tenure (unless for nonpayment); and free sale (payment for

---

[59] For a discussion of Costa's ideas, see especially Maurice & Serrano 1977 and Gómez Benito 2011.

improvements). The limited legal changes in these areas highlight both the continuing influence of landowners, and the difficulties facing small farmers to organize politically. There was also a long history of village conflicts over the recovery of common lands that had been sometimes been appropriated illegally with the liberal land reforms, an issue which became of major political importance during the Second Republic. Finally, many farm workers were unable to rent or buy land and gain a footing on the farm ladder, and those that did were often dependent on labour markets for supplementary wages. Significant strike waves took place in wheat- and olive-producing regions across the country from the late nineteenth century, especially during the years 1903–5, 1918–20, and 1931–3.

Rural conflicts were therefore relatively common. Following Charles Tilly, protest can be divided into two distinct categories. First, *reactive* collective action, which required little organization and was often isolated, 'spontaneous' village-based incidents, such as protests against the state or feudal lord over matters such as taxes, conscription, threats of famine, etc. The second form was *proactive*, which required much greater planning, and often took place over large areas.[60] Given the long periods when trade union activities were banned or severely constrained, even

Table 4.6 *Major land and labour conflicts in the half-century prior to the Second Republic*

Description	Nature of contract	Region	Nature of demands/ conflicts
Rabassa Morta	Perpetual contract for planting & cultivating vines	Barcelona and Tarragona	Full ownership of land
Yunteros	Short-term rental & sharecropping	Extremadura	Right to cultivate/ land invasions
Foros and subforos	Indefinite	Galicia	Full ownership of land
Rental contracts	Short-term rental	Castile-Leon, Aragon, & Central Spain	Security of tenure
Jornaleros	Casual labour – on large estates	Southern Spain	Right to form labour syndicate/improve work conditions
Common lands		National	Recovery of common lands

[60] Tilly 1975, p. 54. Very rarely, major regional-based movements against the central state, such as the Vendée or, in Spain, the Carlists in the nineteenth century.

strike activities often remained reactive, rather than proactive protests. The lack of voice also helps explain their sometimes violent nature. With the Restoration, the agrarian questions began to slowly assume new forms, and especially in periods with greater freedom of association and speech, and when the right to strike was allowed. Local problems, which may have festered for decades, became increasingly politicized by individuals who could organize and create pressure groups to advance their demands. The wide range of conflicts in Table 4.6 makes it difficult to talk about a single agrarian problem, and it would be the ability of political entrepreneurs during the Second Republic to widen and change the cycles of contention that determined which acquired national importance.

Conclusion: Was Spanish Agriculture a Success before 1931?

This chapter suggests that Spanish agriculture performed strongly during the first third of the twentieth century. Productivity growth was achieved by a combination of extending the area cultivated, raising output per hectare, and using fewer labour inputs. The most visible aspect of this change was the appearance of new mechanical technologies, such as the presence of at least 4,000 tractors.[61] Yet most change was less noticeable, although not necessarily less important, with small farmers in Galicia, for example, mixing bracken with manure to produce compost, or share-croppers in Extremadura using small quantities of chemical fertilizers.[62] By 1931, traditional Spanish farming was slowly disappearing, to be replaced by a modern, scientific agriculture dependent on industrial inputs. Recent Spanish historiography rather confusingly has often emphasized both the need for land reform, *and* stressed a successful agricultural performance before 1931, as farmers introduced new production techniques, and land and labour productivity increased. This is examined in more detail in Chapter 7.

In fact, these farming changes were insufficient to eliminate many of the problems facing Spanish farmers. Productivity remained low and, given that about half the active labour force still worked in the sector, a single family produced on average only enough to feed itself and one other. Living standards of many Spaniards remained poor and precarious, as the lack of assets for many workers and small farmers made them especially vulnerable to economic downturns. Problems were contained while surplus farm labour could easily find employment in the cities, but once the Depression set in and workers returned to their villages, the

---

[61] Sabio Alcutén 2002.   [62] Fernández Prieto 1997 and Simpson & Carmona 2017.

limits of traditional agriculture to create employment soon became apparent. It was perhaps little wonder, therefore, that contemporaries in the 1930s were more concerned about the shortcomings of the sector, rather than its achievements. With the advantage of hindsight, a number of factors can be identified that limited the extent, and nature, of agricultural change during the period.

The technical problems associated with expanding the intensity of production under dry farming was a major obstacle to agricultural progress, and indirectly a cause of growing income inequality. Over much of the country, there were still few alternatives to leaving large areas of land in fallow, and major difficulties existed to working the soil more intensely and improving yields. By contrast, mechanization in the interwar period offered the possibilities of growing economies of scale, benefitting large cereal farms, but making small farms or those with highly fragmented holdings, uncompetitive. The direction of technological change with dry cereal farming therefore threatened to eliminate a significant source of seasonal employment for landless labourers, and the livelihood of marginal cereal producers. By contrast, although wine and olive production was ideal for small farms, market conditions in the 1930s were unfavourable for both. Without irrigation, there were very few possibilities for areas of dry-farming to absorb more labour, which made Spanish agriculture unusually dependent on growing industrialization and economic growth to employ surplus rural labour.

Income distribution in rural areas was also strongly influenced by government policy, which remained heavily orientated towards the interest of landowners, rather than those of farmers. As the country had escaped the sufferings from food shortages experienced in most other European countries during the First World War, there were few political demands for the state to create research stations to improve cultivation techniques to raise output. Landowners and their representatives continued to play their traditional role of interpreting and implementing government policy at the village level. The political strength of landowners restricted the appearance of associations of family farmers, which led to the failure to develop adequate capital and mortgage markets to meet the needs of a modernizing farm sector. In comparison with many other Western European nations, family farmers were less likely to belong to a cooperative, and those that did exist, had limited influence in the processing and marketing of farm products or supplying credit. Therefore, if many workers were able to gain a foot on the farm ladder by purchasing or renting small plots of land, many failed to become established 'independent' farmers. The reasons for this are examined in the following chapter.

Part III

Explaining the Weakness of the Family Farm

While the family farm was often efficient in its use of labour, the transition from a traditional organic agriculture to a 'modern' one that used industrial inputs and experienced lengthening food chains from the turn of the twentieth century presented it with new challenges. In response, small farmers over large areas of Europe began to organize credit and producer cooperatives to reinforce their competitive position. As Cleary has noted, 'if technical changes – the mechanization of arable and pastoral farming or the drive for ever greater production and productivity' were the 'most visible aspect of the transformation of rural France, the spread of new forms of cooperation and association' was 'no less important.'[1] As the previous chapter showed, Spain had become a country of small family farmers between 1860 and 1930, as the share of landowners and tenants in the total farm population had increased from 44 per cent to 70 per cent, while the numbers of landless workers more than halved. However, most of these farmers were poor, and remained as 'peasants' rather than 'free farmers'. This section explains both why family farmers were unable to create cooperatives and associations to improve their economic competitiveness and create an effective political lobby, and why the landed elites and Church were able to preserve their political power until much later than in most other European countries.

A large literature since Tocqueville has considered the development of free, independent organizations as being crucial for democracy and economic development.[2] Given the importance of the agricultural sector in pre-industrial societies, many of the first associations appeared in the countryside, linked to activities such as the management of common lands, controlling the access to irrigation, or organizing village festivals. The literature also often stresses the contrast between a high density of civic associations in northern Europe, and the supposed reluctance for villagers to cooperate in southern Europe. Edward Banfield attributed the extreme poverty and backwardness in the southern Italian village he

---

[1] Cleary 1989, p. 167.   [2] See, for example, North et al. 2007.

studied in the 1950s 'largely' to the 'inability of the villagers to act together for their common good' because of a general lack of trust in a society with very unequal landownership.[3] In a similar vein, Putnam suggests that the lack of civic institutions in Southern Italy was the result of unequal agents linked in asymmetric relations of hierarchy, and was negatively associated with good government.[4] By contrast, civic communities in Northern Italy expected, and received, good government and efficient public services. The social infrastructure of civic associations helped create representative government. As Putnam writes, 'Tocqueville was right: Democratic government is strengthened, not weakened, when it faces a vigorous civil society'.[5] The only formal institutions found in Southern Italy were the state which Carlo Levi suggested was, for the peasants, 'more distant than heaven and far more of a scourge because it is always against them', and the Church, which imposed little religion.[6]

Yet these interpretations, even if useful for Northern Italy, appear less so for Spain, despite a somewhat similar north–south divide in property ownership. In particular, as this section argues, the supposed lack of trust noted by Banfield seems insufficient to explain its weak farm cooperative movement. In Spain, there certainly was an absence of effective market-based solutions to small farmers' problems, which left them financially weak and perpetuated the influence of traditional, paternalistic networks. However, this was because of a *lack of interest* by outside hierarchical agencies such as the local elite, church, political parties, or government to help create organizations that reached over wider areas than just the village, rather than any problems of trust. Without this support, village-level organizations remained limited in scope. Farmers in Northern European countries enjoyed higher living standards, partly because economic development allowed them to obtain goods and services from more efficient markets, but also because one or more of these hierarchical groups were willing to help create new organizations to make the family farm more competitive and profitable in exchange for their political support.

This section looks at why Spanish farmers, unlike many others in Western Europe, failed to develop effective credit and producer cooperatives to meet the demands of modern agriculture. Chapter 5 shows that small farmers successfully organized at the village level and that the supposed 'gap' in organizational capacity between the north and south of the country has been exaggerated in the literature. Instead the poor

[3] Banfield 1958, pp. 8–10.   [4] Putnam 1993, p. 174. See also A'Hearn 2000.
[5] Putnam 1993, p. 182.   [6] Levi 1947: 1982, p. 78, cited in Banfield 1958, pp. 36 and 87.

cooperative performance and slow appearance of civic associations was caused by the absence of top-down support to create impersonal networks across wider geographical areas. Chapter 6 explains why, unlike in many other European countries, neither the rural elites nor the Catholic hierarchy had political incentives to help finance cooperatives, or to build provincial and regional networks. The Church was able to remain outside mass politics because of its privileged situation in Spanish society, while the absence of a competitive party system before the Second Republic made it unnecessary for politicians to capture the farm vote.

This had major implications. In the first instance, the landed elites and Church were able to maintain their political and social influence in rural society, at a time when these groups were losing power in other European countries. By contrast, family farmers were weakly represented, explaining why they were politically marginalized during the Second Republic, both by radical, well-organized labour organizations and by landowner groups that organized around the defence of property rights and the Catholic Church. Therefore, if France's Third Republic was dependent on the support of the small family farmer, Spain's 1931 Constitution represented the interests of organized labour and urban republican groups.

5 The Family Farm and the Limits to Village-Level Cooperation

The peasant is 'a rational problem-solver, with a sense of both his own interests and of the need to bargain with others to achieve mutually acceptable outcomes . . . (to resolve) the complex problems of resource allocation, authority, and dispute settlement that every society faces'.[1]

[T]ypically, the peasant cultivator seeks to avoid failure that will ruin him rather than attempting a big, but risky, killing.[2]

The aspiration to become a client, with an accommodating generous, powerful and enduring patron, penetrated deeply into many Italian souls.[3]

Previous chapters have suggested that farm organization and, in particular, the presence of a prosperous network of family farms had a major influence on the political, social, and economic structures of different European countries. Three major ideas were noted. First, from an economic perspective, the low transaction costs associated with the family farm provided strong incentives for its members to work quickly and diligently, caring for valuable assets such as trees crops or protecting soil fertility. Second, agrarian societies were often more egalitarian and produced more democratic institutions in areas where family farms predominated, leading to the creation of 'inclusive' economic institutions that benefitted the majority, rather than a rural elite.[4] Finally, from the mid-nineteenth century, the importance of free family farms – as oppose to 'peasant' ones – grew in most European countries, but they remained relatively rare before the 1930s in Spain and other Southern European countries (Table 2.2).

Across Europe, the growing integration of national and international markets, and the shift from traditional to modern farming practices, presented major challenges to farmers. Although favourable movements in factor price helped the landless workers gain access to land, farmers often faced considerable difficulties to accumulate the necessary capital to move

---

[1] Popkin 1979, p. ix-x   [2] Scott 1976, p. 4   [3] Bosworth 2005, p. 29
[4] Dahl 1971, p. 71, and Acemoglu & Robinson 2012.

up the farm ladder. However, with the extension of suffrage their political influence increased from the turn of the new century, and they began to organize and create new forms of cooperation and associations. In Northern Europe, especially, there was a rapid increase in the numbers of credit and producer cooperatives that improved the competiveness of family farmers in their negotiations with upstream and downstream agents, while farmworkers were increasingly represented by trade unions and syndicates. By contrast, in Spain, as elsewhere in southern Europe, civil associations were fewer and less important; the presence of paternalistic arrangements remained stronger and influence of factor markets weaker; and the position of the rural elites was still formidable in the early 1930s.

This chapter looks at the nature and extent of collective action, and the difficulties associated with creating credit and producer cooperatives. It begins by examining the traditional village economy, and shows how it provided a wide variety of public goods, including controlling access to common lands or creating institutions to help reduce risk. The second section tests the extent that village communities were able to organize and resolve problems of collective action by looking at the persistence from the Old Regime of the *pósitos*, or village grain banks. It suggests two important conclusions. First, that successful village-level collective action was found over most of the country and not just the north, as is often assumed. Second, although the village pósito met the needs of a traditional, organic-based farming system, it was inadequate for one that was becoming increasingly dependent on industrial inputs by the interwar period. In particular, it was the inability to create an organizational structure that might attract savings from a wide geographic area to meet the needs of the small farmers that helps explain the persistence of paternalist relations in the countryside. The third section looks at the limited success of creating producer cooperatives and argues that their major problems originated from the lack of cheap capital and an inability to extend collective action from the village to the regional and national levels. The chapter finishes by providing a background to the changing nature of Spain's farm organizations over the half-century prior to the Second Republic.

The Nature of the Village Economy

Farmers faced a number of major challenges in traditional agricultural societies, including the difficulties for young couples to accumulate sufficient capital to establish a household and gain access to some land; the high seasonality of farm income; and the significant annual fluctuations in harvest size. In the absence of effective formal credit and insurance markets, individuals were dependent on informal mechanisms, provided by the family, the village, or private suppliers. The continued weakness of credit and insurance markets implied that economic activity in Spain during the 1930s was still heavily influenced by the size of the harvest, forcing farmers to reduce consumption following poor harvests, and expand it after exceptional ones, such as those of 1932 and 1934.

The family farm was too small to manage risk effectively, or provide public goods such as public order, crop insurance, maintenance of irrigation systems, or repairing roads. Farmers were therefore required to cooperate with others, making the village community an extension of the family household. The nature of the peasant and village economies has been widely discussed in the historical and sociological literature. In particular, writers such as E. P. Thompson and James Scott have suggested that peasants in traditional societies lived on the margin of subsistence, making them averse to risk. According to Scott, this encouraged economic, social, and political arrangements to guarantee a minimum income each year. Crops were chosen for home consumption rather than the market, and seed varieties preferred that produced a reliable harvest, even though this might result in poorer returns over the long-run. In social matters, it implied a preference for extended kinship and village institutions which guaranteed families access to common property.[5] Nevertheless, because land ownership was usually unequally distributed, village life was often organized along hierarchical lines, in patron-client networks. These involved informal contracts whereby clients, in exchange for good work and loyalty, received not just a subsistence wage, but other goods needed to survive.

Scott's observations came from his work on Asian farming in the mid-twentieth century and, even if true for that specific context, are questionable for Spain's villages in the 1930s. Yet important conclusions can be drawn from his study, and the criticism that it has provoked. First, historians need to understand the social, political, and economic context in which decisions are taken by farmers. Indeed, as this book argues, the nature and speed of economic development, rural social mobility, and state-making had major implications for different farm groups, and the nature of the opportunities and restrictions that each of them faced. A second factor is the role of markets and the nature of risk in peasant farming. Historically, patron–client networks often declined with the appearance of new market opportunities for farmers to specialize in cash crops and the appearance of alternative sources of credit from commercial banks. However, the nature of risk changed rather than disappeared, and

---

[5] Scott 1976, with a useful survey in Bates 1990, pp.6–7. The last major famine in Spain was in 1882, although there was also widespread hunger over much of Andalucia in 1905.

now became linked to the high price volatility originating in urban markets, rather than simply harvest size. Instead of being reliant on paternalist contracts with rural elites, small farmers now found themselves dependent on government intervention in markets. In Spain, the slow development of alternative sources of working capital or unemployment benefits implied that interlinked contracts and paternalism still continued, albeit in widely different forms, over much of the countryside in the 1930s. Indeed, the weak government response to help family farmers during the Great Depression partly explains why this group moved towards the political right during the Republic.

Finally, there is the question of collective action, and the problem of the free-rider. Therefore, even though farmers might want to manage the village commons fairly and efficiently, or create a new cooperative winery, coordination breakdowns often led to the failure to create suitable organizational structures that provided the right incentives to make them happen. In particular, the free-rider problem suggests that mechanisms are needed to ensure that all members contribute their share to the project, as the under-provision of effort or money by some members would discourage others to contribute, resulting in collective action failure.[6]

Collective action and village organizations are believed to have been strongest in northern Spain, and the complex management and control of access to common lands received considerable attention from contemporaries such as Joaquin Costa.[7] Common lands provided basic entitlement rights for village members in the form of grazing, fire wood, wild foods, and temporary cultivation (*suertes*), while the rent from other village lands (*propios*) was used for village expenses, including education.[8] Village experiences could differ significantly, but the study by Ruth Behar of the village of Santa María del Monte (León), illustrates how important the complexity of user-rights over common property and obligations could be. In Santa María, access to common goods was guaranteed to all villagers (*vecinos*), who were defined as married males in possession of a house and land, and resident during most of year.[9] Some 70 per cent of the land was held directly in common, but villagers also enjoyed common grazing rights on the stubble after the harvest on the large open-fields. Children, because of equal inheritance, were guaranteed some property on the death of a parent, as well as the common

---

[6] Popkin 1979.   [7] Costa 1898: 1915, especially chs. 7, 8, 9, and 11.
[8] For the importance of common lands for primary education in the mid-nineteenth century, see Beltrán Tapia 2013.
[9] Widows also enjoyed limited rights, Strict restrictions existed to outsiders becoming *vecinos*. Behar 1991, p. 121.

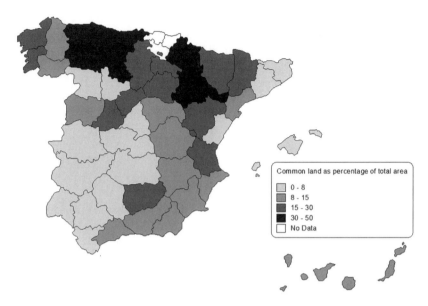

Map 5.1 Area of common lands as a percentage of the total area in 1926
Source: GEHR 1994, Map 4.

inheritance on becoming a *vecino*.[10] Private land was heavily fragmented, which helped individuals climb the farm ladder by purchasing one plot at a time, and common land could be used to build a house. Finally, although the state began to tax common lands from the late nineteenth century, the influence of Santa María's village *concejo* and ordinances continued until well into the second half of the twentieth century.[11]

How far the experience of Santa María del Monte can be extended to other parts of the country depends on several factors, including the amount of common land that was still available in the early twentieth century; the extent that village communities were sufficiently egalitarian to be run democratically and overcome opposition from local landed elites; or the capacity of villagers to create new institutions as their needs changed, and avoid the problems of the free-rider.

In fact, the persistence of common lands on the eve of the Second Republic varied significantly across the country (Map 5.1). Sales had

[10] Ibid., p. 104, notes that although children were able to work parents' land, sometimes as sharecroppers, there was a popular saying that 'parents-in-law (or parents) are like potatoes: they do not bear fruit until they are underground'.
[11] Attempts to standardized village government across Spain in 1887 failed. Ibid., p. 156, and López Morán 1900.

been especially important in the central-southern provinces during the first half of the nineteenth century, and a further 4.8 million hectares were sold between 1859 and 1926, equivalent to 9.6 per cent of the country's total land area, or 41.5 per cent of all the common land in 1859.[12] The geographical differences can be explained partly by the relative ease in converting common lands to arable in some regions compared to the difficulties faced in mountainous and areas with poor communication.[13] In general, common lands persisted most in areas where small farms predominated; summer rainfall was adequate for all-year farming; an active lay and lower clergy existed in relatively closed village communities; high levels of outmigration were experienced from the 1890s; or localized land-tenure regimes were found.

Beltran has recently drawn attention to the geographical coincidence of the persistence of traditional common property, irrigation communities, and small property, with the appearance of farm cooperatives during the first third of the twentieth century.[14] Following Hirschman and others, he argues that the supply of social capital in villages increases through its use, and depletes when idle, so that the continued presence of traditional forms of association such as common land helped create the trust and necessary social capital needed to introduce new organizations, such as producer and credit cooperatives.[15]

While the link between trust, social capital, and successful collective action seems clear, Spain does not appear to have experienced such a strong north–south divide as found in Italy. Furthermore, a quick glance at the map of common lands in 1926 (Map 5.1), and cooperatives in 1933 (Map 5.2), suggests important differences.[16] Neither does the presence of common property rights imply that there were no conflicts, or that hierarchical patron-client networks were absent.[17] The controversial *Contribución territorial* (land tax) was imposed in areas of both latifundios and small family farms and, as noted, it was often enforced in a way that was incompatible with a democratic village society, with fraud being common.[18]

---

[12] GEHR 1994, p. 132.   [13] Gallego et al. 2010, p. 105.   [14] Beltrán Tapia 2012.
[15] Hirschman 1984. Putnam 1993, p. 167, writes: 'Voluntary cooperation is easier in a community that has inherited a substantial stock of social capital, in the form of norms of reciprocity and networks of civic engagement'.
[16] We exclude landless workers, who did not usually belong to cooperatives, which weakens the north-south divide found in Beltrán Tapia 2012.
[17] Even with the relative equality in Santa Maria del Monte, there were conflicts between livestock owners and farmers over whether cultivation on communal lands should be temporary or permanent. Behar, 1991, pp. 230–7.
[18] Pro Ruiz 1995, pp. 101–2.

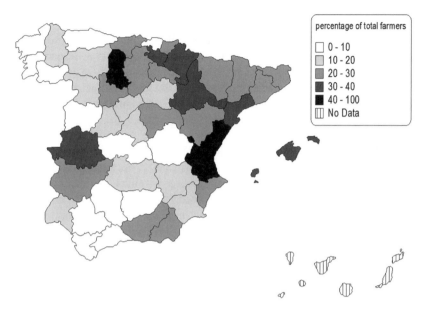

percentage of total farmers

☐ 0 - 10
▨ 10 - 20
▨ 20 - 30
▨ 30 - 40
■ 40 - 100
▥ No Data

Map 5.2 Percentage of farmers who were members of a cooperative in 1933
Note: Figures for Navarra include members of rural *cajas* for 1926, as the legal form of syndicates for this province was different to elsewhere. Muñiz 1926. Strictly speaking, Tables 5.1 and 5.2 show the number of syndicates, rather than cooperatives. There are no independent figures for cooperatives.
Sources: Farmers (landowners and tenants) in 1930, in Carmona et al. 2019; members of cooperatives in Spain. Ministerio de Agricultura 1934.

In fact, as we will argue, there is strong evidence that, *when it was in their interest*, farmers and labourers did organize effectively at a village level, as individual face-to-face monitoring could take place. The real difficulty was to build regional organizations, especially as these had to incorporate neighbouring villages, when levels of trust had historically often been low. To achieve this, hierarchical organizations supported by the landed elites, Church, or labour unions were necessary. Therefore, just as the Church helped organize and shape the demands of small farmers in some northern regions, labour syndicates would help day workers across southern Spain.

Collective Action and the Supply of Working Capital

Low earnings, and the need for farmers to feed their families and work animals during the months before the harvest, created a demand for working capital in all rural societies. The reluctance of Spain's formal credit markets to lend to small farmers, and the high annual interest rates charged in informal ones, often in excess of 25 per cent, made the need for alternative supplies of capital crucial for farmers to climb the farm ladder.[19] The problem was discussed in all the government enquiries from the mid-nineteenth century and in an estimated 56 national and regional farm congresses between 1880 and 1901, because, as Miguel de Unamuno noted, the use of the village usurer was likely to continue until farmers enjoyed alternative sources of credit.[20] The failure to develop an efficient rural banking system before the Civil War was not just an important impediment to building a more prosperous peasant agriculture, but helped perpetuate the power of landowners and paternalistic networks, both obstacles to the creation of a genuine democracy.

The failure of formal credit systems to provide working capital at low interest rates is usually explained by the high costs that commercial banks face collecting information on a small farmer's credit worthiness. Enforcing legal contracts is also often difficult, especially when prohibitive legal fees exist to use property as collateral to secure loans. This explains the success of microcredit schemes in Third World countries today, as they can use neighbours or the village community to monitor borrowers, ensuring that loans are correctly employed and repaid. Perhaps surprisingly, rural credit was provided using village grain banks (*pósito*) which had for several centuries successfully operated over large areas of Spain as a form of microcredit. These not only reinforce the argument that village institutions could operate effectively to provide collective goods, but also that hierarchical organizations were required if they were to make a major contribution to the family farm.

From the sixteenth century, pósitos were created in the Old Kingdom of Castile to guarantee bread supplies for urban consumers, but by 1792, their main function was lending seed to farmers, and from the nineteenth century their activities were limited to cash loans.[21] Despite the civil wars and periodic famines during the nineteenth century, as well as the intermittent raids on their capital by the national exchequer, about 3,500 were

---

[19] For high interest rates, see Senador Gómez 1915: 1993, pp. 92–3, and Sabio Alcutén 1996.
[20] Spain. Ministerio de Fomento 1910, pp. 179-84, Carmona & Simpson 2003, p. 264, and Unamuno in Costa 1982, Vol. 2, p. 368.
[21] Carasa 1983, p. 256.

still operational by the turn of the twentieth century, with around 100 million pesetas on their books, equivalent to 3 per cent of total net farm production.[22] All the pósitos operated within a common legal framework, but their success depended on the day-to-day lending decisions taken by the village council, whose representatives were chosen by the concejo and supervised by the municipal secretary. The pósitos provided short-term loans for the duration of the growing season at interest rates below that demanded by private lenders. At times of hardship, the concejo was legally obliged to give preference to the poorest taxpayers.[23] The fact that pósitos could not take deposits or borrow money from other financial institutions implied that their survival depended entirely on their ability to make borrowers repay loans. However, and as with modern microcredit schemes, borrowers could be easily monitored by neighbouring farmers, who had strong incentives to inform if these village funds were being misused. The presence of an active village pósito is therefore a rough indicator of good management, although not necessarily of a democratic institution, as the role played by the village elite in their day-to-day operations is unknown.

The fact that the pósitos were found over much of the country challenges the idea that farmers could not cooperate in areas of latifundios in southern Spain (Map 5.3). In Valladolid, a province of predominantly small cereal farms, pósitos were found in 46 per cent of the villages on the eve of the First World War, compared to 34 per cent in Caceres, a province of mixed farming with a high concentration of landownership. However, this situation is reversed when measured by the number of villagers who had access to one, reaching 69 per cent in Caceres, and 43 per cent in Valladolid. Their success is also suggested by the fact that the presence of an active pósito in the interwar period made the creation of credit cooperatives less likely.[24]

By the early 1930s, many pósitos were still successfully lending money to poor farmers to purchase seed, but they probably served less 10 per cent of the nation's farmers.[25] Their inability to capture outside capital significantly reduced their possibilities to meet the growing needs of cereal farmers, not just because of the major increase in the area cultivated from the late

---

[22] Anes 1969. The number of pósitos peaked in the late eighteenth century at around 10,000. In 1900, about 77 per cent of their capital consisted of unrecoverable debt, much of it linked to interest that had accumulated on loans conceded before 1866.

[23] Carmona & Simpson, 2014b, pp. 9-10. Carmona & Simpson 2019, fn. 23.

[24] In Valladolid, there was a 70 per cent possibility of a credit cooperative being established in a village where the pósito lent to only 20 per cent of the households, but only a 20 per cent chance when 70 per cent of households received loans. Carmona & Simpson 2019.

[25] Calculations in Carmona & Simpson 2019.

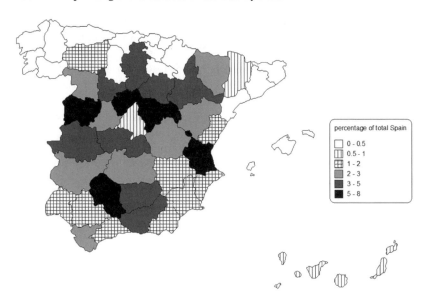

Map 5.3 Geographical distribution of capital lent by *pósitos* in 1923 (%
of Spanish total)
Note: The absence of pósitos along Spain's northern coastline is
explained by the limited amount of wheat cultivation, and in Catalonia
by a different legal system in the Old Regime.
Source: Inspección General de Pósitos 1924, p. 60.

eighteenth century, but also because of the new demands associated with
industrially produced farm inputs.[26] The governments' endeavours to convert the pósitos into genuine rural savings banks to compete with the
Catholic credit cooperatives also failed, partly because of the state's inability
to coordinate activities, but also because successful pósitos were reluctant to
lose control over their own funds.[27]

Small farmers therefore remained dependent on village moneylenders
because most pósitos had only limited supplies of capital, and commercial
banks were unwilling to lend.[28] In developing economies today, Debraj

<hr />

[26] The sixteen pósitos that were reportedly renting out 'simple machinery' in the province of
Burgos in 1919 appear to be exceptions. Martínez-Soto & Martínez-Rodríguez 2015,
p. 264.
[27] Ibid., p. 273. The 1924 Decree that allowed pósitos with idle funds to lend to those with
a shortage consequently failed.
[28] This was not just because the difficulties of monitoring borrowers, but also because land
values were hard to establish as a guarantee, especially in areas where the *amillaramientos*
were still in use. Notary fees to register loans were high.

Ray notes that the 'majority of village moneylenders do not pursue usury as their sole occupation', but are local landlords, shopkeepers, or traders, who both know their clients (and can therefore select), and are happy to accept the borrower's harvest or future farm work as collateral for the loan.[29] Landowners in some parts of Spain used interlinked transactions with their tenants, collecting the rent and payments for seed and fertilizers with the harvest so that, in the case of non-payment, the borrower risked losing not just the possibilities of future loans, but also being evicted from the land.[30] Landlords could reward good tenants, and thereby reinforce their clientelistic relationships. As the quote by Bosworth at the outset of this chapter suggests, this at least had the merit of providing security for the asset-poor in the absence of the impersonal credit markets. Traders, by contrast, might create an informal futures market, by guaranteeing to buy farmers' harvest at a predetermined price, while merchants supplied inputs, especially chemical fertilizers on credit.[31] Some private lenders built up small groups of trusted borrowers over time, although their numbers and the geographic area that they served were strictly limited.[32]

The 1906 Syndicate Law offered, at least in theory, the possibility for village credit cooperatives to take deposits, and then make small loans to local farmers that it could easily monitor. As most village cooperatives had few assets, local landowners were needed to provide the necessary collateral to obtain loans. The most successful was in Badajoz where, under the initiative of the director of the local branch of the Banco de España, Raiffeisen commercial and professional accounting practices allowed landowners to obtain relative large amounts of capital.[33] However, loans were usually restricted to the richer farmers, and the twenty-six banks had just 5,860 members, equivalent to between 10 and 25 per cent of the village households.[34] In other words, risk was reduced by these banks only lending to well-established farmers towards the top of the farm

---

[29] Ray 1998, p. 541.
[30] Extremadura, in Carmona & Simpson 2014b. Commercial banks, unlike some village lenders, were not interested in collateral that took the form of the future harvest or unpaid labour. Ray 1998, p. 534.
[31] Spain. Ministerio de Fomento 1921.
[32] For the Cinco Villas, Sabio Alcutén 1996, pp. 91–108.
[33] Noguer 1912, p. 586, and Carmona & Simpson 2003, p. 292. Between 1906 and 1911, Badajoz's savings banks received 55 per cent of all the loans made by the Banco de España to savings banks. Martínez-Soto 2003, p. 144.
[34] In 1922, Almendralejo had 452 members in a village of 4,253 households (10 per cent); Fregenal, 678 and 2,701, respectively (25 per cent); Fuentes de León, 268 and 1,474 (18 per cent), and Olivenza, 629 and 3,114 (20 per cent). Carmona & Simpson 2003, p. 290, and Spain, Ministerio de Trabajo, Comercio e Industria, 1922, pp. 22–33, Badajoz. The five largest banks doubled their loan portfolios between 1918 and 1933 from 4.6 to 9.8 million pesetas. Martínez-Soto 2003, pp. 133 and 144.

ladder. The Badajoz banks did not form a federation, and remained independent of the official Catholic one (CNCA), despite the attempts of this organization to incorporate them, especially in the period 1917–19.[35]

Another possibility was to federate cooperatives into networks, and use the greater economies of scale to capture loans, sometimes with government help, and monitor village cooperative lending to ensure that the records were kept and loans repaid. Elsewhere in Europe, the initiative and expertise to create a federation and coordinate both credit and producer cooperatives was provided by a variety of groups: the traditional agrarian elite; political parties; the Church; or a government agency. In Spain, the Church was the driving power behind most credit cooperatives. Not only did it have the organizational capacity to build federations across large areas, but parish priests played a key role in screening who was suitable to join the village cooperative. As the agronomist José Cascón noted, 'they are the only ones who know the economic situation of the borrower and, more than anything else, their moral conditions, which are the best and most solid guarantee to give personal credit'.[36]

By the 1920s there were around 500 credit cooperatives with fewer than 60,000 members, with almost half located in just three provinces, Badajoz, Navarra, and Tarragona.[37] Individual loans averaged around 350 pesetas, a similar figure to the more successful pósitos. In Valladolid, for example, the pósitos on the eve of the First World War lent more than the cooperatives did fifteen years later.[38] Many credit (and producer) cooperatives quickly failed, with 30 per cent of those founded between 1906 and 1909 disappearing by 1915, and the cooperatives created after 1927 accounted for half of those operating in 1933.[39] Catholic writers such a Noguer blamed the poor performance of credit cooperatives on the opposition from liberals and local elites (caciques), although a bigger problem was probably the reluctance of the Church to attract more capital, discussed in the next chapter.[40] In conclusion, most farmers received no loans from either a pósito or a credit cooperative, and those

---

[35] Polo Benito 1919, suggests that a federation would have required the banks to have a social function. The CNCA also failed to create their own credit cooperatives in the province, despite the large numbers excluded by the Badajoz banks. Pulido Romero & Villalobos Cortés 2006, p.123.

[36] Cascón 1934, p. 567. Examples of individual initiatives include Rivas Moreno and Nicolás Fontes in Murcia, and Luis Chaves in Zamora.

[37] Carasa 1991, pp. 328–9, and Carmona & Simpson 2003, p. 285.

[38] The 110 pósitos made 4,400 loans of 500,000 pesetas compared to the cooperatives lending 483,000 pesetas to 13,000 members in 1926. Spain. Delegación Regia de Pósitos (1911–15) and Muñiz 1926, pp. 452–60.

[39] Garrido 1995, pp. 134–8.   [40] Noguer 1912, p. 287.

who did, received only sufficient to buy seed and perhaps some fertilizers. This might have been enough in a traditional, organic farming economy, but the lack of cheap credit became a major obstacle to modernizing the sector, especially as there were also relatively few producer cooperatives.

The Limits to Producer Cooperatives in Areas of Dry-Farming

The advantages that small family farmers enjoyed in organizing their own labour was increasingly offset from the turn of the century by the disadvantages of small scale in a rapidly changing market place. As one newspaper complained, as the value chain lengthened, the family farmer was squeezed by 'the abuses of buyers and sellers which try to obtain at misery prices the produce of the countryside, and to sell to the farmer at enormous profits machinery, fertilizers and everything else necessary to live and work on the land'.[41] Producer cooperatives therefore promised to combine the work and entrepreneurial incentives associated with the family farm with the economies of scale found in bulk buying of inputs, processing of farm products, and marketing them in distant urban centres.[42]

'Bottom-up' and 'top-down' interest in Spanish farm cooperatives followed two distinct cycles. First, farmers showed little interest when farm prices were buoyant, and only saw cooperatives as a solution for guaranteeing sales during economic downturns, a moment when it was especially difficult to raise the necessary capital.[43] A second, political cycle emerged with the reaction of the Church to anticlericalism and socialism, with the numbers of cooperatives tripling between 1916 and 1923 during a period of political unrest in the countryside, but then declining following the government's successful repression.

Despite the frequent references in the Spanish literature to the potential of producer cooperatives, few farmers actually belonged to one, and those who did enjoyed limited benefits. With the exception of Catalonia and its powerful regional association, the *Unió de Vinyaters de Catalunya*, there were few village wine cooperatives before 1936, and as late as 1950 they accounted for only a tenth of total production. This absence was in part caused by operational difficulties described elsewhere, but the lack of top-down support left the sector with weak lobbying power, especially for

---

[41] *Voz Social* 1922, cited in Castillo 1979, p. 324.
[42] Valentinov 2007. By contrast, cooperatives since the Second World War have often been created to help stabilize markets, and raise prices. Fernández & Simpson 2017.
[43] The classic example was the wine cooperatives in the Midi in France during the 1900s, the so called *filles de la misère*.

small producers.[44] The lack of credit was a major problem, and wine growers in Utiel (Valencia) were forced to wait twenty-two years before they could build their winery, and those in neighbouring Requena had to build it themselves.[45]

There were also virtually no cooperative olive mills in 1931, despite the significant advantages they offered small growers.[46] There is no obvious reason for their absence, but again they required considerable investment, and the highly volatile olive harvest would have made meeting annual interest payments difficult. However, perhaps the biggest problem was that while wine growers had always traditionally made their own wine, this was never the case with olive growers. Therefore, although small wine growers could continue using their own facilities during the construction of a cooperative, olive growers risked retaliatory action and a lock-out by local olive oil producers.

The reaction of landed elites, especially the caciques, to cooperatives was crucial to their success, as these groups often controlled the processing and selling of local farm produce. With cereals for example, which accounted for more than a third of farm output over much of the secano, most cooperatives limited their activities to bulk purchases of fertilizers and seed for members, ignoring the potential gains to be obtained from creating storage and milling facilities, because of opposition from established businesses and caciques.[47] The experience of the *Sindicato Agrícola de Cervera* (Lerida) was atypical only in the persistence of its members. After the local millers refused to buy the cooperative's grain, the members constructed their own mill. They were then prohibited from selling flour outside the province and in 1923 the mill was destroyed in an arson attack.[48] As late as 1937, only 11 of the 2,700 cooperatives belonging to the Catholic Church's organization (CNCA) owned flour mills.[49]

Yet opposition from caciques or merchants to competition from a new village cooperative was to be expected. The real question therefore is why Spain's landed elites as *a group* showed no interest in organizing small farmers, unlike many of those found in North-Western Europe. Even the most successful producers' organization, the Danish dairy cooperatives, was the culmination of a long process of technological change encouraged

[44] Simpson 2011; Fernández & Simpson 2017. In particular, cooperatives could not design an adequate incentive structure to encourage growers to produce better grapes to improve wine quality.
[45] Piqueras 1981, p. 270.
[46] Fraser 1986, pp. 111–5, for Mijas (Malaga), cited in González Calleja et al. 2015, p. 124.
[47] The use of mineral fertilizers was new, so cooperatives did not compete with established merchants.
[48] EPAPM, 15/1/1928, pp. 24–5 and Simpson 1995, pp. 229–30.
[49] *Voz Social*, dic. 1937, cited in Castillo 1979, pp. 475–9.

by the elites and diffusion of new methods among a rural middle class of owner-occupiers that helped enforce product quality standards to capture foreign markets.[50]

Farm Representation and the State

In Western Europe, the consequences of economic development, growth of the state, and the spread of democracy, transformed the nature of farm representation and the capacity of governments to intervene in the sector. It also changed the nature of organizations that mediated between agriculture and government.[51] As this section argues, change was limited in Spain and the links between the state, elite organizations, and village associations remained weak.

The presence and development of Spanish farm associations can be shown in three distinct time periods (Table 5.1). The first includes those organizations that had developed at a time when traditional, organic agricultural systems predominated, and were still influential at the time of the late-nineteenth-century grain invasion. In some cases, these were classic elite organizations, such as the *Asociación General de Ganaderos del Reino* (AGG), founded in 1836 following the abolition of the Mesta,[52] or the *Sociedades económicas de Amigos del País*, which had been created during the Enlightenment to instruct farmers on new techniques, but by the late nineteenth century played only a minor role. The most dynamic elite organization was undoubtedly the *Instituto Agrícola Catalán de San Isidro* (IACSI) created in 1851, which combined a highly conservative approach to property rights, with the need to develop a competitive, export-orientated agriculture.[53]

These elite organizations contrast with the traditional village ones described earlier, such as that of Santa María de los Montes, or the 3,000 or more village *pósitos*. The First Republic (1868–74) also saw the creation of numerous associations that represented small farmers, such as the short-lived *Asociación Agrícola por la Iniciativa Privada* in Valladolid, which

[50] Henriksen 1999, p. 59 and Lampe & Sharp 2018.
[51] Sheingate 2001, p. 5. However, as noted, state capacity was also a function of previous investment in increasing and improving the administrative branches of government.
[52] From 1917, the AGG was officially responsible for protecting the nation's sheep walks (*cañadas*) and during the Second Republic would represent livestock producers' interests in their fight to stop the conversion of pasture to arable to create more employment. Cabrera 1983, p. 61.
[53] Membership by the end of the nineteenth century was 2,000. Planas 2013 and Pan-Montojo 2000, p. 34.

Table 5.1 *Three waves of creating farm organizations before the Second Republic*

Organization	Interest Group It Represented
Already in existence by 1880	
Asociación General de Ganaderos del Reino (AGG), founded 1836	Livestock interests
Sociedades económicas de Amigos del País	Urban and rural academics
Instituto Agrícola Catalán de San Isidro (IACSI), (1851)	Catalan landowners
Sociedad Valenciana de Agricultores (1859)	Valencian landowners
Asociación de Ingenieros Agrónomos, (1872)	Professional association for agronomists
Pósitos	Village-level granaries
Created between c.1880 and c.1906	
Asociación de Agricultores de España (AAE), (1881)	National 'peak' association
Cámaras agrícolas (law of 1890)	Provincial landowners
Comunidades de Labradores	Rural security in large villages
Federación Agrícola Catalano-Balear (1899)	Regional association of federations
Asociación de Labradores de Zaragoza (1900)	Regional association of federations
Unio de Vinyaters de Catalunya (1901)	Regional lobby of winemakers
Created between 1906 and 1931	
Agrarian Syndicates (1906 law)	Village-level associations and cooperatives
Confederación Nacional Católico-Agraria (CNCA), (1917)	Catholic federation of syndicates (cooperatives)

combined demands for tax reform and higher tariffs with those to encourage agricultural research and education.[54]

A second phase of farm organizations dates from the late nineteenth century, and is associated with the growing threat of cheap food imports, the destruction of the country's vineyards by phylloxera, and the increasing use of industrially produced farm inputs and science-based knowledge. At the same time, state building led to demands for greater information on land ownership and farming, both for tax purposes and to compile statistical information on output, stocks, and consumption.

The *Asociación de Agricultores de España* (AAE) was created in 1881 with the object to modernize farming through scientific methods, rejecting protectionism, and encouraging exports.[55] Membership was open not just to landowners and farmers, but also civil servants, especially

[54] Serrano 1997 and Pan-Montojo 2002, p. 37.
[55] This paragraph is based on Pan-Montojo 2007.

agronomists, as well as most of the country's leading farm associations, allowing it to become the 'lobby of the lobbies' for the sector, rather than simply an instrument for the landowning elite, or cereal interests. Power resided in its network of politicians, civil servants, and large landowners resident in Madrid who enjoyed close contacts with government ministers. Over time, lobbying methods changed from writing letters and informal visits to notables, to organizing press campaigns and public meetings that enjoyed the active presence of a high-ranking minister. The AAE successfully made the transition from liberal democracy to dictatorship in 1923, but it failed to become the sector's peak association, as it was unable to represent all farm interests, or criticize government policy. Even though its membership soared from 423,317 to 668,333 between 1931 and 1933, its lobbying influence declined under the very different political conditions of the Second Republic.[56]

Given that the AAE was unwilling to challenge the political status quo, the first concerted farm campaign to change government policy and raise cereal protection was successfully organized by the short-lived *Liga Agraria* in late 1880s.[57] Some of the groups that had supported the *Liga* were converted into *cámaras agrícolas* after 1890, which the state hoped would reinforce its influence within the sector. The cámaras were controlled by rural elites and the lack of bottom-up interest led to them being significantly reformed in 1919, with membership being made compulsory for all farmers paying more than 25 pesetas tax. This measure met with fierce protests and the government was forced to back down, leaving the cámaras once more without adequate funding.[58] A third of all the cámaras and half their membership were found in Catalonia, while in areas of latifundios their influence was strictly limited, although they effectively stopped other groups from emerging.[59]

The 1887 Law of Associations led to the creation of numerous new organizations although, as Pan-Montojo has noted, many were village groups already in existence and now refounded with new objectives.[60] In Galicia, for example, associations for the provision of mutual insurance for animals, consumer cooperatives, or educational societies were sponsored by diverse groups, including emigrants, Catholic and lay societies and, from the 1920s, socialists.[61] By contrast, in Extremadura, landless

---

[56] Ibid., especially, pp. 114–15, and Cabrera 1983, pp. 62–3.
[57] Other demands included lower land taxes, a reduction in rail freight, and the prohibition of imports of industrial alcohol. Pan-Montojo 2000, pp. 43–4.
[58] Pan-Montojo 2002, pp. 19.
[59] Spain. Anuario estadístico de España, 1926 and Florencio Puntas 1994, p. 99.
[60] Pan-Montojo 2000, pp. 53–4.
[61] Cabo Villaverde 1998, pp. 12–52, Fernández Prieto 1997, p. 154, and Chapter 6.

workers and small farmers organized in formal and informal groups to sublet areas of pasture, which they then divided among themselves to cultivate.[62] The 1887 Law also helped the Catalan IACSI extend its influence by organizing small farmers in their fight against phylloxera, and create its own federation, the *Federación Agrícola Catalano-Balear* (1899). The IACSI was also behind the pressure group, the *Unión Agrícola de Cataluña*, which represented distinct regional federations.[63] However, the attempt in 1903 to create the *Unión Agraria Española* failed, given the deep divisions of interest within Spanish agriculture.[64]

The IACSI was also a major influence behind the 1906 Syndicate Law, which was modelled on the French 1884 Waldeck-Rousseau legislation. As in France, syndicates provided a 'catalyst around which a range of other organizations – cooperatives, mutual, rural banks – could coalesce'.[65] This makes it difficult to identify their exact contribution to farming at the village level, resulting in most historians considering a village syndicate as being a farm cooperative, a custom that is followed here.[66] Many cooperatives belonged to hierarchical structures, with the Catholic *Confederación Nacional Católico-Agraria* (CNCA) being the most important, and operating at the national, diocesan, and village levels. The CNCA was a 'mixed' syndicate and its membership was open not just to small farmers, but also landowners and farm labourers. Another mixed syndicate was IACSI-backed *Unió de Vinyaters de Catalunya* (UVC) in 1911, in this case organized by large farmers.[67]

By the early 1920s a wide variety of agrarian organizations were therefore found in the Spanish countryside (Table 5.2). Some can be described as 'official' or top-down, with the initiative coming directly from the government or the elites, although most were bottom-up, with the legal framework in which they operated established in Madrid, but the organizational initiatives originating with villagers. Nevertheless this division is not as useful as it first appears, because successful organizations usually required the presence of both dynamic local associations and top-down groups, that helped finance and coordinate the activities of village associations over wide geographical areas. Therefore bottom-up and top-down were not mutually exclusive, but rather necessary complements.[68]

---

[62] Carmona & Simpson 2014a, cuadro 10.
[63] Planas 2013, p. 27. The *Asociación de Labradores de Zaragoza* was created in 1900.
[64] Pan-Montojo 2000, pp. 50–1.   [65] Cleary 1989, p. 26.
[66] See, for example, Garrido 2007, figures 1 and 2, and Beltrán Tapia 2012, p. 512 and figure 1.
[67] Planas 2013, pp. 27, 41–4, 49, and 52.
[68] As Banerjee et al. 2008, p. 3145, have argued, 'if public good access were determined primarily by local population characteristics, we would rarely see rapid changes in such access, since many of these characteristics (religion, caste, ethnicity) change very slowly

Table 5.2 *Rural associations and cooperatives in 1920*

	Number of organizations	Number of members	Principal area of influence
Cámaras agrícolas	126	14,223	Province
Comunidades de labradores	124	134,824	Large villages
Federaciones agrícolas	54	28,096	Province /region
Asociaciones agrarias	857	145,885	Local
Sindicatos agrícolas	3,471	302,285	Village
Cooperatives and rural *cajas*	514	55,804	Village
Sociedades económicas de Amigos del País	48	7,302	Province
Sub-total	5,194	688,419	
Pósitos	3,529	97,585[69]	Village
Other formal & informal village associations			

Sources: Banco Urquijo 1924, pp. 342–5, and Spain. Delegación Regia de Pósitos 1920, pp. 77–8.

Finally, two issues were especially important when considering farm representation and the Spanish state before 1931. The first was whether local elites could manipulate the nature and extent of state intervention in the countryside, or whether it was the central government that determined policy, and created its own local farm organizations such as the *cámaras provinciales* to implement it, thereby avoiding the influence of the local elites.[70] Everywhere a growing number of state technicians, planners, and engineers looked to sweep away the old, 'inefficient' farming systems and implement 'scientific' solutions of their choice on the countryside. Local notables usually opposed outside intervention that they could not themselves control, and in Spain the landed elites were in general successful at limiting state capacity intervention and were able to maintain their own influence over local matters before the Second Republic.

A second question concerns the farm groups themselves, and the question of representation. Perhaps only the National Farmers' Union in England and Wales can be considered a single 'peak association' in

over time. It would also be difficult to explain the convergence of under-provided areas with those that have been historically advantaged'.

[69] The figure refers to villagers who enjoyed a loan.

[70] See especially Pan-Montojo 2000. In fact, the nature of local land-tenure regimes made it very difficult for the state to control the *cámaras provinciales*. In Galicia, for example, they were used by local groups against the *foros*, and by the IACSI in Catalonia, to defend the *rabassa morta* contract (Chapter 10).

Europe by the 1920s, as farm groups elsewhere often remained deeply divided along regional, commodity, and ideological lines, as well as increasingly between landowners, farmers, tenants, and labourers. Building national, or even regional, organizations demanded considerable resources, and these could, in theory, have been provided by the elites (landowners, the Church), the state, or by governments requiring farmers as taxpayers to contribute to their running costs. The difference was important, because when the elites paid, it usually demanded a major, if not exclusive, say in its policies. By contrast, organizations funded by taxpayers promised a much wider, even democratic representation. Therefore, the Spanish landed elites created an organizational structure that was sufficiently flexible to allow informal contacts with the leading politicians to meet their needs. However, when the political system changed, and a new group of politicians with different ideas came to power in 1931, the landowners' organizations lost much of their parliamentary influence.

Conclusions

This chapter has argued that villagers were able to cooperate when it was in their interests, especially when face-to-face monitoring was possible. The persistence of the pósitos over much of the country indicates that collective action was also feasible in areas of latifundios. However, the success of credit and producer cooperatives depended not just on the ability of small farmers to cooperate at the village level, but also the incentives that vertical organizations such as the state, Church, or political parties had in providing an organizational structure. Successful farm cooperative movements in Europe before the Second World War were rarely established without hierarchical organizations helping resolve the political obstacles to their creation, and providing capital and the technical expertise needed. Labour organizations would in time play a similar role in coordinating and presenting local workers' demands at the national level.

The weak development of cooperatives across much of Spain had four wider implications for our study. In the first instance, asset-poor farmers had difficulties to climb the farm ladder, leaving them to follow farming systems that were often far from optimal, and dependent on patron-client networks. Despite the important changes that took place in the Spanish countryside during this period, the influence of the rural elite remained strong, because of the difficulties of small farmers to access market-based alternatives to obtain goods and services. A second factor was that this dependence on the elites made it difficult for small farmers to influence government legislation, with the most obvious shortcomings being the delays in creating an efficient and fair land tax and the absence of rural banks. Another consequence was the political implications for the Second Republic, as the presence of a dynamic network of civic associations is often seen as the cornerstone for a democratic society. In particular, the 1931 Constitution might have looked very different had the two and a half million family farmers been already organized in strong civic associations that could represent their interests. Finally, the weakness of village-level civic associations would have important consequences during the Second Republic when governments tried to implement the far-reaching reforms. The governments' inability to gather accurate village level information; to distribute public goods impartially; or to execute reforms efficiently, were important reasons explaining the deep polarization of village society in 1936.

6 The Persistence of the Landed Elites and the Nature of Farm Lobbies

Spanish agriculture was in many respects a success story during the first third of the twentieth century, as labour productivity increased by two-thirds, caused partly by the use of fewer workers, but also by an extension of cultivation, better yields, and the slow switch to higher-value crops and livestock produce (Chapter 4). Yet there were perhaps half a million landless or near landless families in Southern Spain, and their plight will be examined in the next chapter. In addition, many family farmers remained poor and politically weak, despite the fact that around a third of all voters in 1931 could be described as 'farmers'. The political under-representation of such a large group had important consequences for the survival of the Second Republic.

This chapter explains why Spain's traditional elites, the large land-owners and Church hierarchy, remained politically and economically strong before the Second Republic, unlike most other Western European countries. It argues that the landed elites did not have to organize to create a mass party system to attract the farm vote, as their use of patronage and corruption allowed the turno pacifico to successfully determine electoral outcomes. At the same time, parliamentary antic-lericalism remained weak because of the Concordat between the Church and the liberal Restoration regime, allowing the Catholic hier-archy to abstain from party politics most of the time.[1] Finally, the Socialist Party continued to cling to Marxist orthodoxy, and was generally uninterested in organizing small farmers (Chapter 9). The weak political incentives for rural elites, Church, and political parties to encourage grass-root movements and build modern, mass political parties to involve small farmers in national politics explains not just why farm cooperatives had a limited influence, but also why other political groups successfully captured the political agenda after 1931.

Farm lobbies played an important role in determining agricultural policy in the absence of mass political parties. While the late-nineteenth-

---

[1] For the relations between the Church hierarchy and the Restoration, Callahan 2000, p. 27.

century grain crisis and the First World War had the potential to radically change the rural social order, this was limited in Spain because of tariffs that offset falling prices, while the country's neutrality during the Great War avoided any serious food shortages. As a result, the economic power and influence of the traditional landed elites remained largely unaffected. Only when high wartime prices increased farm profitability and squeezed workers' living standards, leading to the 1917–19 *Trienio bolchevique* and some of Europe's highest levels of rural strikes, did the landed elites and Church feel seriously threatened.

The Chapter is organized as follows. The first section provides an alternative explanation of culture or social capital for the failure to create a strong network of farm associations and cooperatives before 1931. Following Kalyvas, it argues that neither the rural elites nor the Church hierarchy were required to participate in mass politics, which limited their interest in building grass-root support and organizing village-level cooperatives into federations. By remaining outside mass politics, both groups were able to preserve their traditional powers. The next section develops these arguments and suggests that the successful farm cooperatives and rural associations in Catalonia are the exceptions that prove the rule. The third section looks at how collective action and the formation of lobbies developed following the 1870s grain invasion. The higher tariffs encouraged an expansion in wheat output that reinforced the position of cereal farmers, and especially large landowners. Finally, the fourth section examines the difficulties for government to respond to the collapse of prices from the late 1920s. The weak farm organizations made it impossible for the government to collect basic, village-level information on production and food stocks, and it lacked the ability to intervene in markets impartially.

The Political Economy of Cooperative Failure

In no rural society have landed elites willingly given up their economic and political powers, and Spain's Restoration settlement effectively allowed the country's 'major power centres' involving rural patron-client chains, religious institutions, and the military to remain virtually undiminished on the eve of the Second Republic.[2] Although small farmers and rural workers showed considerable success in organizing activities at a village level, and despite universal male suffrage from 1890, their

[2] For a discussion of these power centres, Tilly 2007, p. 23. In a similar vein, North and his co-authors emphasize that 'open-access' societies are rich and vibrant, with lots of autonomous organizations, independent of the traditional rural elites and the Church. North et al. 2007, p. 11.

ability to influence national politics remained strictly limited because of the absence of mass politics outside a few major urban centres.

Spain therefore differed to countries such as France, where the rural elites and the Church became involved in peasant politics, and played a major role in helping create cooperatives and associations for small farmers. The Waldeck-Rousseau law of 1884 removed the need for government consent to create an association of more than twenty people, and republican groups needed to capture the farm vote because, as Jules Ferry noted, the 'republic will be a peasants' republic or it will cease to exist'.[3] However, it was the powerful conservative and anti-republican *Société des agriculteurs de la France* that explains the initial growth of small farm syndicates, with one militant describing them in 1910 as 'a marvellous instrument to maintain the religious fervour of our peasants, to improve their living conditions and to prevent the iniquitous spread of socialism into our tranquil villages'.[4] In response, republicans created the *Société nationale d'encouragement à l'agriculture* in 1880 with the same objective of creating cooperatives and mutual-aid groups, and in 1910, the *Fédération nationale de la mutualité et de la coopération agricole.*[5] According to Sheingate:

Like the creation of an independent Ministry of Agriculture, the development of farm groups in the late nineteenth century reflected the same struggle for republican control of rural France. Agricultural syndicates – organisations for the purchase of farm inputs, rural credit, and crop insurance were the result of direct and indirect state action designed to bolster republican political success in the countryside.[6]

This struggle between a centralized, liberal state and a localized, conservative paternalism, resulted in France's small farmers receiving both political support and practical help, with the 2,069 agrarian syndicates and 512,000 members in 1900, increasing to 15,000 and 1.5 million respectively by 1929.[7] For Cleary, the period between 1918 and 1930 in France was a 'golden age', 'when the power and influence of regional syndicates brought in its train a major expansion in the numbers and activity of allied groups such as cooperatives, mutual insurance groups and the agricultural credit movement'.[8] Large producers also organized

---

[3] Cited in Wright 1964, p.1 3.
[4] Barral 1968, p. 107, and *Bulletin de l'Union Catholique Aveyronnaise*, both cited in Cleary 1989, p. 34.
[5] Cleary 1989, p. 34.   [6] Sheingate 2001, p. 65.
[7] Ibid., p. 92. By contrast, class-based syndicates were much less widespread than community-based movements, and the success of socialists and communists to create syndicates was limited. Cleary 1989, pp. 43 and 81.
[8] Cleary 1989, p. 3.

confederations for sugar beet producers (1921) and wheat (1924), but their lobbying strength depended on their ability to represent significant numbers of small farmers demanding 'fair prices' and a more efficient marketing system. To do this, new institutional relations were required, which led to greater government intervention in the market, and the incorporation of farm groups in the regulatory process, so that these associations 'not only amplified the voice of farmers in politics but also supplied government administrators with information, assistance, and political cover in the implementation of agricultural policy'.[9]

France was not an exception. In Italy in the early 1920s, the *Lega Nazionale delle Cooperative* (Socialist), the *Confederazione Cooperativa Italiana* (Catholic), and the *Sindicato Italiano dell Cooperative* (fascist), competed with each other to organize small farmers, although the growth of the cooperative movement slowed when Mussolini ended competitive politics.[10]

Two questions therefore need to be answered. First, why were the landed elites and the Church in these and other Western European countries willing to play a major role in helping to organize small farmers, but not in Spain? A second and related question is why did these two groups then lose a significant part of their influence in village society and national politics by the interwar period? For political scientists, the question is crucial because the voluntary surrender of political power by the landed elites and Church hierarchy was a major step on the road to democracy. In the terminology of North and his co-authors, it helps explain the shift from a 'limited-access', to an 'open-access' society.[11] Paradoxically, the greater participation by the European landed elites and Church in helping small farmers organize was the major cause of their loss of influence and political decline.

Following Stathis Kalyvas, in countries such as Belgium, the Netherlands, Austria, Germany, and Italy between 1870 and 1920, the Church became heavily involved in national politics, not from choice, but rather as an 'unplanned, unintended, and unwanted by-product of the strategic steps taken by the Catholic Church in response to Liberal anticlerical attacks'. At the same time, the position of traditional landed elites was endangered by the rising industrial and urban bourgeoisie, that 'stood for state rationalization and centralization', which directly threatened their control and patronage in village politics.[12] The significant heterogeneity of farming systems and land-tenure regimes, and the essentially

---

[9] Sheingate 2001, pp. 31, 78, and 98.
[10] Simpson 2000, p. 116. For the importance of northern Italian civic associations, see especially Putnam 1993, ch. 5.
[11] North et al. 2007.   [12] Kalyvas 1996, pp. 6 and 51.

local nature of patron-client networks, made it difficult for the landed elites to organize across large areas. Therefore, in what was supposed to be a temporary alliance, the Church mobilized voters and contracted out to the conservative elites the political struggle against anticlerical reforms. It proved to be highly successful. However, as Kalyvas stresses, the creation of a new platform for lay and clerical activists inevitably diminished the Catholic hierarchy's power, while the conservative elites, especially in countries such as France or Italy, were unhappy at forging close links with the Church.[13] Over time, lay Catholics and the lower clergy looked to widen their political constituencies and in doing so removed the restricted influence of the episcopate and traditional conservative elites, thereby creating secular Christian Democratic parties that did not 'carry the baggage of aliberalism, intolerance, and dependence on the church'.[14] From the turn of the century, if not before, small farmers in these countries enjoyed competitive politics based on ideology rather than a system that was linked solely to personal interests. As Kalyvas writes, 'together with Socialist parties, although before them, Catholic movements were the winners of mass politics'.[15] Small family farmers now benefitted not only from dynamic village associations and cooperatives but confessional parties that gave them much greater political voice to demand policies such as tenure reforms, the provision of research and extension services, and market intervention to resolve problems of their weak bargaining power and farm price volatility.

France took a slightly different route, as no confessional parties emerged during the Third Republic. However, a deep ideological divide and political competition existed between those who wanted to restore the monarchy and those who defended the Republic.[16] As noted, republican parties from the 1870s successfully united under a banner of anticlericalism and opposition to the monarchy, and made a conscious effort to capture the peasant vote, and to legislate in favour of small farmers, sometimes at the expense of large landowners. By contrast, the rural elite were still looking for regime change and a return to the monarchy instead of attempting to organize the rural electorate and, as a result, 'kept losing elections' until 1891.[17] With the abolition of the Concordat of 1905, the Church finally began to encourage the growth of local

---

[13] Ibid., pp. 36–7, 108, and 125. Both the Church and conservatives believed they could control confessional parties, and the 'electoral successes took everyone by surprise'. Ibid., p. 105.

[14] Ibid., p. 1, and table 1.   [15] Ibid., p. 93.

[16] This paragraph is based on Kalyvas 1996, ch. 3.

[17] The weak party system and French agriculture in Sheingate 2001, p. 64, and how politics revolved around the viability of the Republican regime, rather than across party lines in Kalyvas 1996, ch. 3.

organizations, but by this time French voters had learnt to keep their religious beliefs separate from their political ones. For Kalyvas, the failure of a confessional party to emerge in France had major political implications, as it 'greatly facilitated the rise of nationalism and antiliberalism among Catholics' and formed the background to the Vichy regime.[18]

In countries such as France or Italy, the landed elites, Church hierarchy, and political parties therefore helped family farmers create producer and credit cooperatives in response to changing political opportunities and demands. These political incentives failed to materialize in Spain, because electoral fraud made party competition unnecessary before the Second Republic, and the 1876 Constitution defined both the Monarchy's and the Church's relations with the state, at least until the dictatorship of Primo de Rivera in 1923, limiting parliamentary anticlericalism. This implied not only that family farms lacked the necessary support to build organizations, but also that both the landed elites and Catholic hierarchy were able to maintain their powers, as they avoided the need to become involved in party politics. Indeed, the Restoration settlement perhaps even strengthened the rural elite, as they played a crucial role in "organizing" local elections in response to demands from Madrid, using a combination of patronage, fraud, and outright threats.[19] Finally, the Socialists showed virtually no interest in organizing small farmers (as oppose to landless labourers), while the major republican groups remained small, and generally concentrated in urban areas.

Accounting for the Regional Diversity of Cooperatives

A major argument advanced here for Spain's weak cooperative performance during the first third of the twentieth century was the lack of incentives for rural elites, political parties, and Church to help build top-down federations to obtain the necessary scale, especially for providing credit and marketing produce. Yet by 1923, there were over 5,000 cooperatives, of which roughly two-thirds belonged to the Church's national organization, the *Confederación Nacional Católico-Agraria* (CNCA) (Table 6.1). It was the fact that cooperatives' activities remained so few, rather than their limited numbers, that was important, something shown by the regional experiences.

The Spanish Catholic Church was perhaps more divided than in any other Western European country over how to respond to the development of a modern, liberal, centralized state. Following three major civil wars, the Concordat and the state's ability to appoint as

---

[18] Kalyvas 1996, p. 166.   [19] Martínez Cuadrado 1969 and Varela Ortega 1977.

bishops only those who accepted the constitutional monarchy gave it greater control over the Church's hierarchy. Yet in the north, many of the clergy 'remained steadfast in their opposition to a political system tainted by liberalism',[20] and held radically different views to those of the Church hierarchy. By contrast, over much of southern Spain, the Church had become dependent on landowners and by the nineteenth century had 'forfeited the allegiance of the pueblo'.[21] This deep social division is reflected by the presence of many more parish priests in northern Spain, increasing the chances that a village cooperative would be created in this area.[22] Yet there were also major regional differences in northern Spain, with 37.7 per cent of all farmers in Catalonia belonging to a cooperative, more than five times the figure in Galicia (6.7 per cent). Cooperatives in Catalonia and the Valencia region between them accounted for over half the nation's capital reserves (Table 6.2). This regional diversity can be explained not only by the interest that hierarchical institutions, especially the Church, had to create federations, but also by the distinctive nature of local land-tenure regimes and the characteristics of local agriculture.

There was rapid growth in the number of cooperatives following the 1906 Agrarian Syndicate Law, with many being integrated in Catholic regional federations linked to the diocese. The CNCA was created in 1917, and two years later it claimed to have 3,143 cooperatives, although this figure had fallen to 1,902 in 1933, less than 45 per cent of the national total (Table 6.1). The initial growth of the Church cooperatives can be explained by the emergence of anarchist and socialist trade unions across Spain during the *Trienio bolchevique* (1917–19), leading to the CNCA's president, Antonio Monedero, spending large sums of money belonging to the Castile-Leon organizations to extend the federations' influence into other rural areas. This recruitment drive ended once the government had restored order and social unrest subsided.[23] The priority for Monedero

---

[20] The Carlist newspaper, *El Siglo Futuro*, founded in 1874, quickly became the most popular newspaper among Spain's lower clergy. Callahan 2000, pp. 32–3 and 61.

[21] Pitt-Rivers 1954: 1971, p. xxi. For the role of the clergy, see especially Callahan 2000, ch. ix. The presence of large numbers of small rural villages in the North, rather than the large 'agro-towns' in the South, was another factor to explain the regional distribution of the clergy.

[22] Gallego et al. 2010, pp. 85–116, argue that the high concentration of family farmers living in small villages involved in a variety of community-based organizations, such as managing the open fields and common lands, as well as the greater presence of parish priests, created favourable conditions for cooperatives.

[23] Monedero was subsequently sacked by the Church hierarchy for the excessively high levels of expenditure on propaganda outside the region Castillo 1979, pp. 147, 150, 166–7, and 197.

Table 6.1 *Estimates of cooperatives and CNCA membership, 1907–37*

	CNCA			All cooperatives	CNCA cooperatives as % of total	Number of credit Cooperatives
	Cooperatives	Members	Federations			
1907				433		
1916				1,754		
1919	3,143	500,000	57	3,471	90.6	503 (1918)
1923	3,212			5,180	62.0	499
1926	3,034			5,821	52.1	
1929	2,276	200,000				
1933	1,902			4,266	44.6	646
1937	2,700		41			

The CNCA was created in 1917.
Sources: Garrido 1994, p. 84, Castillo 1979, pp. 115, 275, and 475, and Martínez-Soto et al. 2012, table 2.

was for the CNCA to defend Catholicism, rather than provide economic support to family farmers.[24]

The fact that the CNCA's polices were closely associated with those of the cereal producers in Castile-Leon, also had important implications. Many farmers in other regions, especially in Galicia and the irrigated areas of the Mediterranean region actually wanted lower, and not higher, cereal and bread prices. For these farmers, the CNCA was a lobby that had little to offer, and while its decision to move its headquarters to Madrid helped the Church's hierarchy maintain control over policy and propaganda, it made it less flexible to respond to local demands. Finally, although the CNCA was a 'mixed' syndicate, it had limited success in helping the landless establish a foot on the farm ladder, especially given the difficulties to intensifying cereal production under dry-farming conditions.[25]

The risks caused by high levels of market volatility also discouraged the CNCA from creating cooperative banks. The export demand for food and strong farm prices during the First World War encouraged cooperatives to increase their lending, and the Valencian federation was one that became heavily indebted to the CNCA. The subsequent collapse in wheat prices bankrupted many of the Valencian cooperatives, as well as some of the more dynamic federations in Castile-Leon, such as that of Rioja.[26] By

---

[24] Castillo 1979, pp. 143–4, and Callahan 2000, p. 147.
[25] For the CNCA, Castillo 1979, pp. 234–54.
[26] The wholesale wheat price fell by a third between 1920 and 1922, and the drop in farm prices is likely to have been even greater.

Table 6.2 *Regional distribution of cooperatives and rural cajas in 1933*

	N° of farmers	% of Spanish total	N° coops	% of total	N° of cooperative members	% of farmers in coop	N° coops with K	N° coop> 100,000 pesetas	capital coop in 000s ptas	% of total	N° of rural cajas	Deposits in rural cajas 000s ptas	% of total
Galicia	363,948	13.4	314	7.4	24,398	6.7	129	2	828	0.9	8	200	0.2
Valencia	276,248	10.2	365	8.6	97,610	35.3	277	41	21,952	22.6	65	28,842	24.0
Cataluña	209,533	7.7	540	12.7	79,018	37.7	344	64	27,600	28.5	76	8,216	6.8
Castile-Leon*	372,473	12.1	1256	29.6	72,115	19.4	450	11	8,397	8.7	124	17,092	14.2
Navarra	65,168	2.4	81	1.9	22,938	35.2	56	4	2,474	2.6	34	4,524	3.8
Sub-total		45.8		60.2		23.0				63.3			49.0
Spain	2,711,961	100	4,251	100	522,414	19.3	2,043	179	96,926	100	522	120,194	100

* Includes Logroño, but not Salamanca. For Navarra, see note for Map 5.2.
Sources: Spain. Ministerio de Agricultura 1934 and, for estimates of numbers of farms, Carmona et al. 2019.

1929, the number of syndicates in Valencia had more than halved and, in 1933, only a quarter of the total, and a third of the membership, were Catholic.[27] Massive market intervention to reduce this market volatility was well beyond the capacity of cooperative federations, although some of the CNCA leaders worked with the dictator Primo de Rivera in his failed attempt at creating a corporatist state between 1923 and 1929, and it was only after the 1950s that the government could intervene effectively in the wheat market (as we shall discuss). Therefore the combination of low levels of social conflict and financial difficulties limited the Church hierarchy's interest in using the CNCA to help small farmers, while its poor showing in Catalonia, and especially Galicia, is also explained by the Church's reluctance to become involved in landownership conflicts (Table 6.1).

In Navarra, the clergy, together with a 'rather modest upper class' provided the 'moral leadership of the local community'.[28] Although Carlism had been defeated as a military force in 1876, local society continued to reject liberalism and the Restoration political settlement. Consequently the two driving forces behind the province's cooperative movement were a highly traditional, but dynamic clergy closely associated with village society, and rural elites such as the Vizconde Val del Erro, a Carlist senator in Madrid, as well as president of Navarra's cooperative federation. This was federated with the CNCA, and therefore controlled by the Catholic hierarchy, although it maintained significant operational independence.[29] The region's special tax status also permitted greater freedom from Madrid. Yet Navarra's cooperatives, despite high levels of social capital and a clergy and rural elites that were willing to contribute to the top-down organization, often did little more than buy fertilizers in bulk.[30] Some attempts were made to organize sugar beet producers, but no granaries or flour mills were built, and there were only two wineries.[31] The endeavours to attract outside finance and create internal sources of credit were also disappointing. Yet rather than an organizational failure, the problem was instead that the levels of scale that cooperatives and their federations offered farmers were inappropriate for most of their needs. In the first instance, the potential economic contribution of cooperatives was

[27] The number of cooperatives fell from 301 in 1920, to 127 in 1929. Castillo, 1979, p. 125, and Martínez Gallego 2010, p. 246–7.
[28] Pitt-Rivers 1954: 1971, p. xxi. However, on the fertile lowlands, landownership was more concentrated and support for the Restoration settlement stronger.
[29] The Federation was organized by leading Carlists, with decisions taken by majority voting and, after 1922, the bishop's representative lost the right to veto. Majuelo & Pascual 1991. p. 66.
[30] These increased from 860 to 5,600 tons between 1910 and 1923. Ibid. p. 148.
[31] Those of Cintruénigo (founded in 1927) and San Martín de Unx (1914).

often greatest for crops with high value added and produced relatively close to large urban markets, or with access to export markets. In general, this was not the case for farmers in upland Navarra. There is also a risk of assessing cooperative activity in isolation, and in Navarra's closely knit, dynamic village societies, they were just one of a number of community-based activities. Indeed, as Majuelo and Pascual argue, cooperatives played an important role in defending village lands against privatization, an important factor even in the 1920s,[32] while the Church in the 1930s, despite its usual reluctance to interfere in the contentious issue of property rights, supported the efforts of Navarra's Cooperative Federation to recover those common lands that had already been sold.[33]

In Castile-Leon, the landowners' associations had few political reasons to organize family farmers, as their support had been already effectively captured during the tariff debates of the late 1880s, and their acceptance of the Restoration settlement was assured.[34] Cereal production in this region accounted for about a half of net farm output, and family farmers faced a growing need for artificial fertilizers, farm machinery, and an effective banking system which would end their dependence on the village usurer. Yet neither the elites nor the CNCA were willing to provide the necessary collateral to attract sufficient capital, and per capita cash deposits found in Castile-Leon's cooperatives and *cajas* were little more than the national average, and equivalent to only the more successful *pósitos* (Table 6.2).[35] Cooperative activity was mainly limited to bulk buying and guaranteeing fertilizer quality at a time when fraud was common, an input that had become crucial for extending the area cultivated.[36]

Galicia, was a region of tiny, family-operated farms, but had only 4.7 per cent of Spain's cooperative members and just 0.9 per cent of capital deposits in 1933, despite accounting for 13.4 per cent of farmers. Nevertheless, collective action was as strong as in any part of the country, but took other forms. A strong regional identity led to a number of government-sponsored organizations – the *Escuela de Veterinaria* (1882), the *Granja Agrícola Regional* (1888) and the *Misión Biológica* de Galicia (1921) – being well supported and playing important roles in the

---

[32] Majuelo & Pascual 1991, pp. 165–9, and Beltrán Tapia 2012, p. 516.

[33] In particular, the owners of the *corralizas*, or disentailed estates sold in the nineteenth century, were opposed to Carlism. Majuelo & Pascual 1991, pp. 182–3.

[34] Large landowners' organizations remained closely linked to the CNCA at a national level. Castillo 1979, pp. 154–60, and Varela Ortega 1977, pp. 269–70 and 278–9.

[35] A few attempts were made to build cooperative granaries, but these faced fierce opposition from established merchants.

[36] Simpson 1995, p. 119. In some cases, cooperatives provided neither the capital nor the storage facilities, but simply helped their members to organize collectively to buy fertilizers. This activity would not appear in their accounts.

local agriculture.[37] Groups of farmers bought fertilizers and farm machinery, sometimes with the support of the middle classes in the small neighbouring towns, with the spectacular diffusion of threshing machines being the most visible.[38] These initiatives were local in scope and professional in nature, which helped reduce ideological conflicts among members.

By contrast, Galician landowners were unwilling to provide the leadership to build cooperative federations and, as rentiers, were usually divorced from farming activities. From the 1890s, tenants demanded the right to purchase their land (*foro*) and this was backed by rent strikes and occasional violence, before the legal right to redemption was granted in 1926.[39] The movement was supported by republicans, liberals, and emigrants, but also attracted large numbers of Catholic groups, as well as Carlists, who were strong in the region.[40] The Church hierarchy initially opposed the movement, thereby siding with conservatives and the local *caciques*,[41] although in time it supported a moderate project that became part of the 1926 law.[42]

Landowners in the Mediterranean regions by contrast were much more active. Catalonia had the greatest penetration of cooperatives in the country, and competitive regional party politics, rather than the Church, can explain its success.[43] Local landowners and farmers began to organize from the late nineteenth century in response to the threats caused by cheap imports and the destruction of vines by phylloxera. They used state legislation to create agricultural chambers at the district level to organize thousands of owners and tenants.[44] These pressure groups were led by big landowners, and resulted in the creation of a conservative regionalist political movement (the *Lliga*), which captured the vote of many small

---

[37] Pan-Montojo 2005, chs. 5 and 6.
[38] Fernández Prieto 1992, pp. 168, 190, and 213, and Fernández Prieto 1997.
[39] Many had already been bought, helped by growing livestock sales and emigrants' remittances. Villares 1982.
[40] The republicans created *Solidaridad Gallega*, which had around 400 agrarian organizations between 1907 and 1911, copying the Catalan model (*Solidaritat*), with the objective of displacing the two Restoration political parties and end the *foro*. However, despite a successful grass-roots movement, they did not create large cooperative federations as in Catalonia. Cabo Villaverde 2006b, p. 254. The number of organizations in Pomés 2000a, p.,114, and failure in Cabo Villaverde 2006b, p. 238.
[41] Lombardero Rico 1997), 537–49, gives the example of the successful Catholic cooperative in Ribadeo, where the absence of *foros* avoided farmers' hostility.
[42] Martínez López 1989, pp.,189–90. According to Vázquez de Mella, an influential Galician Carlist who favoured agrarian syndicates, many parish priests actually sided with the *caciques*, and therefore opposed the syndicates. Rodriguez Lago 1997, p. 322.
[43] In Catalonia, the Church remained close to the rural population, and the clergy often spoke Catalan. Pomés 2000a, pp. 179 ss, Callahan 2000, pp. 158–62, and Lannon 1987, pp. 141–2.
[44] Ramon i Muñoz 1999, p. 18, and Planas 2013, pp. 103–7.

farmers before the Second Republic.[45] The *Lliga* was behind the creation of a regional organization that grouped the representatives of the four Catalan provinces into a single administrative unit (*Mancomunitat*) that helped organize and finance farm cooperatives.[46] This explains the development of increasing numbers of specialist cooperative federations, not just for wine production, but also early potatoes and vegetables, often for export. These attracted many small farmers and led to the creation of the *Unión de Sindicatos Agrícolas de Cataluña* in 1931.[47] The landowners' leadership, however, did not go uncontested. In the most important winegrowing regions, a sharecropping contract – the *Rabassa Morta* – was widely used and proved particularly contentious during the first third of the twentieth century, a time of low wine prices. Sharecroppers (*rabassaires*) helped to create the political party, *Esquerra Republicana de Catalunya* and, with urban republicans, enjoyed significant electoral success in the 1930s.[48] Given their own organizing capacity and political achievements, the rabassaires movement rejected the 'mixed' cooperatives of the landowners, although their own cooperatives had only limited success.[49]

The cooperative movement in the Levante region was also successful. Not only did 35 per cent of farmers belong to one, but almost a quarter of the national deposits of cooperatives with over 100,000 pesetas were found here in 1933, while its rural *cajas* accounted for a similar figure. Large landowners were interested in promoting agricultural advances, especially in the export sector, but regional cooperative federations remained weak. In particular, and unlike Catalonia, the use of regional politics against the dynastic parties failed to create effective organizations, and the most successful, the *Federación Agraria del Levante* (FAL) founded in 1901, was unable to overcome intra-provincial and sectoral rivalries, and its most successful local cooperatives actually left to operate on their own.[50] Instead, cooperative success owned more to high levels of farm specialization, encouraged by irrigation and strong export and urban demand for high-value farm produce.

Although the limited participation of both the Church hierarchy and rural elites restricted the development of Spain's cooperatives and farm associations, there were some important regional differences (Table 6.3).

---

[45] Riquer 2001, p. 210, and for Lerida after 1917, Ramon i Muñoz 1999, p. 17.
[46] Casanova i Prat 1998, pp. 396–408.
[47] Pomés 2000a. Planas 2008 cites the examples of Catholic and Republican cooperatives that left their respective federations to join more professionally orientated ones.
[48] Riquer 2001, p. 211, and Balcells 1980, pp. 150–1.
[49] Conflicts date from after 1918. Pomés 2000a, p. 506.
[50] The FAL in Martínez Gallego 2010 and Martínez Soto 2000. For the difficulties to federate cooperatives, Garrido 1996; the conflicts between provinces, in Martínez Gallego 2010.

Table 6.3 *Explanations for regional cooperative success*

	% of farmers belonging to a cooperative in 1933	Do rural elites actively encourage agricultural change?	Where there major conflicts over land tenure?	Strength of dynastic parties at local level/ caciquismo	Strength of regional cleavage (foralismo)	Political strength of rural Carlism	Importance of wheat farming (% of farm output) [1]	Presence of dynamic 'local' markets
Castile-León	19.4	No	No	High	Low	Parts of Castile	49.0	No
Navarra	35.2	Yes	No	Weak	High	High	34.1	No
Catalonia	37.7	Yes	Yes	Weak	High	Limited	21.1	Yes
Valencia	35.3	Yes	No	Average	Low	High	13.9	Yes
Galicia	6.7	No	Yes	High	Low	High	19.5	No

[1] This is a proxy for the difficulty to shift to higher-value farm products.

Conflicts over local land-tenure regimes (Galicia, Catalonia) and the nature of farming also played a part in shaping the form of collective action most appropriate to regional needs. However, and with few exceptions, the family farmer was poorly represented politically on the eve of the Second Republic.

Farm Lobbies and the Wheat Question

Falling transport costs from the late nineteenth century allowed farmers across the world to export cheap temperate and tropical farm products to European consumers, leaving many of the Old World's farmers uncompetitive almost overnight. In Spain, the farm crisis was delayed, but cereal producers from the early 1880s started to complain of competition from low-cost New World producers, and olive oil growers from cheaper vegetable oils. By the 1890s, livestock producers faced threats from imported meats, while wine producers saw their vines devastated by phylloxera. At the same time as farmers were threatened with lower prices, labour costs were rising because of industrialization and emigration.

The widespread need for dry-farming in Spain limited the possibilities for farmers to increase yields or switch to new crops. Wheat was by far the most important crop, representing about a fifth of total farm output, and perhaps half of all farm households were involved in its production to some extent or another, especially at harvest time.[51] It was the major staple of the national diet, supplying over a third of calorie intake.[52] Cheap imported food and beverages promised to benefit urban workers and threaten a massive switch in purchasing power away from the countryside to the cities. The large modern flour-milling installations located at the ports would also benefit from imports at the expense of the thousands of small, traditional millers, many of whom were local caciques, who bought grain from family farmers. By contrast, tariffs promised not only higher rents for landowners and better prices for farmers, but also revenue for the government.

The grain 'invasion' sparked a major debate, and many European governments held official enquires to gather information on their country's agriculture.[53] In Spain, this led to the publication of the massive *La Crisis Agrícola y Pecuaria* (1887–9), which highlighted the government's

---

[51] Montojo Sureda 1945, p. 15, argued that wheat was grown by two million farmers, equivalent to about 80 per cent of the nation's total, based on figures in Carmona et al. 2019, p. 676.

[52] The figure declined from around 40 per cent in 1900 to 37 per cent in 1930. Simpson 1989, table 5.

[53] For government surveys, see especially Vivier 2014.

very limited knowledge concerning the area cultivated, production, and stocks, even of the major crops. The Liberal government of the day responded to some of the Enquiry's suggestions, including tax reductions, the creation of farm schools and experimental farms, legal changes to encourage irrigation, as well as help in the fight against phylloxera and combating other disease and plagues.[54] Yet relatively little was actually done.[55] Instead, the *Liga Agraria* between 1887 and 1889 lobbied for higher tariffs, as well as lower taxes and rail freight, and an end to the imports of industrial alcohol.[56] The tariff debate allowed cereal and livestock farmers, sectors both dominated by large landowners, to form an alliance with the major industrial groups, and extend tariffs in 1891 to their products.[57] This ensured not only that wheat prices fell less in Spain than in most other Western European nations (Figure 6.1), removing the necessity for the country's farmers to adjust, but it also avoided the need for direct state intervention in the sector and the provision of public goods to make farmers more competitive. The fact that wheat tariffs were set at levels that kept small, marginal producers in Castile-Leon in production would considerably benefit the large commercial farmers on the fertile soils of Andalucia.[58]

The grain invasion not only threatened lower prices, but it radically changed the nature of cereal markets. Previously, a poor harvest had been accompanied by high prices, with low ones following a large harvest. In the Old Regime, Government intervention was therefore associated with attempting to reduce the highly volatile wheat and bread prices that consumers faced.[59] By contrast, the integration of cereal markets across different production zones now left the farmers facing high income volatility, as they were no longer compensated by high prices after poor harvest, while consumers saw much smaller annual price movements.[60] Small farmers found it much harder to adapt, and were forced to sell immediately after the harvest when prices were at

---

[54] The decrees for these changes refer specifically to the final reports of the Enquiry and the need to respond to the agricultural crisis caused by foreign competition through technological change and an intensification of cultivation. Serrano Sanz 1987, p. 101.

[55] As Chapter 5 noted, the powerful AAE enjoyed close connections with the political elites, and was generally unwilling to challenge government policy, although its general philosophy was to modernize agriculture and encourage exports, rather than protection. Pan-Montojo 2007, especially pp. 97–104.

[56] Pan-Montojo 2000, p. 44.

[57] By contrast, both the olive and vine were dominated by small producers and depended on export markets. For the tariff question, see especially Tena 1999.

[58] Bernal 1985, p. 261.   [59] Castro 1987.

[60] Simpson 2001. Fluctuations in wheat yields were exceptionally high for Europe. Montojo Sureda 1945, p. 15, and Hevesy 1940, p. 605.

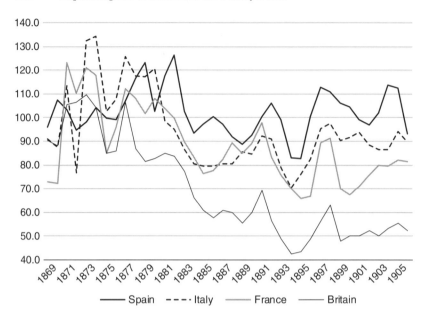

Figure 6.1 Wheat prices in select countries during the late nineteenth
century, 1869/73 = 100
Source: Simpson 2001, p. 102.

their lowest, because they needed cash to pay taxes, repay loans, and
for day-to-day consumption needs. Larger farmers stood to gain, not
only through their activities as moneylenders, but also because they
could hold back wheat to benefit from the higher prices paid later in
the year. Spanish governments could now regulate domestic markets by
allowing grain imports when domestic prices moved too high, as world
prices were much lower.

A major test to this policy was the First World War, when European food
prices soared, and Spanish merchants could now benefit by exporting
wheat and flour. The government tried to manage shortages by restricting
exports, and establishing maximum prices (*tasa*), although it lacked adequate mechanisms to enforce them. Policy from the First World War had
a number of important long-run consequences. In the first instance, high
prices led to a significant increase in the area cultivated, and between 1905/
14 and 1926/35, the area of wheat sown and production increased by just
over a fifth, slightly faster than population growth.[61] The clearing and
preparing of large areas of land to be brought into cultivation created

[61] The area increased by 21 per cent, production by 24 per cent, and population by
19 per cent in Simpson 1995, table 11.4. The increase in wheat production almost

Table 6.4 *Domestic wheat production and consumption of basic foods in various countries, c.1930*

	% Self-sufficiency in wheat (1925/9)	Daily calorie intake	Annual per capital consumption (kgs) in 1930s			Kilos bought with one hour of work by building workers (January 1930)		
			Flour	Meat	Sugar	Bread	Meat	Sugar
Spain	96.9	2,760	146.4	28.1	11.6	1.8	0.27	0.7
France	86.2	2,880	123.7	55.2	24.3	2.3	0.29	1.1
Germany	83.9	3,040	113.0	52.8	26.3	3.1	0.50	2.1
Italy	74.0	2,520	160.4	20.1	7.9	1.5	0.25	0.4
Ireland	na	3,400	131.4	54.9	38.1	2.8	0.64	2.4
GB	21.2	3,110	95.3	62.6	44.5	3.4	0.71	2.7

Sources: Yates 1960, table 2.4, and Simpson 1995, tables 8.1, 8.2, and 8.3.

significant employment opportunities, especially in central Spain (Chapter 7).[62] Another factor was that although tariffs had made Spain virtually self-sufficient in wheat by the late 1920s, basic foods were often more expensive than in other Western European countries, and workers' diets were poorer (Table 6.4).[63] At the extreme, with an hour's wage, a British labourer could buy almost twice the amount of bread than a Spanish worker; nearly three times more meat; and four times more sugar. This difference was the result not only of natural resources and the need for extensive farming practices, but also government policy. Tariffs, including at times an outright prohibition on imports, allowed farmers to increase output, and the government to tax them.

Finally, tariffs protected the economic position of the landowning elites. In Spain, the farm lobby demanded higher farm prices, and not tenure reform or lower rents. David Ricardo had argued that a prolonged fall in wheat prices would produce a fall in farm rents, as tenants would find it unprofitable to renew their old leases, but even in countries with free trade, legislation was often needed to help tenants improve their bargaining power, and reduce that of landowners. This failed to happen in Spain.

certainly began earlier, probably from the late 1890s, but the statistical quality is too poor to be certain. See especially GEHR 1983b.

[62] The greater integration of domestic markets produced by motorized transport and telephone communications reduced the incentives for political parties to demand government research in dry-farming technologies.

[63] See Palafox 1991, pp. 39–40 for the negative impact of high food costs for industry. See also Gallego Martínez 2016.

Wheat and the Crisis of the Family Farm in the 1930s

Jules Ferry's comments that France's Third Republic needed to be a peasant's republic, was just as true for Spain's Second Republic. Yet not only did the Socialist Party struggle to attract the vote of landless workers, but all parties found it difficult to respond effectively to small farmer and tenant demands to maintain their living standards during the economic depression. The failure to find practical solutions for the family farmer would discredit the Republic, and offered political opportunities for the rural elites to widen their support networks and defend themselves against the Republic's attacks on their property (Chapter 9).

The Second Republic inherited a situation of virtual wheat self-sufficiency which combined volatile and often uneconomical grain prices for farmers, with expensive bread for consumers. The area of wheat cultivation reached its twentieth-century peak in 1934 at a massive 4.6 million hectares, and the harvest of that year would only be surpassed in 1967.[64] The problem of overproduction was not unique to Spain, although the relative size of its farm sector and the high cost of food made the situation worse than in most other countries. Governments could reduce food prices for consumers by allowing more imports, but this would have created more unemployment and economic hardship in the countryside, and was therefore seen as politically unacceptable to rural voters.

By the early 1930s, a number of European governments were attempting to intervene directly in the cereal commodity chain. The idea was to create a monopoly to buy the harvest, and then to release the grain onto the market in an orderly fashion over the year. Flour and bread prices were also to be fixed. In theory, farmers would enjoy a guaranteed market, allowing the wheat agency to provide them with credit and working capital. However, large amounts of capital were required to build the grain silos and finance operations, as well as an organizational capacity that even the most advanced governments lacked. Furthermore, successful price support risked encouraging farmers to increase output even more. In France, the state could count on a strong cooperative federation for storing and milling, but it took several years to establish the *Office du Blé* wheat agency, while in Germany the State Food Corporation (RNS) was created with a view of guaranteeing food supplies during a war (Chapter 2).[65] In Spain, discussions for intervention on a major scale began only towards the end of the Republic but, as Rafael del Caño noted, the government had neither the necessary financial resources nor the capacity to operate it.[66] It would be left to the Franco regime to implement a state monopoly after 1939.

---

[64] Barciela López et al. 2005, pp. 302–3 and 307–8.
[65] Chatriot 2016, esp. pp. 62–3, 132, and 394.   [66] del Caño 1933, p. 108.

Instead the Spanish government was forced to use two distinct, but equally inefficient mechanisms to help wheat farmers. The first was to modify the *tasa*, and require merchants to pay farmers a minimum price. This might have worked at times of scarcity, but with overproduction it failed to produce either a fair price for farmers or cheap bread for urban consumers.[67] One problem was that wheat farmers received a falling share of the bread price during the first third of the twentieth century because of a combination of technological changes in transportation, storage, milling, and bread-making. Wheat is relatively homogenous and easily stored, so production can take place at considerable distances from consumption, leading to the lengthening of commodity chains, at a time of falling per capita consumption.[68] Governments during the Second Republic attempted to fix prices at each stage of the commodity chain but, while urban consumers found it relatively easy to organize against 'cheating' by bakers, farmers found it impossible to force merchants to buy their grain, especially following the massive harvests of 1932 and 1934.[69] Even the government price index recorded prices below the official maximum price levels (Figure 6.1).[70] The situation was made worse as large farmers, who had traditionally held back their harvest to benefit from higher prices later in the year, now also sold immediately after the harvest. Merchants preferred to buy from them because of the greater volumes involved and the fact that larger farmers were more willing to accept deferred payments. By contrast, small farmers needed to sell quickly to repay loans and pay taxes but, without a guaranteed market for their wheat, they were effectively excluded from credit markets.

Another problem was that the Spanish governments still lacked good information concerning the area cultivated, the size of the harvest, and stocks (Appendix 1). Indeed, there was considerable debate over whether the wheat area was actually increasing or decreasing, and the Valladolid newspaper, *El Norte de Castilla*, continued to publish its own estimates for

---

[67] Boletín del Instituto de Reforma Agraria (BIRA), 46, April 1936, p. 414.
[68] In the United States in the late 1930s, for example, wheat farmers received just 13 per cent of the retail price of bread, compared to 54 per cent for meat producers; 77 per cent for egg producers; or 35 per cent of fresh fruit and vegetables. Shepherd 1947, table 20.
[69] Small farmers often signed forms saying that they had received the stipulated price, although they were actually paid less. del Caño 1933, pp. 71–4.
[70] Palafox 1991, p. 245.

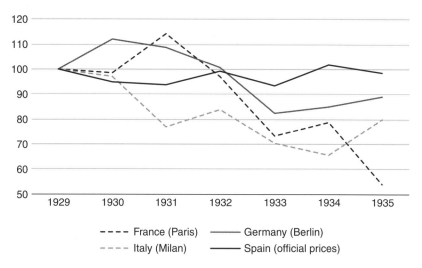

Figure 6.2 Wheat prices in select countries during the Great Depression
Sources: Hevesy 1940, appendix 32, and Barciela López et al. 2005,
p. 337.

the national harvest.[71] The lack of information on stocks held by merchants
and farmers led to the politically disastrous decision to import wheat to
depress bread prices in the months before the 1932 harvest, which would be
the country's largest to date.[72] Government attempts to store surplus stock
(Law of June 1935) proved enormously expensive, and failed to remove
market uncertainty, as merchants could not predict when the government
would release them onto the market. Furthermore, farmers reacted to
a wheat-friendly government by maintaining output, especially as dry-
farming production conditions offered few alternatives. Low wheat prices
and rising production costs now provided large landowners and farmers with
the opportunity to attract small farmers to their cause, and attack the
Republican governments, especially those of the centre-left between
June 1931 and November 1933, for supposedly benefitting urban rather
than rural interests.[73] Therefore a problem caused by the international crisis
and the inherited weak government capacity was portrayed as being produced by incompetent republican politicians.[74]

---

[71] For a discussion, see del Caño 1933, pp. 102–4 and Torres 1944.
[72] Montojo Sureda 1945, pp. 39–40.
[73] Torres 1934 and especially the short survey of the literature in Robledo 1993, pp.
94–100.
[74] Along these lines, del Caño 1933, pp. 9–10.

The Left-Republican and Socialist government in the spring and early summer of 1931 also attempted to improve farm incomes *and* reduce food prices by setting 'fair' rents and protecting tenants from eviction, except in cases of non-payment of rent.[75] 'Fair' rents implied a reduction, and were initially justified because of the 'extraordinary situation' caused by the poor harvest of that year, low farm prices, and rising costs, and were supposed to be a preliminary measure before the introduction of more radical tenancy reforms. When voluntary agreements failed, local tribunals of landowner and tenants settled demands which, given the political conditions across much of Spain in 1931 and 1932, were usually beneficial to tenants. A recent study of the district of Caceres (Extremadura) highlights just how significant the rent reductions could be, as a total of 649 cases were brought before the local tribunal, covering a quarter of all farm land, and perhaps a half of all that was rented. The average reduction achieved was of the order of 28 per cent, benefitting both large and small tenant farmers (Table 6.5).[76]

Rent reductions on this scale promised to improve farm profitability at the expense of landowners, rather than the consumers. However, there

Table 6.5 *Rent reductions demanded and amounts achieved in Caceres in the early 1930s*

		Relative success of demands	
Number of cases	Average % rent reduction demanded	% reduction	Reduction as % of amount demanded
3	25	33	100+%
4	40	40	100%
8	41	37	80–100%
26	49	34	66–80%
53	52	29	50–56%
35	63	26	33–50%
18	54	14	33%+
Total 147	Average 53	Average 28	

Only 156 of the 649 cases provide the necessary information for this table. For a variety of reasons, no reductions were given in nine cases.
Source: Carmona & Simpson 2014a, cuadro 7.

---

[75] Decrees of 11/7/1931 and 29/4/1931. These degrees were just the first of more than a dozen. See Alvarez Jusué 1933 and Carmona & Simpson 2014a, on which this paragraph is based.
[76] Carmona & Simpson 2014a, pp. 190–1 and 193.

were major problems in using rent controls in this way, even if many contemporaries believed that rental agreements, especially subleasing, were a major cause of inefficiency in Spanish farming. In particular there was a problem of calculating a 'market' rent, as the cadastre still covered only 46 per cent of the country, and even in these areas price levels were those that were prevailing when the survey was carried out, rather than those of 1931. Where there was still no cadastre, the tribunals had to use the *amillaramientos*, which were not only notorious inaccurate, but also unfair, making it difficult for even an objective tribunal to decide. In exceptional cases, landowners paid so little tax that the tribunals awarded rent reductions of as much as 90 per - cent.[77] This made it very difficult to achieve voluntary agreements between the two parties, perhaps explaining the large numbers who turned to the tribunals in Caceres. However in Toro (Zamora), where the cadastre was finished, rent reductions of between 15 and 25 per cent were also common.[78] From October 1931 the government required tribunals to estimate a 'fair' market rent, which took into consideration a range of factors, including the economic situation of the landowner and tenant, and placed a maximum permissible reduction of 50 per cent.

With weak prices, the incentive for small family cereal farmers with limited land was to try to produce more by working harder to maintain incomes, as they could not cut wage costs. The problems would have been less dramatic if the demand for labour had been stronger in the cities, or if farmers could have switched to other crops that could be grown under dry-farming conditions. In fact, government policies, such as land reform and irrigation, threatened to *increase* wheat production at a time when per capita consumption was stagnant or even falling, as did the 1931 legislation that prohibited farmers taking land out of cultivation (Chapter 7).

The response to the wine protests in the Midi in 1907 showed how government legislation could provide a legal framework for village organizations brought together in a strong regional federation, to police the sector, and enforce the laws against wine adulteration.[79] By contrast, Spanish governments showed little interest in legislating to help small wine producers, and there were no strong village organizations and federations outside Catalonia. The demands of small producers included a reduction or elimination of the highly regressive

---

[77] Ibid., p. 186.
[78] This was achieved in 69 per cent of cases, with 13 per cent being less than this figure, and 18 per cent more. Ruiz González 2011, p. 107.
[79] Simpson 2011, pp. 65–70.

local taxes, the enforcement of laws against fraud, and the restriction on the use of cheap, industrial alcohol for strengthening wines. Yet while French governments supported small growers' organizations, in Spain they preferred to listen to the demands of wine exporters, and their need to strengthen them with cheap spirits to compete in foreign markets, or the sugar producers, who produced the industrial alcohol, and were happy to pay high taxes in exchange for a guaranteed market.[80]

Conclusions

This chapter has shown how the rural elites and Church were able to maintain their political and economic power by not having to participate in competitive party politics. Chapter 9 will show that the Socialist Party, unlike in France, also showed virtually no interest in helping small farmers. The consequence was that Spanish governments from 1875 to 1931 did little to help the family farmer in the fields of tax reform, provision of cheap credit, tenure reforms, research and farm extension, or infrastructure investment. As a result, although the numbers who owned or rented some land increased from 2.1 to 2.7 million between 1860 and 1930, a jump from 60 to 72 per cent of the total farm population, perhaps only a fifth of them could claim to be independent 'free farmers'. This is considerably less than elsewhere in Western Europe, with the exceptions of Italy and Portugal.[81]

The nature of political competition between the two Restoration parties also created few incentives to improve state capacity, especially as the two major exogenous shocks to hit Western European agricultural sectors before the 1920s, namely the late nineteenth century Agrarian Depression and the food shortages of the First World War, were quickly resolved. Tariffs in the first case were sufficient to protect most producers, although wine and olive farmers faced greater problems to adjust. During the First World War, the Spanish governments continued to depend on landowners, a group that benefited from the high prices. The result was that traditional land-tenure regimes, where the cacique played a crucial role in connecting village society with central government, remained essentially unchanged. Governments were obliged to use these intermediaries whenever they wanted to tax villagers or allocate public goods, and the village cacique was expected to protect and reward his supporters. Weak

---

[80] See especially Pan-Montojo 1994 and Fernández 2008.
[81] Table 4.3. This figure assumes that 90 per cent of those in the North had access to land.

civic associations, as suggested by the cooperative movement, made it difficult for the state to obtain objective farm or even village-level information. Chapter 7 looks more closely at the economic and political effects of the large estates in Southern Spain, and the difficulties that governments of the Second Republic had in implementing reforms and, in particular, wide-reaching land reform.

Part IV

Rural Elites, Poverty, and the Attempts at Land Reform

[T]he profitable running of the large estates is based on minimum wages and periodic unemployment for four or five months a year, during which farm labourers cannot work nor eat.[1]

A long historical tradition suggests that the landed elites in the thirteen latifundio provinces across central and southern Spain were an important obstacle to economic and political change, and the direct cause of large numbers of landless or near landless families living in extreme poverty. Contemporaries such as Manuel Azaña, the Republic's first Prime Minister, was one of many who believed that high farm profits were made by paying starvation wages, and the British journalist Henry Buckley believed that many Spaniards saw the Second Republic as the opportunity to end 'feudal society' and remove a landed elite that supposedly obstructed democracy, restricted economic growth, and caused rural poverty. The fact that an important section of the landed elite supported the July 1936 coup d'état is seen by some historians as further evidence to their opposition to democracy.[2]

The relation between the nature of landownership and long-run economic development has generated a large literature over the past decade or so, especially for the Americas.[3] According to one theory, the landed elites that initially owned the large estates and plantations in Latin America, the Caribbean, and the US South also controlled the governments, and created institutions that helped to perpetuate their political and economic influence for centuries, turning to military force whenever the situation was needed. The 'extractive' nature of these institutions harmed long-run economic growth, and produced high levels of inequality, widespread poverty, illiteracy, a regressive tax system, restrictive franchise, as well as weak state capacity. Only when late industrialization

---

[1] Azaña, cited in Espinosa 2007, p. 27.
[2] For example, Tuñon de Lara et al. 1985, pp. 40–1and 59–60, Preston 1978, p. 239, and especially Casanova 1994.
[3] Major contributions include Acemoglu & Robinson 2012, Engerman & Sokokoff 2012, and the review by Williamson 2012.

began to diversify the economies, and new political demands led to a growth in state capacity, did the influence of the landed elites begin to diminish.[4] By contrast, in societies of small, family farmers that predominated over much of North America, 'inclusive' institutions were created which encouraged economic growth, low levels of income inequality, and the early appearance of democratic society.

Historians are often much more sympathetic to Western Europe's landed elites, emphasizing their contribution as entrepreneurs that stimulated, rather than frustrated, economic change. Their modernizing role had several dimensions, ranging from introducing farming improvements on their estates which were subsequently copied by small, neighbouring farmers to directly intervening to assist their tenants, or creating local organizations, such as annual farm shows, that diffused new practices. In Britain, for example, a significant literature since Arthur Young has stressed the positive role of the landed elites in helping tenant farmers to adapt cultivation practices to compete in a rapidly changing market place.[5] In France, as noted, the rural elites from 1900 encouraged small farmers to create cooperatives and, through the use of sharecropping contracts, introduced improvements in viticulture and livestock farming.[6] A reassessment of Denmark's successful cooperative movement also stresses the crucial role played by the landed elite in the late eighteenth century in improving dairy farming and widening markets for small family farmers.[7]

These contrasting visions of Latin America and Western Europe suggest a better understanding is needed of when landed elites encouraged development, and when they obstructed it. In particular, although Spain's landed elites were able to maintain their political power and failed to help organize small farmers before 1931, it is not obvious why they should want to badly cultivate their estates, which supposedly caused so much rural poverty. In fact, this section argues that landownership was neither static over time, nor did it create the formidable obstacles to economic growth as perhaps it did in Latin America. Farming on Andalusia's latifundios changed significantly from the turn of the twentieth century and social indicators for workers improved considerably, albeit from low levels. Nevertheless, agricultural modernization required a protected cereal market, and widespread rural poverty continued to be found on the eve of the Second Republic.

---

[4] Albertus 2015, pp. 49–58.   [5] Beckett 1990, especially pp. 28–30, for a brief survey.
[6] Cleary 1989, and for viticulture in Beaujolais, Carmona, & Simpson 2012, pp. 900–1, and livestock in western France, Carmona 2006, pp. 245–8.
[7] Lampe & Sharp 2018.

Just as in the US South or Southern Italy, Andalucia in the mid-nineteenth century was a comparatively wealthy region, enjoying the country's second highest GDP per capita, and accounting for nine of the twenty largest cities, despite having only a fifth of Spain's population.[8] Growing market integration from the late nineteenth century led to agricultural specialization, and the industrial sector remained heavily dependent on natural resources, especially food processing and alcoholic beverages, and failed to attract the new, high-productivity industries associated with higher levels of human capital.[9] Mining also became increasingly important although, and unlike the Basque Country, it developed weak linkages with the regional economy and the sector entered a severe downturn from the end of the First World War.[10] By 1930, labour productivity in Spanish agriculture was only 39 per cent of that found in industry and 29 per cent in services, but three-fifths of Andalusia's workforce was still found in this sector. Furthermore, labour productivity in Andalusia's agriculture was only 75 per cent of this low national figure.[11] As a result the region's GDP per capita grew relatively slowly between 1860 and 1930, and on the eve of the Second Republic it had fallen to twelfth of the country's seventeen regions. The experience of Extremadura and La Mancha, the two other regions dominated by latifundios, was even poorer.[12]

This combination of slow economic growth and relatively high levels of rural poverty encouraged the first Republican governments to attempt a major land reform to break up the large estates and create a more egalitarian and democratic society. In theory, a redistributive land reform such as the World Bank might propose today, would change work incentives and encourage small farmers to grow crops that made better use of their labour, increasing farm output and reducing rural poverty. Therefore, a redistributive land reform promised not just political and social benefits but also economic ones. Yet this failed to happen in Spain in the 1930s because weak state capacity greatly exaggerated the possibilities for land reform, while its slow implementation encouraged the

[8] Rosés et al. 2010, table 1. The region's population increased from 18.9 per cent to 19.6 per cent between 1857 and 1930. Nicolau 2005, cuadro 2.32. Parejo 2009, p. 228.
[9] Rosés 2003. However, technical change was also significant in many food industries during the first third of the twentieth century.
[10] Perhaps half of Spain's mining industry was foreign owned in 1913. Although a few companies, such as Rio Tinto, were highly profitable, only one in five made profits. Harvey & Taylor 1987, pp. 199–200.
[11] Calculated from Rosés et al. 2010. Labour productivity refers to value added per workers.
[12] Andalucia was ninth in 1900, and Castilla-La Mancha was fifteenth and Extremadura seventeenth in 1930. Rosés et al. 2010, table 1, and Parejo 2009, p. 228. In 1930, it still had seven of the country's largest cities, but their relative size had declined sharply, and in terms of population fell from 36 to 19 per cent of the total.

landless in western Spain to invade and illegally occupy farms. The experience of land reform therefore frustrated many of those in need, while it alienated not just the landed elite, but also many small farmers.

Chapter 7 shows that despite contemporary opinion, latifundios were not only usually well cultivated by the standards of the day, but living standards for workers had improved in the half-century prior to the Republic. What marks Southern Spain out from Northern European countries is not that the landed elites failed to modernize their farms, but rather that there were few knowledge spill-overs that could benefit small farmers, and the need for dry-farming limited the possibilities to intensify labour inputs. Tariffs kept farm prices high and, because cereals required relatively little labour, the minimum size of a viable family farm under dry-farming conditions was 25 to 30 hectares (Appendix 2). Both the olive and vine were much more suitable for small farmers under dry-farming conditions, but weak farm prices during the 1930s discouraged using large amounts of labour to increase the cultivated area. Chapter 8 looks at the two types of land reform attempted during the period: the highly centralized top-down reform initiative of 1932, and the temporary settlements following the massive land invasions in western Spain. We argue that in both cases improvements in living standards were limited and efficiency gains almost non-existent. Nevertheless, land reform provided a useful platform for the Right to overcome its organizational problems and centre the ideological debate over the legitimacy of private property, rather than the persistence of a powerful landed elite (Part V).

7   Landownership, Economic Development, and Poverty in Andalusia and Southern Spain

> Gavin Wright writing for the US South, notes that 'many of the characteristics of backwardness, such as low-wage, low-skill industry, under-investment in education, even capital scarcity, were rooted in the regional character of the labour market.[1]

> Control of the state implies control of the definition, generation, and appropriation of public services (credit, technology, information, infrastructure, etc.) and policies (terms of trade).[2]

It was the agrarian problem in southern Spain, and especially Andalucia and Extremadura, that most occupied Spanish society in the 1930s. Contemporaries believed that large numbers of landless workers lived in extreme poverty *at the same time* as absentee landowners left significant areas of fertile land abandoned, or under-cultivated. These landowners and their tenant farmers supposedly maintained a privileged position through a combination of patronage and the strict enforcement of law and order by the state, with the Church providing its moral backing. By contrast, landless workers were often forbidden from organizing trade unions, driving political activists underground, and thereby creating Europe's largest rural anarchist movement. The need to resolve the plight of the landless labourers was considered a top priority for most republicans in 1931.

Land ownership in southern Spain was heavily concentrated, both on the rich cereal lands of the Guadalquivir valley (*Campiña*), as well as the huge *dehesas* found in the less populated upland regions. Farms of over 250 hectares numbered just 0.3 per cent of total holdings, but covered 41.2 per cent of the area and produced 27.8 per cent of the taxable income, while in Andalucia, which included the most fertile regions, they represented 51 per cent of the total area, and 33 per cent of income.[3] Around three-fifths of Andalusia's active population worked in agriculture, and perhaps 40 per cent of these were landless in the early 1930s, although Carrión believed that as many as 95 per cent of

---

[1] Wright 1986, p. 52.   [2] Janvry 1981, p. 110.
[3] Malefakis 1970, table 3 and appendix C. Our calculations.

landowners earned less than a peseta a day after expenses from their land.[4] It was also widely believed that landed elites or their agents controlled local and national elections; passed legislation to further their interests; and implemented laws in ways which increased their political patronage.

This chapter examines the historical evidence concerning poor cultivation and the nature and causes of the rural poverty to understand better the demands placed on the new Republic. It argues that the structure of land ownership was not an obstacle to increasing farm output during the half century before the Second Republic and, despite high levels of inequality, living standards improved for most workers, at least until the Great Depression. Instead, the agrarian problem in Southern Spain is explained by a combination of three inter-related factors: the growth in cyclical unemployment; the emergence of new, labour-saving farm technologies for cereal farming; and the difficulties associated with developing labour-intensive crops in areas of dry-farming. Against this worsening economic background, the political events of the Second Republic significantly increased the opportunities for organizing the landless and near-landless workers, sparking widespread conflicts (Chapter 10).

This chapter is centred on Andalucia, the region that most worried contemporaries because of its supposedly greater agricultural potential, although mention is also made of the two other latifundio regions (Extremadura and La Mancha), that were also subject to the 1932 Land Reform. It is divided into three major sections. The first challenges contemporary beliefs that latifundios were inefficient by showing that farmers were quick to respond to changes in factor and commodity prices. In fact, large farms by the late 1920s were especially suitable for extensive cereals and livestock given the growing possibilities for reducing labour costs through mechanization, and the difficulties facing labour-intensive olive and vine cultivation.[5] The second section shows that the living standards of rural workers improved over time, although they were vulnerable to economic downturns because of the erosion of traditional safety nets, and the failure of the state to create new ones. The final section shows the influence of the latifundios on agricultural development and why landowners created limited demands to increase state capacity.

[4] Carmona et al. 2019, Carrión 1932: 1975, p. 104, and Appendix 2.
[5] The area dedicated to other high-value crops in 1931, such as cotton (5,282 hectares), cane sugar (3,833 hectares), sugar beet (28,727 hectares), or oranges (5,249 hectares) was still relatively small. Instituto de Estadística de Andalucía 2002.

Adapting to Markets: Landownership and the Limits to Agricultural Growth

Southern Spain experienced widespread labour unrest at the turn of the twentieth century which was only ended by a severe drought; this left farm workers with eight or nine months of forced unemployment, 'without receiving a day's wage'.[6] The government's concern was such that it instructed the *Instituto de Reformas Sociales* (IRS) to carry out a major enquiry in 1902 to look into the living conditions of rural workers in Andalucía and Extremadura, and the following year it offered a prize for the best report on 'The agrarian problem of southern Spain: suggestions to harmonize the interests of the landowners and workers and raise agrarian output'. This attracted 74 entries, with many contributors believing that the lack of farm employment was caused by large farmers following extensive crop rotations and leaving large areas of fertile land as natural pasture.[7]

Benítez Porral, for example, argued that the persistence of traditional 'organic' agricultural practices explained this under-cultivation, as the lack of working capital made output largely dependent on labour inputs, rather than mineral fertilizers, and led to a damaging cycle of low livestock densities, scarcity of manure, the need for extensive cultivation, and lack of population living in the countryside.[8] High feed costs made intensive livestock farming unprofitable and often left work animals badly fed and weak, explaining the frequent complaints that tillage was poorly carried out, with ploughs doing little more than scratching the surface.[9] This bottle-neck was solved in the seventeenth and eighteenth centuries in Northern Europe when winter fodder allowed an increase in work numbers, but in the south the lack of summer pasture and high cost of feed was only resolved by mechanization. Another problem according to Quevedo was that absentee landowners were divorced from the day-to-day farming problems which limited their interest in the local economy, while Benítez Porral found the indifference of the ruling classes to agricultural and technical studies even more depressing than the ignorance of the general population.[10] Another complaint was that the short-term nature of rental contracts supposedly gave tenants few

---

[6] Díaz del Moral 1928: 1973, p. 207, writing of Cordoba.
[7] The contest was won by Celedonio Rodrigáñez. See Carmona & Simpson 2013.
[8] Noriega y Abascal 1897, cited in Benítez Porral 1904, p. 125. Rodrigáñez 1904: 1977, pp. 280–1, wrote that 'perhaps the main cause of our backwardness is the abnormal relations between cattle ranching and cultivation, which impoverishes national agriculture'.
[9] Benítez Porral 1904, p. 105.
[10] Quevedo y García Lomas 1904, p. 16, and Benítez Porral 1904, p. 130.

incentives to invest in fertilizers to improve soil fertility, which had long-term benefits.[11] Finally, as Peyron had noted a century earlier, the fact that most workers lived in large villages rather than the countryside left large areas unpopulated, making it unprofitable to cultivate the land.[12] Quevedo estimated that cereals produced a profit of 26.5 pesetas per hectare when cultivated within a kilometre of the village, but this figure dropped to 18 pesetas when the distance increased to two kilometres; 9 pesetas at three; 2 pesetas at four; and a loss of 7 pesetas when they were five kilometres away.[13] This author claimed that farmers possessed the necessary scientific knowledge to cultivate their land intensely and create more employment, but it was simply unprofitable. He proposed to redistribute land (*reparto*) in a 'scientific and rational' way, and for workers to live near the fields. Most authors at the turn of the twentieth century still believed that land reform was unnecessary, and even Quevedo argued that it should be limited to those estates that were obviously under-cultivated, and found in areas with widespread unemployment.[14]

Andalusia's agriculture saw major changes over the next three decades, but the complaints concerning absentee landowners and extensive farming practices did not disappear, and the number of contemporaries that considered land reform as necessary to reduce rural poverty increased. Officially, almost 60 per cent of the active male population was still employed in agriculture in Andalucia on the eve of the Second Republic (Table 7.1). However, the classification of labour in farm and non-farm occupations is far more complex than what the official census figures suggest, as workers were often employed part-time in a variety of activities, including farming, construction, transport, mining or charcoal production. Women were rarely included in the census figures (Appendix 1). The lack of full-time farm employment encouraged workers to live in large villages or towns to allow them to exchange information concerning employment opportunities and strengthened social networks. However,

---

[11] Quevedo y García Lomas 1904, pp. 100–1. In theory, when landlords provided the capital, tenants would be tempted to over-cultivate and exhaust the land, and then leave. By contrast, when tenants invested, landowners could evict them before they enjoyed the benefits, and then raise the rent.

[12] Peyron 1808, pp. 30–6.

[13] Quevedo y García Lomas 1904, pp. 73–4. In Castile-Leon, another region of dry-farming, villages were much smaller and closer to each other. Carmona & Simpson 2003, ch. 7, and Carmona & Simpson 2007a, pp. 296–8.

[14] Quevedo y García Lomas 1904, p. 11. The 1907 Colonization Law incorporated many of these ideas.

Table 7.1 *Structure of male employment in
Andalucia, 1860–1930*

	Agriculture	Industry	Services
1860	61 (63)	15	25
1900	70 (71)	15	15
1930	57 (47)	20	23

Source: Instituto de Estadística de Andalucía 2002, p. 78.
Figures for Spain in brackets.

and as noted above, it made intensive cultivation on distant fields difficult.

The relatively large numbers of casual workers and the highly seasonal nature of labour demand also distorts our vision of the region's agricultural performance. Labour productivity in Andalucia between 1910 and 1930 appears to have grown by just 24 per cent compared to a national increase of 65 per cent, with output per farm worker on the eve of the Second Republic little more than two-thirds of that achieved nationally (Table 4.5).[15] However, these figures are calculated by dividing total farm output by the *total* number of agricultural workers, and they ignore the fact that seasonal unemployment was very high in areas of dry-farming. If labour productivity is measured by the *day*, instead of by the *year*, then the figures for Andalucia would probably have been higher than those in the rain-fed northern provinces.[16] Day wages, as shown below, were in fact as high, if not higher than in other regions. Rural poverty was therefore caused by the lack of employment and reflects not so much poor farming decisions as the difficulties of increasing labour opportunities because of the nature of dry-farming technologies available, and the widely dispersed nature of settlements across Southern Spain.

Agriculture in this region was dominated by two farming systems: 'mixed husbandry' based on extensive cereal–legume rotations and livestock, and small-scale olive oil production, which together accounted for about 70 per cent of output in 1930 (Table 7.2). Contemporaries

[15] Output per hectare was 88 per cent of the national figure, but grew by just 12 per cent between 1910 and 1930.

[16] Assuming farm workers were employed 128 days a year in Andalucia in 1926–35, daily output would have been 18.5 per cent *greater* than that achieved in the rain-fed agriculture in the North (assuming farmers worked 256 days a year), rather than being 40 per cent lower as shown in Table 4.5. A figure of at least 256 work days per year seems likely for the North given its intensive farming based on small family farms. Simpson 1992b, p. 16 and 1995, p. 51.

Table 7.2 *Farm population and major crops in Southern Spain, c.1930*

	% of active male population in agriculture	% of rural population landless	Cereal & legumes as % of final output	Olive oil as % of final output
Eastern Andalucia				
Almería	57.8	34	13.4	2.0
Granada	74.5	36	36.6	7.2
Jaén	68.7	28	17.6	53.0
Málaga	62.4	43	20.1	10.0
Total	66.8	35	23.4	22.2
Western Andalucia				
Cádiz	61.9	67	42.4	4.6
Cordoba	64.5	42	29.9	31.0
Huelva	54.0	33	48.9	8.9
Sevilla	54.0	43	37.1	23.9
Total	58.5	46	33.8	21.4
Extremadura (and Salamanca)				
Badajoz	67.7	40	35.0	8.3
Caceres	54.7	53	36.0	5.5
Salamanca	64.4	37	49.6	1.2
La Mancha				
Albacete	66.2	38	44.8	2.3
Ciudad Real	59.8	27	25.7	6.9
Cuenca	80.5	18	51.4	3.8
Toledo	72.8	33	41.6	12.5
Total South	64.1	38	32.7	14.9
South as % of Spanish total % of national figure	41.6	59	36.5	75.5

Sources: Carmona et al. 2019 and Simpson 1995b, pp. 211–2.

believed that farm output could be greatly increased, with Fernando de los Ríos suggesting that Spain had 18 million hectares of idle land which could be cultivated, and Carrión that between 40 to 60 per cent of all the uncultivated land in the South could be farmed.[17] Technically, no doubt some of this land could have been brought under the plough, but was not profitable. In fact, Spanish farmers increased wheat production by about a third during the first third of the twentieth century because of the high prices produced by tariffs. Although the total area of cereal–legume rotations increased only marginally (2.1 per cent) in Andalucia, between

[17] de los Rios 1925, p. 831, and Carrión 1932: 1975, cuadro 45. This is often repeated by historians, such as Preston 1978:2003, p. 83.

1903/12 and 1930/5, the area that was sown rose by a fifth (19.8 per cent), resulting in the amount of uncultivated fallow within the rotation dropping from 47.7 to 38.6 per cent, considerably better than the national figure (from 43.7 to 40.9 per cent). Andalusia's wheat yields grew by 21 per cent, and were 10 per cent higher than the national figure. With the 1932 Land Reform, government agronomists could finally study some latifundios in detail, and they discovered that land was being continuously cultivated on those found on the rich soils of Cordoba's Campiña when fields were within easy walking distance of the village.[18] Although more extensive three-field rotations (*al tercio*) where used when farms were further away, unsown fallow only accounted for a third of the rotation.[19] These agronomists reported that most estates were well cultivated given the labour costs and farm prices of the period, and corroborated Diaz del Moral's argument of rapid changes in farming methods on the latifundios, rather than Carrión's vision of stagnation (Chapter 4). By the Second Republic, even the government's figures suggested that 61 per cent of land in cereal–legume rotations was sown in Andalucia, compared to 59 per cent in the rest of Spain.[20]

Considerable change had also taken place on the large areas of poorer soils. In Extremadura, the area sown with cereal–legumes increased by 61 per cent and in La Mancha by 40 per cent between 1903/12 and 1930/35,[21] although much of this new cultivation obviously depended on wheat prices remaining high. The long summer droughts and high feed costs kept livestock farming densities low and created few jobs, and animal husbandry failed to make a significant contribution to the smallholders economy, as they did in Northern Europe (Chapter 4). The seasonal nature of agriculture affected not just employment opportunities, but also limited the time that work animals could be used, and those small farmers who worked part-time in haulage faced growing competition

---

[18] This shift to continuous cultivation using artificial fertilizers, where wheat alternated with a fallow crop (cotton, maize, beans, chickpeas, sugar beet, sunflowers, etc.) began in the late 1920s, but did not become widespread until after the Civil War. According to (Sumpsi 1978), continuous cultivation using wage labour was only profitable when farms were fully mechanized with tractors, which were still rare in the early 1930s. When traditional farming methods and wage labour were used, continuous cultivation was actually less profitable for employers than extensive rotations. By contrast, it was profitable with family labour, and perhaps explains, together with the growing social unrest, why some landowners preferred to divide their estates and use rental and sharecropping contracts during the 1920s. Naredo et al. 1977. The fact that López Ontiveros & Mata Olmo 1993, pp. 118–19 found few signs of sharecropping in the IRA archives for Cordoba probably reflects the threat of expropriation of rented land in the 1932 Land Reform Act. By contrast, sharecropping on Extremadura's *dehesas* was common. Carmona & Simpson 2014a.
[19] López Ontiveros & Mata Olmo 1993, p. 120.
[20] GEHR 1983b, pp. 316–8. Our calculations.   [21] Ibid., pp. 316–7. Our calculations.

from motorized transport. Indeed, just as farm mechanization was reducing the seasonal demand for labour, better roads were diminishing the
off-peak demand for mules and donkeys in transportation.[22]

By the interwar period, Spain was virtually self-sufficient in wheat,
which eliminated the possibility of creating more employment with
further import-substitution, or provide an excuse for yet higher tariffs.
Labour was an important input in traditional cereal farming, with Rafael
de Caño claiming that it made up 75 per cent of production costs on
family farms, compared to between 30 and 45 per cent on large ones.[23]
However, if the possibilities of increasing output and employment with
dry farming were limited, new farm machinery threatened to reduce costs
and eliminate peak labour demand, especially at the harvest (Table 7.3).
Tractors also had the major advantage over work animals in that they did
not have to be fed when idle, and they could plough in the summer
without waiting for the autumn rains.[24] Mechanization also changed the
most efficient farm size for cereals, encouraging family farmers to increase
their holdings when possible, and large farmers to reduce the number of
workers employed.[25] Therefore in Castile-Leon, a region of small family
farms, the area of cereal–legumes increased by about 25 per cent, while
the labour force fell by a similar amount over the half-century before the
Civil War.[26] In fact, the lack of capital and fragmented farms limited
change and led to demands for land consolidation, rather than land
reform in this region.[27]

While cereal mechanization in Castile-Leon promised to strengthen
the family farm, in Southern Spain it threatened to eliminate an important
source of income for landless and near landless workers, at a time when
there was limited alternative employment. The extent of change was
apparent in the pioneering region of Jerez de la Frontera (Cadiz), where
harvesting and threshing machines had displaced Portuguese harvesting
gangs, and were threatening to make local workers unemployed even

---

[22] The number of automobiles increased by four-fold between 1920 and 1930, from 31,890
to 140,602. By 1928, there were already 32,200 lorries. Uriol Salcedo 1990, pp. 182–3
and 253.

[23] del Caño 1933, p. 74.

[24] Tractors were still relatively rare in Cordoba on the Campiña on account of the difficulty
of carrying out repairs on the farms found at a distance from the main settlements, rather
than a disinterest by landowners. López Ontiveros & Mata Olmo 1993, p. 127.

[25] Olmstead & Rhode 2001.   [26] Simpson 1995, table 7.7.

[27] I Congreso Nacional Cerealista. Valladolid 1927, p. 128. Although the *cámaras
agrícolas* in Valencia and Segovia demanded legislation to help consolidate smallhold-
ings of less than a hectare (p. 117), it was opposed by other regions, especially
Andalucia, (p. 120), presumably because it either created a precedent for state intervention to change property rights, or because cereal prices would drop if small farmers
became more competitive.

Table 7.3 *Mechanization and seasonal demand for labour in Southern Spain*

	Intensive cereal–legumes	Wheat – harvest unmechanized	Wheat – 'semi' mechanized *	Intensive olives
January	0.2	0	0	5.2
February	1.1	0	0	6.2
March	0.9	0.5	0.5	3.4
April	0.4	0	0	4.3
May	0.6	0	0	3.0
June	2.0	1.0	0.1	1.0
July	3.5	6.5	1.9	1.0
August	1.7	3.5	1.0	3.0
September	1.0	1.0	1.0	4.5
October	1.7	3.5	0.8	1.0
November	1.3	1.0	0.3	1.1
December	1.0	0	0	2.0
Total	15.5	17.0	5.5	35.4

Number of days' work required per hectare.
* Reapers and threshers are used.
Source: Sindicato Vertical del Olivo 1946, tables 22, 32, 36, and 40.

before the First World War. One estimate suggests that by the Second Republic there were sufficient machines to fully mechanize cereal cultivation on Jerez's fertile Campiña soils.[28] Rapid mechanization did offer some new employment possibilities, and the landowners' *Unión de Derechas Independientes* claimed in 1932 that there were 300 farm mechanics 'of different categories', and five large workshops, 'which lived from the repair of farm equipment' in the town.[29] Jerez undoubtedly was an exception, but the threat posed by farm mechanization to unskilled harvest employment is clearly seen in the collective bargaining agreements during the Second Republic that frequently contained clauses to limit the use of machinery. The growing economies of scale associated with mechanization in cereal production and the need to use dry-farming techniques would greatly complicate land reform. Both socialists and anarchists therefore preferred to convert the latifundios into mechanized

[28] There were about 50 steam threshing machines operating in Jerez on the eve of the Great War. Cabral gives 200 threshing machines in Cadiz in 1942 (of which 81 were in Jerez); 42 combine harvests in Cadiz (of which 31 were in Jerez); and by the end of the 1930s, 286 tractors in Cadiz (and 190 in Jerez). Cabral Chamorro 2000 pp. 63–4, 73, 76, 80, and 91. The first national farm machine census reported a total of 571 reapers and reaper-binders; 18 combine-harvesters; and 137 tractors in the province of Cadiz in 1932. Spain. Ministerio de Agricultura 1933, pp. 320 and 322.
[29] Caro Cancela 2001, p. 194.

collectives although, as noted in Chapter 8, most workers wanted their own individual plots.[30]

Andalucia also had around a million hectares of olives, accounting for almost two-thirds of the nation's production. Olive oil production nearly doubled during the first three decades of the twentieth century, with exports accounting for almost a quarter in 1930.[31] The olive was especially suited to small family farms, and a significant number of landless labourers planted trees on plots of marginal land, helping them climb the farm ladder to become independent producers. Planting was labour intensive, requiring five times the amount of work that was needed for annual cultivation, although subsistence crops could be planted between the young trees until they came into full production. The first crop was not collected until the sixth or seventh year, and only after fifteen or twenty did olives enter into full production.[32] Labour and capital accounted for approximately 90 per cent of annual production costs, and on poorer soils, the olive required more than twice as much work per hectare than intensive cereal-legume rotations (62.5 days per year as opposed to 25 days). Output was around a third greater.[33]

Despite these advantages, there were limits to how far the olive could transform the regional economy and create a dynamic society of small family producers. As Chapter 4 noted, Spain's competiveness in international markets depended on abundant supplies of suitable land and cheap labour, factors which were widely found across the Mediterranean, especially in Greece, Tunisia, and Algeria. Any upward shift in international demand was met by an expansion in the area cultivated rather than by productivity growth in the orchards, while growers were reluctant to uproot trees during economic downturns.[34] Domestic demand was relatively inelastic, and if prices did not fall more during the Depression it was only because of the disastrous harvest in 1930/1.

Family olive producers also found themselves at a disadvantage within the commodity chain. While olive cultivation, especially the pruning and

---

[30] Collectives not only enjoyed potential economics of scale, but they allowed political parties greater control over their members.

[31] Although quality improved significantly, most oil was still exported in bulk to French and Italian markets for rebranding. Zambrana 1987, Simpson 1995, pp. 167, 214–7, and Ramón Muñoz 2000, pp. 182–92.

[32] Its commercial life was then between fifty and a hundred years. For sharecropping, see Simpson 1985, p. 227.

[33] Carrión 1932: 1975, p. 324. Net output per day was less (4.0 pesetas as oppose 4.8 pesetas), reflecting perhaps the greater proportion of family labour used in olive cultivation. Simpson 1995, p. 235.

[34] This was becoming less true in Spain between 1901/12 and 1926/35, as greater output was achieved by both an extension in the area cultivated (33 per cent) and higher yields (28 per cent). Simpson 1995, p. 216.

harvesting, remained heavily labour intensive, technological change significantly increased the scale in the manufacturing and commercialization of olive oil. Small growers were especially vulnerable during cyclical downturns because of the low prices offered by mill owners, while in Andalucia there were virtually no cooperatives. Therefore, not only were there difficulties in creating a society of prosperous family olive farmers, especially in the 1930s, their demands were often diametrically opposed to those of the landless labourers who collected their harvest: namely higher farm prices and lower production costs, rather than cheap food and higher wages.

Agricultural Growth, Labour Markets, and the Nature of Rural Poverty

Most countries at some point during economic development experience problems of surplus labour in the agricultural sector and large pockets of poverty can persist over decades, especially at the regional level. In this respect, Spain was not necessarily very different. However, the almost total lack of statistic information concerning the numbers involved, the extent of the poverty, or its structural as opposed to cyclical nature, makes cross-country comparisons of rural destitution impossible. This section therefore is limited to showing a number of important changes that occurred over time in Andalucia, and why the problems of the rural landless would produce such a formidable challenge for governments of the Second Republic.

Historians have often argued that southern labour markets remained disconnected to national ones, with workers reluctant to participate in the massive emigration to the Americas before 1914, or move to the growing industrial cities of Barcelona, Bilbao, or Madrid in the interwar period.[35] In addition, landowners are believed to have enjoyed significant monopsony power in rural labour markets.[36] However, this view is challenged by Rosés and Sánchez Alonso who argue that, despite low rates of internal migration, 'substantial' wage convergence took place between 1850 and 1930 across Spanish regions.[37] Furthermore, although rural poverty was very real, living standards improved for many workers in Andalucia before the Depression. If they did not increase more, it probably owed more to Spain's weak industrialization rather than to predatory landowners.

---

[35] For the relative absence of Andaluces migrating to Barcelona and Madrid see Silvestre et al. 2015, and Beltrán Tapia & Salanova 2017.
[36] Robledo Hernández & Esteban 2017, pp. 19–28.
[37] Rosés & Sánchez-Alonso 2004, p. 404.

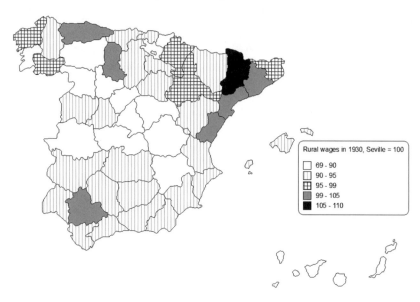

Map 7.1 Day wages for male farm workers, 1930
Source: Rosés & Sánchez-Alonso 2002, wages deflated by local prices.

Real day wages in Andalucia for agricultural and unskilled construction
workers were not especially low compared to the rest of the country
(Maps 7.1 and 7.2). In fact, despite strong demographic growth, the long-
run changes in labour supply and demand in agriculture and real wages
actually produced an improvement in living standards, especially after
1914. A study of four of the most contentious southern provinces (Cadiz,
Cordoba, Granada, and Jaen), which takes into consideration the shifts in
the area cultivated, livestock densities, and technological change, concludes that per capita work opportunities for the rural population
increased by about a fifth between 1886/90 and 1926/30, before dropping
slightly in 1931/35. Furthermore, while real wages were flat before the
First World War, they then increased, especially between 1918–21 and
1927–33.[38] The contrast with Southern Italy is illustrative, as hourly
wages for male agricultural workers in Andalucia grew about three
times more quickly between 1913 and 1929 than in Apulia, and six
times more than in Sicily. This gap widened even more during the early
1930s.[39]

[38] Simpson 1992b, especially pp. 235–8, and Bringas Gutiérrez 2000, cuadro A.4.
[39] Ramón Muñoz 2010, p. 260.

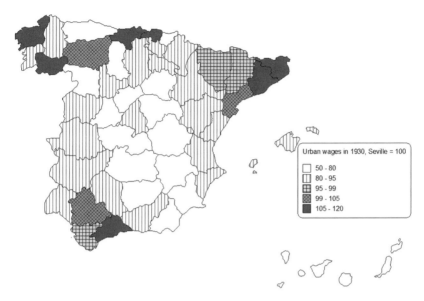

Map 7.2 Day wages for unskilled urban male workers, 1930
Source: Rosés & Sánchez-Alonso 2002, wages deflated by local prices.

Rising wages helped many landless workers to rent or buy some land. In Andalucia, the share of the rural population who were either tenants or owners increased from just 33 per cent of the total in 1860 to 46 per cent in the 1910, before jumping to around 60 per cent in 1930.[40] Even if in many cases they had only small plots of land, the direction of change is important and consistent with other social indicators, such as infant mortality, life expectancy, literacy, and stature that suggest slow, but steady improvements (Table 7.4). As with the rest of the country, Andalucia also probably experienced a narrowing of income inequality.[41] Finally, although many historians have debated why labourers did not leave village poverty for the rapidly growing northern industrial cities, four of the nation's nine provinces that were *attracting* labour from other regions between 1900 and 1930, were latifundio provinces.[42] The pull of Spain's major urban centres was still weak before the Civil War, and the provincial population densities found at the end of the nineteenth century are an important factor in explaining relative population growth over the next thirty or forty years.[43] The combination

---

[40] Carmona et al. 2019, p. 676.   [41] Prados de la Escosura 2008.
[42] García Barbancho 1967, A.3. See also Bernal 1985, pp. 243–8.   [43] Ayuda et al. 2010.

Table 7.4 *Social indicators in Andalucia,* c.*1890–*c.*1930*

Estimated per capita farm work for males (days)	% of rural population with access to land	Real male wages	Infant mortality	Life expectancy	Literacy (*)	Height of male recruits
c.1890	108	39	100 (1874)	221 (1900)	n.a.	31.8 (1887)	163
c.1914	123	47 (1910)	102	177	41.5	38 (1920)	163.5
c.1930	130	60	117	122	49.5	53	164.6

* 1887, adult literacy (31–35 years); for the rest, < 4 years old excluded.
Sources: Simpson 1992b, table 7; Carmona et al. 2019, tables 2 and 3; Rosés & Sánchez-Alonso 2002, p. 32, 1900 = 100; Instituto de Estadística de Andalucía 2002, pp. 69 and 107 and Reher et al. 1993, p. 235, and Quiroga Valle 2003a, pp. 192–3.

of high fertility and the delayed rural exodus led to fast population growth everywhere in Andalucia, except in Almeria and Malaga (Map 4.3).[44] Yet despite these rising incomes, the high seasonal unemployment probably led to living standards for many rural workers declining in relative terms to those in urban areas. Therefore if rural poverty perhaps did not shock the middle classes in Barcelona or Madrid in 1900, it was considered incompatible with modern Spain by 1931, as reflected in Luis Buñuel's film of *Las Hurdes*. This growing awareness of *misère*, namely the presence of widespread involuntary poverty in a rapidly growing economy, was not unique to Spain, but also found, for example, in mid-nineteenth-century France and England.[45]

With the Great Depression, living conditions almost certainly became worse for many, as the end of the farm commodity boom in the late 1920s halted the expansion of cultivation, although population continued to grow rapidly. As noted, the situation was made worse by significant numbers of unemployed workers returning to their villages, increasing the labour supply at a time when the amount of farm work was falling.[46] If

[44] Large numbers of smallholders emigrated from coastal Almeria and Malaga.
[45] For a recent discussion on *misère*, see Nochlin 2018.
[46] For Ciudad Real, BIRA, 1933, 12, p. 426, cited in Ladrón de Guevara 1993, p. 228. In Barcarrota (Badajoz), the disappearance of the cork-stopper industry explained why the 'labour crisis' was one of the worst in the province, while for neighbouring Jerez de los Caballeros the difficulties in mining increased the demand among non-farm workers for employment. Archivo del Instituto de Reforma Agraria (AIRA), *Caja* 6.37, *Informe plan de asentamiento, enero* 1934, p. 3 and *Caja* 6.40, *Tablada, plan de asentamiento.* In Huelva, the decline in activity at the outset of the First World War led to many of the 20,000 laid

the rough calculation in Table 3.7 is anything like correct, then the supply of farm labour increased by around 20 per cent between 1930 and 1936 creating a sharp cyclical downturn in living standards.

The fact that a large share of the farm population were wage earners in areas of latifundios implied that the consequences of the economic crisis were much more visible than in regions of small farmers, especially as the nature of political opportunities and the constraints on collective action for family farmers and rural wage earners were radically changed during the first years of the Second Republic. Traditional demands for land redistribution were now joined with calls for the government to resolve falling farm prices and cyclical unemployment caused by both the economic downturn and adverse weather conditions. In particular, after the two exceptional harvests of 1927–8 and 1929–30, the 1930–1 olive harvest was devastated by drought, with production falling by 94 per cent in the major region of Jaen.[47] Official unemployment figures are poor, but Bernaldo de Quirós calculated over five million work days lost across Andalucia.[48] This combination of traditional seasonal unemployment, exceptional conditions produced by harvest failure, and economic depression, led to widespread demands for help. The question now was whether it was the landowners, the state, village councils, or organized labour that would be responsible for finding and administering aid to the rural poor,

In traditional Spanish agriculture, paternalism was still important, with clients providing not just their labour, but also political support and ritualized patterns of behaviour in exchange for wages and other goods that ensured minimum subsistence needs and protection. This created a relationship between landed elites and peasant clients that was 'multi-faceted, diffuse, face-to-face, and based on personalistic ties not written contracts'.[49] In areas of dehesas in Extremadura for example, landowners often rented small plots of land and advanced working capital, fodder for animals, and even food, to their tenants and sharecroppers. Although paternalism was often believed to be 'exploitive', it was only likely to

---

off miners returning to their villages leading to rural conflicts as they demanded farm employment. Collier 1987, p. 49.

[47] In Jaen, average output fell from 1.28 million metric quintals between 1925 and 1929, to just 0.12 million in 1930: output recovered to average 0.84 million over the next five years. Simpson 1985, p. 365. Previous crises caused by harvest failure occurred in 1905 and 1916. Florencio Puntas 1994, p. 308.

[48] Bernaldo de Quirós 1931, p. 18. This was equivalent to about a sixth of total annual labour requirements, calculated from Simpson 1992b. Although local workers were the worst affected, the harvest traditionally attracted large numbers from other sectors and migrant labourers from other provinces.

[49] Mason 2004, p. 61.

disappear when small farmers and workers had access to specialized markets for capital or insurance, and the state provided social goods, such as compulsory sickness or unemployment benefits.

In Southern Spain, and especially Andalucia, two distinct types of paternalistic relations can be identified. The first involved the classic face-to-face informal contacts between employer and worker. On the estates (*cortijos*), trusted full-time workers were needed to look after the animals and care for the owner's possessions, and these positions were often passed from one generation to the next. Salaries were low, perhaps only half what other workers earned, but there were additional benefits such as housing and other non-monetary remunerations.[50] However in Andalucia, perhaps only one in every four farm workers enjoyed permanent contracts, and for day labourers it was difficult to establish strong personal relations based on trust, either because they usually worked for several different employers during the year, leading to weak face-to-face contacts, or because landowners or farmers were absentee or rental contracts changed too frequently.[51] Instead a 'collective' paternalism developed, whereby patrons established a clientelistic relationship with formal and informal *groups* of clients. Therefore at times of hardship, the village mayor turned to the *alojamiento* system that encouraged farmers to provide employment for groups of workers.[52] This acted as a voluntary village 'poor law', and helped smooth minor downturns in employment, but was of limited use at times of major harvest failure, or severe economic slumps. In addition, while employers might accept the moral need for providing emergency relief when they were still dependent on local labourers, this presumably became less true with mechanization.[53]

The weakness of face-to-face paternalism for day labourers also helps explain the idea of 'pueblo' and the concept of 'shared poverty'. In societies where individual paternalism was important, it was difficult to build effective village-level solidarity. However in Southern Spain, and especially Andalucia, the weak hierarchical bonds contrasted with villagers' needs to resolve problems of shared poverty among themselves. A strong collective identity at the village (*pueblo*) level was used to help

---

[50] Fuentes Cumplido 1904: 1977, pp. 338–9. The wages of shepherds, for example, were often of secondary importance to their right to keep their own animals on the cortijos at the owner's expense (*excusa*). Carmona & Simpson 2003, pp. 99–101 and Mintz 1982. Problems would arise when the Republic attempted to legislate work conditions for these permanent workers.

[51] See Map 10.1.   [52] Bernal 1974, pp. 155–9.

[53] With the growth of commercial agriculture, this practice perhaps had disappeared in half the villages by the turn of the century. Instituto de Reformas Sociales 1905, cited in Florencio Puntas 1994, p. 278.

organize and distribute employment opportunities. As the Socialist Fernando de los Ríos noted in 1925:[54]

In order to give his comrades a chance, the labourer begins late, works slowly, and tries to make his rests as frequent and long as the vigilance of the ganger will allow; as a result output falls. As he so often says, 'What are we to do? If we work hard, there will be too many of us by half'.

This strong collective identity explains better not just village demands for the recovery of municipal and seigneurial lands, but also the reluctance of workers to migrate for more than a couple of months, as village membership provided basic entitlement rights at times of economic stress.[55] Governments during the Second Republic failed to provide an alternative to paternalism in the form of social transfers, and instead passed legislation to make farmers create more work for unemployed workers (*laboreo forzoso*) and strengthen labour syndicates, measures that shifted an important part of the responsibility to help the rural poor onto landowners and farmers, rather than the state. Not surprisingly, given the exceptional nature of the economic depression and the opportunities for collective action in the early 1930s, these policies became an important cause of rural unrest (Chapters 8 and 10).

Latifundios and the State

If most contemporaries mistakenly believed that agriculture in Southern Spain was backward and stagnant during the first third of the twentieth century, or failed to appreciate that rural poverty among small farmers and landless workers was getting less before the outset of the Great Depression, they were perhaps closer to the mark in identifying the landed elite as an obstacle to both the development of a well-functioning democracy and the creation of a modern state. As Chapter 6 noted, the absence of competitive party politics limited reforms that in other countries favoured small farmers at the expense of large landowners, and produced a more inclusive growth. In this section, the role of Southern Spain's rural elites in resisting change is briefly considered in two areas: their limited role in supporting government research programs, and their opposition to collecting farm statistics.

Andalusia's landed elites were clearly interested in agricultural progress, introducing new farm machinery when they thought it could reduce

---

[54] de los Rios 1925, p. 844. For more general comments, see Martínez-Alier 1971, ch. 5.
[55] Behar 1991, p. 132, notes that residents had to be present for most of the year to benefit from user-rights over communal property. Banerjee & Duflo 2007, p. 165, make similar observations on rural–urban migration today in low-income countries.

costs, or experimenting with artificial fertilizers to improve yields or reduce the amount of fallow. However, these farming innovations were strongly linked to movements in factor and commodity prices, and required little government intervention beyond tariffs. Government research and development are public goods, and investment levels depend on political decisions, and in Spain the number of agronomists actually declined in the 1920s.[56] What needs to be explained therefore is why, if large farmers in Southern Spain responded to market signals and were willing to modernize their farms, they appear disinterested in lobbying for more government-funded research in agriculture.[57]

Some Spanish research institutions were in fact successful, and enjoyed active support from the local rural elites. The best known was the *Instituto Agrícola Catalán de San Isidro*, and in particular the help small wine-growers received to replant their vines after phylloxera.[58] A combination of public research stations and private institutions was also important for improving rice production, introducing new varieties of oranges, or improving livestock breeding across Northern Spain.[59] However the evidence for similar advances across much of Spain's dry-farming regions, including Andalucia, remains limited. One explanation is that the technological constraints associated with dry-farming in this period were an important factor to explain the low level of state investment in research and development, especially as there were few obvious advances in other countries that could be easily adapted to Spanish conditions.[60] Furthermore, and unlike some commodities, the technological spillovers from wheat farming were limited for small farmers, not because of a lack of interest among large farmers, but rather because change often involved mechanization.

Nevertheless the fact that high tariffs made dry-farming cereals profitable is also a crucial explanation for the limited interest of landowners in government-sponsored research and development. Lower tariffs would have required Andalusia's farmers to have been more inventive, but lower wheat prices would also have hit small farmers even more, making them politically unfeasible. This, and the fact that there was no exogenous shock on the scale of phylloxera as happened in viticulture, limited their

[56] Pan-Montojo 2005, p. 238. For a more optimistic view of government research, see Fernández Prieto 2001, especially, pp. 137–44. Andalucia provided 13 per cent of Spain's trained agronomists between 1901 and 1936. Florencio Puntas 2005, p. 22.
[57] This was unlike some of the landed elites in Latin America from the 1950s, who used the threat of land reform to capture government research programs, to transform their estates. Janvry 1981.
[58] Balcells 1980, pp. 61 and 67, and Planas 2008, pp. 18–19.
[59] Fernández Prieto 2001, pp. 127–34, for an excellent summary.
[60] Pujol-Andreu 2011, for wheat varieties and technical change in Europe.

interest in government research programs. Indeed, in those areas where farmers did benefit from new government-sponsored research, namely cotton, sugar beet, or tobacco production, import tariffs were again essential for their profitability.

Andalusia's large farmers have also been criticized for their lack of interest in irrigation, especially as this could have eliminated the restrictions associated with dry-farming, and helped create small, labour-intensive family farms. Carrión noted that almost 80 per cent of the land was found on farms of more than 100 hectares in the three new areas of potentially irrigated land in the region in 1929. Yet farmers could not be expected to invest in irrigation if water supplies could not be guaranteed during the critical summer months and, for this to happen, massive capital-intensive water storage schemes were needed.[61] The combination of high infrastructural costs and the need to create small, competitive family farms required major state involvement. The Caulina cooperative project, for example, which settled 75 families on 150 hectares in 1915, was still waiting for water from the Guadalcacín reservoir fifteen years later.[62]

Landowners were active in slowing the creation of an equitable land tax that was both independent of the local cacique and could be adjusted to reflect the annual changes in farm output and prices, and this was an important factor in explaining the state's limited information concerning farming and landownership. Chapter 3 illustrated the arbitrary nature of the nineteenth-century land tax, and the cadastre was supposed to introduce scientific land measurements to create a much fairer system, and increase the state's information on the village economy. Tax reformers however had to choose between two distinct models: a rapid assessment that allowed a significant increase in revenues, but inevitably contained errors and required dependence on the local caciques for information; or an accurate, detailed study, which would be both costly to create, and slow to produce additional revenues. In Spain, it took over a third of a century to survey less than half the country, and even then values were not updated. Attempts to introduce a genuine income tax were unsuccessful.[63] This resistance had important implications because if landowners rejected their traditional social obligations to help the rural poor in low-tax societies, the state needed resources to take on these

---

[61] Many farmers in the Ebro valley continued to plant traditional dry-farming crops despite the presence of irrigation, both because of the unreliability of water supplies in the summer months, and because of the technical difficulties associated with introducing new, high-value crops. Simpson 1995, pp.143–6.

[62] Carrión, in Congreso Nacional de Riegos 1929, 2, p.195 and Montañés 1997, pp.153–4.

[63] See Chapter 3.4 and, for Spanish taxation in general, Comín 1996, pp. 74–84.

responsibilities in the modern, high-tax societies that began to appear in Europe during the 1930s. Without a strong tax base, the state inevitably had only limited capacity.

The weak tax base was accompanied by low government spending on collecting information on Spanish agriculture. Although output figures exist at the provincial level for the major crops and livestock produce, there was virtually none available at the village or farm level. The detailed provincial studies on cereal and livestock production carried out in the late 1880s were not repeated, and farm gate prices for the interwar period are particularly scarce. Crucially, no information was available for the government on how the latifundios operated. Inevitably, without easily accessible information, the level of contemporary debate on the problems facing Spanish agriculture was limited. Only when land reform was itself already underway, did the government begin to collect some of these basic statistics (Appendix 1).

It would have been highly surprising if Andalusia's landowners had voted to reduce their political influence, or demanded lower farm prices and higher taxes. However, what was unusual in the Western European context was that their farm profits remained strong in the 1920s despite falling international prices. This was caused by the absence of dynamic, urban-based political parties demanding cheaper food. Neither did the landed elite have to organize small farmers politically, and help strengthen the family farm by creating more effective cooperatives, rural banks, and tenure reform. Indeed, if landowners generally welcomed Primo de Rivera's dictatorship in 1923, their support quickly disappeared when he threated to introduce tenure reforms.[64]

Conclusion: Was There a 'Southern Problem'?

The traditional thesis suggests that Spain's 'southern problem' was the result of a heavily skewed landownership structure that persisted unchanged over generations, which led many contemporaries on the eve of the Second Republic to associate latifundios with 'feudalism', and believe that landowners cared little for how their estates were run, or the poverty that this caused among the landless in the neighbouring villages. This chapter, and the previous ones, has questioned this thesis in four important ways.

First, land and labour markets were not frozen in time, but responded to economic and political change. Not only did the numbers of landless labourers in Andalucia fall from 60 per cent of the farm population in

---

[64] Pan-Montojo 2002, p. 25.

1890 to 40 per cent in 1930, but the size of latifundios also declined, from around 2,000 to 1,300 hectares between the mid-eighteenth and mid-nineteenth centuries, and to 700 hectares in Cordoba by 1930.[65] Nevertheless, Spain's landed elites survived the political and economic turmoil associated with the late-nineteenth-century depression, industrialization, and the First World War, better than most in Western Europe, while small, family farmers found it difficult to climb the farm ladder.

A second factor was that even the estates belonging to absentee landowners were much better cultivated than what most contemporaries believed. In particular, artificial fertilizers were being used to reduce the area of unsown fallow, and farmers were increasingly using machinery to reduce their dependence on relatively costly labour and animal power. Although cereal yields in Andalucia, and indeed across much of Spain, were low by Northern European standards, this had little to do with the landownership structure or the use of inadequate technologies, but rather the seasonal patterns of rainfall distribution. The fact that the problems of introducing labour-intensive crops using dry-farming techniques was appreciated by politicians only *after* land reform had begun, would have important consequences as shown in the next chapter. Only irrigation promised to bring about radical changes, and the provision of this was inevitably very slow, and depended more on state involvement than on private initiatives.

A third point was that living standards improved for most farm workers from the turn of the century, as suggested by real wages increasing and growing numbers of landless workers being able to rent or buy land. Significant improvements also took place in literacy and life expectancy. This explains, at least in part, why outmigration remained weak. Living standards did not rise faster because of long periods of seasonal unemployment, rather than low wages.

Finally, although strong economic growth during the first three decades of the twentieth century led to important changes in Andalusia's agriculture and improved living standards, the region also became more vulnerable to economic downturns. Indeed many of the causes of rural poverty in the 1930s were the direct result of economic growth and structural change rather than the persistence of a stagnant economy or 'feudalism'. In particular, agriculture had to absorb unemployed workers that returned to their villages. However, although villagers' traditional entitlement rights were being eroded, the state was slow to fill the gap. In some villages, especially on the dehesas, traditional paternalistic

[65] López Ontiveros & Mata Olmo 1993, p. 45.

tenure and labour contracts remained strong, but elsewhere landowners looked to limit their social responsibilities. While it is doubtful that landowners enjoyed monopsony powers in local labour markets, paternalistic contracts allowed them to benefit from the loyalty of their farm workers. Both the Anarchist Confederación Nacional del Trabajo (CNT), and especially the Socialist Federación Nacional de Trabajadores de la Tierra (FNTT), now attempted to create their own monopolies to restrict employment to local workers who were members of their syndicate (Chapter 10). These very different philosophies for organizing factor markets led to major conflicts over who had the right to decide which worker was to be employed and how the land was to be cultivated.

Andalucia was therefore very different to the US South and the Italian Mezzogiorno, two other backward regions found within fast-developing national economies. In particular, and unlike the US South, workers in Andalucia in 1931 were now able to choose 'voice' and protest, rather than 'loyalty' to their employers, and they benefitted from strong wage increases from 1914.[66] Spanish farmers were also able to rely on the state to protect their legal rights and did not have to contract private protection agencies, such as happened in Sicily. Fascist gangs still remained unimportant by 1936. Indeed, Kenneth Snowden's description of the labour market and large estates in Apulia during the early 1920s is virtually identical to those found in Cordoba in the same years, with the single exception that the Spanish government never hesitated to respond to calls from the provincial governor to use the security forces when he felt it was needed.[67]

Given the significant changes in rural Andalucia, it might be tempting to dismiss the need for state intervention in land and labour markets during the Second Republic. This, however, would be wrong. The social consequences of the Great Depression stretched the capability of governments everywhere, and led to regime change in an important number of them. Spain was no exception. However, whereas the social problems associated with unemployment in the most Western European nations were essentially an urban phenomenon, in Spain they affected rural areas the most. This explains perhaps why the new Republican government chose land reform as a solution, although not necessarily its suitability to resolve the problems.

---

[66] However, as in the US South, farm mechanization can quickly end paternalistic labour systems. See especially Wright 1986.
[67] For the rise of the Sicilian Mafia, see Dimico et al. 2017, and Snowden 1986, for labour unrest in Apulia.

8   The Limits to Land Reform

> There are three intimately linked factors: land, freedom and
> democracy ... The definitive consolidation in Spain of a democratic
> Republic is the fundamental aim of the Agrarian Reform.[1]

> Let the experiment be done, then. And let's see what happens.[2]

The Second Republic sparked considerable enthusiasm among republicans concerning the possibilities for land reform. In July 1931, the
Technical Commission proposed settling on a temporary basis between
60,000 and 75,000 families annually over a period of twelve or fifteen
years. The plan was bitterly opposed by the landowners as it included all
farms, not just those that were poorly cultivated, and by the Socialists,
because reform could be easily reversed by future governments, and they
wanted to settle 150,000 during the first year, and 100,000 thereafter. By
contrast, the 1932 Land Reform Law saw only 4,400 families receiving
a total of 24,000 hectares during the first sixteen months to
December 1933, although a further 6,289 peasants were given 81,558
hectares with the centre-right governments between January and
September 1934.[3] A new, revised law of July 1935 allowed most landowners
to avoid having their lands expropriated, and its budget was so inadequate
that José Antonio Primo de Rivera, the leader of the fascist Falange, claimed
it would need 160 years to be carried out.[4] Historians have usually argued
that land reform failed because of the lack of government commitment,
limited budget, and the legal challenges by landowners to the expropriation
of their property. In the words of Edward Malefakis, 'it was the misfortune of
the Republic that Azaña interpreted the revolutionary document to which
his government had given birth in the most limited manner possible and
failed to take advantage of the extraordinary powers it conferred on him'.[5]
While most of these points have some truth, this chapter argues that the

---

[1] Ruiz-Funes, BIRA 48, 21 Junio 1936, p. 714. See also Robledo Hernández & Esteban
2017, p. 10.
[2] 'Hágase, pues, el experimento. Y a ver que pasa', Vazquez Humasqué 1931, p. 44.
[3] Malefakis 1970, p. 281 and 346.   [4] Ibid., p. 360.   [5] Ibid., p. 235.

decisive factors were the lack of suitable land and the limited state capacity to supervise such an ambitious reform.

The limited success of the 1932 Reform Law contrasts with the land invasions in the spring of 1936, which resulted in 110,921 peasants being settled on 572,035 hectares, leading some historians to suggest that a village-level bottom-up reform was much more effective than the earlier, bureaucratic top-down reform.[6] These village-level initiatives helped reduce the information problems that the state faced in identifying both suitable land for settlements and those most in need, but often they were not implemented impartially, and settlers remained dependent on the state for working capital. In particular, they failed to solve the overriding problem of insufficient land, and simply changed who was to decide which groups of workers were to benefit and which ones were to be excluded. Only after July 1936, when the government could, without compensation, expropriate around seven million hectares, or 30 per cent of the useful land in the Republican zone from the rebels, did the state enjoy sufficient land for a reform.[7]

While the experience of land reform during the Second Republic failed to resolve the social problems or increase agricultural efficiency, it offered political opportunities for both the Left and Right to widen their support networks, polarizing village society, and, in time, undermining democracy. This chapter begins by examining the experience of land reforms in Eastern Europe in the interwar period and the expectations of contemporaries in Spain, and then explains both the problems facing the 1932 top-down land reform and those with the bottom-up reforms following the 1930 land invasions.

The Agrarian Question in Europe in the Interwar Period

Between 1919 and 1926, there was an unprecedented wave of redistributive agrarian reforms affecting as many as fourteen of Europe's twenty countries, especially in Central and Eastern Europe, and involving the transfer of 22.8 million hectares.[8] A major objective of land reform was to break up the huge estates of the Russian, German, Turkish, and Austro-Hungarian imperial aristocracies, political groups that had lost their legitimacy under the new regimes following the First World War.[9] Their apparent success

---

[6] Figures for Spain in BIRA, March–July, Malefakis 1970, p. 377. For bottom-up land reform, see especially Robledo Hernández 2014, p. 78.
[7] Robledo 2012, p. 391.
[8] Brassley 2010, pp. 145–64, and table 7.1. There were also limited reforms in Germany and Austria.
[9] Warriner 1939, pp. 35–42.

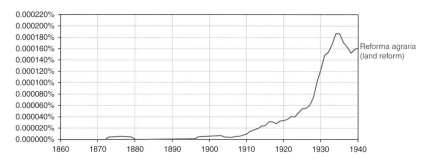

Figure 8.1 Frequency of the words 'la Reforma Agraria' in Spanish literature
Sources: NGram, Google books.

sparked interest in Spain, despite the important differences between these countries (Figure 8.1 and Table 8.1).[10] Not only were Spaniards on average 37 per cent richer in 1930 ($2,724 per capita income compared to $1,988), but fewer people worked in agriculture (47 per cent versus 62 per cent); the country was more urban (48 per cent versus 32 per cent); and agricultural productivity per worker was over 50 per cent higher.[11] There was also an absence of ethnic minorities whose land could be easily confiscated, while Spain's neutrality during First World War implied that it did not have to assimilate new settlers because of frontier changes. In fact, agrarian reforms in Eastern Europe during the 1920s gradually lost their social function to acquire an increasingly ethnic character.[12] In Ireland, which shared similar levels of per capita incomes to Spain, the role of religious and nationalist conflicts were decisive in explaining the mobilization of its population and success of land reform.[13]

The results of the Eastern Europe's land reforms were actually more controversial than suggested in the Spanish literature at the time, although the brevity of the experiment in many countries made an objective balance by contemporaries difficult. Doreen Warriner's study of Central and Eastern Europe, first published in 1939, confirms the reduction in income inequality in most cases, although large-scale land redistribution failed to eliminate landless labourers, and 'dwarf holdings' in countries such as Poland, Romania, or Bulgaria were insufficient to feed

---

[10] de los Rios 1925, Coloma 1928, Caño García 1931, Castro 1931, pp. 83–4, González-Blanco 1931, pp. 26–7, Marichalar 1931, Álvarez Robles 1932, pp. 34–5, Cabezas Díaz 1932, pp. 37–45, Granados 1932, and Peces-Barba 1932, pp. 93–108.
[11] Spanish agriculture also had a much greater diversity that of any of the Eastern European country. Moore 1945, p. 66.
[12] Giordano 2001.   [13] Guinnane & Miller 1997.

Table 8.1 *Selected indicators of countries that carried out land reforms during the interwar period, c.1930*

	Per capita income ($ c.1930)	% employed in agric. (c.1930)	Level of urbanization ** (c.1930)	Labour productivity in agriculture (1930)	National minorities (1930–34) (% of total)	Frontier changes	Year of land reform
Bulgaria	1,405	75	21.4	47	15.5	Yes	1921/4
Czechoslovakia	2,918	33	47.8	105	33.5	Yes*	1919
Estonia	n.a.	55	42.5	99	20.1	Yes*	1919
Finland	2,885	72	22.3	65	10	Yes*	1920
Greece	2,135	51	42.5	50	18.7	Yes	1917
Hungary	2,537	51	42.5	78	7	Yes	1920
Latvia	n.a.	53	34.6	111	26.8	Yes*	1920
Lithuania	n.a.	65	n.d.	73	19.8	Yes*	1918/22
Poland	2,118	60	27.2	49	31.1	Yes*	1921/5
Rumania	1,102	72	20.2	48	26.8	Yes	1918/21
USSR	1,426	78	32.8	39	47.1	Yes	1918/22
Yugoslavia	1,364	76	22.3	38	26	Yes	1919
MEDIA	1,988	62	32	67	24		
Spain	2,724	47	48.5	105	0.3	No	1932/6
Italy	3,241	49	51.9	73	2.7	Yes	1919/21
Ireland	2,823	60	35.5	93		No	1870/1909

Source: Per capita income, Broadberry & Klein 2011; Active population, population density, farm population, and national minorities, Kirk 1946, p. 211, table 17, and appendix 2; Spain, agricultural productivity, Moore 1945; land reform, Brassley 2010, and Peces-Barba 1932.

*Countries that obtained their independence.

**Figures range between 2,000 and 10,000 inhabitants according to country. Figures for Spain refer to 1940.

a family, a major problem in agrarian societies without alternative sources of income.[14] An important factor, and highly relevant for Spain, was the difficulty in creating independent family farms in areas with insufficient rainfall. Not only was farm work too seasonal, but there was a lack of fodder for livestock, making work animals expensive.[15] Warriner recognized the advantages of collectives and mechanization in these areas of dry-farming:

[T]he main reason why the family farm is best for Germany, and the collective farm for Russia, is not that the one accords with Hitler's ideology and the other with Stalin's, but that in Germany the annual rainfall is over 30 inches, and in South Russia less than 15.[16]

In fact, family cereal farms were perfectly compatible with dry-farming. Argentina, Australia, Canada, and the United States, the four largest exporting nations, had wheat yields of 0.97 tons per hectare, little different to the 0.92 tons found in Spain. Where there was a difference was in farm size, and especially the area that a family could cultivate on its own. In the United States, for example, new, labour-saving technologies led to the size of family farms increasing tenfold between 1914 and the early 1970s.[17] By 1930, a typical US cereal farm was around 200 hectares, of which 80 hectares were planted in wheat.[18] For changes on this scale to occur, however, sufficient land had to be available, which could only happen if large uncultivated areas remained, or there was a significant rural exodus.

Spanish governments had a long tradition of intervening in land markets, as shown by the sale of large areas of municipal and church lands from the late eighteenth century.[19] Joaquin Costa in particular was critical of the liberal land reforms for perpetuating large farms and absentee landownership, rather than promoting family farms. The government response was limited, as although the 1907 *Colonización y Repoblación Interior* Law and the *Acción Social Agraria y Emigración* (1926) allowed the state to settle landless labourers, both suffered from budgetary restrictions and their inability to expropriate land.[20] By the 1930s, there was a growing consensus among Spanish politicians that there was a need for some sort of reform, and even conservatives such as Romanones or Severino Aznar defended state expropriation of poorly cultivated

---

[14] Warriner 1939, pp. 140–7 and Urwin 1980, pp. 69–71.
[15] Warriner 1939, pp. 156–67.   [16] Ibid., p. 158.
[17] Drache 1976, cited in Offer 1989, p. 112.   [18] Simpson, 1995, pp. 123 and 227.
[19] For the supposed continuity in these land reforms to the 1930s, see Vergara Doncel, cited in Robledo Hernández 2010, p. 117–22.
[20] Malefakis 1970, appendix e.

farms.[21] However, the reasons advanced for reform were often contradictory.

The economic argument for land reforms rests on the idea that large estates use less labour and achieve lower output per hectare, than small farms using family labour.[22] Therefore a land reform in an economy with abundant labour should in theory increase employment and raise farm output, because family workers face very different incentives than wage labourers. As Carrión argued in 1919, the diverse nature of farm work in Andalucia made it difficult for landowners to create an incentive structure for wage workers to carry out the essential tasks quickly, and with the necessary care. Fernando de los Ríos' comments on farm labourers starting the workday late, working slowly, and extending their breaks to 'create' more employment illustrate the monitoring costs that employers faced, especially during periods of labour unrest.[23] In theory, large farmers would therefore prefer to use extensive cultivation techniques and crops that required little labour. Mechanization would also be encouraged, especially as large farmers could usually borrow more cheaply than smaller ones.[24] By contrast, owner-occupiers or tenant farmers would enjoy strong incentives to work longer hours and could use their entrepreneurial skills to accumulate capital.[25] A land reform that split large estates into small family farms would therefore be expected to lead to more intensive cultivation and the introduction of labour-intensive crops.[26] Carrión actually claimed that output would double from 300 to 600 pesetas per hectare in Andalucia just by parcelling latifundios into family holdings.[27]

Some contemporaries also argued that land reform should be carried out for ethical reasons, as a handful of landowners in some villages controlled employment opportunities, and left large numbers of landless workers in extreme poverty.[28] It was also widely believed that many latifundios had

---

[21] Góngora Echenique 1926. p. 155.

[22] For example, Deininger & Feder 2001, pp. 318–21.   [23] See Chapter 7, fn 66.

[24] In traditional agriculture, the advantages associated with using family labour usually significantly outweighed that of cheap capital. As one development economists notes, the inverse relationship between farm size and average annual output per hectare 'swamps the positive relationship between farm size and average output per hour of work' found on large estates. Lipton 2009, p. 6.

[25] Carrión, in *El Sol*, 15 de junio, 1919. Farm output is highly sensitive to the timing and quality of effort, and deficiencies are often only apparent after the harvest. Carmona & Simpson 2012, pp. 888–9.

[26] See Chapter 2 for the competitive nature of the family farm.

[27] Carrión 1932: 1975, pp. 336–7 and 361. Carrión quotes José Cascón's claim of obtaining wheat yields of 2.7 tons per hectare using dry-farming techniques on the experimental farm in Palencia. See Simpson & Carmona 2017, pp. 49–52.

[28] Cabezas Díaz 1932, pp. 675–6.

been created illegally out of common and seigneurial lands during the nine-teenth century. Attempts at litigation by villagers to recover these lands had often failed because the law required them to provide documentary evidence supporting their claims. With the Republic, the burden of proof was reversed, and it was the landowners who had to supply the written evidence to establish their ownership.

Land reform was also seen as a means to achieve wider economic and political modernization through income redistribution.[29] For many urban politicians the state needed to provide a 'technical' solutions to the pro-blems of the countryside. Some Marxists also wanted to abolish the 'feudal residues', allowing capitalism to develop before the socialist revolution.[30] Finally, land reform was seen by almost all as a necessary palliative to the high levels of rural unemployment during the Great Depression.

These different and sometimes contradictory approaches made it diffi-cult for contemporaries to agree on how land reform should be carried out. In particular, there was tension between those who looked to reform as a means to increase the efficiency of agriculture, and those who saw it as a short-term solution to unemployment. Malefakis also stresses that con-temporaries were forced to choose between a slow reform that respected legal niceties, or a revolutionary one that ignored them.[31] In historical perspective, successful land reforms under democracy have been rare, as opposition groups find it relatively easy to slow, if not block reform completely. As Albertus writes, 'if the executive opposes reform, the legislature cuts off funding, the judiciary raises legal barriers, or the bureaucracy is corrupt or unorganized, redistributive land reform will fail'.[32] In Spain it is sometimes suggested that there were actually two land reforms: the first in 1932 which respected legal norms and was excessively slow and the 1936 land invasions that promised a faster solu-tion which, if not necessarily revolutionary, certainly bordered on the limits of legality.

The 1932 Land Reform

The 1932 Land Reform Law was a 'document of extraordinary complex-ity' and although 'milder' than legislation in Eastern Europe or Mexico, it still envisaged a profound transformation of farm ownership, initially in the fourteen latifundio provinces covering Andalucia, Extremadura, Albacete, Ciudad Real, Salamanca, and Toledo, but eventually for the

---

[29] For example, Díaz del Moral, in *Diario de Sesiones*, 10 de mayo de 1932, 162, 5488–9.
[30] Preston 1978:2003, p. 36.   [31] Malefakis 1970, pp. 393–5.
[32] Albertus 2015, p. 16, argues that most redistributive land reforms have in fact been carried out by autocracies.

whole country. As a 'classical' land reform, it established a maximum threshold for land ownership in each village according to local conditions; levels of compensation for the expropriated land; and mechanisms for allocating land to the new settlers.[33] Land could be expropriated for a variety of reasons, including when it was considered to be poorly cultivated; had been leased continuously for more than twelve years; when a single property occupied more than 20 per cent of the municipality; or where the owner had failed to use irrigation when the facilities were available. Individuals whose land was deemed to have been obtained illegally in the nineteenth century were to lose it without compensation. The state was to assume ownership of the expropriated land and a theoretically autonomous agency, the *Instituto de Reforma Agraria* (IRA), was given the task to organize the new settlements and provide fixed and working capital, as well as a basic income to those most in need until the first harvest. The IRA's farm projects (*planes de asentamiento*) were the first attempt by a Spanish government to systematically collect farm-level information. Tenancy reform was postponed for a later occasion. The prospect of land reform created high expectations, but the combination of lack of suitable land and weak state capacity slowed it to a crawl, leading to frustration and an increase, rather than a reduction, in rural conflicts.

The limited development of state capacity, and especially the lack of reliable statistics, made meaningful debates on the practicalities of a major land reform difficult, if not impossible. In particular, the state had little information concerning the numbers and identity of landless and poor farmers. the potential area of uncultivated land that could be brought under the plough, or the capacity of local agriculture to create more employment (Appendix 1). If the land cadastre recorded farm size, it failed to show whether a low value was the consequence of poor land quality, deficient cultivation, or simply because the figures had not been updated.[34] The often-subjective nature of these variables provided landowners with the possibility of legal recourse to overturn decisions or delay the expropriation of their property.[35] The state also lacked the necessary mechanisms to deliver impersonal public services and identify those most in need. In fact, the number of state agronomists only increased from 321

---

[33] For a discussion on 'classical' land reforms, Lipton 2009, pp. 127–8.

[34] Rents were not updated and could quickly become out of date, making comparison across provinces impossible. Carrión 1932: 1975, p. 98.

[35] Not only was the Land Reform generous in the amount of land that was exempt, but it was estimated separately in each village, so that those with land in a number of municipalities might avoid expropriation, an important factor if the object was to weaken the political and economic influence of landowners.

to 431 between 1923 and 1934, insufficient when the Italian land reform after the Second World War had one technician for every 25 settlers.[36] The government's lack of information on the amount of new land that could be expropriated and brought into cultivation at both the village and provincial levels is illustrated in Pascual Carrión's highly influential book, *Los latifundios de España* (1932). Carrión, using statistical information from the cadastre, showed the extent of land concentration in southern Spain, but his estimate of 5.9 million hectares of available land to settle 930,000 families proved well wide of the mark.[37] A couple of years later, Vazquez Humasqué, the IRA's director, reduced the figures to 407,000 families and 3.66 million hectares, equivalent to an average of 9 hectares per family.[38] Contemporaries never calculated exactly the total amount of land that could be expropriated under the 1932 Law, but one recent estimate puts it at 4,650,000 hectares in the latifundio provinces, or 25 per cent of their productive surface.[39]

The creation of a village census of landless workers and poor land-owners and tenants (*Censo de Campesinos*) also proved difficult.[40] The family was considered the basic economic unit, but virtually no independent information existed to indicate a family's income, while household size could fluctuate sharply for demographic reasons and over the economic cycle. In addition, given the rumours surrounding a possible land reform, 'numerous' workers from outside the sector claimed to be farm labourers.[41] Many villages simply failed to carry out the *Censo*, while the difficulty of establishing objective criteria provided local authorities with the possibility to create lists that rewarded their political followers (Chapter 10).

[36] Pan-Montojo 2005, p. 267 and 274, and Palerm 1962, p. 26.

[37] Carrión believed that 10.4 million hectares was available by expropriating all the land found on estates of over 250 hectares, and assumed that half of this could be cultivated. According to his study, 250,000 landless families required 10 hectares each, and a further 680,000 families had insufficient land, and needed 5 hectares each. Carrión 1932: 1975, p. 362 and cuadro 65. The cadastre was virtually complete in eight provinces (Albacete, Cadiz, Ciudad Real, Cordoba, Granada, Jaen, Malaga, and Toledo), and well advanced in the rest (94 per cent complete in Seville, 83 per cent in Badajoz, 73 per cent in Huelva, 67 per cent in Almeria, 59 per cent in Caceres, and 51 per cent in Salamanca). Ibid., cuadro 3.

[38] Vazquez Humasqué, *El Sol*, 17 de mayo 1934. A recent estimate gives 569,000 landless adult male workers, a figure which perhaps is not too different to the 407,000 families. Carmona et al. 2019, table 3.

[39] Robledo Hernández 2014, p. 91. Most landowners appear to have registered their farms with the government's inventory of expropriable lands, as financial rewards were offered to informants of undeclared land. López Ontiveros & Mata Olmo 1993, ch. 3.

[40] Owner-occupiers who paid less than 50 pesetas tax, equivalent to about 10 hectares of cereal land, were also eligible. Malefakis 1970, pp. 111–12, and Espinoza et al. 2007, p. 310. For the *Censo de Campesinos*, see also Corrionero Salinero 1986.

[41] For example, AIRA, Caceres, 6–7, Alonso Peña, p. 8.

Historically, land reform has had a much greater chance of success when the state has owned large areas of land, or could expropriate it cheaply from a landowning class that had become politically discredited or shown to have acquired it illegally.[42] In Spain, the state owned virtually no farm land, but the Azaña government linked the grandees with the failed 'Sanjurjo' military coup of 1932, and expropriated their lands without compensation. Many contemporaries believed that the nobility owned vast tracts of uncultivated land, but the government now found a much more modest figure of 1.2 or 1.3 million hectares throughout the whole country, equivalent to 'no more than 6 per cent of the 21 million hectares that are normally cultivated', while the grandees accounted for just half these figures, with much of their lands found outside the municipalities with the greatest social need.[43] On the eve of the 1936 military uprising, the government was preparing legislation to recover large areas of the old common lands, although once again it had no information on their potential effect for creating new employment. Indeed, many contemporaries and historians have ignored the fact that both the land belonging to the grandees and the old common lands were often already in cultivation, implying that there was limited possibility for bringing more land under the plough, and that the settling of new farmers would require the expulsion of others.

Historically, land reform also stands a better chance of success when the future beneficiaries are the tenants or sharecroppers already working the land, as they are acquainted with organizing production themselves, limiting the need for state involvement (Table 8.2).[44] By contrast, when land reform attempts to convert landless labourers into farmers, either the state has to provide major investment to build new farm buildings and help manage thousands of small farms, or the old estates have to be run as collectives. In the first instance the reform is often far too slow, while collectives risk falling output and low labour productivity because of the free-rider problem.

In Spain, land reform was attempted on two very different types of latifundios: the large cereal farms (*cortijos*) involving landless labourers, especially in the fertile Guadalquivir river basin (*Campiña*); and on the dehesas, areas of poor soils in the upland regions of Andalucía and

---

[42] Griffin et al. 2002.
[43] Malefakis 1970, p. 73. Robledo 2012, cuadro 2, estimates the grandees owned about half a million hectares in all Spain, and only 4 per cent of the cultivated area in the south. Contemporaries had little information, with Fernando de los Rios, for example, being unable to give any idea of the area of the old seigneurial land that could be expropriated during the cabinet meeting of 10th August 1931. Pan-Montojo 2005, pp. 284–5.
[44] Griffin et al. 2002.

Table 8.2 *The impact of land reform on farm structure and work incentives*

Who receives land?	Impact on farm structure	Impact on work incentives	Examples in Spain
Family farmers (tenants & sharecroppers)	No change	Good	Attempted in Extremadura (dehesas)
Landless workers: to create family farmers	Need to build new farms	Good – but need help to become entrepreneurs	Attempted in Andalucia (cortijos)
Landless workers: to create collectives	No change	Weak	Attempted during the Civil War

throughout Extremadura, involving small tenant farmers and sharecroppers. Despite widespread criticism of poor cultivation by contemporaries such as Carrión, the agronomists' reports for both the expropriated cortijos on Cordoba's *Campiña*, and Badajoz's dehesas, suggest that there were few options to significantly increase output in the short term.[45] In Cordoba, they noted that the creation of state-run experimental stations and extension services might help the asset-poor workers become entrepreneurs, and introduce new crops such as cotton, sugar beet, tobacco, and maize, but there is no suggestion that the previous owners would not have introduced these themselves if commercial conditions had been more favourable.

In Badajoz, agronomists also proposed very few changes in farm practices on the twenty expropriated farms for which information is available, and in about half the reports there were no suggestions for improvements at all. Nevertheless, they projected future output that was 68 per cent higher per hectare than the provincial average, and wheat yields 46 per cent greater, even though land quality according to the cadastre was only 5 per cent better. How this increase in output was to be achieved with only minimum changes in production methods, and on soils little better than the provincial average, is difficult to explain, unless agronomists believed that land reform would change work incentives sufficiently to increase labour inputs.[46] Yet for this to happen, three collective-action

---

[45] López Ontiveros & Mata Olmo 1993, pp. 127–31, and Simpson & Carmona 2017, pp. 46–52. Carrión 1932: 1975, pp. 328–32, gives only one example of a supposedly poorly cultivated farm in all his book, a 444-hectare dehesa in Trujillo in Extremadura, which he claims was similar to other farms in the region. He offers virtually no information concerning ecological restrictions, farm gate prices, or the practical problems associated with settling large numbers of workers at a significant distance from their village homes.

[46] A more detailed discussion in Simpson & Carmona 2017, pp. 46–52.

problems had to be resolved, namely adverse selection (the attraction of low-ability members to settlements), shirking, and the threat of exit by high-ability members.[47] Although settlements existed for only a few years, the evidence suggests that these were formidable problems, and the IRA was frequently required to intervene to keep farms operating, let alone produce efficiency gains.

Settlers were usually chosen from the *Censo de Campesinos* by *Acción Social*, an independent body, according to a rough indicator of economic need, with household heads listed in order according to the number of family members of over 12 years of age that they supported. Not surprisingly, the average age of those receiving land was almost fifty, and the land reform therefore effectively excluded young farmers.[48] Furthermore, despite the fact that many tenants and sharecroppers in Badajoz already owned draft animals and farm equipment and were accustomed to organizing themselves into small groups to rent and cultivate land, the land reform created settlements with individuals who did not necessarily have much in common with each other, except being poor and having large families.[49] The difficulties were further compounded by the fact that many settlements were located in the depths of the countryside, with seventeen of the twenty-eight settlements in this province being five kilometres or more from the nearest village.[50]

The settlers were dependent on the IRA for help managing the farm and for loans to feed their families and work animals, as well as to buy seed and fertilizers, until the harvest. All the settlements were found in areas of cereal farming using dry-farming techniques, and the IRA's agronomists usually recommended that estates be kept as a single unit and worked as collectives, suggesting that the potential economies of scale associated with using farm machinery, draft animals, and grazing land outweighed any change in work incentives found using family labour. However most settlers, perhaps better aware of the difficulties of organizing an average of eighty-one families, such as was the case in Badajoz, wanted farms to be divided into family plots to work individually.[51] In this province, a hybrid

---

[47] Abramitzky 2011.

[48] Simpson & Carmona 2017, table 6. Some settlements also recruited specialist workers, such as shepherds to tend the village flock. The 1932 Land Reform Act (*Base* 11) gave preference to cultivators with families, and within this category, those with the most children.

[49] For tenant associations see Simpson & Carmona 2017, p. 54, and Carmona & Simpson 2014a for traditional collective tenancies. Article 12c of the 1932 Land Reform Law gave preference to 'collective cultivators' when allocating uncultivated land. Malefakis 1970, p. 229.

[50] Only three were found within a kilometre of a village. Simpson & Carmona 2017.

[51] AIRA, Badajoz, Caja 6.7. Settlements in some cases outsourced activities, such as grazing or harvesting cork.

situation developed whereby each family cultivated their own plots on the open fields, but the common flock, the payment of rent, and the responsibility for repaying capital were communal responsibilities.[52] The combination of large families and small plots implied that settlers were forced to seek off-farm employment making it harder to monitor their work effort, leading to complaints about workers' underperforming or simply disappearing. On the Ramira Alta estate, for example, 153 settlers were expelled for absenteeism, while another 53 were fined for not working their plots adequately. The fact that a foreman kept daily accounts of each settler's work, reinforced the idea that they were still essentially wage labourers rather than independent farmers, and on one farm in Cádiz, the 'farmers' actually went on strike demanding more 'pay' from the IRA.[53] The nature of agency problems and transaction costs were therefore changed rather than reduced, and the need for dry-farming implied that output increased not through labour-intensive improvements, but rather by extending the area of subsistence cereals on marginal soils, and collecting wood for charcoal production.

The government was divided over the objectives for land reform, with the cabinet demanding a rapid response to rural poverty, while those in the IRA and the Ministry of Agriculture wanted to restructure agriculture and create a society of independent family farms. For example, in July 1933, Manuel Azaña, the Prime Minister of the Republic, rejected a proposal by the Ministry of Agriculture to provide land and loans of 12,000 pesetas, equivalent to a subsistence income for six years, to each of the 4,000 families to be settled, as it would have failed to resolve the severe regional unemployment.[54] Likewise the plan by the IRA to create twenty-three family farms, each with its own plough team on the 596-hectare Merinillas Altas estate (Badajoz), was rejected by the government in favour of giving 5 hectares each to 119 families, sufficient perhaps to cover their basic needs, but leaving families dependent on labour markets for seasonal employment. Just as in Eastern Europe, land reform would lead to the creation of farms far too small to be economically viable.

In conclusion, most contemporaries failed to appreciate not just the rapid changes that had taken place in southern agriculture over the

---

[52] It was believed that workers would sell the land if they were given full possession. Following the 1935 Land Reform, the rent was paid to the old landowners. Sales were made collectively and any surplus distributed among settlers after rent and credit repayments had been made to the IRA.

[53] Macarro Vera 2000, p. 233.

[54] 6 July 1933, in Azaña 1997, p. 383. The farm was probably in Andalusia. Azaña also noted it was totally impractical, and believed that his Minister of Agriculture (Domingo) was unaware that the 4,000 mule teams would be left seriously under-employed during the year.

previous two or three decades, but also the lack of suitable new land that could be brought into cultivation. There were certainly plenty of open spaces, but these often suffered from fragile soils, were too far away from the village to allow intensive cultivation, and the available dry-farming technologies made it difficult, if not impossible, to increase yields.[55] In addition, although only a relatively small number of estates were ever confiscated, land reform was also seen as a risk to family farmers. This was not just because a future government might reduce the maximum farm size permitted before expropriation, or confiscate properties that had previously been common lands, but because it threatened farmers already on the farm ladder. In Extremadura, for example, the high cereal prices from the First World War had encouraged an enormous expansion of cultivation, which had often been carried out by small or medium-sized tenants, subleasing lands from larger tenants.[56] The 1932 Land Reform imposed a limit of 20 hectares, while village authorities placed a maximum of 10 hectares of rented land for those listed on the *Censo de Campesinos*.[57] In Extremadura, farmers usually needed considerably more than 20 hectares to maintain a fully employed plough team because of the poor soil quality (Appendix 2).

Finally, the 1932 Land Reform permanently settled less than 5 per cent of those in need in southern Spain, but it was seen as being irrelevant by those most in need at the foot of the farm ladder, namely the young. Large numbers of the landless in western Spain looked instead for an alternative solution.

Land Reform by Invasion: the Role of Village-Level Institutions

The slow implementation of the 1932 Land Reform contrasts with the dramatic land invasions during the night of 24–25 March 1936, which would lead to 110,921 farmers being officially settled by the IRA on 572,035 hectares.[58] These invasions were geographically concentrated in areas of dehesas, especially in Extremadura, where many small farmers owned work-animals and farm implements, and were accustomed to working small plots of land on short leases, either as individuals, or in

---

[55] Chapter 7. Simpson & Carmona 2017, pp. 49–54.
[56] Carmona & Simpson 2016, table 2, for the contribution of small and medium farms in expanding output.
[57] Ley de Bases, base 12, j and k. Simpson & Carmona 2017, pp. 53–5.
[58] Malefakis 1970, pp. 369–78. Some 72 per cent of the peasants and 42 per cent of the area were found in Extremadura. See Chapter 10 for details.

small groups.[59] Poor soil quality implied that the land could only be cultivated for a couple of years before it had to be returned to pasture, and tenants were therefore dependent on being given new contracts to different plots of land on the estate at regular intervals. According to many contemporaries, the first invasions in 1932 were caused by local landowners refusing to renew tenancies, either because of the economic crisis, or as part of an organized lockout in response to Republican legislation.[60] The government's response was the *Intensificación de cultivos* decree, which allowed the settlement of 33,000 farmers on 100,000 hectares for a maximum of two years. The government automatically renewed the leases in 1934 for another year, but many tenants were evicted by landowners following the 1935 harvest.

The invasions after the Popular Front's victory in 1936 followed a decree that gave village councils powers to identify suitable land that could be cultivated by the landless in those areas of major social need.[61] The occupations required the formal approval of the IRA before planting could begin to ensure that there was indeed social deprivation; that the settlements were carried out in accordance with the law; and that the settlers were only those listed in the *Censo de Campesinos*.[62] In practice, it seems that permission was almost always given, either because of local pressure, or because of the difficulties for the IRA's agronomists to assess such large areas in the short time period before planting, and the impossibility of verifying whether those occupying the land were actually in need. For many Socialists, the land invasions were to be the start of a larger movement of legalized occupations driven by local initiatives, which included the recovery by villagers of their old common lands.[63]

Some historians have argued that these bottom-up reforms were more effective than the highly centralized 1932 Land Reform for settling large numbers of workers quickly, and would have been successful if they had not been interrupted by the outbreak of the

[59] In reality, as Chapter 10 explains, they usually rented or sharecropped the land from other tenants.
[60] Government statistics, however, show no significant falls in the cultivated area and Chapter 10 argues that the conflicts probably originated over whether it was the landowners, or the Socialist FNTT, who decided which tenants should have access to the insufficient amounts of land for cultivation. Changes in the area cultivated are discussed in Carmona & Simpson 2016, pp. 125–9.
[61] BIRA, junio 1936, pp. 735–38; Riesco Roche 2006, pp. 317–18. This was the social utility clause found not just in the 1935 Land Reform Law, but also in the 1931 Constitution (article 44).
[62] Ruiz Funes in Parliament, in Ladrón de Guevara 1993, p. 426.
[63] Riesco Roche 2006, pp. 321, notes that in thirteen municipalities of Caceres, 45,000 hectares were identified for future occupation.

Civil War in the summer of 1936.[64] Certainly the village authorities had much greater local information and flexibility than the IRA bureaucracy. However, the reforms were not without their problems. In the first instance, the rapid expansion of the settlements created demands by settlers for seed, fertilizers, and the family's subsistence which stretched the IRA's resources, as it not only had to make the loans, but also to assume the very high supervision costs to enforce their repayment from asset-poor settlers. There were numerous complaints of the failure of the state, and some settlers abandoned their land.[65] In reality, neither the IRA nor village organizations were in a position to substitute the traditional channels for financing farming or marketing their output, which had often been in the hands of landowners or large tenants.

There was also a risk of opportunistic behaviour on the part of tenants. For the asset-poor, the major preoccupation was gaining employment and sustenance for their family and animals over the coming year, while landowners had to balance the attraction of an immediate rental income (which in theory was guaranteed by the IRA) with the long-term need to preserve soil fertility. Land shortages now not only risked pasture lands being ploughed under and livestock farmers having to dispose of their animals, but also soil mining by tenants on the arable. Given the short-term nature of contracts, and the fact that many landowners would be unlikely to voluntarily renew them to those who had invaded their land, there were few incentives for tenants to practice good husbandry and maintain soil fertility. In fact, although rents were often assessed below the market rate, landowners complained that neither the tenants, nor the IRA, actually paid them.[66]

Finally, it is not clear whether it was those families in greatest need that received land, or those with the greatest capacity for mobilization. Some information exists on the identity of those settled under the 1932 Land Reform, but very little is known about the individuals who participated in the land invasions.[67] The only characteristic that is repeated in the different studies is that many belonged to the Socialist FNTT, and the syndicate itself claims to have coordinated the

---

[64] This is the hypothesis, for example, of Robledo Hernández 2014, p. 78, or Iriarte & Lana 2016.

[65] Malefakis 1970, p. 383.

[66] Rent was assessed on tax returns which, where the amillaramientos was still in use, such as in Caceres (40 per cent) or Salamanca (49 per cent), could be significantly below the real value. Even if the cadastre was in use, values were sometimes those of before 1914.

[67] For example, Carmona & Simpson 2016. No information is given in Riesco Roche 2006, Espinosa 2007, or Ladrón de Guevara 1993.

invasions.[68] The fact that the Socialist press complained that land-owners and employers discriminated against FNTT members in 1931 and 1932, and again in 1935, makes it likely that FNTT membership was a necessary criterion to receive land following the 1932 and 1936 invasions that they organized.[69] In fact, as Chapter 10 argues, the possibility of conflict between different groups of workers and small farmers were much greater with bottom-up reforms than top-down ones.

Conclusion: the Limits to Land Reform

By the 1930s, Spain was too rich for a classic land reform that involved the large-scale permanent redistribution of property. There were strict limits to increasing output by using more labour under dry-farming conditions, and the growing economies of scale associated with cereals, especially on the heavy, fertile Campiña soils, suggests that there was no longer a clear inverse relationship between farm size and land productivity, as capital inputs were becoming increasingly important.[70] Furthermore, although labour organizations such as the FNTT preferred cereal production to livestock farming because it created more employment, per capita bread consumption had already peaked, and the country had become virtually self-sufficient in wheat. By contrast, the ploughing up of large areas of pasture threatened livestock production despite a growing demand for meat and dairy products. The vine and olive were the traditional, labour-intensive crops suitable to dry-farming conditions, but both were suffer-ing from overproduction, and in any case required between four and seven years to become productive.[71] Only a 'green-revolution' could have absorbed the surplus labour, but the technological problems to extend the area of irrigation and grow commercially viable crops would not be resolved until several decades later, and even then irrigation was only found in highly specific geographical areas.

Two major restrictions to land reform in Southern Spain were the fact that most of the new land that could be brought under the plough was marginal pasture land, and that dry-farming cultivation techniques were usually required. This severely limited the possibilities of changing work

[68] Malefakis 1970, pp. 370; Ladrón de Guevara 1993, pp. 410–12, and 424, for the rejection of non-socialist workers; Riesco Roche 2006, p. 145, for the systematic exclu-sion of anarchist workers.

[69] Carmona & Simpson 2016, pp. 136–7, for evidence that they were not always the poorest groups in the locality.

[70] Lipton 2009, p. 65. The relationship would be expected to exist with specialist tree crops and market gardening, but these usually needed irrigation.

[71] Vázquez Humasqué, for example, makes no mention of either in *El Sol*, 17 de mayo 1934.

incentives as small farmers found it difficult to increase output by working the land more intensely. Therefore if land reform could not increase production, its success would be limited to simply reducing land and income inequality. In fact, if it is assumed that there were half a million families in the thirteen latifundio provinces identified by Malefakis who were either already farmers or landless workers, then average gross farm output was 5,088 pesetas in 1931, a figure that drops to around 3,360 net of rent and capital inputs. Although this figure is two-thirds higher than the basic income required to support a family, it could only have been achieved by a massive redistribution of farmland over a region with some 12.6 million hectares.[72] By contrast, the 1932 Land Reform settled at most 5 per cent of those in need.[73] Even more so than in most countries, living standards for farmers and workers in this region by the 1930s had become much more dependent on the changes in the demand for labour in the non-farm sector, than the ability of agriculture itself to create more employment.

Given the difficulties that the state faced in carrying out a permanent land reform, there were some advantages in allowing village-level organizations a greater role, as they could identify better under-cultivated land, or select the workers most in need. Yet temporary settlements obviously could not resolve the problem of a shortage of land, and the 3 hectares or so that each family received in Badajoz, for example, under the *Intensificación de cultivos* (1932) or the *Yunteros* decrees (1936), produced an annual income of only 216 pesetas net, or 342 pesetas including rent, little more than a quarter of family's basic needs (Appendix 2). These small plots of labour-intensive cereals on the poor dehesa soils were never going to be competitive with other Spanish regions, and their impact on living standards was limited by the need to pay rent. Eliminating rent was only possible in a democratic society when the state had sufficient fiscal capacity to compensate landowners, which was not the case in Spain.[74] Temporary settlements were also restricted by the fact that significant numbers of the landless were effectively excluded because they had no work animals or basic farm equipment. Indeed, the geographic

---

[72] Vázquez Humasqué (1934) gives a figure of 407,000 families in need, while Martínez de Bujana 1935 calculated a total of 800,000 families in the latifundio provinces. We assume rent and capital accounted for a third of gross farm output. For details, Appendix 2.

[73] At most, 20,000 families were settled under the 1932 Land Reform compared to Vázquez Humasqué's figure of 407,000 in need. A further problem was that the population most in need often lived in villages with limited amounts of uncultivated land. Even if land reform had not been interrupted by the Civil War, it is unlikely to have resolved the region's underlying problems.

[74] Foley-Fisher & McLaughlin 2016, note that in Ireland the British government was willing to guarantee the loans. A further problem in the areas of dehesas was that settlers needed access to large areas of land to be able to rest the soil every two or three years, as well as animals to graze the pasture and fallow.

distribution of the farms that experienced invasions to cultivate land, as opposed to illegally remove timber or gaze an animal, was almost exclusively on the dehesas. On the large cortijos in Andalucia, especially in the Campiña, there were virtually no invasions.

Even the temporary settlements in regions of dehesas increased, rather than diminished, conflicts. There were many small farmers in Southern Spain, and latifundios in some villages were relatively unimportant.[75] The fact that land reform only addressed the interests of the landless labourers could lead to clashes with small tenant farmers, as they needed significantly more land to keep their mule team fully employed.[76] Land shortage also risked over-cultivation, especially as settlers had weak incentives to respect rotations and natural pastures, and not exhaust the soil. Finally, conflicts arose over which group had the right to allocate scarce resources: local farmers; the IRA; village authorities; or syndicates (Chapter 10).

The experience of land reform therefore had only a limited impact on poverty, but the laws and decrees fuelled political tensions in the countryside and weakened, rather than strengthened, democracy. The political consequences of policies that excluded such a large section of the rural poor, especially among the young, was destabilizing for the Republic as support flowed to the FNTT and the far-right *Juventudes de Acción Popular* (JAP). Indeed, it could be argued that the Spanish land reform should not be seen as some sort of World Bank experiment at changing economic incentives, but rather as a political instrument designed by both the Left Republican-Socialist coalition, and the parties of the right, to attract political support.[77] In this respect, they found three controversial clauses of the 1932 Land Reform Law especially helpful. First, land reform was seen as national problem, as it was eventually to be applied to the whole country, resulting in 71 per cent of the 879,371 farms identified for expropriation being found outside the fourteen latifundio provinces.[78] Second, the provision to expropriate all land in the latifundio provinces that had been rented for more than twelve years included many plots belonging to workers who had recently migrated to the cities, as well as widows and those too old to work the land themselves.[79] Finally, landowners with more than 20 hectares of cereal land, or its equivalent,

---

[75] See especially the case of La Solana (Ciudad Real) in Rey 2008.
[76] Carmona & Simpson 2015, cuadro 5.
[77] Pérez Yruela 1979, pp. 93–5, for example argues that the land reform was essentially political.
[78] Malefakis 1970, pp. 216–17.
[79] In the rest of Spain this law only applied to owners who rented more than 400 hectares. Malefakis 1970, p. 212.

that was found in the immediate vicinity of villages (*ruedos*) also faced expropriation, thereby potentially affecting quite modest farmers. Yet while these clauses certainly helped the Left build support outside the latifundio provinces, it is less clear how they helped the traditional landed elites, as opposed to the new right-wing parties. The landed elites were closely linked with the monarchical parties, and many refused to accept either the Republic or the 1931 Constitution, and were behind the failed Sanjurjo coup-d'état in August 1932. This effectively removed them from mass party politics, and it was a new democratic Right, first the Radical Party, and then increasingly the right-wing *Confederación Española de Derechas Autónomas* or CEDA, that tried to organize small farmers on a national basis (Chapter 9).[80] Rural poverty in the South was a major social problem, but it was the ability of strong labour organizations, especially the Socialist FNTT, that turned it into a national, rather than a regional problem. Therefore, although by 1931 Spain had become a country of family farmers who accounted for around a third of the country's electorate, and the latifundios contributed little more than 3 per cent of Spain's GDP and employed only 5 per cent of the nation's workforce, the Socialist FNTT and Anarchist CNT successfully used the latifundios question to set the political agenda, and test the new Republic.[81] The next chapter will explain how.

---

[80] Rey 2008, p. 186 claims that small farmers in La Solana organized themselves.

[81] The thirteen latifundio provinces produced 28 per cent of Spanish farm output in 1931, and within this area major taxpayers (> 5000 pesetas) accounted for half (48 per cent). As agriculture contributed 24.2 per cent to GDP, the contribution of latifundios was 3.3 per cent. The thirteen provinces employed 27 per cent of the nation's agricultural work force. We assume that 38.7 per cent of these were landless and worked on latifundios, giving 10.4 per cent of the agricultural labour force, equivalent to about 5 per cent of the national work force. Carrión 1932: 1975, Carmona et al. 2019, Prados de la Escosura 2003, and Simpson 1995b.

Part V

Rural Conflicts and the Polarization of Village Society

[E]ffective political competition requires credible guarantees that losers will not be expropriated and that losing political organizations continue to enjoy access to future competition.[1]

This book began with some comments on Luis Buñuel's film *Las Hurdes* that illustrated for urban audiences the acute rural poverty found in this isolated region of western Spain. At one point, it shows groups of males walking desolately back to their village after being unable to find work in the cereal harvest in Castile and Andalucia. No explanation for this failure is given, although the fact that the film was made in the early 1930s suggests that it was for political rather than economic reasons, and caused by the so-called *Términos Municipales* decree that banned the use of migrant labour in villages when local workers were unemployed. Well-intentioned government reforms which aimed at strengthening the bargaining power of local workers by reducing competition, inadvertently shifted hardship onto other workers, while increasing production costs for both large and small farmers at a time of weak farm prices. The state's inability to implement legislation impartially effectively gave significant powers to village politicians over how farm incomes were to be distributed. Village disputes arose over whether it was the local employers and landowners who decided which workers, tenants, and share-croppers were to be contracted, and under what conditions, or whether these rights belonged instead to the Socialist FNTT or the Anarchist CNT. As village societies became more polarized, farm labourers and small farmers were forced to choose between their 'loyalty' to traditional landowners and employers, or 'voice' and join a labour syndicate. Crucially, given the economic conditions of the 1930s, 'exit' was no longer an option.[2]

The popular acclaim for the new democratic republic following the abdication of the king in April 1931 did not guarantee its success. Indeed, with hindsight, the chances of consolidating a genuine democracy at this time appear small. This was not because of any obvious shortcoming of

[1] North et al. 2009, p. 117.   [2] See Hirschman 1970.

the leading politicians who, even if lacking in experience, were as able as any that Spain produced over the twentieth century, but rather to the Republic's inheritance of a weak state capacity, the absence of genuine political parties, and the deep economic depression.

Political power would change hands three times during the Second Republic: favouring the Left Republican-Socialist coalition during the *Primer Bienio* (December 1931 and November 1933); then a Centre Right Coalition in the *Bienio Conservador* (November 1933 to February 1936); and finally, the Left Republicans, without the Socialists, after February 1936. At the village level, representatives of the employers and syndicates alternated in controlling local patronage and only implementing labour and social legislation if it was in their interests. The February 1936 election results show a deeply divided country, with the *coalición antirrevolucionaria* or anti-revolutionary coalition, gaining almost as many votes nationally as the Popular Front.[3] Although a map immediately following the military uprising in July 1936 suggests a country split geographically between regions of family farmers that supported the uprising and others of landless labourers and latifundios remaining true to the Republic, the real division was often within villages, in areas of both latifundios and small farmers.

The tensions that these political swings produced are vividly described in George Collier's study of 'Los Olivos', a village in the Sierra de Aracena (Huelva). According to Collier, electoral competition among the rural elites before the Second Republic was essentially over who controlled the patronage networks rather than ideological issues. This changed when the Socialists came to power in the village in early 1932, as they only employed FNTT members for public works, and fully implemented the 1931 and 1932 legislation that required farmers to hire more workers than they needed, and attempted to determine which ones they could employ.[4] This situation was reversed following the Asturias Revolution of October 1934, as the new centre-right municipal government closed the village's *Casa del Pueblo*, arrested the local Socialist leaders, and eliminated names of their opponents from the electoral census. Judicial citations by the Guardia Civil increased thirty times in 1935, as landowners became highly sensitive over who they allowed to collect fire-wood or

---

[3] The Popular Front had a common electoral program, although various parties, including the Socialists, announced beforehand that they would not participate in a government. The anti-revolutionary coalition lacked even a common program, and its sole purpose was to defeat the Popular Front. Juliá 1989.

[4] This went against the owners *autonomía*, which was the 'cultural construct embodying the proprietors' claim to the right to manage their own affairs in the sphere of production and more broadly in social life'. Collier 1987, p. 5.

graze a couple of animals freely on their land. Policies changed dramatically once more following the Popular Front's victory in February 1936, but these were cut short by the military uprising. During the first year of the Civil War, thirty-eight Socialist men, the equivalent of 12 per cent of the village's adult males were dead, most having been summarily executed, their household possessions looted, and family members 'terrorized and humiliated'.[5]

This section argues that village society became polarized as a result of the difficulties to implement even modest social and economic polices because the Republic inherited a weak party system and limited state capacity to implement legislation. Governments failed to reduce poverty because the state could not organize social transfers impartially at the village level, leaving traditional, undemocratic systems of corruption and clientelism to continue. This benefitted those who controlled village institutions, at the expense of those who were excluded. At first, it was the Left, which took over traditional patronage systems to benefit their own followers. This involved discriminating against those workers and tenants belonging to the traditional patron-client networks, and benefitting instead their own supporters. Membership of the Socialist FNTT soared, but higher living standards were now dependent on the Left Republican-Socialists remaining in power. When the Right returned to power, it too resorted to policies that maximized its partisan advantage, rewarding its supporters, and discriminating against those of the Left. Against a background of falling living standards and the growth of fascism in other European countries, the Marxist influence increased, and drove many socialists away from democratic politics, terminating in the Asturias uprising in October 1934. Yet equally to blame was the failure to create a moderate, Christian Democratic party that could respond to both the economic and social problems of the time, and attract the active support of the landed elites and Church. By using its temporary control of power to blatantly reward its own supporters at the expense of the opposition was not sustainable in a democracy. When the CEDA, in alliance with other right-wing groups, lost the elections in February 1936, it faced the same stark choice as the Socialists had in November 1933: either accept a drop in living standards of many of its supporters and falling party membership, or move towards an authoritarian solution that would permanently exclude their rivals. Ultimately democracy failed because both groups increasingly believed that if their opponents gained political power, they would discriminate against their members, close their newspapers, and attempt to destroy their political organization. As

[5] Ibid., pp. 146 and 162.

Levitsky and Ziblatt have recently argued, 'one thing is clear from study-ing breakdowns throughout history, it's that extreme polarization can kill democracies'.[6] In conclusion, it makes little sense to try and establish whether it was the Left or the Right that was most to blame, as both groups had failed in the formidable tasks in building new, broadly based democratic parties.

This section explains not only why the main parties on both the political extremes failed to play the democratic game, but also why conflicts deeply polarized village society. Chapter 9 shows that just as the failure of Christian Democracy to develop before 1931 had allowed the landed elites and Catholic hierarchy to remain outside mass party politics, so the Socialist Party's limited political experience delayed the appearance of revisionist Marxism and Social Democracy. The result was that neither of the two main parties during the Republic, the PSOE and the CEDA, had a strong commitment to attract moderate voters and defend democracy, which led to their supporters quickly moving towards the political extremes following electoral setbacks. Indeed, after February 1936, both the main parties were outside the government. The final chapter looks at the nature of rural conflicts and why they were often between different groups or workers or tenants, rather than between social and economic classes.

[6] Levitsky & Ziblatt 2018, p. 9.

9 Creating Parties, Political Alliances, and Interest Groups: Rural Politics in the 1930s

Ortega y Gasset (June 1931): [W]ith the exception of the Socialist Party, all the other parties that engage in politics are not really parties nor anything worthy of it.[1]

Engels (1894): [I]t is the duty of our party to make clear to the peasantry again and again that their position is absolutely helpless so long as capitalism holds sway, that it is absolutely impossible to preserve their holdings as such, and that capitalist large scale production is absolutely sure to run over their impotent and antiquated system of small scale production as a train runs over a pushcart.[2]

A range of theories have been advanced to explain the difficulties of sustaining democracy in Spain during the early 1930s. For some historians, democratic failure was caused by the rural elites who from the outset supposedly opposed even moderate reforms to improve the material conditions of landless workers and poor tenant farmers.[3] By contrast, others blame the Left for policies that threatened to ruin the national economy, and especially agriculture, and culminated in a revolutionary uprising in Asturias in October 1934, which left up to 2,000 dead across the country.[4] A glance through the pages of *El Socialista* or *ABC*, the leading monarchical daily, provides plenty of evidence for both arguments. Yet while it is hardly surprising to find extremists in the 1930s on either side of the political spectrum, what needs explaining here is why the consensus found at the beginning of the Republic for moderate reforms to improve living conditions among the rural poor so quickly broke down, and why the countryside then became so polarized. This chapter looks at the difficulties of creating democratic political parties that could respond to the demands of a highly diverse rural electorate, while Chapter 10 shows how the persistence of clientelistic networks and weak state capacity led to the polarization of village society.

---

[1] Linz 1967, p. 228   [2] Cited in Berman 2006, pp. 37–8.
[3] Robledo Hernández & Esteban 2017, pp. 28–9, Preston 2000, p. 34 and Gonzalez Calleja 2012, p. 395.
[4] Rey 2011, pp. 38–39, Macarro Vera 2017 and Payne 2005, p. 543. For estimates of mortality, see especially González Calleja 2015, pp. 203–44.

As Chapter 3 argued, political parties before 1923 were weak and organized around clientelistic networks and patronage, rather than ideology. Election results were planned in Madrid, and implemented by local elites (*caciques*). The attempts during the Primo de Rivera dictatorship (1923–9) to bring about change by creating a single party and corporatist government proved unsuccessful. The 1931 Constitution changed the legal framework but, unsurprisingly, failed to transform a weak party system based on clientelistic politics to one with dynamic civic associations and competitive party politics. During the Second Republic, the party that could appoint provincial governors and control municipal government continued to have a significant electoral advantage, especially in rural areas. For example, when the Left Republican-Socialist coalition came to power in 1931, new elections were ordered for over 2,000 municipalities where irregularities had supposedly taken place, leading to the monarchists being heavily defeated, and they failed to win a single one of the 889 seats in the province of Seville.[5] An electoral system that had been run exclusively by the rural elites for control over local patronage was now embraced by other political groups, including the well-organized Socialist Party and its syndicate to reward their supporters. The fact that universal male suffrage had existed since 1890 led many voters to associate the electoral box with patronage, something that no party was going to abandon now, and the classical patronage system of the Restoration (1876–1923) simply changed to state clientelism and a single party under Primo de Rivera (1923–30), and to party clientelism under the Second Republic.[6]

The weak state capacity to implement policies can be illustrated by the government attempts to compile a *Censo de Campesinos*. This was carried out with considerable delays, if at all, in those villages where the rural elites enjoyed significant influence. However, in other villages it was collected in the Socialist *Casa del Pueblo*, thereby discouraging workers loyal to landowners from signing, and the control by the supposedly neutral village secretary, a professional civil servant.[7] Likewise, the decisions of the *jurados mixtos*, which fixed land rents and work conditions, often reflected the interests of those who were in political power in the

---

[5] According to Townson, although the republican civil governor was politically neutral in theory, they, 'like the monarchist ones before them, invariably went to great lengths to promote the cause of the particular party which had sponsored them'. For example, Manuel Portela, the prime minister and leader of the new *Partido del Centro Democrático* in 1935, actually believed that his control over the electoral system would result in it gaining a third of the seats, making it the largest party. Townson 2000, pp. 46–9 and 338–9.

[6] Gómez Benito 2011, p. 24. In fact, the system underwent considerable changes during the Restoration period, as suggested by Rey 2008, p. 56.

[7] Collier 1987, p. 93.

village.[8] The village worker in Casas Viejas (Cadiz) who claimed that everyone belonged to the Anarchist CNT, 'because you had to in order to get work', acted no differently to those workers in other villages who decided to join the Socialist FNTT, or support the Catholic CNCA.[9]

What did change however was that the two monarchical parties, the Conservatives and Liberals, effectively disappeared, as they won only nine of the fifty provincial capitals in the municipal elections of April 1931. The 1931 Constitution encouraged a proliferation of small and often local parties, requiring politicians to form alliances to govern. In fact, no single party in the three national elections (1931, 1933, and 1936) obtained even a quarter of the parliamentary seats (Table 9.1).[10] An unknown, but important section of the traditional rural elites now belonged to groups on the extreme right, which never recognized either the 1931 Constitution, nor the Republic. But in numerical terms, these were very small, and their political influence limited until 1936. Most landowners and tenants did initially accept the Republic (but perhaps not the Constitution because of its anti-Catholic clauses), and they voted for Lerroux's Radical Party, and later for Gil Robles and the CEDA. The Left was divided between Left-Republicans of the groups around Azaña, and the Socialist Party (PSOE), which split in 1936. The Anarchists were never represented in parliament. There were also important regional parties, especially in Catalonia and the Basque Country.

For these new political parties, the farm sector was crucial, as 84 per cent of all the members of parliament were chosen from an area where agriculture still employed 55 per cent of active work force and, with few exceptions, even the cities in this region 'were inhabited by an upper and middle class dependent on agriculture, with little or no understanding of democratic processes and ideological issues.'[11] The major urban and industrial regions of Madrid, Barcelona, Guipuzcoa, and Vizcaya, accounted for the rest (Table 9.2).[12]

However, agriculture, as this book has shown, was divided along commodity, regional, and social cleavages, and no single peak association had emerged to represent the sector. Not only did wheat farmers,

---

[8] Largo Caballero claimed in 1933 that landowners and workers could agree on jury presidents and vice-presidents in only a fifth of the cases, leaving the government to appoint the rest. Malefakis 1970, p.168, fn.15.

[9] In Mintz 1982, p. 165, cited in Domenech 2013b, p. 93.

[10] The Socialist Party was the largest in the 1931 elections with 24.6 per cent of the seats, and the CEDA with 21.4 in 1933 and 21.8 per cent in 1936. Linz et al. 2005, pp. 1099–1100.

[11] Linz 1967, p. 203.

[12] The metropolitan areas of Barcelona, Madrid, Malaga, Murcia, Sevilla, Valencia. Vizcaya, and Zaragoza accounted for just 14 per cent of seats.

Table 9.1 *The fragmentation of Spanish political parties and election results*

	Constituent assembly June 1931	Legislature – November 1933	Legislature – February 1936
Extreme Left	Isolated deputies	1 PCE	19 PCE et al. 49 maximalists PSOE
Moderate Left	105 PSOE	61 PSOE	50 moderate PSOE
Bourgeois Left	194 Azaña	38 Azaña	162 Iz.Rep. or Unión Rep
Bourgeois Left tending to Right	70 Lerroux		
Republican Centre-Right	39 minor groups Miguel Maura	129 Lerroux	40 minor groups, Radicals, PNV
Centre Right		95 Agrarians Lliga	
Right – accept Republic but not '31 Constitution	42 Agrarios	105 Gil Robles	116 CEDA
Extreme Right	Monarchists, extreme Catholics	40 Calvo Sotelo et al.	22 Calvo Sotelo
Other	3	5	5
Total	470	474	474

The combination of fragmented parties, local political alliances, and a complicated voting system implies that different estimates for results exist.
Source: Linz 1967, p. 261

Table 9.2 *Agriculture and parliamentary representation during the Second Republic*

	% employed in agriculture in 1930	Number of parliamentary seats in 1936	Relative importance of rural groups*		
			Employers	Essentially family farmers	Essentially hired labourers
Basque Country	26.5	17	10.9	79.5	9.6
Catalonia	26.2	54	24.2	57.1	18.7
Madrid	9.0	25	17.8	28.4	53.9
Latifundia Spain	58.2	154	17.5	25.7	56.9
Rest of Spain	53.2	221	19.9	57.0	23.1
Spain	47.1	471	19.1	46.4	36.4

* Figures refer to 1956, when a more detailed breakdown of the farm population is available.
Sources: Simpson 1995b, p. 212, Álvarez Tardío & Villa García 2017, tabla 1, and Junta Nacional de Hermandades 1959, pp. 4–5.

olive growers, or livestock farmers face very different economic problems, but the large variety of land-tenure regimes contributed to important regional cleavages. Four major social groups with different economic priorities in the sector can be identified. At one end of the social scale were the large landowners and farmers, who had traditionally played a major role in representing village interests in Madrid, either directly or indirectly. At the other end were the landless and near-landless workers, who depended on casual farm labour for an important part of their livelihood. In between was a large group of small owner-occupiers and tenant farmers who were divided by those who needed to use dry-farming techniques, and those free from this constraint. These social differences are reflected in the fact that in the areas of latifundios, about 57 per cent of the agricultural population were hired labourers, a figure that is almost identical to the numbers of family farmers found in the rest of the country (Table 9.2).

This chapter examines the role of different political groups in organizing the rural sector during the Second Republic. It begins by looking at how Marxist ideas concerning agriculture and historical materialism changed over the half century before the Great Depression, encouraging some European Socialist parties to develop policies to attract votes from family farmers. In Spain, this influence was much less, and the Socialists, especially the UGT syndicate (*Unión General de Trabajadores*), remained heavily influenced by orthodox Marxism. As a result, its farm policies were centred almost exclusively on improving the living standards of the landless labourers which, given the constraints imposed by dry-farming and the economic depression on productivity growth, was achieved only at the expense of both large and small family farmers. The legislation of the Left Republican-Socialist coalition governments of 1931 and 1932 threatened traditional property rights and religious privileges, finally drawing both the Church and landowners into mass party competitive politics. While a small, but influential sector never accepted either the 1931 Constitution or a democratic republic, most were initially willing to build a new conservative party (CEDA) which attracted support from across the country in defence of property rights, the Church, and Spain's political unity. By 1933, it claimed around 800,000 members. The chapter ends by showing how the significant regional land-tenure regimes helped develop strong regional political movements in Galicia and Catalonia.

Farm Labourers and the Shift to the Left

Historically, the Left has had difficulties in attracting support in rural societies. In part this stemmed from orthodox Marxist theory that the huge, mechanized estates would replace peasant farming in a future socialist society, and in part from the practical problems of organizing a large and highly heterogeneous group, which included not just landless workers, but also small tenants and poor family farmers, and which were spread over a large geographical area.[13] The contrast with industrial workers undertaking repetitive tasks in huge modern factories could not be greater. The difficulties of adapting theoretical Marxism to the day-to-day realities of the Second Republic and successfully organizing rural workers provides the background to one half of the intransigent nature of Spanish society in this period.

The fact that the PSOE was still a self-proclaimed Marxist Party in 1931 had important consequences.[14] The idea of historical materialism and capitalism containing the seeds of its own destruction, encouraged orthodox Marxists to wait for economic development and the resulting class struggle, for socialism to appear. This believe in 'economic forces rather than political activism' being the prime mover of history was first challenged by German and French socialists, with Bernstein arguing, for example, that not only was capitalism unlikely to collapse on its own accord, but that political passivism risked losing support among the masses. For Bernstein, democracy was the key to achieving social reforms and improving the conditions for the working class.[15] French revisionists such as Jaurés also argued that policies were needed to attract both workers and the small farmers and producers, as these were suffering from the late nineteenth century economic depression, and their votes were crucial for the survival of the Third Republic. As democratic revisionism spread, socialists in alliance with other parties increased their representation in Western European parliaments, although the jump from the day-to-day struggle for social reform to that of actually participating in a 'bourgeois' government was something that many parties found difficult before the Second World War.[16]

Political conditions in Spain before 1931 severely restricted the development not just of Christian Democracy, but also democratic revisionism and Social Democracy. This can be partly explained by the fact that despite universal male suffrage, the *turno pacífico* offered few possibilities for the PSOE, even in alliance with republicans, to obtain more than a handful of parliamentary seats. Therefore the PSOE could neither offer

---

[13] Marx had denigrated the French peasantry by writing that 'their site of production, the smallholding, does not allow any division of labour in its cultivation, no application of science and therefore no diversity in development, no diversification of talents, no wealth of social relationships'. Marx 2002, p. 100.
[14] Preston 1978:2003, p. 2.   [15] Berman 2006, pp. 13–15.
[16] Ibid., especially chapters 5–7.

the electorate the possibilities of parliamentary social reforms, nor argue that an extension of the franchise would lead to socialism, as in Sweden.[17] Instead, a continued belief in historical materialism and the class struggle made many socialists suspicious of 'bourgeois' governments, with major consequences for the countryside. Helping workers become small farmers was seen not just as futile, but risked turning them into the petite bourgeoisie, and delay the appearance of commercial agriculture that was necessary for capitalism. As *El Socialista* in 1896 noted, 'Socialism must relieve the intense pains that small farmers suffer from land concentration, but in no way should this concentration be interrupted'.[18] For orthodox Marxists, land reform was not seen as a means to create a stable society of small farmers, but to eliminate 'feudalism' to foster commercial agriculture, thereby preparing the conditions for a socialist revolution.

Democratic revisionists were not the only critics of orthodox Marxism, and in Spain anarchism was often seen as a more practical response, promising the violent overthrow of the existing political order. It was strongest in both Barcelona, the country's leading industrial centre, and among the poor landless day-labourers on the Campiña of western Andalucia.[19] In the late nineteenth century, secretive revolutionary syndicates sprung up as trade unions were banned and political representation restricted. The presence of anarchist thinkers and outrages were common in Europe at this time, but in Spain the Anarchist CNT became a mass-movement that represented an important part of the working classes, especially between 1917–21 and 1931–7.[20] A strategy of direct action responding to local problems and involving the whole village community was particularly effective in organizing workers and maintaining strike discipline. Anarchism was very strong in villages where there were large numbers of landless labourers and the farm ladder was weak, if not absent, resulting in a relatively homogeneous working class with common interests.

The CNT also benefited from the Socialists largely ignoring farm workers before the First World War, while widespread anticlericalism restricted Catholic syndicates in Andalucia.[21] Following the failed general strike of 1917, the Socialist UGT changed tactics and rejected revolutionary actions, influenced no doubt by the fact that its Madrid

---

[17] For Sweden, see ibid., ch. 7.
[18] 4 September 1896, cited in Acosta Ramírez et al. 2009, p. 190.
[19] For rural anarchism, see Díaz del Moral 1928: 1973, Brenan 1962, Hobsbawm 1959, and Álvarez Junco 1976, and for anarcho-syndicalism in Catalonia, Smith 2007 and Balcells 1974.
[20] Casanova 2010a, p. 8.   [21] Acosta Ramírez et al. 2009, p. 135.

strike committee was 'very nearly subjected to summary execution'.[22] Over half the agricultural strikes that took place between 1904 and 1929 occurred between 1918 and 1920, and the agricultural section of the UGT grew rapidly from 8,000 in 1917, to 61,000 by 1920.[23] Unlike the Anarchist CNT, the UGT created a centralized bureaucracy in Madrid to coordinate village grassroots organizations. The weak electoral influence of the PSOE increased the relevance of the UGT, especially as the syndicate cooperated with the dictator Primo de Rivera between 1923 and 1929, allowing it to maintain its organizational structure, while making the CNT illegal. The experience helped it appreciate the potential advantages of corporatism, where political alliances substituted market decisions. After 1919, the UGT began to slowly develop a policy for tenant farmers and sharecroppers, but there still remained very little in the Socialist program that might attract small farmers, and their policies during the Second Republic drove many farmers to conservative parties. To coordinate its policies, the UGT in April 1930 created an agricultural section, the *Federación Nacional de Trabajadores de la Tierra* (FNTT).[24]

The Socialist Party schism of 1921 saw the expulsion of 15,000 members and helped create a more moderate, revisionist party. The PSOE during the Second Republic never won more than a quarter of the seats, but it was the most voted party in 1931; came third in 1933; and second in 1936, creating the dilemma of whether to join with other political groups and participate in government. Its initial alliance with the Left Republicans in 1931 gave it control over three important ministries (Finance, Justice, and Labour) and it was active in passing a series of decrees and laws between 28 April and 14 July 1931 that radically changed the nature of land and labour markets (Table 9.1). Landowners could now only evict tenants if they failed to pay the rent, or left the land uncultivated, while tribunals revised, and in many cases reduced rents. To stop tenants subletting, landowners had to give preference to formally constituted workers' societies, one of the few measures that were welcomed by both the Socialist FNTT and Catholic CNCA.[25] Farm workers now benefitted from an eight-hour day, arbitration boards that determined local wages, and employers' restrictions on the hiring of migrants if local workers were unemployed. In an attempt to avoid a lockout, farmers were obliged to cultivate their land and employ the same

[22] Preston 1978:2003, pp. 11–12
[23] Acosta Ramírez et al. 2009, pp. 125–30. Between 1918 and 1920 the number of Socialist municipal councillors increased from 82 to 946, while in Andalucia the figures went from 11 to 204.
[24] Acosta Ramírez et al. 2009, p. 315.   [25] Malefakis 1970, p. 167. See Chapter 10.

number of workers as before. As Chapter 8 showed, land reform also attempted to redistribute private property from large landowners to landless workers, and the Intensification of Cultivation decree gave workers temporary access to land that state agronomists believed could be brought under the plough to increase employment.

The objectives of these reforms were to address rural social injustices, and to mitigate the effects of the economic crisis. Given the practical difficulties of organizing rural workers, the FNTTs aimed to increase its membership and then, from a position of strength, negotiate wideranging regional agreements with employers. Local conflicts, such as those that the Anarchist CNT encouraged, were seen as a distraction and a waste of resources.[26] There were, however, two interrelated problems with this strategy. First, membership was often fickle, with workers joining in large numbers when they felt the syndicate could offer immediate rewards, but then failing to pay their dues when conditions changed. To avoid this and maintain its negotiating strength, it needed to be in a position to implement labour laws which, given the clientilistic nature of municipal government, required the socialists to remain in the government. This obliged the PSOE to pact with other parties, something that deeply divided the party, with many socialists wanting to leave the government once the Constitution was approved in December 1931. As a result, the influence of the PSOE declined and it was the syndicate that would dominate the socialist left.

The Anarchists rejected a centralized state, and their usual decision not to participate in local elections left them unable to reward their followers to the same extent as the Socialist FNTT. Therefore, while the national membership of the FNTT jumped from 27,340 to 392,953 between 1930 and June 1932, the Anarchist CNT saw a drop from 350,000 in Andalucia in December 1931, of which about half were agricultural workers, to 243,000 by March 1933.[27] The rapid growth of the FNTT changed the UGT from 'a predominately elite union of the working-class aristocracy to a mass union of unsophisticated unskilled workers and rural labourers, at a time of economic depression and rising unemployment'.[28] However, not only are these figures provided by the syndicates and likely to be inflated, but membership had probably peaked, and would fall significantly in 1934 and 1935 because of employer victimization and

---

[26] This led to the rank and file on occasions being more militant than the FNTT leadership. See, for example, Preston 1978:2003, pp. 29 and 88.

[27] Caro Cancela 1987, p. 145, Maurice 1990, p. 28, and Bizcarrondo 2008, pp. 199 and 205.

[28] Preston 1978:2003, p. 78. The FNTT accounted for 43 per cent of the UGT membership in 1932. Bizcarrondo 2008, p. 205.

Table 9.3 *Major agrarian reforms during the Second Republic*

	Objectives	Date	Region to be applied
Land	Land reform	Law Sept. 1932 (significantly changed July 1935)	Latifundio provinces initially, then rest of Spain
	Abolition of 'feudal' rights	Decree Nov. 1933	Spain
	Recovery of common lands	Projects	Spain
	Minimum & intensification of cultivation	Decrees May 1931 & Nov. 1932	Latifundio Spain
Tenure	Rent tribunals	Decrees July & Oct 1931	Spain
	Redemption of *foros*	Decree November 1931	Galicia
	Redemption of *rabassas*	Law March 1934 – regional parliament	Catalonia
	Tenure reform	March 1935	Spain
Labour	Limits to migrant labour	Decrees May & July 1931	Spain
	Wage tribunals	Law Nov. 1931	Spain
	Eight-hour day	Decree July 1931	Spain

Source: Adapted from Robledo & Espinoza 1999, p. 411.

state repression. Nevertheless, the two syndicates between them succeeded in converting the problems of the landless labourers in the latifundio provinces into a national issue, despite the fact that they represented less than 5 per cent of county's active labour force.

They also helped deeply divide local society. Even accepting their own figures, only a third of the workers and small farmers registered in the *Censo de Campesinos* in the latifundio provinces belonged to the FNTT at its peak in June 1932, and only in Jaen did it reach half (Table 9.3). When the total active farm population is considered, the figures drop to 17 per cent. Assuming that half of the Anarchist CNT members were farm workers increases the figures in Andalucia a further 6 per cent, but even so less than a quarter of the active population belonged to a left-wing syndicate.[29] A significant share of the rural poor clearly rejected the Left even in areas of latifundios, a fact illustrated by the election results of November 1933 and February 1936.

[29] The CNT estimates, based on 146,712 members in 1936, in Maurice 1990, p. 30; and the FNTT 125,617 in 1932, in Calero 1976, p. 153; and 885,454 farm workers in 1930, Simpson 1995b.

Table 9.4 *Membership of farm associations and the FNTT in the latifundio provinces, 1932–4*

	Registered in the Censo Campesino	FNTT affiliated in 1932	% FNTT/registered in the Censo Campesino	Agricultural labour not registered in the Censo Campesino	Affiliated syndicates (mainly Catholic)	% affiliated in syndicates / active population not registered in the censo	Landowners + 250 hectares
Badajoz	97,398	36,673	38%	60,107	28,020	47%	2,495
Cáceres	72,997	20,708	28%	31,274	14,500	46%	729
Ciudad Real	48,878	18,278	37%	43,464	9,635	22%	658
Córdoba	64,141	21,003	33%	68,404	2,792	4%	1,455
Salamanca	43,414	8,008	18%	25,943	4,358	17%	643
Sevilla	69,397	15,397	22%	69,259	4,897	7%	2,344
Huelva	30,311	9,191	30%	34,541	7,799	23%	157
Albacete	35,453	11,317	32%	17,968	7,050	39%	579
Cádiz	36,123	5,169	14%	14,929	2,486	17%	802
Jaén	65,262	32,633	50%	82,481	3,560	4%	1,257
total	563,374	244,128	43%	448,370	118,094	26%	13,871
% over active population	57%	17%		42%	8%		1%

Information for Granada, Malaga, and Toledo are incomplete

Source: Carmona & Simpson in press.

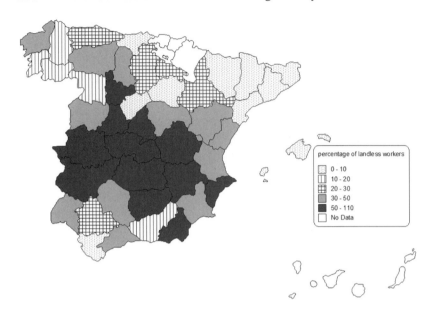

Map 9.1   Estimated share of landless labourers affiliated to the FNTT,
June 1932
Sources: FNTT 1933, p. 322 and Carmona et al. 2019.

Another feature of the FNTT's growth was that two-fifths of its membership in June 1932 was found outside the latifundio provinces, in areas
of small farms (Map 9.1). To increase its potential constituency, the
FNTT helped tenant-farmers carry out massive farm invasions in
Extremadura, organized landless labourers during the cereal harvest in
areas of small farmers, and lobbied for legislation to allow villagers to
recover their old common lands (Chapter 10). Rural conflicts were therefore confined not just to areas of latifundios; indeed the FNTT claimed
that between the declaration of the Republic and 30 June 1932, almost
half (49 per cent) of the strikes that it had organized took place outside
these provinces.[30]

The Socialists withdrew from the government in September 1933, and
then lost 42 per cent of their parliamentary seats in the November elections, when a centre-right coalition came to power. According to *El
Socialista*, the new provincial governors and municipal governments
now ignored labour agreements and syndicalists complained of being

[30] FNTT 1933, p. 224. Our calculations.

blacklisted. The dilemma for both the party and the syndicate was whether to continue its democratic revisionism and compromise, or move further to the left and pursue revolutionary politics. The FNTT, in an effort to bring to a halt the drop in living standards of its members and the erosion of its influence, called a national harvest strike in June 1934. The government declared this a 'revolutionary' act and made it illegal, thereby allowing employers to ignore labour legislation and contract migrant workers. The revolutionary uprising in Asturias in October followed in response to the inclusion of CEDA members in the government, and the repression that followed effectively ended the syndicate's activities until 1936. However, the split within the party continued to deepen, with Largo Caballero resigning from the PSOE's national executive in December 1935, and associated now exclusively with the UGT. This left the Socialists with 'two political leaderships which were not only entirely independent of each other but also diametrically opposed'.[31] The so-called Popular Front was limited to an electoral pact for the elections of February 1936, with the PSOE ruling out participating in a future government.

Farmers, Tenants, and the Shift to the Right

Farm policy during the *Primer Bienio* (1931–3) was primarily aimed at helping farm workers with a land reform, and far reaching changes to labour laws. Although attempts were also made to support small farmers by introducing rent controls, and future legislation was promised on tenure reform, the provision of cheap rural credit, and the recovery by villages of common lands, these were not immediate priorities. There was also interest in irrigation, but this required long-term planning, was hugely expensive before the appearance of new labour-saving construction technologies, and required higher farm prices. Therefore, the immediate effect of government policies was to raise labour costs but not improve farm prices. This led to large numbers of small farmers and tenants voting for centre-right parties in the November 1933 elections, at the same times as considerable numbers of workers stayed away from the polls, frustrated at the slow progress in reducing rural poverty.

The Radical Party, founded in 1908, was perhaps the closest that could be described as a moderate centre party which stressed the need for 'reconciliation rather than reform' to consolidate the Republic.[32] However, the party was notoriously weak, as policy was determined almost exclusively by its aging leader, Alejandro Lerroux, whose drive

---

[31] Juliá 1989, p. 32.   [32] Townson 2000, p. 31. This paragraph is based on this work.

and democratic credentials by 1930s were decidedly limited. It held no party congresses before the Republic, and failed to build a political organization, relying instead on its ability to control provincial governors and municipal government to capture votes using clientelism and corruption. It was asked to form a government following the November 1933 elections but, with the exception of the *Términos Municipales* decree, failed to repeal the labour legislation of the Left Republican-Socialist governments. In fact more workers were settled under the 1932 Land Reform Law than previously, and those who received land following the invasions in Extremadura of the same year were permitted to stay until late 1935. The Radical Party quickly alienated many family farmers as it was believed to be too closely aligned with urban interests, was mildly anticlerical, and lacked energy in its attempts to build rural networks to attract voters. The party's drift to the right and complaints of growing unemployment led to it splitting in May 1934. In reality, the Radical Party neither protected farm workers, as landowners often ignored the labour tribunals, nor restored profitably for small farmers. Increasingly farmers looked to the CEDA (*Confederación Española de Derechas Autónomas*), a new party to the right of the Radicals that had emerged out of *Acción Nacional* and then *Acción Popular*, to restore their fortunes.

The CEDA has been described both as a nascent Christian democratic party, and an embryonic fascist one.[33] As a broad-based coalition, it contained individuals from both political groups, but the relevant question here is the extent that it was possible for the CEDA to resolve the economic problems facing landowners and tenant farmers within a democratic republic. In fact, the CEDA's experience of government was very similar to that of the Socialists, and followed three distinct stages. First, both parties failed to resolve the basic problems of their main constituencies when they initially participated in a coalition government. Then, following its electoral loss in February 1936, the CEDA believed that the incoming government would use its control of institutions to maximize partisan advantage, negatively affecting the livelihoods of many of its supporters, just as the socialists had experienced after the November 1933 elections. Finally, both parties faced the dilemma over whether to accept a decline in the living standards of their main constituents and lose members to more extreme groups, or whether to move the party itself in that direction.[34] The groups to the right of the CEDA

---

[33] See especially, Álvarez Tardío 2011.
[34] Linz et al. 2002, p. 65, writes, 'Both parties, and the PSOE after 1933 in particular, were internally divided between those who wished to operate legally within a reformed system, and the "maximalists" who no longer believed that the system deserved their loyalty'. Cited in Álvarez Tardío 2011, p. 64.

included the authoritarian monarchists and many of the traditional landed elites who were affiliated to *Renovación Española* and later the *Bloque Nacional* of José Calvo Sotelo.[35] Although their parliamentary influence was limited, they provided a Catholic alternative to the CEDA and those who rejected parliamentary democracy. The political failure of centre parties representing moderate republicans and socialists on the one hand, and Catholics on the other, was therefore behind the polarization of village society that created the conditions for the military uprising of 18 July 1936.

As previously noted, confessional parties were virtually absent in Spain before 1931 because the Restoration settlement allowed the Church to maintain its privileged position, especially in areas of education, and the traditional landed elites continued to control national and local politics, making it unnecessary for either to enter into a strategic alliance to defend jointly their interests.[36] This had a major implication for the new Republic as small farmers were poorly represented compared to the interests of the urban liberal elites and organized labour in drawing up the 1931 Constitution. This Constitution excluded the Catholic Church from education, removed the crucifix from classrooms, and required education to be mixed, and was interpreted over large areas of rural Spain as an attempt to legislate partisan policy, rather than determine new political procedures.

In response to the Left Republican-Socialist government decrees that began to reform the land and labour markets in 1931, new right-wing regional parties were formed such as *Derecha Regional Valenciana* or *Acción Agraria Manchega*. In February 1933, the CEDA was created as a national body to represent these organizations, and help establish new ones, such as *Acción Popular Catalana*. The CEDA was a Catholic organization, but it was not subordinated to the Church hierarchy, and was organized in a way similar to other European confessional parties, with both the party and its press being run by lay Catholics who accepted freedom of worship and parliamentary government.[37] Many of its leaders

---

[35] Gonzalez Calleja 2012, pp. 106–9 and Artola Blanco 2015, pp. 196–7. It also included CEDA's own youth branch, the *Juventudes de Acción Popular* (JAP). See especially, Lowe 2010, p. 18.

[36] Ángel Herrera's attempts to build a Catholic political movement to compete electorally in the early twentieth century enjoyed only limited success, but suggests that the origins of the CEDA was more than just a 'counter-revolutionary' movement to the republican left-socialist coalition. Tusell 1986, and Álvarez Tardío 2011, pp. 64–5.

[37] Álvarez Tardío 2016, pp. 92–3. Giménez Fernández, who would become the Minister of Agriculture, claimed that the party elite, its main newspaper *El Debate*, and the policy initiatives were inspired by Christian Democracy, although this was not necessary true of either its parliamentary deputies, or its electorate.

had previously collaborated with Primo de Rivera's dictatorship. For the November 1933 elections, the CNCA associations were used to mobilize the electorate against the 'Catholic persecution' of the Left Republican-Socialist government, although it was the opposition to the government's farm policies that were perhaps even more important to voters.[38] The combination of rising labour costs, falling farm prices, and growing anticlericalism led to the CEDA winning 105 parliamentary seats, or 22 per cent of total, and making it the country's second largest party after the Radicals (Table 9.2). Its electoral success was found across large areas of Spain, being weak only in Catalonia, Galicia, and western Andalucia.

The Spanish president Alcalá-Zamora now asked the Radical Party to form a government, and successfully opposed the entry of the CEDA to the cabinet until October 1934, an event which sparked the Asturias uprising and subsequent repression. By gaining three major cabinet seats (Justice, Labour, and Agriculture), the party enjoyed a major influence on policy, although it had only limited success in the controversial areas of farm prices, tenure reform, and labour costs. The CEDA's largest constituency were small farmers, especially cereal producers, who faced problems of overproduction and low prices. This was also the key constituency of the *Partido Agrario* (Agrarian Party), which was both an ally and rival to the CEDA, but which had stronger links with landowners' associations than with the Catholic syndicate, the CNCA.[39] The CEDA proposed a system of price support to regulate stocks, with the state to guarantee the capital that the banks would lend to farm cooperatives and associations, which were controlled by the CNCA.[40] Technicians associated with the CEDA, such as Manuel de Torres or José Larraz, also debated the possibilities of reducing the cultivated area, although, even if this could have been enforced, it would have been rejected by small farmers. In reality, just as land reform failed to resolve the problems of landless workers for the Socialists, intervention in the cereal market could not help the CEDA solve problems of low prices for small producers.[41]

The fact that the CEDA was independent of the traditional conservative rural elite helped reduce the class barriers to attracting small farmers to the party, and it successfully used other social cleavages, especially

[38] Ibid., p. 82.   [39] Gil Cuadrado 2006, p. 19.
[40] The Agrarian Party wanted the state to guarantee banks loans of 300 million pesetas, although it criticized the 50 million pesetas that was allocated to the IRA for land reform.
[41] The CEDA, and by extension the CNCA, had only limited interest in cooperatives to process farm produce.

religion, property, and even nationalism, to mobilize.[42] However, and as Ziblatt has recently argued, the absence of a traditional landed elite from a hierarchical mass party such as the CEDA was more likely to undermine democracy, than reinforce it.[43] In fact, although the CEDA took advantage of the CNCA's grass-root organizations, it remained vulnerable to the influence of outside interest groups determining its political agenda which, in this case, would drive the party further to the right. In particular, the Association of Landowners (*Agrupación de Propietarios de Fincas Rústicas* or APFR), which had been created in September 1931 to organize opposition to land and tenancy reforms, was strongly influenced by the landed elites, some of whom also held positions of influence in the CEDA. A second group, the Spanish Confederation of Farm Employers (*Confederación Española Patronal Agrícola* or CEPA), was created in April 1932 to represent employers' interests on the new joint commissions, and planned to establish itself in each village offering 'a single front of agricultural producers in the odious, imposed and provoked class struggle'.[44] The CEPA organized a massive demonstration in Madrid for 18 September 1933 which was banned by the Lerroux government, further discrediting the Radical Party among farm groups.

The area which caused the greatest tensions within the CEDA and Agrarian Party was Giménez Fernández's project for tenure reform of March 1935. The April 1931 decree, supposedly a temporary measure, had given tenants the right to remain on their land, except when they failed to pay the rent. Previous efforts at reform by Marcelino Domingo in April 1933, and Cirilo del Río in February 1934, had both failed, making the need for legislation urgent. Giménez Fernández, a Christian democrat, saw tenure reform as a practical alternative to land reform as it helped those who were already cultivating the land, a key CEDA constituency, and he hoped that it would result in all rental contracts disappearing within fifteen to twenty years.[45] Sharecropping by contrast was to be encouraged as landowners were supposed to make a greater contribution to farming than with rental contracts. Fierce opposition within the CEDA led to the proposals being significantly watered down, which is usually interpreted in the historical literature as reflecting the intransient

---

[42] Class was a major cleavage for conservatives in the late nineteenth century. Ziblatt 2017, pp. 46–7.
[43] Ibid., p.49.
[44] Cabrera 1983, pp. 66–71. The new commissions included Jurados Mixtos de Propiedad y Trabajo, as well as those associated with land reform.
[45] Montero Díaz 1977, 2, pp. 182–3. Although Malefakis 1970, p. 401, interpreted it differently.

nature of Spanish absentee landowners to accept any social reforms.[46] Yet while it is undoubtedly true that the failure to pass a comprehensive tenancy law left large numbers of small farmers facing considerable uncertainty at a time of major economic difficulties, the proposed law was significantly more radical than any found in Europe at the time, with the exception of Ireland. Landowners were certainly unhappy about restrictions to property rights, but a major fear was how it was to be implemented, as supposedly independent commissions had to be created to determine a 'fair' rent and the value of any farm improvements made by the tenant. The recent experience of rent controls described above was not a happy precedent. In addition, the lack of cheap farm credit would have made it problematic for tenants to provide landowners with sufficient guarantees that they could actually pay the proposed instalments to buy their land, especially in years of poor harvests. Just as with the Socialists, the experience of the CEDA showed the difficulties for political parties to carry out reformist policies in the middle of a major economic recession and with limited state capacity.

Instead, the CEDA, like the Socialists earlier, resorted to using policies that simply allocated resources to their own members, by restoring the negotiating powers of landowners and farmers in the land and labour markets. As Chapter 10 shows, the fact that there were virtually no strikes during 1935 was not because workers now enjoyed higher living standards, but because the Socialist and Anarchist syndicates' organizational structures had been devastated, union leaders blacklisted, and Socialist village councils removed. With the Popular Front's victory in February 1936, tensions increased once more, as political power switched back again to organized labour.

Giménez Fernández believed that 'the great defect of the CEDA was that in reality *it was never a party*',[47] and its divisions became brutally exposed over the 1935 tenancy law. Its organizational weaknesses, just as with other conservative parties in Spain at this time, allowed independent groups to capture the political agenda from the party leadership. In the CEDA, groups closely linked with fascism such as its own youth group, the *Juventudes de Acción Popular* (JAP), pushed the party to the right and toward support for the military uprising.[48] Yet this was clearly not just a problem of weak party organization, because for many small farmers the

---

[46] Malefakis 1970, pp. 347–55. Giménez Fernández's was opposed by the CEDA's principal representatives on the Agricultural Committee (Azpeitia, Casanueva and Rodríguez Jurado), as well as Lamamié de Clairac and others on the extreme Right.
[47] Lowe 2010, p. 69, cited in Ziblatt 2017, p. 349.   [48] Ziblatt 2017, p. 352.

Popular Front's victory in the February 1936 elections threatened not just farm profitability, but property ownership itself.

In fact, the anti-revolutionary coalition lost the February 1936 elections to the Popular Front by a relatively small margin. Just as the Socialist FNTT had been able to organize large numbers of landless workers and achieve important gains in provinces of family farmers such as Valladolid or Logroño, so the CNCA and the CEDA found support in many latifundio provinces. In Extremadura (Badajoz and Caceres), for example, a figure that was equivalent to almost half of the farm population that was not listed in the *Censo de Campesinos* belonged to some type of association, many of them Catholic, and significant numbers were found in other provinces such as Albacete (39 per cent), Huelva (23 per cent), Ciudad Real (22 per cent), and Cadiz and Salamanca (17 per cent) (Table 9.2).

Regional Land-Tenure Regimes and Politics: Galicia and Catalonia

Galicia and Catalonia were both regions of family farmers, and not only was the 1932 Land Reform Law, the labour laws, and worries concerning low cereal prices, much less important than elsewhere, but the political influence of the PSOE and the CEDA was also limited. The nature of the agrarian problems in both regions was heavily influenced by the nineteenth century liberal land reforms which had failed to unite the eminent and useful domain in a single person. However, their subsequent histories were very different, and if in Galicia the problems had been effectively resolved by 1931, in Catalonia they played a decisive role in the growing nationalist movement during the Second Republic.

In Galicia, the advantages that farmers enjoyed from a rain-fed agriculture were offset by a lack of land that could be easily cultivated, and a land-tenure regime (*foros*) which required them to pay rent to absentee landowners. While tenants could not be easily evicted, their ability to use credit markets and capture returns from the high labour inputs that the miniscule farms required was hampered. Following a long campaign involving both reactive and proactive contentious collective action, landowners began to sell from the late nineteenth century, and in 1926 tenants gained the legal right to purchase the *foro*. By the 1930s, the agrarian problems in Galicia were little different to those facing family farmers everywhere in Europe, namely concerns over the lack of rural credit and low farm prices.[49] The irrelevance of much of the Left Republican-Socialist

---

[49] See especially Villares 1982, chs. six to eight. The major debates now were over the question of the Zamora-Orense railway and meat imports from Uruguay. Cabo Villaverde 2006a.

legislation of 1931 and 1932, and the limited influence of the Socialist Party in rural areas, implied that social tensions were less than in most regions, and centrist parties, often originating from the old rural clientelistic networks, played a greater political role.[50]

Rural conflicts played a major role in Catalan politics, despite the fact that it was the country's most industrialized and urbanized region, and few casual workers were employed in agriculture. The major source of contention was the *rabassa morta* or 'dead vine' contract, which was found exclusively in viticulture, and gave sharecroppers (*rabassers*) indefinite use of the land so long as it was used to produce only grapes. The contacts first appeared in the seventeenth century, although these were effectively ended when phylloxera destroyed the vineyards, requiring new ones to be drawn up to replant. Unlike Galicia, the landowners were not rentiers, but often played an active role in viticulture, owning commercial winemaking facilities or acting as wine merchants. They were therefore unwilling to sell the land as they were dependent on the growers' grapes for their wine production, and winemaking technologies were highly asset-specific.[51] Viticulture in this region faced significant economic difficulties, and producers from the late nineteenth century found it increasingly difficult to compete with La Mancha, while everywhere growers in the 1920s and 1930s had to adapt to the problems of overproduction and low wine prices.[52] By contrast, rapid industrialization led to the higher urban wages, and therefore a relative decline in sharecroppers' living standards (Figure 9.1). Where they could, sharecroppers responded by shifting some of their labour and capital to other occupations such as rearing pigs, market gardening, as well as non-agrarian activities, although in practice their contracts did not permit changes in land use. The combination of lower labour inputs and ageing vines led to yields falling from 32 to 20 hectolitres per hectare between 1922 and 1935, at a time when they stagnated in the rest of Spain.[53]

Protests by the *rabassers* followed distinct cycles, being especially strong in periods of low wine prices, phylloxera, and during the Bolshevik Trienio. In 1922, Lluís Companys created the *Unió de Rabassaires*, a pressure group which not only demanded legislation to allow growers to buy the land, but also looked to build political alliances with non-Catholic, urban workers' organizations. The *rabassa morta* now became

---

[50] For example, *Organización Republicana Gallega Autónoma* (ORGA) controlled by Casares Quiroga. For *caciquismo*, see Prada Rodríguez 2013.

[51] The importance of winemaking facilities helps explain the opposition of the rabassers to the landowners' cooperatives. Pomés 2000.

[52] For a cost comparison of the two regions, see Simpson 1992a, pp. 124–8.

[53] Garrido 2017, p. 995, and Pomés 2000, who argues that relative prices encouraged growers to switch to early potatoes. For the problem of old vines, Simpson 1985.

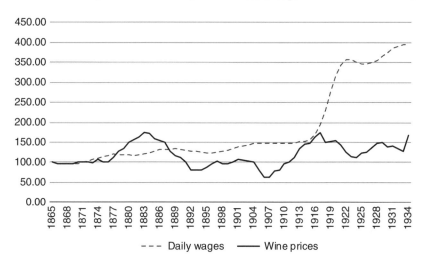

Figure 9.1 Long-run changes in wages and wine prices in Barcelona
(1822–30 = 100)
Sources: Balcells 1980, pp. 376–9, and Garrabou et al. 1991, pp. 40–2
and 46. Five year moving averages have been used.

the rural symbol in the struggle to create regional self-government, not
just because the contract was unique to Catalonia, but also growers
believed that it had been misinterpreted by the Spanish Civil Code.
The Second Republic provided the *Unió de Rabassaires* with the political
opportunity to resolve their long-term grievances, and play a major role in
Esquerra Republicana de Catalunya (ERC). This party included social
reformists, federal republicans, and radical nationalists, and was Spain's
fourth largest parliamentary group in 1931, with 29 deputies. The ERC
formed part of the new Left Republican-Socialist government that establish Catalonia's autonomous government in 1932.[54] Attempts by the
Unió de Rabassaires to use the 'fair rent' tribunals were often rejected,
either because landowners were able to show that rents had not risen since
1914, or because it was ruled that the law did not apply to the *rabassa
morta* contracts.[55] Instead, the ERC revitalized the political campaign for
tenants to gain full ownership of the land, and the Catalan Parliament

---

[54] Nuñez Seixas 2018, pp. 280–1.
[55] Catalonia accounted for about a third of the 67,719 demands in Spain by April 1932,
although there were significant differences between villages. Cabrera 1983, p. 165, and
Balcells 1980, pp. 131–42.

passed the *Llei de contractes de conreu*, or the Tenure Law, in March 1934.[56]

The landowners bitterly opposed the law. These had formed the *Lliga Regionalista* in 1901, a conservative, Catholic party closely identified with Catalonian interests which, in 1907, won more seats in the region for the Spanish parliament than the two dynastic parties of the *turno*.[57] Its rural support was built on the important network of farm associations and cooperatives, created by the IACSI, and the powerful Catalan cooperative federation, the USAC (Chapter 6). In 1933, it became the *Lliga Catalana*, but landowners now threated to leave the party unless it challenged the legality of the 1934 Tenure Law in the Spanish Parliament and Constitutional Court. Many nationalists interpreted this as an affront to the legitimacy of Catalonia's newly obtained autonomy. The Constitution Court declared that the Catalan Parliament did not have the powers to legislate agrarian contract law and, following the October revolution of 1934, the *Generalitat* and Catalan autonomy was suspended. However, the Right had split, and landowners and the IACSI created another political party, the *Acción Popular de Cataluña* in October 1934, which became part of the CEDA.[58] With the Popular Front's victory in 1936, the ERC was returned to power and modified the Contract Law shortly before the military uprising.

As a result, while the *Lliga*, a 'powerful regional interest group' was forced to turn to the central government for support, the 'regional government transformed a local class conflict into a nationalistic issue'.[59] Yet the ERC also united farmers and urban political interests in a way that Luebbert has noted for Scandinavia.[60] By contrast, the failure to resolve the problems of landownership and low farm incomes led to the rabassers moving further to the left, and the landowners to the right.

Conclusion

Before 1931, there was no genuine electoral competition and, despite universal male suffrage from 1890, the two parties of *el turno* failed to reduce the influence of the local elites, allowing them, through clientelistic networks, to adapt at both the village and national levels to the changing demands brought about by economic development. As the power of

---

[56] *Tribunal de Garantias Constitutionales*. Tenants were guaranteed the right to cultivate the land for six years, and redemption if they had cultivated it uninterruptedly for eighteen years. The contract was redeemable 'at the will of the grower', at a price equivalent to twenty times the rent. The law effectively allowed the splitting up of the large estates.
[57] Pomés 2000, p. 464   [58] Balcells 1980, pp. 213–22, 236–8, and 250.
[59] Linz, 1978, p. 158.   [60] Luebbert 1991. For Catalonia, see Soler 2011.

neither the Church nor the landed elites was challenged, they showed little interest in making the necessary investment to build a mass party structure to incorporate small farmers and tenants, which might in time lead to a Christian Democracy, as happened in many Western European countries. It was this weak representation of small farmers, rather than the opposition of the landed elites, that was important in 1931. At the other extreme, the exclusion of the Socialist Party from day-to-day power allowed orthodox Marxism ideas to go largely unchallenged, and left its rank and file to distrust liberal democracy. Neither the Right nor the Left, in their different ways, were prepared for democratic government.

Even in mature European democracies, governments found it difficult to meet the demands to respond to poverty and cyclical unemployment caused by the Great Depression. In Spain, the narrow tax base hampered the efforts to provide public goods, while the state's inability to allocate them impartially, rather than using them to feed party patronage, alienated large numbers of voters. As a result, democracy failed in the Second Republic because it lacked two basic norms for success: mutual tolerance, the willingness to accept opposition parties as legitimate rivals, and forbearance; and the need for political parties to resist the temptation to use their temporary control of power to 'maximize partisan advantage'.[61] Clientelistic politics and outright corruption had effectively reduced the moderate centre, leaving voters facing an increasingly intolerant Left and Right, with both the major political parties, the PSOE and the CEDA, remaining outside the government in the spring of 1936.

It is true that a small, but influential sector of the landed elites rejected both the Republic and the 1931 Constitution, and backed the military uprisings of both 1932 and 1936. Yet it was not so much the traditional landed elites that brought the Republic down by backing the military uprising, but rather the frustrations of millions of small farmers, who saw their economic situation being undermined by ineffective government price policies and higher labour costs, and their religion being attacked in a Constitution which they had not voted for. Without the family farmers' support, there could have been no military uprising.

---

[61] Levitsky & Ziblatt 2018, p. 9.

10 The Growing Polarization of Rural Society during the Second Republic

> Even small and temporary groups of collective actors can have explosive effects on powerful states.[1]

> [G]roups that can capture the agenda of political parties can influence democratic policy to a greater extent than their numbers would indicate.[2]

Although most Spaniards were not politically organized in 1931, and had welcomed the Republic, five years later many had become disillusioned and voted for one of two broad coalitions: either the Popular Front, or the very loosely organized anti-revolutionary coalition. This final chapter explains why farm workers and farmers moved from the political centre towards the extremes in such a short period of time. In some European countries in the interwar period, social democrats, fascists, or national socialists offered a 'third way' to liberalism and communism, but the struggle in the Spanish countryside was often less ideological, but rather over who was to control factor markets, and which groups of workers and small farmers were to benefit from the allocation of scarce resources.[3] Rural conflicts were not just between employers and workers, but also between landowners and employers attempting to maintain their traditional hiring practices and patronage systems, and the Socialist FNTT efforts to build alternative ones to protect, and reward, their members.

Strike levels in Spain in 1933 were some of the highest in interwar Europe, and rural workers accounted for about a third of strikers.[4] Economic conditions were probably worse than they had been in the 1920s for many, but the intensity and nature of contentious collective action during the Second Republic was determined not so much by rural poverty as by changes in the organizational costs facing the socialist and anarchist syndicates, and the capacity of farmer associations to defend themselves.[5] The FNTT was particularly successful in transforming what

---

[1] Tarrow 2011, p. 5   [2] Acemoglu & Robinson 2006, p. 114.
[3] Berman 2006, p. 126, for interwar Europe.   [4] Domenech 2013a, p. 254.
[5] Díaz del Moral 1928: 1973, pp. 45–6 and 63, observed for Cordoba in the 1920s that better-off, rather than poor, workers were most likely to go on strike.

226

had been periodic village unrest associated with landless workers in regions of latifundios into a national problem for the new Republic. Nevertheless, as Marx would have predicted, its attempts to build a strong labour movement among casual farm workers not only deeply divided rural society, but split the socialist movement. Small family farmers moved rapidly to the right after 1931 not because they were necessarily conservative by nature, but because the demands of the FNTT and Socialist municipal governments were perceived as threatening their economic position as much, if not more, than the economic crisis.

As Chapter 9 noted, the cycle of conflicts deepened as political power and the control of the labour markets swung dramatically three times in just the five years, favouring first the Socialist FNTT during the so called *Primer Bienio* (December 1931 and November 1933); then the landowners and employers in the *Bienio Conservador* (November 1933 to February 1936); and finally back to the workers again after February 1936. The workers' and tenants' gains of 1931 and 1932 were checked, and sometimes reversed, during the second phase, allowing landowners and large farmers to once more regain their dominant position in local society. As the prohibition and repression of workers' organizations reappeared, especially after the Asturias uprising of October 1934, the nature of contentious behaviour changed from open, proactive protests to traditional, reactive ones. The situation was radically reversed once again following the elections of February 1936, as illustrated by the massive land invasions in March. The combination of unemployment, low organization costs for political actors on both sides, and radical swings in political power, acted as a catalyst that polarized villages across the country. As a result, many workers and tenants felt the need to become associated either with farmers or the Socialist FNTT and Anarchist CNT to find work.

This final chapter therefore attempts to answer two questions which are crucial to explaining why so many people had become disillusioned with parliamentary democracy. First, it shows why apparently modest reforms, such as the introduction of collective bargaining or the providing of emergency assistance to workers through temporary land settlements, become so contentious and, in particular, why employers and labour organizations were so intransigent. Second, it explains why conflicts became widespread across Spain, appearing not just in areas of latifundios, but also in villages where land was not heavily concentrated. The chapter is divided into four sections. After briefly examining the theoretical literature on rural conflicts and the scale and scope of contentious behaviour in the Spanish countryside between 1931 and 1936, it looks at three case studies to show why conflicts involving casual labourers, tenant farmers, and sharecroppers divided society.

Rural Conflicts: From the Village to the Nation

Economists such as Olson or Tullock have argued that the free-rider problem is an important obstacle to effective collective action.[6] A successful village strike, for example, is a public good and because it benefits *all* workers, rational self-interested individuals will *not* want to pay the costs of participating because they cannot be excluded from the gains. In these circumstances the strike is likely to fail, and working conditions remain unchanged. However, as Chapter 5 noted, the social costs and exclusion that individuals might face within their village society from not participating in collective action could easily swamp any short-term material benefits they might gain if they continued to work.[7] Anthropologists have often stressed the strong *pueblo* solidarity found in Andalucia where, according to Victor Magagna, 'villages and agro-towns can be accurately described as economies of shared poverty in which local communities practice an enforced distribution of risk and benefits according to a finely graded hierarchy of locally defined rights and responsibilities'.[8] The fact that many disputes were essentially local, and most small farmers and farm workers lived cheek by jowl rather than on isolated farmsteads in the countryside, helped reduce the monitoring costs of fellow workers, especially when the village square functioned as a highly visible informal labour market. Group solidarity was further strengthened by a tradition of contentious collective action stretching back to the liberal land reforms and sales of common lands in the nineteenth century.[9]

In reality, village society in the latifundio provinces was much more heterogeneous than this vision suggests. In the first instance, the use of inter-linked contracts and the persistence of paternalism and weak factor markets sometimes created high levels of dependence between landowner and tenant. A different form of dependence was found between employers and those farm workers on annual contracts living on isolated estates. As noted, most village workers were hired on a temporary basis not on annual contracts, and resented migrant laboureres taking 'their work'. The fact that some rural workers earned an important part of their income from non-farm activities added a further dimension, especially when agriculture

---

[6] Olson, 1965, and Tullock 1971.
[7] Mason 2004, p. 87. For example, from the 1910s, the anarcho-syndicalists demanded that workers and employers *boicot* those who failed to respect a strike. Díaz del Moral 1928: 1973, pp. 337–8.
[8] Magagna 1991, p. 173.
[9] Bernal 1974, pp. 112–16, Calero 1976, p. 6, and Pérez Yruela 1979, pp. 25–6 and 32. For collective action as a resource to increase group solidarity, see Tarrow 2011, especially p. 29.

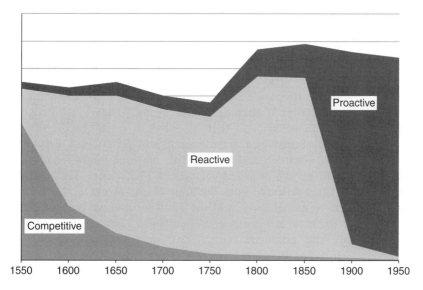

Figure 10.1 Hypothetical evolution of collective action in France
Source: Tilly et al. 1975, p. 54.

was the employer of last resort, and had to accommodate the unemployed urban workers returning to their villages. Another crucial division was age, as rural poverty fluctuated over the life cycle, being especially high among youngsters struggling to get onto the farm ladder, while older workers often became part-time farmers with family responsibilities, making them reluctant to play a prominent role in organizing labour because of their fear of being blacklisted by local employers.[10] Finally, not only would it be very wrong to suppose that all villagers in Andalucia had similar interests to participate in collective action, but anthropologists have also stressed a lack of solidarity *between pueblos*.[11]

Tilly's description of three types of collective action that reflect the demands and organizational capacity of French villagers and the likely response of the local elites and the state, is useful to understand conflicts in Spain (Figure 10.1). First, 'competitive' collective action describes disputes between different communal groups, such as villages over such issues as the use of common pasture lands. Second, 'reactive' rural protest was essentially local and unplanned, and responded to the

---

[10] In the Third World today this represents about a third of rural poverty. World Bank 1990, p. 35, cited in Lipton 2009, p. 18.
[11] Pitt-Rivers 1954: 1971, pp. 8–9.

intrusion by the state, or the negative consequences associated with a widening market economy. Targets were often local landowners or their representatives, who could be both employers and government agents. In years of dearth, therefore, villagers might react by stopping the local landowners' grain being taken to be sold elsewhere, or poach on their land when they were considered to have infringed the community's 'moral economy'. It often followed seasonal patterns, with poaching, collecting fire wood, and theft of olives frequent in the winter months, and crop burning, illegal gleaning, and destruction of harvest machinery in the summer, and the numbers involved might range from a handful to one or two hundred villagers.[12] These 'everyday forms of peasant resistance' reflected both the logic of organizing at the village, rather than the regional level, and the need for anonymity, given the landowners' ability to arbitrarily end clientelistic arrangements, significantly raising the potential costs for those who challenged their authority.[13] Finally 'proactive' describes situations when 'at least one group is making claims for rights, privileges, or resources not presently enjoyed', and collective action takes place over large areas involving considerable numbers of individuals. In this case, the ability of villagers to organize bottom-up activities had to be complemented by outside groups creating top-down structures. The presence of these outside organizations greatly increased the 'repertoire of contention', allowing villagers to mobilize in different ways according to their needs and possibilities.[14] As Tarrow notes, 'where the old repertoire had been parochial, direct, and segmented, the new one was national, flexible, and based on modular forms of action'.[15]

Tilly's three forms of collective action illustrate how groups can adapt to changing political scenarios. In this respect, the proclamation of the Second Republic in April 1931 represented a dramatic shift in the opportunity structures for contentious collective action, as the new government not only stopped repressing trade unions, but also introduced major labour market reforms which altered 'the costs and benefits of participating in unions and gave unions a greater ability to punish neutrals and strike breakers during strikes',[16] thereby challenging landowners' paternalistic networks. As noted in Chapter 9, a Socialist Minister of Labour approved decrees which, among other things, required farmers to maintain the intensity of the cultivation on their lands (*Laboreo Forzoso*) and offer work to local unemployed workers before hiring migrants, even if these came from the next village (*Términos Municipales*). It also created

---

[12] Rey 2008, p. 292.   [13] This is the subtitle of Scott's 1985 book.
[14] The expression in Tilly 2008.   [15] Tarrow 2011, p. 55.   [16] Domenech 2013b, p. 90.

Table 10.1 *Forms of collective action and the response of the authorities, 1931–6*

Activity	Objectives	Collective action restrictions	Results
Petty 'theft'	Survival/revenge	Individuals-none	Immediate
Violence against property	Revenge	Few	Immediate
'Minimum work' *	Create employment	Few	Immediate
Harvest strikes *	Higher wages	Significant	Immediate
Land invasions *	Create employment	Few	Future

* Requires tolerance by local (and sometimes national) authorities

a closed shop and allowed village authorities to determine which workers were to be employed (*Turno Riguroso*), and local arbitration boards (*Jurados Mixtos*) to regulate not just the wages and hours of work, but also to restrict the use of piece work and harvest machinery.[17] Indeed, the clause found in collective bargaining agreements that determined the share of the harvest to be collected by hand rather than by machines was often as important to workers' incomes as the wage itself. The favourable political situation between April 1931 and November 1933, and again after February 1936, saw strikes and land invasions become common, as syndicates attempted to enforce the decrees and collective bargaining decisions. As a result, and despite the deep economic recession and growing unemployment, rural strikes in 1932–3 measured as a proportion of those employed in agriculture increased six fold compared to the previous peak in 1918–20.[18] When the political tide turned, and syndicates and labour organizations were repressed again, especially after October 1934, village workers returned to traditional forms of resistance, in part to survive, and in part to challenge landowners and employers, creating a highly charged atmosphere. Finally, the fact that the state often used the municipality to coordinate economic activity, such as with the highly contentious *Términos Municipales* Decree, implied that conflicts between villages were also common, resulting in all three forms of contentious collective action being present at one moment or another during the Second Republic.

[17] The *Jurados Mixtos* consisted of equal numbers of worker and employer representatives with a government-appointed chairman holding the deciding vote.
[18] Domenech 2013b, p. 89

Casual Labour and the Harvest

A major characteristic of dry-farming was the highly seasonal nature of labour demand. The first detailed statistical study is only available in 1956, and shows that 77 per cent of all workers in the south were classified as day workers, compared to 81 per cent in the Mediterranean, and 67 per cent in Old Castile and Upper Ebro (Map 10.1). What makes Southern Spain so different, however, was the presence of large estates and the fact that most workers had little or no land, leaving them highly dependent on seasonal employment. The harvest was one of the few moments of the year when labour requirements were significantly greater than what the village could supply, and the failure to collect it quickly had major economic consequences for employers, as it represented a large part of their annual income. Indeed, strikes had a tendency to increase in years of a good harvest, when farmers could afford to pay higher wages, and decline in those with poor ones. In these areas, the organizational problems facing labour syndicates in the interwar period were more akin to those found in the market gardens of California, rather than in Northern Europe.

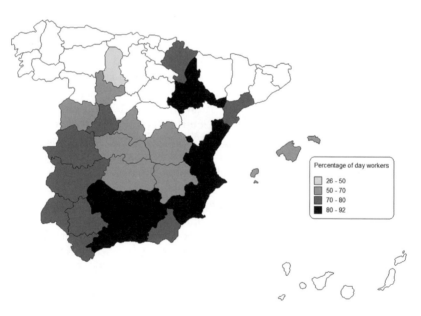

Map 10.1 Day workers as a share of farm labourers in 1956
Source: Junta Nacional de Hermandades 1959.

Across Spain, cereals and legumes accounted for 72 per cent of the crop area, and harvest demand was equivalent to perhaps 20 per cent of all farm work in Cadiz, Cordoba, Jaen, and Seville, four of the most contentious provinces in Andalucia. The figures for the olive could be even greater.[19] At the extreme, there were 305,000 hectares of olives in Jaen where the harvest provided an average of 15 workdays per hectare, implying an annual average of 4.25 million workdays between 1926 and 1935, or 28.5 days for every male employed in agriculture in the province.[20] When harvest volatility is accounted for, labour demand fluctuated from about 47 workdays per male worker in 1929/30, to just 11 in 1930/1.[21] Although the olive was often cultivated on small family farms, labour requirements on this scale implied that even modest producers needed to employ some harvest labour.

Harvest work provided employment not just for farm labourers but also small farmers and many who were normally employed in industry or services. On Andalusia's latifundios three types of workers can be identified, each with their own demands. First, a small number of permanent workers lived on the *cortijos* and enjoyed annual contracts and small perks in exchange for their loyalty. This patron-client relationship made it unlikely they would become unionized.[22] A second and much bigger group consisted of casual workers including women and children living in the village. These demanded to be paid by the day, rather than by piecework, in order to prolong the harvest as long as possible to maximize their total earnings. Finally, migrant labour was attracted from both neighbouring villages, often in the sierras, as well as from long distances. Migrant gangs were especially attractive to employers when a fixed price to collect all the harvest could be negotiated, as this effectively subcontracted the problems of monitoring work effort to the group itself. When this was not possible, piecework provided workers with an incentive to collect the harvest quickly and thereby spend as little time as possible away from their homes.

---

[19] Unsown fallow and rough pasture are excluded from crop area, and harvest operations assumed to account for half of labour inputs. In the four provinces of Cadiz, Cordoba, Jaen, and Seville, the olive accounted for 32 per cent of the final output, and 46 per cent of farm work in the in 1930/5. In Jaen, the level of dependence was even greater, reaching 53 per cent and more for employment. Simpson 1992b, table 7, and 1995b, pp. 188, 196 and 211–12.

[20] Simpson 1985, p. 239. López Estudillo 2006, p. 105, gives twenty workdays / hectare for Cordoba in 1900.

[21] Simpson 1985, p. 412, for collecting olives, and 1992, p. 13, for 1.6 days to process one ton. Some three million workdays were lost in the 1930/1 harvest in Jaen compared to employment levels in the previous five years.

[22] However in Ciudad Real workers on annual contracts did strike. Ladrón de Guevara 1993, pp. 72–8. For paternalism, see Chapter 7.

Legislation during the Old Regime had sometimes forced villagers to collect the local harvest because of the low population densities and labour shortages.[23] However, by the early twentieth century, employers benefitted from a better transport system that encouraged temporary internal migrations, weak syndicates, and provincial governors who were usually willing to provide police protection for workers who wanted to work during strikes. Although labour became increasingly organized from the First World War, employers' negotiating position was also strengthened by population growth, harvest mechanization, and the development of motor transportation to bring in outside labour to break strikes.[24] On the eve of the Republic, complaints were still common that landowners agreed over drinks in the village casino on the coming harvest wage and blacklisted union organizers. Nevertheless, the high wages noted in Map 7.1 suggests that labour scarcity, especially following a good harvest, still gave organized labour significant negotiating strength.

For a harvest strike to be successful, syndicates needed both the full backing of local workers, especially in the larger municipalities where farms were highly dispersed, and the ability to stop employers hiring migrant workers or using machinery. Therefore, even when there was a high level of village solidarity, the local syndicates needed to create regional organizations to control migrant workers and enforce agreements on employers. In Andalucia, union capacity and employers' institutions took place in 'waves', marked by the series of harvest strikes of 1882–3, 1902–5, 1918–20, 1931–3, and 1936, with the two major labour organizations in the countryside, the Anarchist CNT and Socialist FNTT, developing very differently.[25]

The strength of the Anarcho-Syndicalists was their highly flexible and essentially local organizational structure which made it easy for them to respond to village demands, which were often parochial. Their dislike of bureaucratic structures was well suited when organizing labour was illegal, and syndicates repressed. Labour discipline was sometimes enforced by calling a general strike for the whole town, which both helped reduce monitoring problems, such as having to determine whether small farmers were going to work their own plot or to break the strike by working for others, as well as pressuring other employers to intervene and convince landowners to concede. Yet while this might be sufficient to control local

---

[23] Florencio Puntas & López Martínez 2000.
[24] Montañés & Simpson 2015, pp. 128, for the use of motor transport.
[25] Franzosi 1995, for organizational change and cycles of unrest. Catholic worker syndicates were also important, but faced very different organizational problems to both the CNT and FNTT.

workers, it failed to deal adequately with migrant labour. The logical response was therefore to call for a revolutionary strike over a larger area, something that the CNT did in 1932, 1933, and 1934. The acrimony between the Anarcho-Syndicalists and their bottom-up organizational structure and the Socialist FNTT, with its top-down approach, frequently led to open disputes, and the CNT sometimes found itself as much in conflict with the FNTT as with the employers.[26] Only in 1934 did the CNT make any attempt to coordinate its activities with the FNTT.

The Socialists responded to the problem of transforming local village conflicts into a general struggle to improve living standards by attempting to institutionalize collective action, rather than encouraging isolated local actions. As Shorter and Tilly found for France, successful strike outcomes were much more likely when the state was sympathetic to worker demands.[27] In theory, the provincial governor, the state's local representative, could intervene and make both sides accept arbitration; it could remain neutral, allowing market forces and the local power struggle in the countryside to determine the outcome; or it could back either the employers (for example, by declaring a strike illegal), or the syndicate (by failing to guarantee the freedom to work during a strike). The state was not neutral, and during the 1930s it switched from first sympathizing with organized labour, then the employers and, finally, back to labour once again.

The Socialists had attempted to influence government legislation, first by working with the Primo de Rivera dictatorship's endeavours to create a corporatist state, and then by introducing the labour legislation of 1931 and 1932. Their objective was to create a legal structure that obliged employers to participate in collective bargaining and respect its decisions, as well as protecting union officials and members from discrimination. To enforce legislation however, the Socialists needed to control the municipal government and, ideally, enjoy the support of a sympathetic provincial governor. Collective action now took on a form of 'rightful resistance', with the primary objective being to oblige employers to compile with the law and

---

[26] In Cordoba, a province where both the Anarchists and Socialists were strong, strikes became on occasions 'more of a struggle between syndicates than a labour conflict'. Pérez Yruela 1979, p. 128. For Cadiz, Caro Cancela 2001, p. 180. Azaña talked of an 'authentic civil war' between the two syndicates.

[27] Shorter & Tilly 1974. State intervention that obliged employers to negotiate effectively gave legitimacy to 'what was after all, an insurgent political movement' before the Second Republic.

Table 10.2 *Indicators of conflicts and collective action, Cordoba, 1931–6*

	Agricultural strikes	Nature of government	Size of cereal harvest (3)	Theft and robbery	Arson
1931 (1)	69	+	75	27	6
1932	30	+	135	52	13
1933	95	+	53	29	21
1934	51	-	158	15	6
1935	–	-	79	37	9
1936 (2)	24	+	?	67	1
Total					

(1) April to December; (2) to 18 July; (3) 1931–5 = 100; Governments favourable to collective action +
Sources: Pérez Yruela 1979, pp. 116, 184, and 208.

legally abiding agreements.[28] These changes gave the Socialist FNTT full control of labour markets, because the Anarchist CNT refused to participate in the new labour institutions, and the Catholic worker syndicates could not legally represent workers on arbitration boards. As a result, the FNTT membership soared tenfold, from 27,340 in 1930 to 392,955 by the end of June 1932, with its activities being limited not just to latifundio provinces, but also including areas of small farms. In Valladolid, a province of essentially small family farmers, there were thirty harvest strikes in 1933, and seventeen the following year.[29]

The cycle and nature of contentious collective action can be illustrated in the province of Cordoba, with good cereal harvests (1932 and 1934), and a government sympathetic towards workers' interests (1931–3 and 1936), encouraging 'proactive' strike activities and a switch to 'reactive' activities such as theft or arson when these were absent (Table 10.2). However, it is clear that there were also other factors at play. Strike activity was unusually high in 1931 because of the local struggle between the Anarcho-Syndicalists and Socialists, while the low levels found in 1932 reflect the weak bargaining strength of the employers. The 1933 harvest was half the normal size, and the provincial section of the FNTT launched a massive strike that was ended by the delegate of the Ministry of

---

[28] For example, in Salamanca in late 1932 and early 1933. Cabrera 1983, pp. 154–5, and Jaen, Cobo Romero 2003, p. 23. More generally, FNTT 1933, pp. 196–223. For 'rightful resistance', see O'Brien & Li 2006.
[29] Prado Moura 1985, pp. 107 and 116, and Gil Andrés 2013, pp. 110–12, for la Rioja.

Table 10.3 *Changes in official farm prices and wage costs in Southern Spain, 1931–6*

	National farm prices			Collective agreements for wheat harvest work (male day wages)		Other estimates for male day wages		
	Wheat	Olive oil	Wine	Cordoba collecting by hand (in pesetas)	Cadiz threshing	Cordoba	Spain max. male wages	Spain real-day wages
1913	100	100	100		100	100	100	100
1931	146	153	105	7.75		316	256	141
1932	155	153	107	9.40	221		266	142
1933	146	135	98	8.50	243		275	152
1934	159	134	105	9.00	243		277	152
1935	154	131	97		219	272	281	154
1936				9.00	219		303	155

1913 = 100.
Sources: Carreras and Tafunell, 2005, 1, pp. 335–6, and 3, pp. 1220–1; Pérez Yruela 1979, pp. 293, 321, 354, 377, and 422; Montañés & Simpson 2015, table 4; Bringas Gutiérrez 2000, A.4.

Employment imposing conditions that were generally favourable to the workers.[30] The growth of the FNTT's membership was the result of its initial success during the harvests of 1931 and 1932, leading Malefakis to write that 'Spain had probably been the only nation in the world in which wages had actually risen during the Depression'.[31] This success was inevitably resented by larger farmers, especially as wages grew considerably faster than wheat prices between *c.*1913 and 1930/35 (Table 10.3). In addition, employers complained that both the length of the workday and the physical effort provided by workers fell significantly, particularly when piecework was prohibited. Small farmers who needed to hire labour for the harvest were worst hit because they also had greater difficulties in selling their harvest. The *Términos Municipales* Decree in particular was immensely unpopular, as migrant workers were frequently excluded from all forms of harvest work, not just the harvesting gangs such as those from Las Hurdes that for generations had crossed the country, but also workers living in neighbouring villages. By segmenting local labour markets, some workers suddenly found themselves with plenty of work, while others, where the land/ labour ratio was unfavourable or where the village

---

[30] Pérez Yruela 1979, pp. 141, 161–5.   [31] Malefakis 1970, p. 329.

specialized in a single crop, faced long periods of unemployment. In Jerez de la Frontera (Cadiz), for example, numerous workers from the neighbouring villages settled in the municipality so that they could work there, with some also taking advantage of the Anarchist boycott to the 'Socialist' land reform and joining the IRA's settlement program.[32]

Although the government legislation of 1931 and 1932 benefitted some groups of workers, it was often at the expense of others, producing conflicts between local workers and migrants, syndicalists and non-syndicalists, anarchists and socialists, etc. It also pushed up production costs for small farmers at a time of low farm prices. Conflicts turned to polarization because the Madrid government was unable to implement the legislation impartially, being dependent instead on municipal authorities. As a result, an 'independent' village council quickly became pressured by different groups to enforce legislation in their favour. Control of the village council therefore became crucial, and was a major reason why central government changed village councils following each of the national elections, in 1931, 1933 (and especially after Asturias) 1934, and February 1936.

With the victory of the Centre-Right coalition in November 1933, the FNTT found it hard to enforce labour laws, and complained that farmer organizations encouraged their members to ignore collective bargaining agreements.[33] The dilemma now facing the FNTT was therefore whether to continue to consolidate its hierarchical movement and cooperate with a government that was moving further to the right, and risk losing members whose living standards it claimed were deteriorating by the day, or whether instead to move in the opposite direction, and challenge the state. It chose the latter, and called a national strike on the eve of the country's largest ever cereal harvest, starting on 5 June 1934. Although the government declared the harvest 'of national interest', thereby effectively ensuring that it would be collected, it also appears to have met most, if not all, of the FNTT's demands four days before the announced strike. However, these demands were increased two days later to include clauses that would allow labour organizations to designate which workers could be contracted; introduced a ban on farm machinery across the country; and extended the high harvest wages for the whole of the agricultural year. Historians remain divided over whether it was the government, and especially the conservative Salazar Alonso, the Minister for Home

---

[32] Caro Cancela 2001, pp. 128 and 203.
[33] In La Solana, even before November 1933, the Socialist *El Obrero de la Tierra* (15 April, 10 June, 15 July, 17 August, and 9 September 1933) complained about work agreements not being respected, employers hiring workers on their own account, and the lack of cooperation with village authorities. Rey 2008, pp. 343–5.

Affairs, or the belligerence of the FNTT that was to blame for the strike.[34] Press censorship also makes it impossible to know how widespread it was, but it almost certainly greater than the official figures, but perhaps less than suggested by Preston, who argues that stoppages were 'almost complete' in Jaen, Granada, Ciudad-Real, Badajoz, and Caceres, and 'substantial' elsewhere in the south.[35]

In fact the importance of the strike lies elsewhere, as it strengthened the arguments of the extremists both on the Left, who argued that neither the Centre-Right government nor indeed democracy could protect workers' interests against the employers, and those on the Right, who now demanded the immediate dismantlement of the FNTT and its *Casas del Pueblo*. Following the revolutionary uprising in Asturias in October 1934, the government did repress the labour movement in this way, jailing many syndicalist, as well as removing the Socialists from office in hundreds of village councils, and closing the *Casas del Pueblo*. As a result, there was an almost total absence of strikes in 1935, although rural poverty undoubtedly increased, and landowners and employers frequently ignored the labour legislation and blacklisted union organizers (Table 3.7). Instead, there was a massive increase in reactive activities, including poaching, collecting firewood or fallen olives, or pasturing animals on private land.[36]

The failure of the 1934 harvest strike highlights the limits of the FNTT's strategy, and that of the Socialists in general, in terms of building a hierarchical centralist organization. Although the FNTT had successfully made regional rural poverty a national issue, membership at its peak in June 1932 represented less than a third of those listed as landless or poor farmers in the *Censo de Campesinos* in the latifundio provinces (Table 9.3).[37] More importantly, the Socialists failed to build a lasting alliance with any other major political group, leaving the FNTT as a narrow and highly specific organization that antagonized most sections of rural society.[38]

---

[34] According to Malefakis 1970, p. 338, Townson 2000, pp. 246–8, and Rey 2008, p. 392, the demands were impossible for the government to accept, an idea disputed by Pérez Yruela 1979, p.193.

[35] Preston 1978:2003, pp. 152–3.

[36] Table 10.2 undoubtedly severely underestimates this reactive response. In 'Los Olivos' for example, citations by the Civil Guard 'increased by an astonishing thirtyfold in 1935', Collier 1987, p. 128, while in La Solana a certificate of proof of ownership was required for those who sold grapes to wineries. Rey 2008, pp. 401 and 441.

[37] The FNTT failed to publish national figures after June 1932. However, provincial figures suggest significant declines. In Valladolid, for example, membership fell from 11,009 in June 1932, to 7,729 in March 1933, and 6,554 in May 1936. Serrano Garcia 2016, pp. 4–5.

[38] Calls to admit tenants and smallholders to the FNTT or the creation of specific sections are frequent in *El Obrero de la Tierra* (27 August 1932, 6 May 1933, July 8, 1933, or 16 Sept. 1933). Candido Pedrosa (6 August 1932) complained about the lack of 'solidarity'

This made it impossible to negotiate a corporatist agreement whereby farmers would be willing to guarantee workers a living wages and employment package in exchange for state intervention in commodity markets, and enforce minimum farm prices. Yet neither was the Right willing to abandon its partisan advantage when it was in power in 1934 and 1935, nor the state able to offer adequate guarantees that it could actually implement an agreement.

The *Yunteros* and Land Invasions in Extremadura

Some of the most dramatic events of the Second Republic were the land invasions, first in 1932, but especially in March 1936, when over 100,000 small tenants, sharecroppers, and landless workers occupied over half a million hectares in western Spain. These occupations resulted in the rapid redistribution of considerably more land than the bureaucratic 1932 Agrarian Reform organized by the IRA from Madrid. However they bitterly divided the countryside in Extremadura, not just vertically between landowners and tenants, but also horizontally between different farm groups.

The provinces of Badajoz and Caceres were at the epicentre of the invasions, a region where 70 per cent of the workforce was still employed in agriculture. Around 44 per cent of the farm population was landless, and 88 per cent of those with access to land had less than ten hectares.[39] In Caceres in 1956, when better information is available and conditions had not changed significantly, only 15 per cent of the active farm population lived 'comfortably' from their farms; while another 28 per cent were dependent on other sources of income (usually working as casual labourers), and 57 per cent were landless.[40] Per capita incomes in Extremadura were the lowest of Spain's 17 regions, and illiteracy remained above 40 per cent.[41]

The large estates were farmed as dehesas because soil quality was poor, and combined extensive livestock farming (animal breeding, wool, meat), with small-scale cereal production, as well as forestry (acorns for fodder, wood, cork). These estates were usually rented for their winter pastures to owners of large flocks from northern Spain, much as under the Mesta

of the tenants and settlers with field workers, but went on to warn that 'anyone who confronts the legitimate aspirations of the proletariat will suffer the consequences'.
[39] Carmona & Simpson 2016, pp. 131–2.   [40] García Pérez 1982, p. 223.
[41] Rosés et al. 2010, p. 249, and Núñez 1992, p. 163. Labour productivity in agriculture was 82 per cent of the national average and land output 48 per cent. Simpson 1995b, pp. 211–12. For those areas where the cadastre was complete (59 per cent in Caceres, and 83 per cent in Badajoz), 1.8 per cent of landowners owned 63 per cent of the land, and 2.4 per cent paid 59 per cent of the land tax. Carrión 1932: 1975, table 3.

before its abolition in 1836.[42] The landowner, or a large tenant, would rent or sharecrop small areas to local farmers to prepare and cultivate for a couple of years, before the land was allowed to return to grass. Before the Second Republic, local workers were often organized in associations or collectives, which helped both the landowners find suitable tenants and allowed large numbers of poor workers access to land that otherwise would have been impossible.[43] The fact that new land, and therefore new contracts, was needed every two or three years gave tenants strong incentives to conserve soil fertility.

The Great Depression marked the end of a period of rapid growth in farming in Extremadura, with the area of cereals and livestock numbers almost doubling between 1900 and 1930. Further expansion was now discouraged by weak cereal prices and rent controls, just at a time when the demand for work was growing because of population growth and unemployed workers returning to their villages. The usual explanation for the land invasions is that landowners responded to the new government decrees and the threat of land reform by instigating a 'lock-out' and converting arable land to pasture.[44] Yet while some landowners undoubtedly failed to renew leases to those tenants who were considered politically active, there is no evidence of a generalized decline in the area cultivated.[45]

In fact, a better explanation for the first land invasions was the uncertainty caused by the 1932 Land Reform Law which abolished subletting.[46] Village collectives enjoyed preference to rent the dehesas, but they usually lacked the necessary capital to stock the farm for grazing.[47] Many landowners were no doubt more sympathetic to these traditional collectives which were already known to them and often Catholic, rather than the recently founded Socialist ones which tended to attract members with less capital. As a result, the Socialist FNTT

---

[42] In Extremadura, slightly over half of all farm land was rented or sharecropped, although there is no information concerning the exact amount on the dehesas, or the amount that was sublet. Instituto de Reforma Agraria 1934, p. 35.

[43] There were 144 authorized societies with 22,965 members that rented land collectively in Extremadura in January 1934. Instituto de Reforma Agraria 1934, p. 35. In the Caceres region, 21 per cent of tenants signed contracts involving ten or more individuals, and 47 per cent of the subletting contracts. Carmona & Simpson 2014a, table 10.

[44] See, for example, Riesco Roche 2006, pp. 130–6.

[45] Carmona & Simpson 2016, pp. 121–6.

[46] The reformist legislation of 1931 and 1932 aimed to protect tenants against eviction, but abolish subletting. However, the fact that contracts were between tenants and subtenants implied that the law could not oblige owners to keep the subtenants if the tenant left. See Alvarez Jusué 1933, pp. 97–100.

[47] Torrequemada (Cáceres), for example, rented the pasture. Archivo Histórico Provincial de Cáceres (AHPC), Jurados Mixtos, Caja 2, legajo 72.

organized the land invasions in the autumn of 1932, and began cultivating the land, challenging the government to either evict them, or legalize their occupation.[48] The government response was the Intensification of Cultivation decree of November 1932, which provided workers with land for a couple of years – the first to prepare the fallow and grow a catch crop, and the second to plant a major cereal crop. The IRA supervised the choice of suitable land, selected the tenants, and guaranteed the landowners their rent. As very few tenants actually paid their rents, the IRA was held responsible.[49] By October 1933, almost 30,000 peasants had been settled on just under 100,000 hectares in Extremadura, giving an average of just over three hectares each.[50] The IRA allowed leases to be renewed for another year in December 1934, but landowners were free to evict tenants after the 1935 harvest.[51] Many appear to have done so, offering the land now to other *yunteros* of their choice.[52] The decree of 3 March 1936 following the Popular Front victory allowed those tenants evicted in 1935 to reclaim the land once more, and was followed by massive invasions on 25 March 1936, in time to sow a spring crop.[53] Once again the IRA intervened, and around 81,000 peasants received almost 240,000 hectares.[54] While about a third of Extremadura's villages had participated in 1932 invasions, the figures had grown to 82 per cent in 1936, suggesting that the FNTT was more successful at extending its influence over a wider geographical area, rather than recruiting new members in those villages where it already had a presence.[55] It also suggests that many of those who invaded lands in 1936 could not have participated in those of 1932 and consequently evicted in 1935. The area occupied in 1932 and 1936 was equivalent to 13 per cent and 32 per cent of land in cereal rotations respectively.

The Socialist FNTT, and the state IRA, successfully evoked a picture of the poor tenant farmers (*yunteros*) unable to feed their families and work animals, as the victims of economic decisions taken by absentee

---

[48] Malefakis 1970, pp. 237–43, García Pérez 1985, and, for Caceres, Riesco Roche 2006, for Badajoz, Espinosa 2007.

[49] RD de 23 de octubre y 3 de noviembre 1932. See especially Riesco Roche 2006, pp. 157–61.

[50] BIRA, Oct. 1933, pp. 52–60. Malefakis 1970, p. 242. The settling of large numbers of peasants and ending uncontrolled land invasions was considered a success by the IRA. BIRA, 1933, 11, pp. 258–66.

[51] Malefakis 1970, pp. 343–7.

[52] See, for example, Espinosa 2007, p. 144, for the election results.

[53] The 14th March 1936 Law allowed the social utility clause to be used on all dehesas, and that of 20 March for all land. For invasions, see Malefakis 1970, pp. 369–71; Riesco Roche 2006, pp. 131–4, 137, 147–8, and 303–4.

[54] BIRA, March-June, 1936, Malefakis 1970, p. 378, and Tuñón de Lara 1985, pp. 172–7.

[55] Carmona & Simpson 2016, pp. 130 and 136.

landowners.[56] Yet rather than a simple class-based conflict, disputes were frequently between different groups of workers and tenants, not all of whom were necessary poor. In Torreorgaz, for example, the 182 individuals, or 37 per cent of villagers, who invaded the Duchess of Campo-Giro's estate, possessed between them 62 per cent of the village's work animals, and eight actually owned more than one mule team. These were at the top end of the income scale, as a fully equipped mule team required 30 hectares of land, implying that even some rich farmers needed to invade lands (Appendix 2).[57] Across Badajoz, the numbers of those who participated in land invasions in 1936 were equivalent to only 47 per cent of those registered in the *Censo de Campesinos*, suggesting that most workers and tenants did not participate, perhaps because they still benefitted from strong paternalistic relations with their landowners. This is also indicated by the fact that in the essentially rural province of Badajoz, the conservative anti-revolutionary coalition actually won in seven of the fifteen judicial districts in the elections of February 1936.[58]

The lack of suitable land to cultivate led to the FNTT to challenge traditional mechanisms of control by landowners and farmers over how it was to be allocated. The invasions led to bitter conflicts, not just between invaders and landowners, but also between different groups of tenants. One obvious source was land that was traditionally used for grazing, thereby denying large livestock farmers winter pastures, especially as most villagers had very few animals that could use it. As the Socialist deputy Cabrera noted, 'the use as pasture was much more remunerative but condemned whole villages such Mestanza to starve because of the limited work it provided at a time of unemployment'.[59]

A second possible source of uncultivated land was the fallow found within the long cereal rotations. Keeping this land uncultivated was necessary because of the poor soil quality, and represented a capital investment by landowners to be realized in the distant future. However, reaching an objective measurement of soil fertility in this period was very difficult, and impossible for an outside agency such as the IRA with its limited resources, and the huge geographical area to inspect. For the invading tenants it was also unnecessary, as they were encouraged to follow short-term objectives of land-mining, as the possibilities of being given land in the future now depended on the political strength of the

---

[56] See, for example, the IRA film, *Los Yunteros de Extremadura*, made in the spring of 1936 (http://ruralmedia.eu/2017/02/yunteros-de-extremadura/).

[57] Carmona & Simpson 2016, p. 135 and figure 4.

[58] For the election results, see Espinosa 2007, p. 97.

[59] Cited in Ladrón de Guevara 1993, p. 246. The quote refers to the Valle de Alcudia in Ciudad Real, but similar debates were found for Extremadura.

244 Rural Conflicts and Polarization of Village Society

FNTT, rather than the goodwill of the landowner. Finally, a significant number of land occupations involved the expulsion of other tenants, a clear indicator of the scarcity of fertile and easily accessible uncultivated land.[60] Even some of the IRA's Land Reform settlements were invaded.[61] In this way, land invasions and their subsequent formalization by the IRA, not only threatened the property rights of large landowners and the interests of large livestock farmers, but also the continuity of small and medium-sized tenants, especially those belonging to Catholic associations.

Land reform through local invasions also generated problems because of the significant differences in the quantity and quality of land available to inhabitants in different villages, even neighbouring ones. In Jerez de los Caballeros (Badajoz) for example, land availability as measured by per capita taxable income ranged from 11 pesetas in Valle de Santa Ana to 248 pesetas in Jerez itself, a ratio of 1:25.[62] As noted previously, the *Términos Municipales* legislation increased inter-municipal conflicts over resources, and disputes now also arose over land invasions by neighbouring villagers. The plans to recover their common lands would undoubtedly have had similar effects, because a village that recovered its old common lands would have faced demands from other villages for access to them.[63]

Finally, the *Censo de Campesinos* and the 1932 Land Reform (Base 11, c9 and d) placed an upper limit of ten hectares for farmers to benefit from land redistribution. While this was perhaps effective in sharing the limited amount of available land and work and allowing the landless a foot on the farm ladder, it was insufficient to keep a family and effectively blocked the possibilities for them to climb the farm ladder (Appendix 2). As such, it benefitted the landless at the expense not just of the large tenants, but also the smaller ones.

It is difficult to know to what extent the land invasions actually reduced rural poverty in Extremadura, as opposed to just fuelling rural conflicts between those groups of poor farmers and landless workers who remained attached to the traditional patronage networks, and others who joined the FNTT. The land that was invaded was equivalent to 17 per cent of the cultivated area in 1936, and those invading represented only 40 per cent of those considered in

---

[60] Riesco Roche 2006, pp. 145–7 and 303–10, Espinosa 2007, pp. 152–237 and Ladrón de Guevara 1993, p. 422. For the context of province in Andalucia, see Cobo 2013.
[61] Riesco Roche 2006, p. 304.
[62] Carrión 1932: 1975, pp. 187–91. España. Dirección General del Instituto Geográfico 1932. It refers to 1930.
[63] This is ignored in the most recent studies, such as Iriarte Goñi & Lana Berasain 2016 or Robledo 2012. For the 'exclusive' nature of common resources being reserved for community members in Ostrom 1990, pp. 30–2.

need.[64] Most landless workers therefore had either already been able to rent land, or chose for some reason not to invade. Membership of the Socialist FNTT was 57,000, or a third of those on the *Censo de Campesinos*, and although this was sufficient to organize mass actions, it was too small to represent rural society. By contrast, 42,000 farmers belonged to cooperatives and other associations, equivalent to 47 per cent of those that did not qualify to be listed on the *Censo* (Table 9.2). These were almost certainly opposed to the land invasions, but the opinion of the other half is unknown. Therefore the experience of land reform appears to have left Extremadura highly polarized, without resolving the fundamental problems of the lack of employment and rural poverty. The fact that the invasions received widespread national coverage in newspapers did little to reassure small farmers and tenants in other regions.

Conclusion: The Village and the Polarization of Rural Society

Despite the FNTT's propaganda, rural unrest was not limited to conflicts between just capital and labour, but rather resulted from landowners, village councils, labour unions, and the state, all attempting to control access to the limited amounts of available work and land. Conflicts arose between different groups, including livestock and arable farmers; between workers and farmers who lived in a village with plenty of land and work, and those next door who lacked resources; and between tenants and workers who continued to enjoy strong paternalistic contracts with landowners, and those who looked instead to the *Casa del Pueblo*, the Socialist FNTT, or Anarchist CNT. Village life became highly polarized because it was the local authorities who determined whether legislation was implemented to help organized labour, or whether instead farmers could ignore it. Farm groups now became increasingly organized as political power changed hands three times between 1931 and 1936, and many became intolerant not just of the other faction, but also those who attempted to follow a neutral, middle path. The fact that the state lacked the ability to collect village-level information, or create impersonal mechanisms to determine which workers were most in need, allowed political groups to fill the void, thereby intensifying conflicts.

---

[64] There were 292 thousand employed in agriculture, and 81 thousand settled in 1936. The population in need is assumed as 80 per cent.

Some of the policy difficulties can be illustrated with the farm ladder. The 1931 and 1932 decrees often attempted to improve the living standards of the poorest individuals found in the *Censo de Campesinos* and at the bottom of the ladder. However, because of the scarcity of resources, these policies actually made upward mobility considerably harder for those farmers who owned more than ten hectares, the maximum permitted to be listed on the *Censo*. These farmers therefore suffered not just from low farm prices, but also faced difficulties to rent enough land to provide work for their animals. The bitterness of the conflicts in southern Spain were caused, at least in part, because there few possibilities for low-paid workers to exit the rural labour market and move to the cities in the 1930s.

The attempts by political activists to create class-based syndicates to achieve permanent improvements in living standards therefore had only limited success. However, this was also true for casual farm workers everywhere, whether they were organized locally by independent syndicates, or by moderate bureaucratic socialist ones. The long-term solution in most other Western European countries would be some form of corporatism, which involved the substitution of political bargaining for market-determined wage settlements.[65] Britain was at the extreme, as the majority of workers felt integrated in the democratic system, and where the exceptional wartime economy produced in 1917 'what 50 years of trade union agitation had failed to', namely a guaranteed national minimum wage and a fixed working week for farm workers.[66] Fascist Italy, and later Spain, produced a different form of corporatism, which organized the farm sector vertically, giving only limited guarantees to farm labour. By contrast, class-based syndicates, such as the Anarchist CNT and, after 1934, the Socialist FNTT, were never going to obtain sector-wide agreement with employers and government in a democratic society, especially when market forces and the availability of relatively cheap harvesting and threshing equipment were working against them.

[65] Luebbert 1991, p. 2
[66] Howkins 1985, p. 121, and, more recently, Howkins & Verdon 2009.

Conclusion

This book has argued that weak state capacity and the absence of competitive mass political parties that the Second Republic inherited severely limited the possibilities of its success. As Juan Linz has noted, weak state capacity can create problems of efficacy, or the ability of governments to find adequate solutions to resolve basic demands, as well as a lack of effectiveness in policy implementation.[1] Land reform is an excellent example because it failed to resolve the problems of the landless, leading to frustration among a large section of rural society, while providing a platform for an even larger group to organize against the Republic. Although land reform initially had widespread support within Spanish society, the state lacked basic information on the crucial questions of how the latifundios were actually being run; how many landless workers were in need; or how many families could realistically be settled. There was also a profound misunderstanding of the state's capacity to carry out a reform of this magnitude, as well as the possibilities for creating employment using dry-farming technologies.

The success of the Restoration political system of *el turno* had owed much to the fact that the two major parties – the Conservative and Liberals – accepted the unwritten rule that power would automatically change hands with each election, and it only began to have difficulties when an increasing number of groups in society found themselves excluded. By contrast, the Second Republic and the new Constitution were opposed by large sections on both sides of the political spectrum from the outset. The experience of *el turno* was therefore a poor preparation for creating a genuine democracy. As argued in Chapter 6, competitive parliamentary politics in most Western European countries had forced the landed elites and Church to join forces and create mass political parties to defend their interests in parliament. Their success in attracting large numbers of conservative voters, especially among small farmers, encouraged the appearance of new independent political entrepreneurs and development of

[1] Linz 1978, chapter 2.

Christian Democracy, leading to the declining influence of the Church and landed elites. In Spain, this did not happened because the Restoration system protected the interests of these two groups, and this goes a long way to explaining why both the Church hierarchy and landed elites were still politically influential, and why their rejection of democracy and the liberal Constitution of 1931 set the tone for confrontation from the outset. Even in 1931, two basic norms for democratic success were therefore missing; namely, a mutual tolerance of competing parties to accept others as a legitimate rivals, and forbearance, implying 'that politicians should exercise restraint in deploying their institutional prerogatives'.[2]

The Left was also unprepared for democracy because the Socialists had enjoyed only a very limited parliamentary presence, and their trade unions were frequently suppressed, discouraging the appearance of a democratic revisionism of Marxism and social democracy. The secretive nature of the labour movement in particular left it deeply divided, and a strong anarchist movement developed in both the country's industrial heartland (Barcelona) and among the landless workers of Andalucia. From the start, the Anarchists opposed the 1931 Constitution and engaged in ferocious attacks on the Socialists, especially as these had supported Primo de Rivera (1923–9), a dictator that had repressed them. By contrast, although the Socialists played a major role in creating the Republic, the ineffectiveness of its social reforms and the illegal resistance of the conservative elites led many to become disillusioned with parliamentary democracy. Just as a significant section on the Right was happy to take its opposition outside parliament, so too would the Left when they saw their reforms being blocked, and then reversed.

Nevertheless, the indifferent support for the Republic by family farmers greatly increased the political influence of the traditional conservative elites and the anti-republican left. This group, by far the largest in countryside and representing around a third of the total electorate, is usually ignored in the literature, which focuses instead on the landed elites and landless labourers. As in most of Western Europe in the decades before 1930, the favourable movements in real wages and farm rents allowed large numbers of landless workers to become tenants or landowners in their own right. By 1930, Spain was a country of small farmers, although most remained 'peasant' rather than the prosperous, independent producers found throughout Northern Europe. As shown, small family farmers suffered from both natural resource constraints imposed by dry-farming,

---

[2] Levitsky & Ziblatt 2018, p. 8.

and institutional arrangements created during the Restoration that limited their organizational capacity. As a result, they were largely unrepresented in the new Constitution, severely weakening the legitimacy of
the Second Republic in rural Spain.

The long summer droughts over much of the country implied that dry-
farming techniques were needed for cultivation, leading to low output per
hectare and a highly seasonal labour demand. Therefore, while young
farm workers in Northern Europe were able to climb the farm ladder by
working long hours on their land to increase output and accumulate
savings, this was not possible over four-fifths of Spain without irrigation.
Dry-farming made land reform impossible, because asset-poor farmers
could not use their underemployed labour to switch from extensive
cereals into high-value labour-intensive crops. It is true that New World
family farmers who used dry-farming techniques were highly competitive
in international markets, but these enjoyed ample supplies of farmland
and mechanization allowed them to reduce the peak labour demand to
increase farm size. Extensive cereal cultivation was also competitive on
Spain's latifundios, but left many farm workers unemployed and in
poverty, something that was politically and morally unacceptable given
the economic conditions of the 1930s. Only with vine and olive cultivation could employment be increased, but the vine needed four years
before it came into production, and the olive at least seven, and both
were dependent on export markets, which were closed in the 1930s.

Another problem with creating a society of prosperous independent
family farmers was the institutional constraints to build new organizations. This was not because Spanish farmers were unable to cooperate, as
shown by the persistence of the village grain banks that were found
throughout most of the country, but rather because of the lack of top-
down support to create provincial or regional federations of cooperatives
and associations. In France, the landed elites, Church, or republican
groups had provided this role in their attempts to build political support,
and create mass political parties. In Spain, by contrast, the Restoration
settlement made this unnecessary and, barring the few years of social
unrest at the end of the First World War, the Church hierarchy showed no
interest in organizing small farmers. The Second Republic was defined by
the centre-left as a 'Republic for Republicans', rather than one that
attempted to win over the poor, but usually Catholic and conservative
small farmers. The liberal, urban agenda of social reforms, which also
included the separation of Church and State and land reform, offered
little that was attractive to the family farmer. Indeed, the split between
urban-rural interests was intensified by the governments' dilemma over
whether to support a policy of high wheat prices that favoured farmers

and landowners, or one of higher wages and cheaper food that benefited workers.

The lack of parliamentary experience and high levels of mutual intolerance between competing parties is insufficient however to explain why rural society became so polarized. The major source of friction was over how to allocate the insufficient amounts of work and land that were available at a time of deep economic depression. Even in the most advanced democracies, governments faced severe difficulties of how to create and implement social transfers efficiently, so it is hardly surprising to find in Spain that landowners and farmers continued to use the traditional patronage systems, or that the Socialist FNTT attempted to reward its own followers with land and work when it was in power. The state's inability to implement policies impartially led to corruption and manipulation of local politics continuing with the Republic, and the political orientation of the village council determining how decrees and laws were enforced. Paternalistic networks simply evolved to include new players, most notably the FNTT, resulting in farm work and land being given to the supporters of whatever political party was in power. Conflicts were essentially local, and when employers ignored laws and refused work to members of the FNTT or CNT, it was the village mayor and council that were held responsible. Likewise, it was the republican or socialist mayor that obliged landowners to employ more workers than they wanted, or enforced collective bargaining agreements that caused them to lose money with the harvest.

The problems of efficacy and effectiveness implied that first the moderate Socialists, and then the moderate Centre-Rigth, moved away from supporting parliamentary government to other, non-democratic, solutions. The failure of land reform, together with the difficulties of realizing other social reforms, split the Left Republican-Socialist government coalition, and allowed a disorganized and divided conservative opposition to consolidate. By 1933, landowners and farmers began to ignore the labour legislation and blacklist trade unionists. Once out of government, Fernando de los Ríos told the ex-Prime Minister Azaña of the 'incredible and cruel persecutions that the workers' political and union organizations were suffering at the hands of the authorities and the employers. The Civil Guard was daring to do things it had never dared do before.'[3] Work was given only to those who were not unionized. The Socialist leadership was therefore faced with a stark choice: accept the falling living standard of their constituents, and the declining party and syndicate membership, or

---

[3] Cited in Preston 2012, p. 57.

move further to the left, and illegality. The October 1934 Asturias uprising was the answer.

Yet the same three stages that began with the inability to legislate
effective and lasting reforms, to coalition splits, and finally to illegitimate
resistance, were also experienced by the Centre-Right. The fact that the
government was unable to regulate the wheat markets to raise farm prices
encouraged farmers and employers to cut wages, and employ only those
workers that made commercial sense for them. Once again the success of
this policy was dependent on the government remaining in power to
repress trade unions. This was possible throughout 1935 but, following
the Popular Front victory in February 1936, and the land invasions of the
following month, increasing numbers of small farmers began to question
the CEDA's moderation, and pushed for more radical, and undemocratic
solutions. In particular, just as the youth movement of the *Federación de
Juventudes Socialistas*, which merged with the Communist youth movement in March 1936, had started pushing moderate socialists to the left
and outside parliamentary politics in 1934, so now the youth movement
of the CEDA, the *Juventudes de Acción Popular*, acted as a magnet for the
extreme right and fascism.

This shift to the political extremes was encouraged by the electoral
system that greatly favoured the formation of broad coalitions and joint
lists. Most voters in the elections of February 1936 were offered the
choice between either the Popular Front or the Anti-Revolutionary
Coalition, and the certainty that victory for whichever group would
further divide the country, as the new government would be subject to
tremendous pressures to maximize their partisan advantage and crush
their opponents. In the countryside, farmers feared a Popular Front
victory as it would lead to higher production costs and weak farm prices,
but for workers it promised better living standards, a more ambitious land
reform, the continued separation of the Church from the State, and an
amnesty for political prisoners of October 1934. By contrast,
a government emerging from the Anti-Revolutionary Coalition would
allow farmers to cut labour costs, prohibit strikes, and blacklist workers.

In fact, these two major political groupings were largely fictitious and
existed only to win the election, but they obliged moderate, regime-
supporting parties, to give legitimacy to other parties that were clearly
disloyal to the Republic.[4] The Left was split, not just between the two
major syndicates (FNTT and CNT), but also with the revolutionary and
reformist wings of the Socialist syndicate and party. By contrast, the
CEDA had no clear ideological boundaries and included both Christian

---

[4] Juliá 1989 and Linz 1978b, p. 168.

Democrats and would-be fascists. When the opposition rejected moderate policies, it was relatively easy for voters to move further away from the centre.

The degree that the Spanish countryside was split is illustrated by the closeness of the February 1936 election even in regions of latifundios, and the fact that considerable debate exists even today over who actually won.[5] One recent estimate suggests that the Anti-Revolutionary Coalition won in five of the thirteen latifundio provinces, and lost by only 1.8 per cent of the votes in Jaen, and 2.9 per cent in Caceres. In total, the Popular Front obtained 1.294 million votes in the latifundio provinces compared to 1.289 million by the Anti-Revolutionary Coalition a difference of just 0.39 per cent.[6]

The military uprising in July 1936 was not in response to the call of any political party, but rather by generals who wanted to assume control of the government. As with all civil wars, the brutalities on both sides were immense. However, it was the republicans and members of labour organizations who suffered most, accounting for around three-quarters of the 200,000 people assassinated and summarily executed across the country.[7] As many local historians have documented, anybody who had anything to do with political or trade union activities was significantly at risk. While the slaughter was greatest in the latifundio provinces, it was also widespread in areas of small family farmers. Everywhere, the victors made off with the belongings and land of those who had supported the Republic.

The agrarian problems obviously did not disappear following Franco's victory in 1939 but, with the military firmly in control, it became possible to devise policies that benefitted landowners and farmers, at the expense of labour. Limited resources, now even scarcer because of government policy and the effects of the Second World War, benefited the clients of

---

[5] In particular, Álvarez Tardío & Villa García 2017, and the replies by Santos Juliá (*El País*, 04/05/2017) who doubts that the existence of a true 'counterrevolutionary coalition'; Lopez Villaverde (CTXT, 05/03/2017), who questions the counting centralist and counterrevolutionary candidates as one. By contrast, Payne (*ABC*, 05/07/2017), supports the existence of a coalition.

[6] The Popular Front won in the provinces of Badajoz (with a margin of 18 per cent over the anti-revolutionary coalition), Caceres (3 per cent), Cadiz (52 per cent), Cordoba (43 per cent), Huelva (19 per cent), Jaen (2 per cent), Malaga (61 per cent), and Seville (23 per cent), and the anti-revolutionary coalition won in Albacete (31 per cent over the Popular Front), Ciudad Real (30 per cent), Granada (49 per cent), Salamanca (53 per cent), and Toledo (60 per cent). Álvarez Tardío & Villa García 2017, pp. 580–99. Electoral results are calculated by comparing the number of votes obtained by the leading candidate for both coalitions. Figures for Seville and Malaga only include rural areas.

[7] Preston 2012, p. xviii.

the regime at the expense of the defeated. However, in the long run, the problems of land shortage and the limits to dry-farming would be resolved by rural emigration. Irrigation also made its contribution, and the Franco regime was lucky both to inherit the expertise of the Second Republic in this area, as well as the appearance of new technologies.

Appendix 1

Agricultural Statistics in Spain, France, and Italy in the Early 1930s

The poor quality of statistical data in Spain significantly limited government attempts during the Second Republic to respond to social problems. A brief comparison with France and Italy suggests that Spain lacked information on many economic and social aspects of agriculture, farm organization, and the nature of farming, precisely the information needed to carry out a land reform. Some additional statistical information was obviously available in local and provincial archives, and an unknown amount in the Ministry of Agriculture's archives that has been lost. Yet it was the material in the public domain that was crucial for informed debates on the need for land reform and how it should proceed. Neither France nor Italy were at the statistical frontier, but governments in both countries had considerably better information that had been collected more scientifically, covered a greater number of variables, and was often available at the municipal level (Table A1.1).

France published decennial agrarian statistics from 1836 to 1892 that gave detailed information, not just on the cultivated area and the production of the major crops and farm animals, but also concerning farm organization (farm size, nature of tenure, use of capital), as well as market prices for farm inputs and output at department level.[1] Although the series was interrupted in 1892, it began again in 1929, being published in 1936.[2] These studies were complemented with annual production statistics (*Statistique Agricole Annuelle*), which, by 1901, depended on a specialized statistical office enjoying significant technical support (Table A1.1).[3]

The French experience suggests a number of general problems associated with collecting farm statistics. First, the reluctance of villagers to disclose reliable information required outside agents to monitor and investigate the facts, adding to both cost and time in obtaining the data.

---

[1] The first was in 1836, and then followed by others in 1862, 1873, 1882, 1892, and 1929. For the possibilities that these offer, see, for example, Clout 1980 or Carmona & Simpson 2012.

[2] France: Ministère de l'Agriculture 1936.   [3] Alfroy 1976, p. 290.

Table A1.1 *Summary of statistics available in Spain, France, and Italy in the early 1930s*

	SPAIN Anuario Estadístico de España	FRANCE Enquête 1929	ITALY Catasto 1929
Population according to professional category	provincial	department	municipality
Population census	municipal	municipal	municipality
Farmers and workers by categories	no	department	municipality
owners/tenants mixed/ wage labourers	no	department	municipality
family size by categories	no	department	municipality
farm labourers – fixed and casual		department	municipality
fixed farm labourers – by age and gender	no	department	
temporary workers by activity, gender & place of origin	no	department	municipality
Farms – by ownership, tenure, sharecropping, etc.	partial	department	municipality
- by size	no	department	municipality
- by nature of labour used (family, wage labour, etc.)	no	department	municipality
Livestock census	provincial	department	municipality
Machinery and farm equipment	census 1932	department	municipality
Fertilizer consumption	provincial (1921)	department	municipality
Fuel consumption	no	no	municipality
Area sown and production	provincial	department	municipality
Farm sales (number and value)	no	no	municipality
Official farm credit, annual loans	provincial	department	regions
Fertilizer prices	no	state	regions
Cost of seed	no	no	regions
Agricultural wages unspecified and according to gender	provincial	department	municipality
by farm activity	no	department	no
by farm activity, gender, and food and board	no	department	no
by farm activity, gender, and month	no	no	municipality
Farm-gate prices	provincial (AEPA)	no	regions
monthly prices in certain locations	no	no	yes
Farm accounts	no	only large	large and small

A second factor was the importance of learning by doing, and building on previous experiences. This was often behind the changes in methodology, such as switching from a system of having local information sent directly to Paris (1882) to one of regional organizations collecting information (1892), or the incorporation of farm associations to support technicians at local level (1929). A third factor was how the political demand for information changed over time. For example, while the debate in the late nineteenth century was over farm size and the future of the small, peasant holding, during the First World War the concern was over who benefited from the high food prices. In particular, the lack of price information led many to wrongly believe that farmers had prospered excessively during the War. Criticism continued in the early 1920s:

The statistics published by the Ministry of Agriculture are drawn up by officials who do not dispose of funds sufficient to enable them to adopt satisfactory methods of observation; nor are these officials qualified for the scientific observation of economic facts. The statistics are very incomplete even in respect of cultivation areas and crops. As regard certain crops and certain categories of animal produce they are completely silent. They furnish, for instance, no information whatever on food products of such importance as milk and eggs.[4]

By the 1930s, the debate had changed again to concerns over low farm prices, and the difficulties of adapting the new labour legislation. The 1929 *Enquête* offered significant material on farmworkers (over 120 pages), and also incorporates two novelties: the elaboration of monographic volumes by department that provided detailed qualitative evidence at the regional level, and greater rigour in collecting local statistical information using the technical support and assistance from agrarian associations.

Italy published annual production figures from 1860, but it was only with improvements in collecting local data and the creation of statistical sections organized by agricultural regions after 1906 that their quality and reliability acquired acceptable levels for some regions before the First World War, and the whole country in the 1929 *Catasto*. The *Catasto* was comparable to the French *Enquête* of the same year, and devoted significant amounts of space to questions of farm size and organization, labour and credit markers, capital investment and livestock, as well as detailed price information on farm inputs (fertilizers, seeds) and local farm prices. Significantly, it contained detailed published information at the municipal, as well as the provincial levels.[5]

[4] Augé-Laribé & Pinot 1927, pp. 2–3 and 141–3.   [5] Annali di statistica 1958.

Spain's first statistical yearbook (*Anuario Estadístico de España*) was published as early as 1858, but information was very limited, and no volumes appeared between 1868 and 1912, a gap of forty-five years. The yearbooks summarized the most important statistics produced by the different ministries and, by 1930, contained provincial information on the cultivated area of the main crops, some basic data on farm wages, the number and declared value of farm properties sold over the previous year, loans made by the pósitos, and basic information on agrarian associations. The great dispersion in the nature and quality of the data shows the lack of systematization and interest in completing the missing information. Very limited and highly generalized information was published on the working population, and only minimum and maximum farm wages are given by gender and province.

In many respects, the situation had been better in the 1880s. The late nineteenth century agrarian crisis had seen governments across Europe create special parliamentary commissions to study the sector and assess the most appropriate measures to revive its fortunes.[6] In Spain, this led to the country's first major agricultural survey, which was published in eight volumes as the *Crisis agrícola y pecuaria* (1888).[7] It highlighted the lack of available information, and most reports were of voluntary contributions by local notables, often responding to a wide range of questions. Its deficiencies however led to a number of other government incentives, and in particular to the *Junta Consultiva Agonómica* compiling what would be the most detailed studies on different branches of Spanish agriculture before the 1950s.[8] The government also commissioned a number of reports on specific topics, first by the *Comisión de Reformas Sociales* and then, between 1903 and 1923, by the *Instituto de Reformas Sociales*. However, these remained essentially qualitative rather than quantitative, and again depended heavily on information provided by local notables.

Figures were also published from the last decade of the nineteenth century on the area cultivated and annual production for the major crops and the Statistical Yearbook of Agricultural Production (AEPA) from 1928 includes areas, yields and prices by province for most crops and, on occasion, livestock products. The questionable quality of these figures is suggested by the newspaper *El Norte de Castilla*, still publishing

---

[6] See especially the collective volume edited by Vivier 2014.

[7] Crisis Agrícola y Pecuaria 1887–9.

[8] Detailed reports were published on cereals and their rotations in Spain: Dirección General de Agricultura Industria y Comercio 1891 and livestock in Spain: Dirección General de Agricultura Industria y Comercio 1892. Other published studies include wine (1891), olive oil (1891), phylloxera (1892), irrigation (1904), and pasture land (1905). Carmona & Simpson 2014c, pp. 218–19.

258 Appendix 1

its own estimates for the cereal harvest. Following recommendations from the International Institute of Agriculture, local associations and provincial agronomists began to check the information provided from producers.[9] One major statistical deficiency is the virtual total absence of information at the municipal level. Practically no information is available on different types of tenure used, or the number and basic characteristics of farms. Considerable difficulties also exist in interpreting the population censuses, not only because women are usually excluded, but because many male workers were employed in a variety of occupations, including working part-time on their own land or doing non-farm work.[10] The first agricultural machine census only took place in 1932, but local historical studies for Galicia and Andalucia have shown the figures to be grossly inaccurate, underestimating the true levels of farm mechanization.[11] In conclusion, information was still very limited in 1931, and it was not until the first agrarian census in 1962 offered data at municipal levels that was comparable to the Italian *Catasto* or French *Enquête* of 1929.[12]

[9] GEHR 1991.   [10] Information is only available at the provincial level.
[11] Spain. Ministerio de Agricultura 1933, pp. 318–26.
[12] Spain. Instituto Nacional de Estadística 1966.

Appendix 2

Dry-Farming and the Economics of the Family Farm

The question of how much land was needed to meet the basic consumption needs of a family was crucial to whether land reform could succeed or not. The IRA estimated a minimum family income of 2,000 pesetas net of expenses a year, and the 1932 Land Reform placed a ceiling of ten hectares on the amount of land to be distributed. As this appendix suggests, while the income figure appears reasonable in the light of other estimates, considerably more land was usually needed to reach this figure producing cereals under dry-farming conditions.

Elsewhere we have estimated that the average male worker was employed 126 days a year in agriculture in Andalucia but, even if it is assumed that this represented only half family income, it still only produces about three-quarters of the IRA's figure of 2,000 pesetas (Table A2.1). However, the difference is not so great if the family also enjoyed the income from three hectares of their own land (1,877 pesetas). These estimates are significantly higher than a basic needs budget calculated using Robert Allen's methodology, which in Badajoz was only 1,129 pesetas in 1930 (Table A2.2). By contrast, estimates of per capita output in the agrarian sector are considerably greater (2,988 pesetas) but, as farm inputs and rent have to be discounted, the actual figure would be much closer to the 2,000 pesetas. Carrión, in his book *Los latifundios* (1932), believed that farmers could produce between 2,000 and 3,000 pesetas net on ten hectares with intensive cultivation. Although the 3,000 pesetas figure is similar to the 2,880 pesetas produced per worker in Andalucia in 1931 on all farmland, including olives, vines, and livestock (Table 4.4), capital costs and rent have to be deducted once more.

As Chapter 8 argues, the major problem facing Spanish agriculture was how to increase output per hectare using dry-farming methods. Carrión dedicates only two pages to the problem and offers no evidence to support his figures of 200–300 pesetas net income per hectare. Vazquez Humasqué, the IRA's director, provides other figures and assumptions in 1933, but again without much evidence. In fact, only with land reform

Table A2.1 *Estimates of family income, 1930 (in pesetas)*

	per capita	Family – 4 members	IRA basic income = 100
GDP per capita	1,494		
GDP agrarian sector *	747	2,988	149
Basic needs budget, Badajoz 1930	282	1,129	56
Wage-earners' family income, based on 126 male working days providing half annual income, Badajoz 1930 **		1,512	76
Idem + small holding producing one peseta net income per day		1,877	94
IRA basic income		2,000	100

* Agricultural productivity per worker is taken as half the national average. In 1930, agriculture accounted for 22.8 per cent of gross value added and 45.7 per cent of employment. (Prados de la Escosura 2017), tables S15 and S19.

** Simpson 1992b, table 7. Using local wages, income varies between 1,048 pesetas in Caceres, 1,656 pesetas in Badajoz, and 1,932 pesetas in Seville. Farm income is calculated assuming that these male wages represent half the total income, based on Borderías Mondejar & Abeledo 2017. Salaries in *Anuario Estadístico de España*, 1930. For basic needs budget and IRA basic income, see text.

Table A2.2 *Basic diet, Badajoz, 1930*

	Quantity	Price per unit in pesetas	Total pesetas	%
Flour (wheat), kg	195	0.68	132.6	47
Pork, kg	5	2.95	14.8	5.2
Chickpeas, kg	20	0.95	19.0	6.7
Potatoes, kg	50	0.19	9.5	3.4
Olive oil, litres	3	1.6	4.8	1.7
Total food			180.7	64
Housing				11
Other costs				25
Total per person			282	100
Basic basket, family with 4 members			1,129	100
Family income with 4 members in Badajoz (1930)			1,656	146
IRA estimate for basic income			2,000	176

Sources and methodology: The basic basket follows (Allen 2013), and provides about 1,700 calories per capita/day. Prices are for Badajoz, *Anuario Estadístico de España*, 1930. The *Anuario* does not give prices for other basic goods such as heating or lighting, and these are taken as 25 per cent of total expenses, a similar weight to those found in other low-income countries today (Allen 2017), table 12. Rent is estimated as 11 per cent of the family needs (Carmona et al. 2017), table 3.

itself was the state able to collect the necessary information concerning the capacity of agriculture to increase output.

Production costs and output for a family farm are shown using two types of evidence. The first comes from family farms owning a mule team using dry-farming techniques with different cereal rotations (Table A2.3).[1] For these, gross output ranged from 7,700 and 9,043 pesetas, figures which are considerably above the basic family needs, but the costs for maintaining the mule team, depreciation, rent, and, in the case of Palencia and probably also in Badajoz, hiring some wage labour for activities such as the harvest have to be discounted.[2] These figures also assume that farmers could sell at the official 1930 prices, even though there were widespread complaints that merchants failed to respect them. Nevertheless, although the net family income from the family farm was still between 28 and 60 per cent higher than the IRA's basic income of 2,000 pesetas, the area required in Badajoz and Palencia to achieve this figure was between thirty-two and fifty-one hectares, well above the ten hectares contemplated in Carrión's calculation and the 1932 Land Reform.[3] In Seville, twenty hectares were sufficient, but the land quality was considerably better and no unsown fallow was required.

A second group of estimates come from the different reform proposals of the early 1930s (Table A2.4). The farm size under the 1932 Land Reform (ten hectares) and Vázquez Humasqué's project (twelve hectares) were arrived at by calculating the numbers in need, and the land available. Even accounting for the inadequacy of ten hectares to support a family, the 1932 Land Reform required an area that was twice that of all the land found on farms with more than 250 hectares in the latifundio provinces.[4] Váquez Humasqué's estimates were based on around 407,000 rather than 930,000 families needing land, although this still required more than all the farmland area on these estates. Domingo's Lease Reform Law (1933) guaranteed up to twenty hectares for those tenants who were already renting the land in areas of short supply when the Law was passed. By contrast, the Intensification of Cultivation Law was not intended to create family farms, but rather provide land on a temporary measure to address emergency needs. The final two columns offer the feasibility estimates made by agronomists on two expropriated farms with a view to establishing peasant communities. In the first four cases we use production and output data from the previous table

---

[1] Virtually no genuine farm accounts exist in Spain.
[2] In Mazariegos, a seasonal worker was employed for three months between mid-June and September and another month between October 20 and November. Cascón 1934, p. 495.
[3] In Badajoz, a plough team needed seven days to prepare the fallow and five days to sow wheat (2.50 for barley), equivalent to 192 days in total. Instituto de Reforma Agraria 1934, pp. 88 and 167.
[4] Simpson & Carmona 2017, table 1.

Table A2.3 *Estimates of production costs for family cereal farms in the early 1930s*

	1		2		3		4		5	
	1930*		1930*		1933		1933		1934	
Province	Palencia		Palencia		Badajoz		Badajoz		Seville	
Municipality	Mazariegos		Dueñas		Villanueva del Fresno		Villanueva del Fresno			
Farm size in hectares	32		43		51		48		20	
Area sown	16.2		21.5		16		20		20	
		%		%		%		%		%
Gross output	7,733	100	8,344	100	8,295	100	9,043	100	7,700	100
Arable	7,005		8,286		6,814		7,680			
Livestock	728		58		1,481		1,363			
Output per ha. (in ptas)	242		194		163		188		385	
Inputs	3,187	41.2	3,997	47.9	2,560	30.9	2,686	29.7		
Seed	830		1,402		689		881			
Fertilizers	0		0		629		620			
Animal feed	1,474		1,416		1,242		1,185			
Depreciation & cost of capital	693		864		439		570			
Wages – non-family labour	190		315		0		0		0	
Net income	4,546		4,347		5,296		5,787			
Rent	1,910	24.7	1,322	15.8	1,752	21.1	2,909	32.2		
Farm income including wages	2,636	34.1	3,026	36.3	3,199	38.6	2,554	28.2	2,880	37.4
% 2,000 family income	132%		151%		160%		128%		144%	

Sources and notes: Palencia (columns 1 and 2): half the land sown with wheat and barley, and the other half unsown fallow, and workers hired for 100 days. Data refers to 1912, but corrected with 1930 prices. Cascón 1934, pp. 490–507. Badajoz (columns 3 and 4) refer to the dehesas Las Cabras Bajas (1,384 hectares) and Cerrollano (544 hectares), with wheat being the major crop, and part of the fallow sown with chickpeas. Some income from pasture. AIRA, caja 6.24 and 6.25. Seville (column 5), wheat, cotton, maize, and chickpeas. Naredo et al. 1977, anexo 3.

Table A2.4 *Land reform estimates of production costs and farm income, 1932–4*

	1		2		3		4		5		6	
	1932		1933		1934		1932		1934		1934	
	Land Reform		Lease Reform Law		Vázquez Humasqué project		Intensificación de cultivos Decree		Las Cabras Baja farm		Ramira Alta farm	
Farm size in hectares	10		20		12		3		12		14	
Area sown	5		10		6		3		4		4.5	
Gross ouput	1,740	100%	3,480	100%	2,088	100%	522	100%	2,436		2,338	
Arable												
Livestock												
Output pr ha. (in ptas) (a)	174		174		174		174		203		167	
Inputs (excluding labour)	522	30%	1,044	30%	626	30%	157	30%	787	32%	810	35%
Seeds and fertilizers									333		325	
Animal feeds									271		292	
Depreciation and cost of capital									183		193	
Net income	1,218		2,436		1,462		365		1,649		1,528	
Rent (b)	435	25%	870	25%	522	25%	126	24%	427	18%	398	17%
Farmer income (including labour)(c)	783	45%	1,566	45%	940	45%	239	46%	1,222	50%	1,130	48%

Table A2.4 (*cont.*)

	1	2	3	4	5	6
	1932	1933	1934	1932	1934	1934
	Land Reform	Lease Reform Law	Vázquez Humasqué project	*Intensificación de cultivos* Decree	Las Cabras Baja farm	Ramira Alta farm
% 1,129 basic basket for 4 persons	69%	139%	83%	21%	108%	100%
% 2,000 family income IRA	39%	78%	47%	12%	61%	57%

Sources:

[1.] 1932 Land Reform Law: maximum size of family farm (owned or leased) to receive land or register in the *Censo de Campesinos*. Rent is average from table 3.

[2.] Tenancy Law: maximum area that can be leased in areas of dry-farming. Proyecto de ley de arrendamientos, 1933, Diario de Sesiones. Rent as in (1).

[3.] Vázquez Humasqué 17 de mayo 1934, project ranged from between seven and fifteen hectares according to the province, with an average of nine. The figure of twelve hectares corresponds to Badajoz. Rent as in (1).

[4.] Average area received by family under the Law of Intensification of Cultivation. Malefakis 1970, table 30. Rent calculated as from the average of nineteen farms in four municipalities in Badajoz, AIRA, caja 6.85.

[5 and 6.] Based on the IRA agronomists' estimates for a family. AIRA, caja 6.24 and 6.38.

Notes:

(a) The output figures and percentages for 1, 2, 3 and 4 from the Zahinos estate (Badajoz); for 5 and 6 we use the values of the technical report.

(b) The rent for 1, 2 and 3 as the average of the 6 farms in Table A2.3; 4, is the average of 19 farms from 4 villages (41.9 pesetas per hectare); 5 and 6 as in the technical report of each farm.

(c) The disposable settler income, excluding taxes.

(174 pesetas per hectare), and assume that seed, fertilizers, and animal feed only for days worked represented 30 per cent of costs (Table A2.4). Rent in the first three columns is given in the previous table, and the other figures are from the original source. In all cases, the net family income is lower than 2,000 pesetas, and often around or even less than 1,000 pesetas.

Glossary

Cacique. Local political boss.

Caja rural. Rural credit cooperative.

Carlismo. Carlism. Political anti-liberal movement created in the 1830s and which fought three civil wars during the nineteenth century.

Casa del Pueblo. Local Socialist group headquarters of either the PSOE or UGT.

Confederación Española de Derechas Autónomas (**CEDA**). Spanish Confederation of Autonomous Rightist, the largest political organization of the right.

Censo de Campesinos. A village census of landless workers and poor landowners and tenants established by the Land Reform Law of 1932.

Confederación Nacional Católica-Agraria (**CNCA**). National Catholic-Agrarian Confederation created in 1917 and the main Catholic cooperative federation.

Esquerra Republicana de Catalunya (**ERC**) Catalan Republican Left. A federation of Catalan republican and nationalist parties created in 1931.

Foro. Land tenure contract widely used in North-Western Spain, especially in Galicia.

Intensificación de Cultivos. Decree of November 1932, which allowed temporary settlements by landless workers (*yunteros*) on uncultivated land.

Jurados mixtos. Mixed juries created during the Second Republic to enforce legislation and arbitrate disputes between workers and employers (*Jurado mixto del trabajo*), or between tenants and landowners (*Jurado mixto de la propiedad rústica*).

Laboreo forzoso. A decree of May 1931, which required farmers to create work to reduce local unemployment.

Lliga. A Catalan Catholic conservative and regionalist party created in 1901 (initially *Lliga Regionalista* and, from 1933, *Lliga Catalana*)

Pósito. Local public granary, which provided short-term lending to small cereal farmers.

Rabassa morta. A sharecropping contract for vine cultivation common to Catalonia.

Ruedo. Cultivated land found in the immediate vicinity of the village.

Secano. Dry-farming.

Términos municipales, Ley de. Law of 20 April 1931. This compelled farmers to employ workers living in the same municipality as the farm before hiring those from elsewhere.

Turno pacífico (or turno, turnismo). Name given to the Restoration (1875–1923) political system which saw the two major political parties controlling parliamentary elections.

Unió de Rabassaires. Union of *rabassers*, the main *rabassers* (sharecroppers) pressure group created in 1922.

Unio de Vinyaters de Catalunya. Regional lobby of winemakers created in 1901.

Yunteros. Small tenants, sharecroppers, and landless workers who invaded land in 1932 and 1936 in areas of dehesas, especially in Extremadura.

Bibliography

Archival Sources

Archivo General de la Guerra Civil Española
Archivo del Instituto de Reforma Agraria (AIRA)
Archivo Histórico Provincial de Cáceres (AHPC)
Archivo Histórico Provincial de Cádiz
Archivo Histórico Provincial de Salamanca
Archivo Histórico Provincial de Sevilla
Archivo Histórico Provincial de Toledo
Archivo Histórico Provincial de Zamora
Archivo Histórico Provincial de Zaragoza
Archivo Municipal de Carmona
Archivo Municipal de Casar de Cáceres
Archivo Municipal de Jerez de la Frontera
Archivo Municipal de Malpartida de Cáceres

Primary and Secondary Sources

A'Hearn, B., 2000. Could Southern Italians Cooperate? Banche Popolari in the Mezzogiorno. *Journal of Economic History* 60, 67–93.

Abramitzky, R., 2011. Lessons from the Kibbutz on the Equality–Incentives Trade-off. *Journal of Economic Perspectives* 25, 185–208.

Acemoglu, D., & Robinson, J. A., 2006. *Economic Origins of Dictatorship and Democracy.* Cambridge University Press, Cambridge.

Acemoglu, D., & Robinson, J. A., 2012. *Why Nations Fail: the Origins of Power, Prosperity and Poverty.* Princeton University Press, Princeton.

Acosta Ramírez, F., Cruz Artacho, S., & González de Molina Navarro, M., 2009. *Socialismo y democracia en el campo (1880–1930): Los orígenes de la FNTT.* MAPA, Madrid.

Afton, B., & Turner, M., 2000. The Statistical Base of Agricultural Performance in England and Wales, 1850–1914. In Collins, E. J. T. (ed.) *The Agrarian History of England and Wales, 1850–1914.* Cambridge University Press, Cambridge, pp. 1757–2140.

Albertus, M., 2015. *Autocracy and Redistribution: the Politics of Land Reform.* Cambridge University Press, Cambridge.

Alfroy, M., 1976. *La statistique agricole française.* Etude 140, Ministère de l'Agriculture.

Alonso, G., 2011. Dudas y desencantos de una sociedad civil emergente: La secularización de la España rural decimonónica. In Ortega Lopez, T. M., & Romero, F. C. (eds.) *La España rural, siglos XIX y XX: Aspectos políticos, sociales y culturales*, Comares, Granada, pp. 1–20.

Álvarez Junco, J., 1976. *La ideología política del anarquismo español*. Siglo XXI, Madrid.

Álvarez Junco, J., 2002. *The Emergence of Mass Politics in Spain*. Sussex Academic Press, Brighton.

Álvarez Junco, J., 2013. Spanish National Identity in the Age of Nationalisms. In Centeno, M. A., & Ferraro, A. E. (eds.) *State and Nation Making in Latin America and Spain: Republics of the Possible*, Cambridge University Press, Cambridge, pp. 307–328.

Alvarez Jusué, A., 1933. *Los jurados mixtos de la propiedad rústica*. Góngora, Madrid.

Álvarez Robles, A., 1932. *La reforma agraria española*. Palencia.

Álvarez Tardío, M., 2011. The CEDA: Threat or Opportunity? In Álvarez Tardío, M., & del Rey Reguillo, F. (eds.) *The Spanish Second Republic Revisited: From Democratic Hopes to Civil War (1931–1936)*. Sussex Academic, Brighton, pp. 58–79.

Álvarez Tardío, M., 2016. *Gil Robles*. FAES, Madrid.

Álvarez Tardío, M., & García, R. V., 2017. *1936 Fraude y Violencia en las elecciones del Frente Popular*. Espasa, Barcelona.

Allen, D. W., & Lueck, D., 2002. *The Nature of the Farm: Contracts, Risk, and Organization in Agriculture*. MIT Press, Cambridge, MA, and London.

Allen, R. C., 2003. *Farm to Factory: a Reinterpretation of the Soviet Industrial Revolution*. Princeton University Press, Princeton.

Allen, R. C., 2011. *Global Economic History: a Very Short Introduction*. Oxford University Press, Oxford.

Allen, R. C., 2013. *Poverty Lines in History, Theory, and Current International Practice*. Economics Series Working Papers 685, Oxford, Department of Economics.

Allen, R. C., 2017. Absolute Poverty: When Necessity Displaces Desire. *American Economic Review* 107, 3690–3721.

Allen, R. C., & Weisdorf, J. L., 2011. Was there an 'Industrious Revolution' before the Industrial Revolution? An Empirical Exercise for England, c.1300–1830. *Economic History Review* 64, 715–729.

Anes, G., 1969. *Economía e Ilustración en la España del siglo XVIII*. Ariel, Madrid.

Annali di statistica, 1958. *La rilevazioni statistiche in Italia dal 1861 al 1956*. 87, 1–96.

Ansell, B., & Samuels, D., 2014. *Inequality and Democratization: an Elite-Competition Approach*. Cambridge University Press.

Arenas Posadas, C., 2009. *Una de las dos Españas: Sevilla antes de la Guerra Civil*. Mergablum, Sevilla.

Artola Blanco, M., 2015. *El fin de la clase ociosa: De Romanones al estraperlo (1900–1950)*. Alianza, Madrid.

Augé-Laribé, M., 1907. *Le problème agraire du socialisme: la viticulture industrielle du Midi de la France*. Paris.

Augé-Laribé, M., 1950. *La Politique agricole de la France de 1880 à 1940*. Paris.

Augé-Laribé, M., Pinot, P., 1927. *Agriculture and Food Supply in France during the War.* Carnegie Endowment for International Peace: Yale, New Haven.

Ayuda, M. I., Collantes, F., & Pinilla, V., 2010. From Locational Fundamentals to Increasing Returns: the Spatial Concentration of Population in Spain, 1787–2000. *Journal of Geographical Systems* 12, 25–50.

Azaña, M., 1997. *Los cuadernos robados, 1932–1933.* Crítica, Barcelona.

Baines, D. E., 1994. European Emigration, 1815–1914: Looking at the Migration Decision Again. *Economic History Review* 47(3), 525–544.

Balcells, A., 1974. *Trabajo industrial y organización obrera en la Cataluña contemporánea (1900–1936).* Laia, Barcelona.

Balcells, A., 1980. *El problema agrario en Cataluña: La cuestión Rabassaire.* Ministerio de Agricultura, Madrid.

Banco de Urquijo, 1924. *La riqueza y el progreso de España.* Samarán, Madrid.

Banerjee, A. V., & Duflo, E., 2007. The Economic Lives of the Poor. *Journal of Economic Perspectives* 21, 141–167.

Banerjee, A. V., Iyer, L., & Somanathan, R., 2008. Public Action for Public Goods. In *Handbook of Development Economics.* Elsevier, pp. 3118–3153.

Banfield, E., 1958. *The Moral Basis of Backward Society.* The Free Press, Illinois.

Barciela López, C., Giráldez, J., Grupo de Estudios de Historia Rural, & López, I., 2005. Sector agrario y pesca. In Carreras, A., & Tafunell, X. (eds.) *Estadísticas históricas de España.* Fundación BBVA, Bilbao, pp. 245–356.

Barral, P., 1968. *Les agrariens français de Méline à Pisani.* Armand Colin, Paris.

Bartolini, S., 2000. *The Political Mobilization of the European Left, 1860–1980.* Cambridge University Press, Cambridge.

Bates, R. H., 1990. Macropolitical economy in the field of development. In Alt, J. F., & Shepsle, K. E. (eds.) *Perspectives on Positive Political Economy.* Cambridge University Press, Cambridge, pp. 31–54.

Bayly, C. A., 2004. *The Birth of the Modern World 1780–1914.* Blackwell, Malden, MA.

Beckett, J., & Turner, M. E., 2007. End of the Old Order?: F.M.L. Thompson, the Land Question, and the Burden of Ownership in England, c1880–c1925. *Agricultural History Review* 55, 269–288.

Beckett, J. V., 1990. *The Agricultural Revolution.* Blackwell, Oxford.

Behar, R., 1991. *The Presence of the Past in a Spanish Village: Santa María del Monte.* Princeton University Press, Princeton.

Beltrán Tapia, F., 2012. Commons, Social Capital, and the Emergence of Agricultral Cooperatives in Early Twentieth Century Spain. *European Review of Economic History* 16, 511–529.

Beltrán Tapia, F., 2013. Enclosing Literacy? Common Lands and Human Capital in Spain, 1860–1930. *Journal of Institutional Economics* 9, 491–515.

Beltrán Tapia, F., 2015. Goths and Vandals. *Explorations in Economic History* 47, 244–257.

Beltrán Tapia, F., & Miguel Salanova, S. de, 2017. Migrants' Self-Selection in the Early Stages of Modern Economic Growth, Spain (1880–1930). *Economic History Review* 70, 101–121.

Benítez Porral, C., 1904. *Memoria que obtuvo accésit en el Concurso . . . el problema agrario en el Mediodía de España.* Instituto de Reformas Sociales, Madrid.

Berman, S., 2006. *The Primacy of Politics: Social Democracy and the Making of Europe's Twentieth Century*. Cambridge University Press, Cambridge.

Bernal, A. M., 1974. *La propiedad de la tierra y las luchas agrarias andaluzas*. Ariel, Barcelona.

Bernal, A. M., 1979. *La lucha por la tierra en la crisis del antiguo regimén*. Taurus, Madrid.

Bernal, A. M., 1985. La llamada crisis finisecular (1972–1919). In García Delgado, J. L. (ed.) *La España de la Restauración*. Siglo XXI, Madrid.

Bernaldo de Quirós, C., 1931. Informe acerca del paro de los jornaleros del campo de Andalucía durante el otoño de 1930. In Ministerio de Trabajo, Estudios y documentos, *La crisis agraria andaluza de 1930–1*, Madrid, pp. 8–35.

Besley, T., & Persson, T., 2011. *Pillars of Prosperity: the Political Economics of Development Clusters*. Princeton University Press, Princeton.

Bizcarrondo, M., 2008. *Historia de la UGT (vol. 3): entre la democracia y la revolución, 1931–1936*. Siglo XXI, Madrid.

Blattman, C., & Miguel, E., 2010. Civil War. *Journal of Economic Literature* 48, 3–57

Boix, C., 2003. *Democracy and Redistribution*. Cambridge University Press, Cambridge.

Boletín del Instituto de Reforma Agraria (1933–1936), published by the Instituto de Reforma Agraria.

Boone, C., 2014. *Property and Political Order in Africa: Land Rights and the Structure of Politics*. Cambridge University Press, Cambridge.

Borderias Mondejar, C., & Abeledo, L. M., 2017. Family Budgets According to the 1924 Census, Catalonia and Galicia. In *XII Congress of the Spanish Association of Economic History*, Salamanca.

Bosworth, 2005. *Mussolini's Italy: Life Under the Dictatorship, 1915–1945*. Allen Lane, London.

Boyd, C. P., 2000. The Military and Politics. In Álvarez Junco, J., & Schubert, A. (eds.) *Spanish History since 1808*. Arnold, London, pp. 64–79.

Brassley, P., 2010. Land Revolution and Reallocation in Interwar Europe. In Congost, R., & Santos, R., (eds.) *Contexts of Prosperity in Europe: the Social Embeddedness of Property Rights in Land in Historical Perspective*. Brepols, Turnhout, pp. 147–162.

Brenan, G., 1969. *The Spanish Labyrinth*. Cambridge University Press, Cambridge.

Bringas Gutiérrez, M. Á., 2000. *La productividad de los factores en la agricultura española (1752–1935)*. Banco de España, Madrid.

Broadberry, S., & Harrison, M., 1995. *The Economics of World War I*. Cambridge University Press, Cambridge.

Broadberry, S., & Klein, A., 2012. Aggregate and per capita GDP in Europe, 1870–2000: continental, regional and national data with changing boundaries. *Scandinavian Economic History Review* 60, 79–107.

Buckley, H., 1940: 2014. *The Life and Death of the Spanish Republic: a Witness to the Spanish Civil War*. Tauris, London.

Burdiel, I., 2000. The Liberal Revolution, 1808–1843. In Álvarez Junco, J., & Schubert, A., (eds.) *Spanish History since 1808*. Arnold, London.

Cabezas Díaz, A., 1932. *El agro y el municipio: La reforma agraria (Legislación de la República), Ordenada, comentada y con formularios*, Madrid.

Cabo Villaverde, M. A., 1998. *O Agrarismo*. A Nosa Terra, Vigo.

Cabo Villaverde, M. A., 2006a. El foro gallego en su fase final: entre la redención y la prescripción. In Dios, S. d, Miguel-Motta, J. I., Hernández, R. R., & Pérez, E. T. (eds.) *Historia de la propiedad: costumbre y prescripción*. Servico de Estudios del Colegio de Registradores, Salamanca, pp. 665–688.

Cabo Villaverde, M. A., 2006b. Solidaridad gallega y el desafío al sistema de la Restauración, 1907–1911. *Ayer* 64, 235–259.

Cabral Chamorro, A., 2000. *Renovación tecnológica y mecanización de la agricultura en Cádiz (1850–1932)*. Universidad de Cádiz, Cadiz.

Cabrera Calvo-Sotelo, M., & Comín, F. C., 1989. *Santiago Alba: Un programa de reforma económica en la España del primer tercio del siglo XX*. Ministerio de Economía y Hacienda, Madrid.

Cabrera, M., 1983. *La patronal ante la Segunda República: Organizaciones y estrategia, 1931–1936*. Siglo XXI, Madrid.

Calatayud, S., 1990. Los inicios de la mecanización en el regadío valenciano, 1850–1930. *Áreas* 12, 201–211.

Calatayud, S., & Carrión, J. M. M., 1999. El cambio técnico en los sistemas de captación e impulsión de aguas subterráneas para riego en la España Mediterránea. In Garrabou, R., & Naredo, J. M. (eds.) *El agua en los sistemas de agrarios: Una perspectiva histórica*. Argentaria /Visor, Madrid, pp. 15–39.

Calero, A. M., 1976. *Movimientos sociales en Andalucia (1820–1936)*. Siglo XXI, Madrid.

Callahan, W. J., 2000. *The Catholic Church in Spain, 1875–1998*. Catholic University of America, Washington DC.

Caño García, R. d, 1931. *Ante la reforma agraria (cómo está parcelado física, jurídica y agrícolamente el suelo español)*, Madrid.

Capoccia, G., 2005. *Defending Democracy: Reactions to Extremism in Interwar Europe*. Johns Hopkins University Press, Baltimore.

Carasa, P., 1983. Los Pósitos en España en el siglo XIX. *Investigaciones Históricas* 4, 247–304.

Carasa, P., 1991. El crédito agrario en España durante la Restauración. Entre la usura y el control social. In Yun Casalilla, B., (ed.) *Estudios sobre capitalismo agrario, crédito e industria en Castilla (siglo XIX y XX)*. Junta de Castilla y León, Valladolid, pp. 289–343.

Carmona, J., 2006. Sharecropping and Livestock Specialization in France, 1830–1930. *Continuity and Change* 21, 235–259.

Carmona, J., Lampe, M., & Roses, J., 2017. Housing Affordability During the Urban Transition in Spain. *Economic History Review* 70, 632–658.

Carmona, J., Rosés, J., & Simpson, J., 2019. The Question of Land Access and the Spanish Land Reform of 1932. *Economic History Review* 72, 669–690.

Carmona, J., & Simpson, J., 1999. The "Rabassa Morta" in Catalan Viticulture: the Rise and Decline of a Long-Term Sharecropping Contract, 1670s–1920s. *Journal of Economic History* 59, 290–315.

Carmona, J., & Simpson, J., 2003. *El laberinto de la agricultura española: Instituciones, contratos y organización entre 1850 y 1936*. PUZ, Zaragoza.

Carmona, J., & Simpson, J., 2007. El papel de la organización rural en el desar-
rollo agrario en España, 1850–1936. In *México y España: ¿Historias Económicas
Semejantes?* FCE Press, Mexico, pp. 293–314.
Carmona, J., & Simpson, J., 2012. Explaining Contract Choice: Vertical Co-
ordination, Sharecropping, and Wine, Europe 1850–1950. *Economic History
Review* 65, 887–909.
Carmona, J., & Simpson, J., 2013. L'enquête agricole: le XIXe siècle. *Annales du
Midi* 125, 543–56.
Carmona, J., & Simpson, J., 2014a. Los contratos de cesión de la tierra en
Extremadura en el primer tercio del siglo XX. *Historia Agraria* 63, 183–213.
Carmona, J., & Simpson, J., 2014b. Pósitos agrarios y acción colectiva: una visión
desde el estado. In *XI Congreso Internacional de la AEHE.* Madrid.
Carmona, J., & Simpson, J., 2014c. Spanish Agriculture and the Government
Enquiry: La Crisis Agricola y Pecuaria, 1887–9. In Vivier, N., (ed.) *The Golden
Age of State Enquiries: Rural Enquiries in the Nineteenth Century.* Brepols,
Turnhout, pp. 201–222.
Carmona, J., & Simpson, J., 2015. ¿Campesinos unidos o divididos? La acción
colectiva y la revolución social entre los yunteros durante la Segunda República
en España (1931–1936) UC3M, Instituto Figuerola, Working paper in
Economic History, 15–10.
Carmona, J., & Simpson, J., 2016. ¿Campesinos unidos o divididos? La acción
colectiva y la revolución social de los yunteros durante la Segunda República en
España (1931–1936). *Historia Social,* 123–144.
Carmona, J., & Simpson, J., 2019. El microcrédito antes de las cooperativas.
Pósitos y crédito público agrario en España en vísperas de la Gran Guerra.
Historia Agraria 77, 169–99.
Carmona, J., & Simpson, J., in press. Capacidad del estado, democracia y política
enla Segunda República (1931–1936) : el fracaso de la reforma agraria en
España. *Ayer.*
Caro Cancela, D., 1987. *La Segunda República en Cádiz. Elecciones y partidos
políticos.* Diputación Provincial, Cádiz.
Caro Cancela, D., 2001. *Violencia política y luchas sociales: La Segunda República en
Jerez de la Frontera.* Ayuntamiento de Jerez, Jerez.
Carreras, A., & Tafunell, X., 2005. *Estadísticas históricas de España.* Fundación
BBVA, Bilbao.
Carrión, P., 1932: 1975. *Los latifundios en España.* Ariel, Madrid.
Casanova i Prat, J., 1998. La Mancomunitat de Catalunya i el foment del
sindicalisme agrari (1919–1923). In Barrull, J., Busqueta, J. J., & Vicedo, E.
(eds.) *Solidaritats pageses, sindicalisme i cooperativisme.* Institut d'Estudis
Ilerdens, Lérida, pp. 395–415.
Casanova, J., 1994. Guerra civil, ¿lucha de clases?: El difícil ejercicio de recon-
struir el pasado. *Historia social* 20, 135–150.
Casanova, J., 2010a. Introducción. In Casanova, J. (ed.) *Tierra y Libertad.* Crítica,
Barcelona.
Casanova, J., 2010b. *The Spanish Republic and Civil War.* Cambridge University
Press, Cambridge.
Cascón, J., 1934. *Agricultura española.* Dirección General de Agricultura, Madrid.

Castillo, J. J., 1979. *Propietarios muy pobres. Sobre la subordinación política del pequeño campesino. La Confederación Nacional Católico-Agraria (1917–1942)*. MAPA, Madrid.

Castro, C.d., 1931. *Al servicio de los campesinos. Hombres sin tierra. Tierra sin hombres*. Morata, Madrid.

Castro, C.d., 1987. *El pan de Madrid. El abasto de las ciudades españolas del Antiguo Régimen*. Alianza, Madrid.

Ceballos Teresi, J. G., 1931. *La realidad económica y financiera de España en los treinta años del presente siglo*. El Financiero, Madrid.

Centeno, M. A., & Ferraro, A. E., 2013. Republics of the Possible: State building in Latin America and Spain. In Centeno, M. A., & Ferraro, A. E. (eds.) *State and Nation Building in Latin America and Spain: Republics of the Possible*. Cambridge University Press, Cambridge, pp. 3–24.

Clar, E., & Pinilla, V., 2009. The Contribution of Agriculture to Spanish Economic Development, 1870–1973. In Lains, P., & Pinilla, V. (eds.) *Agriculture and Economic Development in Europe since 1870*. Routledge, Abingdon, pp. 311–32.

Clark, G., 1991. Labour Productivity in English Agriculture. In Campbell, B. M. S., & Overton, M. (eds.) *Land, Labour and Livestock: Historical Studies in European Agricultural Productivity*. University Press, Manchester, pp. 211–35.

Cleary, M., 1989. *Peasants, Politicians and Producers: the Organisation of Agriculture in France since 1918*. Cambridge University Press, Cambridge.

Clout, H., 1980. *Agriculture in France on the Eve of the Railway Age*. Croom Helm, London.

Cobo, F., 2013. La cuestión agraria y las luchas campesinas en la II República, 1931–1936. *Hispania Nova* 11.

Cobo Romero, F., 2003. *De Campesinos a Electores. Modernización agraria en Andalucía, politización campesina y derechización de los pequeños propietarios y arrendatarios. El caso de la provincia de Jaén, 1931–1936*. Biblioteca Nueva, Madrid.

Coloma, J., 1928. *El problema social de la tierra*. Marvá, Madrid.

Collier, G., 1987. *Socialists of Rural Andalusia: Unacknowledged Revolutionaries of the Second Republic*. Stanford University Press, Stanford.

Collins, E. J. T., 1969. Labour Supply and Demand in European Agriculture, 1800–1880. In Jones, E. L., & Woolf, S. J., (eds.) *Agrarian Change and Economic Development: the Historical Problems*. Routledge, London.

Comín, F., 1996. *Historia de la Hacienda pública, 2 España*. Crítica, Barcelona.

Comín, F., 2012. La Gran Depresión y la Segunda República. *El País*, 29 January.

Comín, F., & Díaz, D., 2005. Sector público administrativo y estado del bienestar. In Carreras, A., & Tafunell, X. (eds.) *Estadísticas históricas de España*. Fundación BBVA, Bilbao, pp. 873–964.

Congreso Nacional de Riegos, 1929. *IV Congreso Nacional de Riegos: celebrado en Barcelona en mayo y junio de 1927*, Barcelona.

Corrionero Salinero, F., 1986. El censo de campesinos: la jerarquización del proletariado rural. *Studia historica. Historia contemporánea* 4, 181–203.

Costa, J., 1904. El pueblo y la propiedad territorial. *Alma Española*, 2–10, pp. 6–10.

Costa, J., 1898: 1915. *Colectivismo agrario en España*. Biblioteca Costa, Madrid.

Costa, J., 1982. *Oligarquía y caciquismo como la forma actual de Gobierno en España: urgencia y modo de cambiarla: información en el Ateneo de Madrid, 1901* Guara, Zaragoza.

Cox, G., Lowe, P., & Winter, M., 1991. The Origins and Early Development of the National Farmers' Union. *Agricultural History Review* 39, 30–47.

Crisis Agrícola y Pecuaria, L., 1887–9. *Actas y dictámenes de la comisión creada por el Real Decreto de 7 de julio de 1887 para estudiar la crisis que atraviesa la agricultura y la ganadería*. Sucesores de Rivaneyra, Madrid.

Curto-Grau, M., Herranz-Loncán, A., & Solé-Ollé, A., 2012. Pork-Barrel Politics in Semi-Democracies: the Spanish 'Parliamentary Roads', 1880–1914. *Journal of Economic History* 72, 771–796.

Chatriot, A., 2016. *La politique du blé*. IGPDE, Paris.

Dahl, R. A., 1971. *Polyarchy. Participation and Opposition*. Yale, New Haven.

de los Rios, F., 1925. The Agrarian Problem in Spain. *International Labour Review*, 830–51.

De Vries, J., 2003. The Industrious Revolution and Economic Growth, 1650–1830. In David, P, & Thomas, M. (eds.) *The Economic Future of Historical Perspective*. Oxford University Press, Oxford, pp. 43–72.

Deininger, K., & Feder, G., 2001. Land Institutions and Land Markets. In Gardner. B., & Rausser, G. (eds.) *Handbook of Agricultural Economics*, North Holland, pp. 288–331.

del Caño, R., 1933. *Producción y mercado del trigo*. Rotativa, Madrid.

Díaz del Moral, J., 1928: 1973. *Historia de las agitaciones campesinas andaluzas*. Alianza, Madrid.

Dimico, A., Isopi, A., & Olsson, O., 2017. Origins of the Sicilian Mafia: the Market for Lemons. *Journal of Economic History* 77, 1083–1115.

Dincecco, M., Federico, G., & Vindigni, A., 2011. Warfare, Taxation, and Political Change: Evidence from the Italian Risorgimento. *Journal of Economic History* 4, 887–914.

Domenech, J., 2013a. Land Tenure Inequality, Harvests, and Rural Conflict: Evidence from Southern Spain in the 1930s. *Social Science History* 39, 253–86.

Domenech, J., 2013b. Rural Labour Markets and Rural Conflict in Spain before the Civil War (1931–36). *Economic History Review* 66, 86–108.

Drache, H. M., 1976. Midwest Agriculture: Changing with Technology. *Agricultural History*, 290–302.

Ellman, M., 2014. *Socialist Planning*, Cambridge University Press, Cambridge.

Engerman, S., & Sokokoff, K. L., 2012. *Economic Development in the America since 1500. Endowments and Institutions*. Cambridge University Press, Cambridge.

Ertman, T., 1998. Democracy and Dictatorship in Interwar Western Europe Revisited. *World Politics* 50, 475–505.

Espinosa, F., 2007. *La primavera del Frente Popular. Los campesinos de Badajoz y el origen de la guerra civil (marzo-julio de 1936)*. Crítica, Barcelona.

Espinoza, L. E., Robledo, R., Brel, M. P., & Villar, J., 2007. Estructura social del campo español: El Censo de Campesinos (1932–1936). Primeros resultados.

In Robledo, R., & López, S. (eds.) ¿*Interés particular, bienestar público? Grandes patrimonios y reformas agrarias.* PUZ, Zaragoza.

Espuelas, S., 2015. The Inequality Trap. A Comparative Analysis of Social Spending between 1880 and 1930. *Economic History Review* 68, 683–706.

Federico, G., 2006. *Feeding the World.* Princeton University Press, Princeton.

Feinstein, C., Temin, P., & Toniolo, G., 1997. *The European Economy Between the Wars.* Oxford University Press, Oxford.

Fernández, E., 2008. El fracaso del lobby viticultor en España frente al objetivo industrializador del Estado, 1920–1936. *Historia Agraria,* 113–141.

Fernández, E., & Simpson, J., 2017. Producer Cooperatives, Institutional Change, and Politics in the Wine Industry, 1880–1980. *Economic History Review* 70, 122–142.

Fernández Prieto, L., 1992. *Labregos con ciencia. Estado, sociedade e innnovación tecnolóxica na agricultura galega, 1850–1939.* Edicións Xerais de Galicia, Vigo.

Fernández Prieto, L., 1997. *Selección de innovaciones en una agricultura atlántica de pequeñas explotaciones. Galicia, 1900–1936. La adopción de las trilladoras mecánicas.* Noticiario de Historia Agraria, 133–163.

Fernández Prieto, L., 2001. Caminos del cambio technológico en las agriculturas españolas contemporáneas. In Pujol, J., Molina, M. G. d., Prieto, L. F., Martínez, D. G., & Garrabou, R. (eds.) *El pozo de todos los males. Sobre el atraso en la agricultura española contemporanea.* Crítica, Barcelona, pp. 95–146.

Fitzgerald, D., 1996. Blinded by Technology: American Agriculture in the Soviet Union, 1928–1932. *Agricultural History* 70, 459–86.

Flora, P., 1983. *State, Economy, and Society in Western Europe, 1815–1975,* 2 vols. Campus Verlag, Frankfurt.

Florencio Puntas, A., 1994. *Empresariado agrícola y cambio económico, 1880–1936.* Diputación Provincial de Sevilla, Sevilla.

Florencio Puntas, A., 2005. *La ingeniería agrónomica en Andalucía: Formación y trayectorias profesionales.* Fundación de Ingenieros Agrónomos de Andalucía, Sevilla.

Florencio Puntas, A., & López Martínez, A., 2000. El trabajo asalariado en la agricultura de la Baja Andalucía, Siglos XVIII-XIX. *Historia Agraria* 21, 99–126.

Flores de Lemus, A. 1926. Sobre una dirección fundamental de la producción rural Española. Reprinted in *Moneda y Crédito,* 1951, 36, 141–168.

FNTT, 1933. *Memoria del II Congreso.* Gráficas socialistas, Madrid.

Foley-Fisher, N., & McLaughlin, E., 2016. Capitalising on the Irish Land Question: Land Reform and State Banking in Ireland, 1891–1938. *Financial History Review* 23, 31–39.

Font de Mora, R., 1954. *El Naranjo, su cultivo, explotación y comercio.* Espasa Calpe, Madrid.

Frader, L.L., 1991. *Peasants and Protest: Agricultural Workers, Politics, and Unions in the Aude, 1850–1914.* University of California Press, Berkeley, Los Angeles, and London.

Fraile Balbín, P., 1991. *Industrialización y grupos de presión: La economía política de la protección en España, 1900–1950.* Alianza, Madrid.

France: Ministère de l'Agriculture, 1936. *Statistique agricole de la France: Résultats généraux de l'enquête de 1929.* Imprimerie Nationale, Paris.

Franzosi, R., 1995. *The Puzzle of Strikes: Class and State Strategies in Postwar Italy.* Cambridge University Press, Cambridge.

Fraser, R., 1986. *Escondido: El calvario de Manuel Cortés.* Instituciò Alfons el Magnànim, Valencia.

Fuentes Cumplido, F., 1904: 1977. Memoria que obtuvo accésit en el Concurso ... el problema agrario en el Mediodía de España, (Lema: El problema agrícola resuelto por los obreros agrícolas). *Agricultura y Sociedad* 3, 337–46.

Fukuyama, F., 2014. *Political Order and Political Decay: From the Industrial Revolution to the Globalisation of Democracy.* Profile, London.

Gallego, D., 2001. Historia de un desarrollo pausado: integración mercantil y transformaciones productivas de la agricultura española (1800–1936). In Pujol, J., Molina, M. G. d., Prieto, L. F., Martínez, D. G., & Garrabou, R. (eds.) *El pozo de todos los males. Sobre el atraso en la agricultura española contemporanea.* Crítica, Barcelona, pp. 147–214.

Gallego, D., Iriarte, I., & Lana, J. M., 2010. Las Españas rurales y el estado (1800–1931). In Garrabou, R. (ed.) *Sombras del Progreso.* Crítica, Barcelona, pp. 85–116.

Gallego Martínez, D., 2016. Obstáculos comerciales y salariales a la transición nutricional en la España de comienzos del siglo XX. *Investigaciones de historia económica* 12, 154–64.

García Barbancho, A., 1967. *Migraciones interiores españolas: estudio cuantitativo desde 1900.* Instituto de Desarrollo Económico, Madrid.

García Pérez, J., 1982. *Estructura social y conflictos campesinos en la provincia de Cáceres durante la II República.* Institución cultural El Brocense, Caceres.

García Pérez, J., 1985. La II República y la Guerra Civil en Extremadura. In García Pérez, J., Sánchez Marroyo, F. & Merino Martín, J. (eds.) *Historia de Extremadura.* Universitas, Badajoz, pp. 996–1018.

García Sanz, A., 1985. Introducción. In García Sanz, A. & Garrabou, R. (eds.) *Historia agraria de la España contemporánea.* Crítica, Barcelona, pp. 7–99.

García Sanz, A., 1991. La ganadería Española entre 1750–1865: los efectos de la reforma agraria liberal. *Agricultura y Sociedad* 72, 81–120.

Garrabou, R., Barciela, C., & Jiménez Blanco, J. I., 1986. *Historia agraria de la España contemporánea. 3. El fin de la agricultura tradicional (1900–1960).* Crítica, Barcelona.

Garrabou, R., Pujol, J., & Colomé, J., 1991. Salaris, us i explotació de la força de treball agrícola (Catalunya 1818–1936). *Recerques* 24, 23–51.

Garrabou, R., & Sanz, J., 1985a. Introducción: La agricultura española durante el siglo XIX: ¿inmovilismo o cambio? In Garrabou, R. & Sanz, J. (eds.) *Historia agraria de la España contemporánea. 2. Expansión y crisis (1850–1900).* Crítica, Barcelona, pp. 7–191.

Garrabou, R., & Tello, E., 2002. Salario como coste, salario como ingreso: el precio de los jornales agrícolas en la Cataluña contemporánea, 1727–1930. In Carrión, J. M. M. (ed.) *El nivel de vida en la España rural, siglos XVIII-XX.* Publicaciones de la Universidad de Alicante, Alicante.

Garrido, S., 1994. El cooperativisme segons l'Esglesia. Els inicis del sindicalisme catolico-agrari a Espanya. *Recerques*, 69–85.

Garrido, S., 1995. El cooperativismo agrario español del primer tercio del siglo XX. *Revista de Historia Económica* 13, 115–144.

Garrido, S., 1996. *Treballar en comú. El cooperativisme agrari a Espanya.* Institucio Alfons el Magnànim, Valencia.

Garrido, S., 2007. Why Did Most Cooperatives Fail? Spanish Agricultural Cooperation in the Early Twentieth Century. *Rural History* 18, 183–200.

Garrido, S., 2017. Sharecropping Was Sometimes Efficient: Sharecropping with Compensation for Improvements in European Viticulture. *Economic History Review* 70, 977–1003.

Gatrell, P., & Harrison, M., 1993. The Russian and Soviet Economies in Two World Wars: a Comparative View. *Economic History Review* 425–52.

GEHR, 1978–9. Contribución al análisis histórico de la ganadería española, 1865–1929. *Agricultura y Sociedad*, Vol. 8, 129–182 and Vol. 10, 105–169.

GEHR, 1980. *Los precios del trigo y la cebada en España, 1891–1907.* Banco de España, Madrid.

GEHR, 1983b. Evolución de la superficie cultivada de cereales y leguminosas en España, 1886–1935. *Agricultura y Sociedad*, 285–325.

GEHR, 1991. *Estadísticas históricas de la producción agraria española, 1859–1935.* Mapa, Madrid.

GEHR, 1994. Más allá de la propiedad perfecta: El proceso de privatización de los montes públicos españoles (1859–1926). *Noticiario de Historia Agraria*, 99–152.

Germany. *Statistisches Jahrbuch für das Deutsche Reich.*

Gerschenkron, A., 1966. *Economic Backwardness in Historical Perspective.* Harvard University Press, Cambridge, MA.

Gil Andrés, C., 2013. 'Esas luchas pueblerinas': Movilización política y conflicto social en el mundo rural republicano (La Rioja 1930–1936). *Ayer*, 93–119.

Gil Cuadrado, L.T., 2006. *El partido agrario español (1934–1936): Una alternativa conservadora y republicana Complutense*, Madrid.

Giordano, C., 2001. Réformes agraires et tensions ethniques en Europe centrale et orientale. *Études rurales*, 205–228.

Gómez Benito, C., 2011a. *Joaquín Costa y la modernización de España.* Congreso de los Diputados, Madrid.

Gómez Navarro, J.L., 1932. *Saltos de Agua y Presas de Embalse.* Herrera, Madrid.

Góngora Echenique, M., 1926. *El problema de la tierra.* Madrid.

González-Blanco, X., 1931. *La tierra de España y la Reforma Agraria*, Valencia.

Gonzalez Calleja, E., 2012. *Contrarrevolucionarios: Radicalización violenta de las derechas durante la Segunda República 1931–1936.* Alianza, Madrid.

González Calleja, E., 2015. *Cifras cruentas: Las víctimas mortales de la violencia sociopolítica en la Segunda República Española (1931–1936).* Comares, Granada.

González Calleja, E., Cobo Romero, F., Martínez Rus, A., & Sánchez Pérez, F., 2015. *La Segunda República Española.* Pasado y Presente, Barcelona.

González de Molina Navarro, M., Infante Amate, J., & Herrera González de Molina, A., 2014. Cuestionando los relatos tradicionales: desigualdad, cambio liberal y crecimiento agrario en el Sur peninsular (1752–1901). *Historia Agraria*, 55–88.

Grafe, R., 2012. *Distant Tyranny: Markets, Power, and Backwardness in Spain, 1650–1800.* Princeton University Press, Princeton.

Granados, M., 1932. *La reforma agraria en Europa y el proyecto español: Los métodos y resultados.* Castro, Madrid.

Griffin, K., Rahman Khan, A., & Ickowitz, A., 2002. Poverty and the Distribution of Land. *Journal of Agrarian Change* 2, 279–330.

Guinnane, T. W., & Miller, R., 1997. The Limits to Land Reform: the Land Acts in Ireland, 1870–1909. *Economic Development and Cultural Change* 45, 591–612.

Haggblade, S., Hazell, P., & Reardon, T., 2007. *Transforming the Rural Non-farm Economy: Opportunities and Threats in the Developing World.* Johns Hopkins, Baltimore.

Harley, C. K., 1991. Substitutes for Prerequisites: Endogenous Institutions and Comparative Economic History. In Sylla, R., & Toniolo, G., (eds.) *Patterns of European Industrialization.* Routledge, London, pp. 29–44.

Harvey, C., & Taylor, P., 1987. Mineral Wealth and Economic Development: Foreign Direct Investment in Spain. *Economic History Review* XL, 185–207.

Hatton, T., & B.E. Bray, 2010. Long Run Trends in the Heights of European Men, 19th–20th centuries. *Economics and Human Biology* 8, 405–413.

Henriksen, I., 1999. Avoiding Lock-In: Co-operative Creameries in Denmark, 1882–1903. *European Review of Economic History* 9, 365–397.

Henriksen, I., 2014. The 1896 Parliamentary Report in Denmark. In Vivier, N., (ed.) *The Golden Age of State Enquiries.* Brepols, Turnhout, pp. 223–238.

Hevesy, P. d., 1940. *World Wheat Planning and Economic Planning in General.* Oxford University Press, Oxford, London, New York, Toronto.

Hirschman, A. O., 1970. *Exit, Voice, and Loyalty: Responses to Decline in Firms, Organizations, and States.* Harvard University Press, Cambridge, MA.

Hirschman, A. O., 1984. *Getting Ahead Collectively: Grassroots Experiences in Latin America.* Pergamon, New York.

Hobsbawm, E., 1959. *Primitive Rebels: Studies in Archaic forms of Social Movements in the 19th and 20th Century.* Norton, New York.

Hoffman, P., Jacks, D., Levin, P., & Lindert, P., 2002. Real Inequality in Europe since 1500. *Journal of Economic History,* 322–355.

Hooker, E. R., 1938. *Re-adjustments of Agricultural Tenure in Ireland.* North Carolina Press, Chapel Hill.

Howkins, A., 1985. *Poor Labouring Men: Rural Radicalism in Norfolk 1870–1923.* Routledge & Kegan Paul, London.

Howkins, A., & Verdon, N., 2009. The State and the Farm Worker: the Evolution of the Minimum Wage in Agriculture in England and Wales, 1909–24. *Agricultural History Review* 57, 257–274.

I Congreso Nacional Cerealista. *Valladolid,* 1927. Zapatero, Valladolid.

Infante Amate, J., 2013. 'Cuántos siglos de aceituna'. El carácter de la expansión olivarera en el sur de España (1750–1900). *Historia Agraria* 58, 39–72.

Inspección General de Pósitos, 1924. *Memoria con referencia a los años 1920 al 1923,* Madrid.

Instituto de Estadística de Andalucía, 2002. *Estadísticas del siglo XX en Andalucía Junta de Andalucía,* Sevilla.

Instituto de Reforma Agraria, 1934. *Datos recopilados sobre las provincias de Badajoz, Cáceres y Huelva*, Madrid.

Instituto de Reformas Sociales, 1905. *Resumen de la información acerca de los obreros agrícola en las provincias de Andalucía y Extremadura*, Madrid.

International Institute of Agriculture, *International yearbook of agricultural statistics*, 1933–4. IIA, Rome.

Iriarte Goñi, I., & Lana Berasain, J. M., 2016. Hopes of Recovery: Struggles over the Right to Common Lands in the Spanish Countryside, 1931–1936. In Congost, R., Gelman, J., & Santos, R. (eds.) *Property Rights in Land*. Routledge, Abington, pp. 132–153.

Jacobson, S., & Moreno Luzón, J., 2000. The Political System of the Restoration, 1875–1914: Political and Social Elites. In Álvarez Junco, J., & Shubert, A. (eds.) *Spanish History Since 1808*. Arnold, London, pp. 93–109.

Janvry, d. A., 1981. *The Agrarian Question and Reformism in Latin America*. Johns Hopkins University Press, Baltimore and London.

Johnson, B. F., & Mellor, J. W., 1961. The Role of Agriculture in Economic Development. *American Economic Review* 51, 566–593.

Johnson, N. D., & Koyama, M., 2017. States and Economic Growth: Capacity and constraints. *Explorations in Economic History*, 1–20.

Juliá, S., 1989. The Origins and Nature of the Spanish Popular Front. In Alexander, M. S., & Graham, H. (eds.) *The French and Spanish Popular Fronts*. Cambridge University Press, Cambridge, pp. 24–37.

Juliá, S., 2008. En torno a los orígenes de la Guerra Civil. In Fuentes Quintana, E., & Comín, F. (eds.) *Economía y economistas españoles en la guerra civil*. Galaxia Gutenberg, Madrid, pp. 171–189.

Junta Nacional de Hermandades, 1959. Encuesta Agropecuaria de la población campesina: 1956. *Revista Sindical de Estadística*.

Kalyvas, S. N., 1996. *The Rise of Christian Democracy in Europe*. Cornell University Press, Cornell, Ithaca, and London.

Kirk, D., 1946. *Europe's Population in the Interwar Years*. Gordon & Breach, New York.

Kitchens, C., & Fishback, P., 2015. Flip the Switch: the Impact of the Rural Electrification Administration 1935–1940. *Journal of Economic History* 75, 1161–1195.

Koning, N., 1994. *The Failure of Agrarian Capitalism: Agrarian Politics in the UK, Germany, the Netherlands and the USA, 1846–1919*. Routledge, London, and New York.

Ladrón de Guevara, M. P., 1993. *La Esperanza Republicana: Reforma agraria y conflicto campesino en la provincia de Ciudad Real (1931–1939)*. Diputación de Ciudad Real, Ciudad Real.

Lampe, M., & Sharp, P., 2018. *A Land of Milk and Butter: How Elites Created the Modern Danish Dairy Industry*. University of Chicago Press, Chicago.

Lannon, F., 1987. *Privilege, Persecution, and Prophecy: the Catholic Church in Spain 1875–1975*. Clarendon, Oxford.

Levi, C., 1947: 1982.*Christ Stopped at Eboli*. Penguin, Harmondsworth.

Levitsky, S., & Ziblatt, D., 2018. *How Democracies Die*. Viking, New York.

Lewis, W. A., 1978. *Growth and Fluctuations, 1870–1913*. Allen & Unwin, London.

Lindert, P., 1991. Historical Patterns of Agricultural Policy. In Timmer, C. P. (ed.) *Agriculture and the State: Growth, Employment and Poverty in Developing Countries*. Cornell University Press, Cornell, Ithaca, and London.

Lindert, P., 2004. *Growing Public: Social Spending and Economic Growth Since the Eighteenth Century*. Cambridge.

Linz, J. J., 1967. The Party System of Spain: Past and Future. In Lipset, S. M., & Rokkan, S. (eds.) *Party Systems and Voter Alignments: Cross-National Perspectives*. The Free Press, New York.

Linz, J. J., 1978a. *Crisis, Breakdown, and Reequilibration*. John Hopkins University Press, Baltimore and London.

Linz, J. J., 1978. From Great Hopes to Civil War: the Breakdown of Democracy in Spain. In Linz, J. J., & Stefan, A. (eds.) *The Breakdown of Democratic Regimes: Europe*. John Hopkins University, Baltimore and London, pp. 142–215.

Linz, J. J., Jerez, M., & Corzo, S., 2002. Ministers and Regimes in Spain: from the First to the Second Restoration, 1874–2002. *South European Society and Politics* 7.

Linz, J. J., Montero, J. R., & Ruiz, A. M., 2005. Elecciones y política. In Carreras, A., & Tafunell, X. (eds.) *Estadísticas Históricas de España*. Fundación BBVA, Bilbao, pp. 1027–1154.

Lipton, M., 2009. *Land Reform in Developing Countries: Property Rights and Property Wrongs*. Routledge, Abingdon.

Lombardero Rico, X., 1997. O asociacionismo agrario en Ribadeo no primeiro terzo de seculo In Fernández Prieto, L., Nuñez Seixas, X. M., Artiaga, A., & Balboa, X. (eds.) *Poder local, élites e cambio social na Galicia non urbana (1874–1936)*. Universidade de Santiago de Compostela, Santiago de Compostela, pp. 537–49.

López Estudillo, A., 2006. Los mercados de trabajo desde una perspectiva histórica: el trabajo asalariado agrario en la Andalucía Bética (la provincia de Córdoba). *Revista Española de Estudios Agrosociales y Pesqueros* 211, 63–119.

López Morán, E., 1900. *Derecho consuetudinario y economía popular de la provincia de León*, Madrid.

López Ontiveros, A., & Mata Olmo, R., 1993. *Propiedad de la Tierra y Reforma Agraria en Córdoba (1932–1936)*. Servicio de publicaciones de la Universidad de Córdoba, Córdoba.

Lowe, S., 2010. *Catholicism, War and the Foundation of Francoism: the Juventud de Acción Popular in Spain, 1931–1939*. Sussex Academic, Portland.

Lowi, T. J., 1979. *The End of Liberalism: the Second Republic of the United States*. Norton, New York.

Luebbert, G. M., 1991. *Liberalism, Fascism, or Social Democracy: Social Classes and the Political Origins of Regimes in Interwar Europe*. Oxford University Press, Oxford.

Macarro Vera, J. M., 2000. *Socialismo, república y revolución en Andalucía*. Universidad de Sevilla, Sevilla.

Macarro Vera, J. M., 2017. La quiebra del socialismo en la II Republica. *Bulletin d'Histoire Contemporaine de l'Espagne* 51, 25–40.

Maddison-Project, T., www.ggdc.net/maddison/maddison-project/home.htm, 2013 version.

Maddison, A., 1995. *Monitoring the World Economy, 1820–1992*. OECD Paris.

Maddison, A., 2003. *The World Economy: Historical Statistics*. OECD, Paris.

Magagna, V. V., 1991. *Communities of Grain: Rural Rebellion in Comparative Perspective*. Cornell, Ithaca, NY.

Majuelo, E. M., & Pascual, A., 1991. *Del sindicalismo catolicismo agrario al cooperativismo empresarial: Setenta y cinco años de la Federación Cooperativas navarras, 1910–1985*. MAPA, Madrid.

Malefakis, E., 1970. *Agrarian Reform and the Peasant Revolution in Spain: Origins of the Civil War*. Yale University Press, New Haven.

Malenbaum, W., 1953. *The World Wheat Economy, 1885–1939*. Harvard, Cambridge, MA.

Maluquer de Motes, J., & Llonch, M., 2001. Trabajo y relaciones laborales. In Carreras, A., & Tafunell, X. (eds.) *Estadísticas históricas de España*. BBVA, Bilbao, pp. 1155–1245.

Mann, M., 1993. *The Sources of Social Power. 2. The Rise of Classes and Nation States, 1760–1914*. Cambridge University Press, Cambridge.

Mann, M., 2004. *Fascists*. Cambridge University Press, Cambridge.

Mann, M., 2012. *The Sources of Social Power. 3. Global Empires and Revolution, 1890–1945*. Cambridge University Press, Cambridge.

Marfany, J., 2012. *Land, Proto-industry and Population in Catalonia*. Ashgate, Farnham.

Marichalar, L., 1931. *La reforma agraria en España*. Minuesa de los Ríos, Madrid.

Martínez-Alier, J., 1971. *Labourers and Landowners in Southern Spain*. Oxford University Press, Oxford.

Martínez-Carrión, J. M., 2011. La talla de los europeos, 1700–2000: ciclos, crecimiento y desigualdad. *Investigaciones de Historia Económica* 8, 176–187.

Martínez-Soto, A., 2000. Cooperativismo y crédito agrario en la Región de Murcia. Historia Agraria, 123–67.

Martínez-Soto, A. P., 2003. El cooperativismo de crédito en España, 1890–1934, modelos, sistemas de gestión y balance de su actuación. *Historia Agraria* 30, 119–150.

Martínez-Soto, A., & Martínez-Rodríguez, S., 2015. Granaries (pósitos): a source of finance for Spain's small farmers, 1900–1950. *Continuity and Change* 30, 251–277.

Martínez-Soto, A., Méndez, I., & Martínez-Rodríguez, S., 2012. Spain's Development of Rural Credit Cooperatives from 1900 to 1936: the Role of Financial Resources and Formal Education. *European Review of Economic History* 16, 449–468.

Martínez Cuadrado, M., 1969. *Elecciones y partidos políticos de España (1868–1931)*. Taurus, Madrid.

Martínez de Bujana, E. 1935. The development of the Agrarian Reforms in Spain, *International Institute of Agriculture, International Review of Agricultural Economics*, 26, July, 252–63.

Martínez Gallego, F., 2010. *Esperit d'associació: Cooperativisme i mutualisme laics al País Valencià, 1834–1936*. PUV, Valencia.

Martínez López, A., 1989. *O cooperativismo catolico no proceso de modernizacion da agricultura galega, 1900–1943.* Diputacion Provincial, Pontevedra.

Marx, K., 2002. The Eighteenth Brumaire of Louis Bonaparte. In Cowling, M., & Martin, J. (eds.) *Marx's Eighteenth Brumaire.* Pluto, London.

Mason, T. D., 2004. *Caught in the Crossfire: Revolutions, Repression, and the Rational Peasant.* Rowan & Littlefield, Lanham.

Maurice, J., 1990. *El Anarquismo Andaluz: Campesinos y sindicalistas, 1868–1936.* Crítica, Barcelona.

Maurice, J., & Serrano, C., 1977. *J. Costa: Crisis de la Restaración y populismo (1875–1911).* Siglo XXI, Madrid.

McLaughlin, E., 2016. Capitalising on the Irish Land Question: Land Reform and State Banking in Ireland, 1891–1938. *Financial History Review* 23(1), 71–109.

Mellor, J. W. (ed.) 1995. *Agriculture on the Road to Industrialization.* Johns Hopkins University Press, Baltimore, MD.

Meltzer, A. H., & Richard, S. F., 1981. A Rational Theory of the Size of Government. *Journal of Political Economy* 89, 914–927.

Milanovic, B., 2016. *Global Inequality: a New Approach for the Age of Globalization.* Harvard University Press, Cambridge, MA.

Milward, R., & Baten, J., 2010. Population and Living Standards, 1914–1945. In Broadberry, S. & O'Rourke, K. (eds.) *The Cambridge Economic History of Modern Europe, Volume 2: 1870 to the Present.* Cambridge University Press, Cambridge, pp. 232–263.

Mintz, J., 1982. *The Anarchists of Casas Viejas.* University of Chicago, Chicago.

Mitchell, B. R., 1992. *International Historical Statistics, Europe, 1750–1988.* Macmillan & Stockton Press, Basingstoke and New York.

Montañés, E., 1997. *Transformación agrícola y conflictividad campesina en Jerez de la Frontera, 1880–1923.* Universidad de Cádiz, Cádiz.

Montañés, E., & Simpson, J., 2015. Casual Workers, Collective Action and anarcho-syndicalism in Southern Spain: Jerez de la Frontera, 1882 to 1933. *Agricultural History Review* 63, 113–131.

Montero Díaz, J., 1977. *La CEDA, El catolicismo social y político en la II República.* Revista de Trabajo, Madrid.

Montojo Sureda, J., 1945. *La política española sobre trigos y harinas (Años 1900–1945),* Madrid.

Moore, B., 1967. *Social Origins of Dictatorship and Democracy: Lord and Peasant in the Making of the Modern World.* Allen Lane, London.

Moore, W., 1945. *Economic Demography of Eastern and Southern Europe.* League of Nations, Geneva.

Moradiellos, E., 2016. *Historia mínima de la guerra civil española.* Turner, Madrid.

Moreno Luzón, J., 2007. Political Clientalism, Elites and Caciquismo in Restoration Spain (1875–1923). *European History Quarterly* 37, 417–441.

Muñiz, L., 1926. *La Acción Social Agraria en España.* Palomeque, Madrid.

Nadal, J., 1975. *El fracaso de la Revolución Industrial en España, 1814–1913.* Ariel, Barcelona.

Naredo, J. M., Ruiz-Maya, L., & Sumpsi, J. M., 1977. La crisis de las aparcerías de secano en la postguerra. *Agricultura y Sociedad* 3, 9–67.

Nicolau, R., 2005. Población, salud y actividad. In Carreras, A., & Tafunell, X. (eds.) *Estadísticas históricas de España*. Fundación BBVA, Bilbao, pp. 77–154.

Nochlin, L., 2018. *Misère: the Virtual Representation of Misery in the 19th Century*. Thames & Hudson, London.

Noguer, P. N., 1912. *Las Cajas rurales en España y el Extranjero*, Madrid.

Noriega y Abascal, E., 1897. *La tierra labrantía y el trabajo agrícola en la provincia de Sevilla*, Madrid.

North, D., Wallis, J., & Weingast, B., 2007. *Violence and Social Orders: a Conceptual Framework for Interpreting Recorded Human History*. Cambridge University Press, Cambridge.

North, D., & Weingast, B., 1989. Constitution and Commitment: the Evolution of Institutional Governing Public Choice in Seventeenth-Century England. *Journal of Economic History* 49, 803–832.

Núñez, C. E., 1992. *La fuente de la riqueza: Educación y desarrollo económico en la España Contemporánea*. Alianza, Madrid.

Nuñez Seixas, X., 2018. *Nueva Historia de la España Contemporánea (1808–2018)*. Galaxia Gutemberg, Barcelona.

O'Brien, K. J., & Li, L., 2006. *Rightful Resistance in Rural China*. Cambridge University Press, Cambridge.

O'Brien, P., & Prados de la Escosura, L., 1992. Agricultural Productivity and European Industrialization, 1890–1980. *Economic History Review* 45, 514–536.

O'Rourke, K., & Williamson, J. G., 1994. Late Nineteenth-century Anglo-American Factor-price Convergence: Were Heckscher and Ohlin Right? *Journal of Economic History* 54, 892–916.

O'Rourke, K., & Williamson, J. G., 1997. Around the European Periphery, 1870–1913: Globalization, Schooling and Growth. *European Review of Economic History* 1, 153–190.

Offer, A., 1989. *The First World War: an Agrarian Interpretation*. Clarendon, Oxford.

Olmstead, A. L., & Rhode, P.W., 2001. Reshaping the Landscape: the Impact and Diffusion of the Tractor in American Agriculture, 1910–1960. *Journal of Economic History* 61, 663–698.

Olmstead, A. L., & Rhode, P. W., 2002. The Red Queen and the Hard Reds: Productivity Growth in American Wheat, 1800–1940. *Journal of Economic History* 62, 929–966.

Olmstead, A. L., & Rhode, P. W., 2009. Conceptual Issues for the Comparative Study of Agricultural Development. In Lains, P., & Pinilla, V. (eds.) *Agriculture and Economic Development in Europe Since 1870*. Routledge, London, pp. 27–51.

Olson, M., 1965. *The Economics of the Wartime Shortage: a History of British Food Supplies in the Napoleonic War and in World Wars I and II*. Duke University Press, Durham.

Ostrom, E., 1990. *Governing the Commons*. Cambridge University Press, Cambridge.

Palafox, J., 1991. *Atraso económico y democracia: La Segunda Republica y la economía española, 1892–1936*. Crítica, Barcelona.

Palerm, A., 1962. *Observaciones sobre la reforma agraria en Italia*. Panamericana, Washington.

Pan-Montojo, J. L., 1994. *La Bodega del Mundo: La vid y el vino en España, 1800–1936* Alianza, Madrid.

Pan-Montojo, J., 2000. Las Asociaciones Rurales y el nacimiento del Sindicalismo Agrario en España, 1834–1907. In Tortosa, F. F. G. (ed.) *Actas 1er Congreso sobre Cooperativismo Español.* Fundación Fernando Garrido Tortosa, Cordoba, pp. 27–64.

Pan-Montojo, J., 2002. Asociacionismo agrario, administración y corporativismo en la dictadura de Primo de Rivera. *Historia Social,* 15–30.

Pan-Montojo, J., 2005. *Apostolado, profesión y technología: Una historia de los ingenieros agrónomos en España.* B&H, Madrid.

Pan-Montojo, J., 2007. La Asociación de Agricultores de España y la clase política, 1881–1942. *Ayer,* 85–115.

Pan-Montojo, J. L., 2009. Los liberalismos y la agricultura española en el Siglo XIX. In Calatayud, S., Millán, J., & Cruz Romero, M. (eds.) *Estado y periferias en la España del siglo XIX. Nuevos enfoques.* Universitat de València, Valencia, pp. 131–158.

Parejo, A., 2009. *Historia económica de Andalucía contemporánea.* Sintesis, Madrid.

Pasour, E. C., & Rucker, R. R., 2005. *Plowshares and Pork Barrels: the Political Economy of Agriculture.* The Independent Institute, Oakland.

Paul, H. W., 1996. *Science, Vine, and Wine in Modern France.* Cambridge University Press, Cambridge.

Paxton, R. O., 1997. *French Peasant Fascism.* Oxford University Press, Oxford.

Payne, S., 2005. *El colapso de la República.* La Esfera, Madrid.

Peces-Barba, G., 1932. *Ley de Reforma Agraria.* Valdecilla, Madrid.

Pérez Moreda, V., 1985. La modernización demográfica, 1800–1930: Sus limitaciones y cronología. In Sánchez-Albornoz, N. (ed.) *La modernización económica de España 1830–1930.* Alianza, Madrid, pp. 25–62.

Pérez Yruela, M., 1979. *Conflictividad campesina en la provincia de Córdoba (1. 931–1. 936).* MAPA, Madrid.

Perren, R., 2000. Milling. In Collins, E. J. T. (ed.) *The Agrarian History of England and Wales, 1850–1914.* Cambridge University Press, Cambridge, pp. 1062–75.

Peyron, M., 1808. *Modern State of Spain.* Stockdale, London.

Pierson, P., 2004. *Politics in Time, History, Institutions, and Social Analysis.* Princeton University Press, Princeton.

Piqueras, J., 1981. *La vid y el vino en el País Valenciano.* Insitució Alfons el Magnanim, Valencia.

Pitt-Rivers, J., 1954: 1971. *The People of the Sierra.* Criterion, New York.

Planas, J., 2008. El Instituto Agrícola Catalán de San Isidro y la organización de los intereses agrarios (1880–1936). *Revista de Estudios agrosociales y pesqueros* 13–47.

Planas, J., 2013. *Viticultura i cooperativisme: La comarca d'Igualada, 1890–1939.* L'Abadia de Montserrat, Barcelona.

Polo Benito, J., 1919. *El problema social del campo de Extremadura,* Salamanca.

Pomés, J., 2000. *La Unió de Rabassaires.* L'Abadia de Montserrat, Barcelona.

Pomés, J., 2000a. Sindicalismo republicano en la España de la Restauracion. *Ayer* 39, 103–32.

Popkin, S., 1979. *The Rational Peasant: the Political Economy of Rural Society in Vietnam.* University of California Press, Berkeley.

Prada Rodríguez, J., 2013. *Clientelismo y poder local en la II República.* Hispania Nova. https://e-revistas.uc3m.es/index.php/HISPNOV/index.

Prado Moura, A.d., 1985. *El movimiento obrero en Valladolid durante la II República.* Junta de Castilla y León, Salamanca.

Prados de la Escosura, L., 1988. *De imperio a nación: crecimiento y atraso económico en España (1780–1930).* Alianza, Madrid.

Prados de la Escosura, L., 1989. La estimación indirecta de la producción agraria en el siglo XIX: réplica a Simpson. *Revista de Historia Económica* 7, 703–18.

Prados de la Escosura, L., 2003. *El progreso económico de España (1850–2000).* BBVA, Madrid.

Prados de la Escosura, L., 2007. Growth and Structural Change in Spain, 1850–2000: a European Perspective. *Revista de Historia Económica / Journal of Iberian and Latin American Economic History* 25, 147–81.

Prados de la Escosura, L., 2008. Inequality, Poverty, and the Kuznets Curve in Spain, 1850–2000. *European Review of Economic History* 12, 287–324.

Prados de la Escosura, L., 2017. *Spanish Economic Growth, 1850–2015.* Palgrave Macmillan, Cham.

Preston, P., 1978. *A Concise History of the Spanish Civil War.* Fontana, London.

Preston, P., 1978:2003. *The Coming of the Spanish Civil War.* Routledge, London.

Preston, P., 2000. *La Guerra Civil española.* Plaza y Janés, Madrid.

Preston, P., 2012. *The Spanish Holocaust, Inquisition and Extermination in Twentieth-Century Spain.* Harper, London.

Pro Ruiz, J., 1995. Ocultación de la riqueza rústica en España (1870–1936): acerca de la fiabilidad de las estadísticas sobre la propiedad y uso de la tierra. *Revista de Historia Económica* 13, 89–114.

Pujol-Andreu, J., 2011. Wheat Varieties and Technological Change in Europe, 19th and 20th Centuries: New Issues in Economic History. *Historia Agraria,* 71–103.

Pujol, J., Molina, M. G. d., Prieto, L. F., Martínez, D. G., & Garrabou, R. (eds.) 2001. *El pozo de todos los males. Sobre el atraso en la agricultura española contemporanea.* Crítica, Barcelona.

Pulido Romero, M., & Francisco Villalobos Cortés, 2006. *100 años del crédito cooperativo extremeño (1905–2005): la Caja Rural de Extremadura.* Caja Rural de Extremadura, Badajoz.

Putnam, R., 1993. *Making Democracy Work,* Princeton University Press, Princeton.

Quevedo y García Lomas, J., 1904. *Memoria que obtuvo accésit en el Concurso . . . el problema agrario en el Mediodía de España.* Minuesa de los Ríos, Madrid.

Quiroga Valle, G., 2001. Estatura, diferencias regionales y sociales y niveles de vida en España (1893–1954). *Revista de Historia Económica* XIX, 175–200.

Quiroga Valle, G., 2003a. Literacy, Education and Welfare in Spain (1893–1954). *Paedagogica Histórica* 39, 559–619.

Quiroga Valle, G., 2003b. Medidas antropométricas y condiciones de vida en la España del siglo XX. University of Alcalá thesis. https://ebuah.uah.es/dspace/handle/10017/16341

Rafael Serrano Garcia, 2016. Socialismo y ugetismo en el medio rural castellano: Valladolid (1931–1936)/Old and New Worlds: the Global Challenges of Rural History. International Conference, 27–30 January, Lisbon.

Ramon i Muñoz, J. M., 1999. *El sindicalisme agrari a la Segarra*. Pagès, Lleida.

Ramón Muñoz, R., 2000. *Specialization in the International Market for Olive Oil before World War II*. Routledge, London and New York.

Ramón Muñoz, R., 2010. Globalisation and the International Markets for Mediterranean Export Commodities: the Case of Olive Oil, 1850–1938. EUI PhD thesis. https://cadmus.eui.eu/handle/1814/14700

Ray, D., 1998. *Developing Economics*, Princeton University Press, Princeton.

Reher, D.-S., Pombo, M .N., & Noguerás, B., 1993. *España a la luz del Censo de 1887*. Institutio Nacional de Estadística, Madrid.

Reher, D. S., 1998. Family Ties in Western Europe: Persistent Contrasts. *Population and Development* 24, 203–34.

Rey, F. del, 2008. *Paisanos en lucha: exclusión política y violencia en la Segunda República española*. Biblioteca Nueva, Madrid.

Rey, F. del, 2011. Introducción. In Rey, Fd. (ed.) *Palabras como puños: la intransigencia política en la Segunda República española*. Tecnos, Madrid.

Riesco Roche, S., 2006. *La Reforma agraria y los orígenes de la Guerra Civil (1931–1940)*. Biblioteca Nueva, Madrid.

Riley, D., 2010. *The Civic Foundations of Fascism in Europe: Italy, Spain, and Romania, 1870–1945*. John Hopkins University Press, Baltimore.

Riquer, B.d., 2001. *Escolta Espanya: La cuestión catalana en la época liberal*. Marcial Pons, Madrid.

Robledo Hernández, R., 2010. *Sombras del progreso: las huellas de la historia agraria: Ramón Garrabou*. Crítica, Barcelona.

Robledo Hernández, R., 2014. Sobre el fracaso de la reforma agraria andaluza en la Segunda República. In González de Molina, M. (ed.) *La cuestión agraria en la Historia de Andalucía. Nuevas perspectivas*. Junta de Andalucía, Sevilla, pp. 63–96.

Robledo Hernández, R., & Esteban, Á. L. G., 2017. *Tierra, trabajo y reforma agraria en la Segunda República española (1931–1936): algunas consideraciones críticas*. Historia Agraria, 7–36.

Robledo, R., 1993. *Economistas y reformadores españoles: la cuestión agraria (1760–1935)*. MAPA, Madrid.

Robledo, R., 2012. La expropiación agraria de la Segunda República (1931–1939). In Dios, Sd. (ed.) *Historia de la Propiedad: la expropiación*. Servicio de Estudios del Colegio de Registradores, Salamanca, pp. 371–412.

Robledo, R., & Espinoza, L. E., 1999. La reforma agraria en la II Republica: el proceso de asentamiento de comunidades de campesinos en la provincia de Salamanca. In Dios, Sd. (ed.) *Historia de la propiedad en España: siglos XV–XX*. Centro de Estudios Registrales, Madrid, pp. 403–40.

Rodrigáñez, C., 1904: 1977. Memoria que obtuvo el premio ofrecido por S.M. el Rey en el Concurso abierto por Real Orden ante el Instituto de Reformas Sociales (Lema: Progreso en el cultivo). *Agricultura y Sociedad* 3.

Rodriguez Lago, J .R., 1997. Sociología y comportamientos políticos del clero parroquial en la Galicia rural (1898–1936) In Fernández Prieto, L., Nuñez Seixas, X. M., Artiaga, A., & Balboa, X. (eds.) *Poder local, élites e cambio social na*

Galicia non urbana (1874–1936). Universidad de Santiago de Compostela, Santiago de Compostela, pp. 287–325.

Rosés, J., 2003. Why Isn't the Whole of Spain Industrialised? New Economic Geography and Early Industrialisation, 1797–1910. *Journal of Economic History* 63, 995–1022.

Rosés, J., & Sánchez-Alonso, B., 2002. Regional Wage Convergence in Spain: 1850–1930. UC3M, Working Papers in Economic History, WP 02–11.

Rosés, J., & Sánchez-Alonso, B., 2004. Regional wage convergence in Spain, 1850–1930. *Explorations in Economic History*, 41–4, 404–25.

Rosés, J. R., Martínez-Galarraga, J., & Tirado, D. A., 2010. The Upswing of Regional Income Inequality in Spain (1860–1930). *Explorations in Economic History* 47, 244–57.

Roses, J. R., & Wolf, N., 2010. Aggregate Growth, 1913–1950. In Broadberry, S. & O'Rourke, K. (eds.) *The Cambridge Economic History of Modern Europe, Volume 2, 1870 to the Present*. Cambridge, pp. 181–207.

Roses, J. R., & Wolf, N., 2019. *The Economic Development of Europe's Regions: a Quantitative History since 1900*. Routledge, London and New York.

Rosique Navarro, F., 1988. *La Reforma agraria en Badajoz durante la II\u1d43 República: la respuesta patronal*. Diputación Provincial, Badajoz.

Ruiz González, C., 2011. La comarca de Toro en la II República y primer Franquismo (1931–1945). University of Salamanca thesis. https://gredos .usal.es/handle/10366/83344.

Ruiz Torres, P., 1996. Reforma agraria y revolución liberal en España. In García Sanz, A., & Fernández, J. S. (eds.) *Reformas y políticas agraria en la historia de España*. MAPA, Madrid, pp. 201–45.

Ruiz Torres, P., 2004. La historiografía de la "cuestión agraria" en España. In Fontana, J., (ed.) *Historia y Proyecto Social Crítica*, Barcelona, pp. 149–238.

Sabaté, O., 2016. Do Democracies Spend Less on the Military? Spain as a Long-Time Case Study (1876–2009). *Revista de Historia Económica* 34, 385–415.

Sabio Alcutén, A., 1996. *Los mercados informales de crédito y tierra en una comunidad rural aragonesa (1850–1930)*. Banco de España, Madrid.

Sabio Alcutén, A., 2002. *Tierra, comunal y capitalismo agrario en Aragón: Uso de los recursos naturales y campesinado en Cinco Villas, 1830–1935*. Institución 'Fernando el Católico', Zaragoza.

Sánchez Alonso, B., 2000. Those Who Left and Those Who Stayed Behind: Explaining Emigration from the Regions of Spain, 1880–1914. *Journal of Economic History* 60, 732–57.

Scott, J. C., 1985. *Weapons of the Weak: Everyday Forms of Peasant Resistance*. Yale University Press, New Haven.

Scott, J. C., 1976. *The Moral Economy of the Peasant: Rebellion and Subsistence in Southeast Asia*. Yale University Press, New Haven.

Scott, J. C., 1998. *Seeing like a State*. Yale University Press, New Haven.

Schultz, T. W., 1945. *Agriculture in an Unstable Economy*. McGraw-Hill, New York and London.

Schultz, T. W., 1964. *Transforming Traditional Agriculture*. Yale University Press, New Haven.

Self, P., & Storing, H. J., 1963. *The State and the Farmer: British Agricultural Policies and Politics*. University of California Press, Berkeley.

Senador Gómez, J., 1915: 1993. *Castilla en escombros*. Ámbito, Valladolid.

Serrano, R., 1997. *Revolución liberal y asociación agraria en Castilla (1869–1874)*. Universidad, Valladolid.

Serrano Sanz, J. M., 1987. *El viraje proteccionista en la Restauración: La política comercial española, 1875–1895*. Siglo XXI, Madrid.

Sheingate, A. D., 2001. *The Rise of the Agricultural Welfare State: Institutions and Interest Group Power in the United States, France, and Japan*. Princeton University Press, Princeton.

Shepherd, G. S., 1947. *Marketing Farm Products*. Iowa State College, Ames.

Shorter, E., & Tilly, C., 1974. *Strikes in France, 1870–1968*. Cambridge University Press, Cambridge.

Shubert, A., 1990. *A Social History of Modern Spain*. Unwin, Boston.

Silver, B., 2003. *Forces of Labor: Workers' Movements and Globalization since 1870*. Cambridge University Press, Cambridge.

Silvestre, J., Ayuda, M. I., & Pinilla, V., 2015. The Occupational Attainment of Migrants and Natives in Barcelona, 1930. *Economic History Review* 68, 985–1015.

Simpson, J., 1985. *Agricultural Growth and Technological Change: the Olive and Wine in Spain, 1860–1936*. University of London, London.

Simpson, J., 1989. La producción agraria y el consumo español en el siglo XIX. *Revista de Historia Económica* 7, 355–88.

Simpson, J., 1992a. Los limites del crecimiento agrario: España, 1860–1936. In Prados de la Escosura, L., & Zanagni, V. (eds.) *El desarrollo económico en la Europa del Sur: España e Italia en perspectiva histórica*. Alianza, Madrid, pp. 103–38.

Simpson, J., 1992b. Technical Change, Labor Absorption and Living Standards in Rural Andalucía, 1886–1936. *Agricultural History* 66, 1–24.

Simpson, J., 1995. *Spanish Agriculture: the Long Siesta, 1765–1965*. Cambridge University Press, Cambridge.

Simpson, J., 1995b. Spanish Agricultural Production and Productivity 1890–1936. In Martín-Aceña, P., & Simpson, J. (eds.) *The Economic Development of Spain since 1870*. Edward Elgar, Aldershot, pp. 181–220.

Simpson, J., 2000. Cooperation and Cooperatives in southern European Wine Production. In Kauffman, K. (ed.) *Advances in Agricultural Economic History*. Elsevier, pp. 95–126.

Simpson, J., 2001. La crisis agraria a finales del XIX: una reconsideración. In Sudrià, C., & Tirado, D. (eds.) *Peseta y Protección. Comercio exterior, moneda y crecimiento económico en la España de la restauración*. Edicions Universitat de Barcelona, Barcelona, pp. 99–118.

Simpson, J., 2011. *Creating Wine: the Emergence of a World Industry, 1840–1914*. Princeton University Press, Princeton.

Simpson, J., & Carmona, J., 2017. Too Many Workers or Not Enough Land? Why Land Reform Fails in Spain during the 1930s. *Historia Agraria*, 37–68.

Sindicato Vertical del Olivo, 1946. *El paro estacional campesino, Madrid*.

Smith, A., 1776: 1970. *The Wealth of Nations*. Penguin, London.

Smith, A., 2007. *Anarchism, Revolution and Reaction: Catalan Labour and the Crisis of the Spanish State, 1898–1923*. Berghahn Books, New York.

Smith, H., 1975. Work Routine and Social Structure in a French Village: Cruzy, Hérault in the Nineteenth Century. *Journal of Interdisciplinary History* 5, 357–82.

Snowden, F., 1986. *Violence and Great Estates in the South of Italy: Apulia, 1900–1922*. Cambridge University Press, Cambridge.

Snowden, F., 1989. *The Fascist Revolution in Tuscany, 1919–1922*. Cambridge University Press, Cambridge.

Soler, R., 2011. La Esquerra de los «rabassaires». La participación política del campesinado en el Penedès, 1931–1936. XIII Congreso de Historia Agraria, Sociedad Española de Historia Agraria, Lleida.

Spain. Delegación Regia de Pósitos, 1920. *Memoria que eleva al Gobierno de S.M. el delegado regio Don Rafael Marín Lázaro*, Madrid.

Spain. Delegación Regia de Pósitos (1911–1915), *Delegación Regia de Pósitos (1911–1915), Memorias y Apéndices*, Madrid.

Spain. Dirección General de Agricultura, Industria y Comercio, 1891. *Avance estadístico sobre el cultivo cereal y de leguminosas asociadas en España, formado por la Junta Consultiva Agronómica, 1890. Quinquenio 1886 a 1890, ambos inclusive*, Madrid.

Spain. Dirección General de Agricultura, Industria y Comercio, 1892. *La ganadería en España. Avance sobre la riqueza pecuaria en 1891, formado por la Junta Consultiva Agronómica conforme a las memorias reglamentarias que en el citado año han redactado los ingenieros del Servicio Agronómico*, Madrid.

Spain. Dirección General de Agricultura, Industria y Comercio, 1980. *Anuario Estadístico de las Producciones Agrícolas*, Madrid.

Spain. Dirección General del Instituto Geográfico y Estadístico, 1891. *Censo de la Población según el empadronamiento hecho en 31 de diciembre de 1887*. Imprenta de la Dirección General del Instituto Geográfico y Estadístico, Madrid.

Spain. Instituto Nacional de Estadística, 1966. *Primer Censo Agrario de España*. INE, Madrid.

Spain. Ministerio de Agricultura, 1933. *Anuario estadístico de las producciones agrícolas. Año 1932*. Madrid.

Spain. Ministerio de Agricultura, 1934. *Censo Estadístico de Sindicatos Agrícolas y Comunidades de Labradores*. Viuda de Navarro, Madrid.

Spain. Ministerio de Agricultura, Dirección General de Agricultura, 1934. *Tres estudios económicos. Apéndice al Anuario estadístico de las producciones agrícolas. Año 1933*. Madrid.

Spain. Ministerio de Fomento, 1910. *Apuntes para el proyecto de Ley de Crédito presentado a las Cortes por el Excmo. Sr. Ministro de Fomento D.Fermín Calbetón*. Madrid.

Spain. Ministerio de Fomento, 1921. *Material fertilizante empleado en la agricultura. Resumen hecho por la Junta Consultiva Agronómica de las Memorias de 1919 remitidas por los ingenieros del Servicio Agronómico Provincial*, Madrid.

Spain. Ministerio de Trabajo, Comercio e Industria, 1922. *Censo de la población de España el 31 de diciembre de 1920*. Talleres de la Dirección General del Instituto Geográfico, Madrid.

Steckel, R. H., & White, W. J., 2012. Engines of Growth: Farm Tractors and Twentieth-Century U.S. Economic Welfare. NBER Working Paper 17879.

Stone, L., 1972. *The Causes of the English Revolution, 1529–1642*. Routledge & Kegan Paul, London.

Sumpsi, J. M., 1978. Estudio de la transformación del cultivo al tercio al de año y vez en la campiña de Andalucía. *Agricultura y Sociedad* 6, 31–70.

Tarrow, S. G., 2011. *Power in Movement: Social Movements and Contentious Politics*. Cambridge University Press, Cambridge.

Temin, P., 2002. The Golden Age of European Growth Reconsidered. *European Review of Economic History* 6, 3–22.

Tena, A., 1999. Un nuevo perfil de proteccionismo español durante la Restauración, 1875–1930. *Revista de Historia Económica* 17, 579–621.

Tena, A., 2005. Sector Exterior. In Carreras, A., & Tafunell, X. (eds.) *Estadísticas históricas de España*. BBVA, Bilbao, pp. 573–644.

Thompson, M., 2007. The Land Market, 1880–1925: a Reappraisal Reappraised. *Agricultural History Review* 55, 289–300.

Tilly, C., 1975. *The Formation of Nation States in Western Europe*. Princeton University Press, Princeton.

Tilly, C., 2007. *Democracy*. Cambridge University Press, Cambridge.

Tilly, C., 2008. *Contentious Performances*. Cambridge University Press, Cambridge.

Tilly, C., Tilly, L., & Tilly, R., 1975. *The Rebellious Century*. Harvard University Press, Cambridge, MA.

Tocqueville, A. de, 1835–40/ 2000 edition. *Democracy in America*. University of Chicago Press, Chicago.

Tooze, A., 2001. *Statistics and the German State, 1900–1945: the Making of Modern Economic Knowledge*. Cambridge University Press, Cambridge.

Tooze, A., 2006. *The Wages of Destruction: the Making and Breaking of the Nazi Economy*. Penguin, London.

Torrejón y Bonete a, A. de, 1934. *Economía y valoración agrícola, forestal y urbana*. Agro Español, Madrid.

Torres, M. de, 1934. La coyuntura triguera en los últimos treinta años. *Agricultura*.

Torres, M. de, 1944. *El problema triguero y otras cuestiones fundamentales de la Agricultura española*, Madrid.

Tortella, G., 1985. Producción y productividad agraria en España, 1830–1930. In Sánchez-Albornoz, N. (ed.) *La modernización económica de España*. Alianza, Madrid, pp. 63–88.

Tortella, G., 1994. Patterns of Economic Retardation and Recovery in South-Western Europe in the Nineteenth and Twentieth Centuries. *Economic History Review*, 1–21.

Townson, N., 2000. *The Crisis of Democracy in Spain: Centralist Politics under the Second Republic, 1931–1936*. Sussex Academic, Brighton.

Tracy, M., 1989. *Government and Agriculture in Western Europe, 1880–1988*. Harvester Wheatsheaf, New York & London.

Tullock, G., 1971. The Paradox of Revolution. *Public Choice* 11, 89–99.

Tuñón de Lara, M., 1985. *Tres claves de la Segunda República*. Siglo XXI, Madrid.

Tuñon de Lara, M., Viñas, A., & Aróstegui, J., 1985. *La Guerra Civil Española: 50 años después*. Labor, Barcelona.

Turner, M. E., 1991. Agricultural Output and Productivity in Post-Famine Ireland. In Campbell, B. M. S., & Overton, M. (eds.) *Land, labour and livestock. Historical studies in European agricultural productivity*. Manchester University Press, Manchester.

Turner, M. E., 2000. Agricultural Output, Income and Productivity. In Collins, E. J. T. (ed.) *The Agrarian History of England and Wales*. Cambridge University Press, Cambridge, pp. 224–320.

Tusell, J., 1986. *Historia de la Democracia Cristiana en España*. Madrid.

UNESCO, 1953. *Progress of Literacy in Various Countries: Monographs on Fundamental Education*, VI. UNESCO, Paris.

Uriol Salcedo, J. I., 1990–2. *Historia de los Caminos de España: Colegio de Ingenieros de Caminos*, Canales y Puertos, Madrid.

Urwin, D. W., 1980. *From Ploughshare to Ballot Box: the Politics of Agrarian Defence in Europe*. Universitetsforlaget, Oslo.

Valentinov, V., 2007. Why Are Cooperatives Important in Agriculture? an Organizational Economics Perspective. *Journal of Institutional Economics* 3, 55–69.

Vallejo Pousada, R., 2014. Las catastróficas secuelas de las guerras en los siglos XIX y XX. In Comín, F., & Hernández, M. (eds.) *Crisis Económicas en España, 1300–2012*. Alianza, Madrid, pp. 253–78.

Van Zanden, J. L., 1991. The First Green Revolution: the Growth of Production and Productivity in European Agriculture, 1870–1914. *Economic History Review* 44, 215–39.

Vanhanen, T., 1984. *The Emergence of Democracy: a Comparative Study of 119 States, 1850–1979*. Finnish Society of Sciences and Letters, Helsinki.

Varela Ortega, J., 1977. *Los amigos políticos: Partidos, elecciones y caciquismo en la Restauración (1875–1900)*. Alianza, Madrid.

Vazquez Humasqué, A., 1931. *Mi proyecto de reforma agraria*. Madrid.

Vázquez Humasqué, A., 1934. Contribución al estudio económico de un plan decenal de reforma agraria. *El Sol*, 17 May 1934.

Villares Paz, R., 1997. Agricultura. In *Historia de España, Los Fundamentos de la España Liberal (1834–1900)*, Ramón Menéndez Pidal. Espasa-Calpe, Madrid.

Villares, R., 1982. *La propiedad de la tierra en Galicia, 1500–1936*. Siglo XXI, Madrid.

Vivier, N., 2014. *The Golden Age of State Enquiries: Rural Enquiries in the Nineteenth Century*. Brepols, Turnhout.

Warriner, D., 1939. *Economics of Peasant Farming*. Oxford University Press, Oxford.

Weber, E., 1977. *Peasant into Frenchmen: the Modernization of Rural France, 1870–1914*. Chatto & Windus, London.

Whitehead, L., 1995. State Organization in Latin America since 1930. In Bethell, L. (ed.) *The Cambridge History of Latin America: 1930 to the Present: Economics, Society and Politics*. Cambridge University Press, Cambridge, pp. 1–96.

Williamson, J. G., 1995. The Evolution of Global Labor Markets since 1830: Background Evidence and Hypotheses. *Explorations in Economic History* 32, 141–96.

Williamson, J. G., 2012. Review of *Economic Development in the Americas since 1500: Endowments and Institutions*. By Stanley L. Engerman and Kenneth L. Sokoloff. *Journal of Economic Literature* L, 809–18.

World Bank, 1990. *World Development Report*, Washington DC.

Wright, G., 1964. *Rural Revolution in France: the Peasantry in the Twentieth Century*. Stanford University Press, Stanford.

Wright, G., 1986. *Old South. New South*, New York.

Yates, P. L., 1960. *Food Production and Manpower in Western Europe*. Macmillan, London.

Zambrana, J. F., 1987. *Crisis y modernización del olivar español, 1870–1930*. MAPA, Madrid.

Zhu, X., 2012. Understanding China's Growth: Past, Present, and Future. *Journal of Economic Perspectives* 26, 103–24.

Ziblatt, D., 2017. *Conservative Parties and the Birth of Democracy*. Cambridge University Press, Cambridge.

Zumalacárregui Prat, J. M. d., 1934. La crisis económica y la organización de la producción. In Semana Social de Madrid (ed.) *La crisis moral, social y económica del mundo*. Madrid, pp. 603–762.

Index

social spending, 28; and Spain, 43; First
World War, 24; impact of Spain
neutrality, 25; in Spain, 57, 59, 125;
limits in Spain, 70; Spanish burocracy,
73; tax collection, 25; to collect and
process information, 25
statistics, 186; limitations of Spanish
statistics, 70
Stone, Lawrence: on the causes of the
English Revolution, 2
strikes, 99; and good harvests, 232;
Cordoba, 236; harvest strike, 234;
harvest strikes in Andalucia, 234; levels in
1933, 226
structural change: Western Europe, 25
subletting: abolition in Land Reform
law, 241
Syndicate Law of 1906, 117, 134

tariffs, 174; and landed elites, 145; cereals,
143, 145
Tarragona, 118
Tarrow, Sidney, 226, 230
tasa. See cereals
taxes. *See land taxes*; and fiscal capacity in
Spain, 71; expenditure, 71
tenancy, 85, 171, 194; fair' rents, 149;
regulation, 98; rent, 149; sub-leasing,
150; tenant farmers and access to land,
58; tenants subletting, 210
tenant farmers, 197
tenants subletting, 241
tenure reform, 186, 212, 215, 219
Términos Municipales decree, 199, 216, 230,
231; and land invasions, 244;
impopularity of, 237
Thompson, E.P., 109
Tilly, Charles: on democratization, 17; on
state capacity and war, 24; rural conflicts,
99; types of collective action, 229
Tocqueville, Alexis de, 103, 104
Tooze, Adam, 54; and fascism, 33
Toro (Zamora), 150
Torres, Manuel de, 218

Tracy, 52
Tracy, Michael, 54
*Trienio bolchevique. See Bolshevik
Triennium*
turno pacifico, 208, 224
turno riguroso: labour reforms, 231

UGT, 207, 209, 211, 215
Unamuno, Miguel, 114
unemployment, 170, 173
Unió de Rabassaires, 222, 223, 267
Unió de Vinyaters de Catalunya, 119, 124
Unión Agraria Española, 124
Unión de Sindicatos Agrícolas de Cataluña,
140, 224
Union General del Trabajo. See UGT
United States, 183; Gavin Wright on
US South, 157; US South, 178

Valencia, 134, 135, 140, 141; and
irrigation, 94
Valladolid: *pósitos*, 115
Van Zanden, Jan Luiten, 37
Vanhanen: definition family farm, 49;
independent family farms, 49
Vazquez Humasqué, Adolfo, 179, 187
viticulture, 81, 94, 150, 222; in
Catalonia, 139
Vizcaya, 205

wages, 168, 170; improvement in Western
Europe, 27; urban wages, 169
Warriner, Doreen, 89, 181
Weber, Eugene, 73
wheat, 147, 162, 163, *See cereals*; prices,
147; wheat farming, 174

Young, Arthur, 154
yunteros, 99; eviction in 1935, 242
Yunteros decrees, 196

Ziblatt, Daniel, 1, 202; and landed elites in
mass parties, 219; and mass conservative
political party, 22